THE JOURNAL OF PRIVATE FRASER
Canadian Expeditionary Force

Private Donald Fraser in full battle gear, 1916.

The Journal of Private Fraser

1914-1918

Canadian Expeditionary Force

Edited and with an Introduction by
REGINALD H. ROY

1985

Sono Nis Press
Victoria, British Columbia

Canadian Cataloguing in Publication Data

Fraser, Donald, 1882-1946.
  The journal of Private Fraser, Canadian
Expeditionary Force

  Includes index.
  ISBN 0-919203-62-0

  1. Fraser, Donald, 1882-1946.   2. World
War, 1914-1918—Personal narratives,
Canadian.   3. Canada.   Canadian Army.
Battalion, 31st—Biography.   4. Soldiers—
Canada—Biography.   I. Roy, Reginald H.,
1922-   II. Title.

D640.F73A3 1985   940.4′81′71   C85-091012-9

49877

This book has been published with the assistance
of the Canada Council Block Grant Program.

Published by
SONO NIS PRESS
1745 Blanshard Street
Victoria, British Columbia

Designed and printed in Canada by
MORRISS PRINTING COMPANY LTD.
Victoria, British Columbia

To Joan and Bob, whose father also served in the 31st Battalion (CEF) and to Ardith, whose father served with the 36th Battery, Canadian Field Artillery which sometimes gave artillery support to the 31st Battalion

Contents

Preface

In 1980 Miss Deirdre Fraser came to my office at the University of Victoria. She had been directed to me by a mutual friend. She left with me copies of a journal written by her father, Donald Fraser, who had served overseas first with the 31st Battalion, CEF and later with the 6th Brigade Machine-Gun Company. When I had completed reading Fraser's journal, I realized that it was one of the most vivid, personal descriptions of trench life by a Canadian soldier I had ever read. With her permission, I decided to prepare the manuscript for publication. It was something that should have been done years earlier, but since this year marks the seventieth anniversary of the beginning of the Great War, I thought this work would help to remind the descendants of the 1914-1918 veterans what their grandfathers had endured in France and Flanders.

I wish to thank Stella Higgins, Franklyn Snedden and Lt.-Col. W. E. J. Hutchinson for their assistance in helping me edit and proofread the journal. I also wish to acknowledge the financial support given me to complete this task by the University of Victoria. In particular, I owe a great debt to Gloria Orr who typed the manuscript, helped to proofread it, and remained cheerful throughout the entire process. I must also express my thanks to my wife Ardith as, once again, she put up with my disappearances into the den for several hundred hours while mentally I turned back the years to serve with Fraser on the Western Front.

Reginald H. Roy
University of Victoria, 1984

Introduction

On November 24, 1914 Donald Fraser, together with a number of other civilians at the Recruiting Depot in Calgary, raised their right hands and swore: "I do make Oath that I will be faithful and bear true Allegiance to His Majesty King George the Fifth, His Heirs and Successors, and that I will as in duty bound honestly and faithfully defend His Majesty, His Heirs and Successors, in Person, Crown and Dignity, against all enemies, and will observe and obey all orders of His Majesty, His Heirs and Successors, and of all the Generals and officers set over me. So help me God."

With his medical examination satisfactory and the oath completed, Fraser was allotted a regimental number—79720—and became a private soldier in the 31st (Alberta) Battalion, Canadian Expeditionary Force. He was 32 years old at the time, almost six feet tall with light brown hair, blue eyes and a good, athletic build. Like many others in his battalion, he had come to Canada from Great Britain some years earlier, and as soon as he opened his mouth to speak he would be recognized as an immigrant from Scotland.

Fraser was born in Edinburgh on March 15, 1882. His father, Hugh Fraser, was a dealer in spirits and owned the Loch Ness Vaults, a business which had a good income and permitted him to raise his six children (two sons and four daughters) in upper middle-class comfort. Like his older brother, Donald was educated at George Watson's College in Edinburgh. Following his father's death in 1903, he tried his hand as a wine merchant and then immigrated to Canada in 1906. He worked for a short time as a farm labourer in Manitoba but soon found a job as a clerk in the Merchant's Bank in Calgary.

11

In 1911, he moved to Vancouver where he worked as a clerk with the Royal Trust Company and left that job to enlist at Calgary in 1914.

There is no record of Fraser having had any military experience in Scotland or Canada prior to 1914. This would be true also of most of the tens of thousands of men who flocked to the recruiting stations on the outbreak of war. At that time Canada's Permanent Force was small—only a few thousand were available in the entire country. There were over 50,000 reserves or militiamen, however, but their military training was very limited. One or two drill nights at the local armoury supplemented by an annual seven- or ten-day training period at a summer camp left much to be desired. Traditionally, Canada had remained content in her semi-isolation, happy to be part of the British Empire and secure in the feeling that the wide Atlantic was dominated by the strongest navy in the world.

When the Great War broke out in Europe, there was a tremendous surge of patriotism throughout Canada. Few were more enthusiastic than the Minister of Militia and Defence, Colonel Sam Hughes. Instead of following the mobilization plan prepared by his military staff officers, Hughes decided to "raise the fiery cross" and called upon the dozens of militia regiments across the country not to mobilize to full strength in some sort of orderly sequence, but rather to contribute drafts of officers and men. These drafts, in turn, were ordered to proceed to Camp Valcartier, a huge tented military camp a few miles from Quebec City. The drafts were collected together and new, numbered battalions were created, assigned officers, formed into brigades and then sent overseas for further training.

The First Contingent of the Canadian Expeditionary Force had been rushed overseas late in 1914. From these men the 1st Canadian Infantry Division was formed and sent to France early in 1915. By that time, the 2nd Canadian Infantry Division was preparing to leave Canada. The 31st Battalion, in which Donald Fraser enlisted, was one of four battalions in the 6th Brigade. All were from Western Canada—the 27th and 28th Battalions from Winnipeg, the 31st ("Bell's Bulldogs") Battalion from Calgary and the 29th Battalion ("Tobin's Tigers") from Vancouver.

It took time to recruit, outfit, arm and teach even the elements of military drill and discipline to such a large body of men. Canada manufactured very little in the way of war material or armaments in 1914 and it was not until some time later that she began to produce a volume of shells, ships, aircraft and weapons which the war was to consume in vast quantities. There was one weapon which it did produce—the Ross rifle—which Colonel Sam Hughes thought was better than the rifle used by the British Army, the Lee-Enfield. We shall see Fraser's opinion of that weapon later. At the time Fraser joined up, however, there was considerable trouble trying to provide enough uniforms to clothe the swarm of recruits coming in and finding quarters for them until sufficient barracks were built.

The 31st Battalion, fully equipped and eager for battle, left Calgary in mid-May, 1915. Within a week the men were packed on board a troopship at Quebec en route for England. By the end of the month, after a long and unpleasant crossing, the unit arrived at Dibgate Camp in Kent, only a few miles from Shorncliffe. Five days later, Lt.-Col. A. H. Bell, commanding the battalion, prepared his unit for inspection by Maj.-Gen. S. B. Steele, recently appointed General Officer Commanding of the 2nd Canadian Division. With that over, the 31st began four months of hard training before crossing over to France.

There was much to be done. As the regimental historian wrote:

Company and battalion drill and manoeuvres, trench digging, and similar work occupies most of the time. Courses of special instruction in bayonet fighting, grenade throwing, machine-gunnery, musketry, signalling and map reading were also inaugurated. . . .[1]

In July there was further practice on the rifle ranges, more route marches, lectures on first aid, military law and administration, all interspersed with periodic inspections by high ranking Canadian and British officials. Now and then there was a ripple of excitement when a German zeppelin came over to drop its bombs on targets of opportunity. Manoeuvres on a brigade and divisional scale took place in August but, as the men were to find out in France, manoeuvres imply mobility, and trench warfare offered little opportunity for movement on the battlefield. Fraser, in his journal, gives an excellent description of what it was like to fight in the trenches and it would probably be true to say that not one man in the battalion really appreciated what he was getting into until he arrived in the front line himself to experience the conditions of warfare in France and Flanders.

Although much secrecy generally surrounds the movement of large bodies of troops, when the entire division was reviewed by His Majesty King George V and Lord Kitchener, it was felt that this was a prelude to the division's departure for France. As it turned out, this assumption was correct. In mid-September, all 28 officers and 890 other ranks of the 31st Battalion were warned they would be leaving in a few days' time. On the 16th, in heavy marching order and carrying 120 rounds of rifle ammunition, the battalion left for

[1] H. C. Singer, *History of the Thirty-First Battalion, C.E.F.*, Calgary, n.p., 1938, p. 22.

France. By the end of the month, the men entered the trenches for the first time.

Possibly because he had been an accountant, when his unit was in England, Private Donald Fraser had been a clerk helping to look after company stores. According to him, however, he "ran away from the work the night we made for the line."[2] Until he was wounded late in 1917, he was never far from the front, whether he was with his company or, for a period, with the Quartermaster Stores where his task was helping to bring food and ammunition to the front.

On several occasions Fraser could have been promoted. Certainly he had the intelligence and experience required to be a non-commissioned officer or an officer. On January 12, 1917, for example, Fraser mentioned that he was offered sergeant's stripes but turned down the offer because the job was "too dull and uninteresting." Possibly there was more to it than that. Fraser would see many of his friends promoted to sergeants and others to lieutenants, but he also realized that the casualty rates among these ranks were exceptionally high. There was some merit and perhaps a greater degree of safety in being among the mass of private soldiers and not having to assume the responsibilities of leadership, even on a modest scale. In any event Fraser, although time and again showing the qualities of leadership as a private, does not accept any rank until he is appointed "No. 1" on a machine-gun crew and accepts the lowest possible rank of a Lance-Corporal.

In some ways his refusal to accept rank must have frustrated his officers who were always on the lookout for suitable men with leadership potential. Within every battalion there was a constant stream of men entering and leaving the unit. Some are killed or wounded; there are some transfers to other units (as was Fraser himself) or to other corps, some were withdrawn owing to battle fatigue and shell-shock, and so on. To replace them there was a constant flow of reinforcements coming to the front-line units. Most of these came from battalions raised and trained in Canada, sent to Great Britain, and there broken up to fill gaps caused by the attrition of war at the front. Most of these new reinforcements were inexperienced, including the officers. It is interesting to note that Fraser blames one of these new reinforcement officers for the severe wounds he received at Passchendaele. After two years of war Fraser had developed a keen instinct about the intentions of the enemy, and he knew from experience when to move along a road under shellfire and when to wait. The officer did not—and casualties resulted.

[2] See his diary entry for 11 January 1916.

The strain and tension which was part of serving in the trenches affected all soldiers, some to a greater degree than others. Fraser, in his journal, describes several incidents where both officers and other ranks, unable to bear the mental anguish and fear of constant shellfire, or perhaps seeing their comrades killed or wounded, broke under the strain and had to be led to the rear. Some never recovered while others were able to perform military duties well behind the line beyond the reach of artillery. Most men steeled themselves to perform the task which had to be done, and in the cauldron of fire there was forged a camaraderie among the veterans which never died. There was a very distinct line, however, between those who served at the front and those whose duties lay out of the range of enemy shells.

Even among those who seemed steady and solid under the constant danger from enemy fire, the stress of service at the front had a cumulative effect on the soldier. Many years after the war Fraser, at that time receiving a partial pension for his wounds, wrote a long letter to a doctor at the Calgary office of the Canadian pensions office. His physical condition was giving him some cause for concern and in his letter, a portion of which is given below, he describes one or two close scrapes with death which would be similar to those experienced by thousands of other Canadian veterans. He wrote in part:

I joined up in November 1914, was in France from September 1915 until put out of commission by wounds at Passchendaele in November, 1917, a period of 2 years and 2 months, continuously at the front with the exception of two short leave trips to Britain and one rest trip to near Wimereux, France. I was an infantryman for 1 year in France, and a machine-gunner for 1 year and 2 months. All the time I was in France I never once reported sick. Apart from being in every line the 6th Brigade was in, I was in the following engagements either in the front in a very direct way or in the supports: St. Eloi; Hooge (3rd battle of Ypres); Somme; Vimy; Arleux-Fresnoy, Lens; Passchendaele. On September 15th, 1916, at the Somme I went over the top with the first wave, and was the first into the enemy line on a frontal of at least 150 yards. At Vimy on April 9th, 1917, I was attached to a unit as a machine-gunner that finished the final objective on the reverse side of the ridge close to the village of Farbus. At Lens I went forward into the enemy terrain, but under orders had to fall back, as we were surrounded on three sides. The other engagements were either of a defensive character or developed into that. I mention these things only to show that I had very close actual fighting until disposed of at Passchendaele. Any stress or strain that went with service during that period I consider I had far more than most men and lasted much longer than 90 per cent of those that went over with me.

Apart from anything in a general way likely to cause my condition, a few things stand out in my opinion, where damage to the blood vessels could have taken place. One occurred in the support line at the Bluff, Belgium, immediately behind the International Trench and about 100 yards from the front line. While talking with four of my comrades, the enemy was firing individual shells which angled over our heads, bursting a few hundred yards beyond in the supports on the south. Not much attention was paid to the shelling as the gunners were ranging over us. We heard the gun firing and knew by instinct and experience that although the shells were coming in our direction they were too high to bother us. Suddenly a report that sounded like a premature or a short made us bolt out of the way. Two of the fellows threw themselves into the nearby dug-out and stuck in the entrance. Another ran north up the support line, while the fourth rushed up the communication trench towards the firing line. Bordering the trench and behind the dug-out was a little wall of sandbags not more than two feet high. I rounded the end of the wall and threw myself flat behind it on the side nearest the line. At that moment the shell burst with a tremendous explosion on the other side of the sandbag wall where I was standing a second ago and not more than a yard away from where I lay. The report of the explosion dazed me and I was hit with all sorts of debris as they fell on me in their downward course. The concussion or whatever it is called created a terrific strain on the tissues. I felt as if I was being pulled apart, as if some unseen thing was tearing me asunder, particularly the top part of the body, and especially the head. I know I could not have stood a fraction more without bursting, the outward pull on the tissue was so immense. Getting over the daze I quickly pulled myself together and got out of range for the time being. The incident passed off, although the bursting effect on the body rankled in my mind. It was the greatest body strain I have ever experienced.

Another time at Vimy, on the memorable April 9th, while awaiting the signal to move forward from an old trench south and adjoining Neuville St. Vaast to complete the final objective, another shell burst on the parapet, almost in my face, and in a moment my breathing stopped; there seemed to be no air to breathe in or out, my mouth was open and completely stuck, I could not even gasp or choke. In a trice I had my gas helmet on and was breathing freely shortly afterwards. It was a peculiar experience and for a moment or two I thought I was finished.

Again, at Passchendaele, my gun crew having been in the attacks at the Somme, Vimy, Fresnoy and Lens, it was decided that we would be held in reserve near Potize for the Passchendaele engagement. However, our transport having received casualties on the way up to Passchendaele, my gun crew was called upon to relieve them. Leaving one man to look after the tent and belongings, the rest of us were placed in charge of horses, carrying cans of water, ammunition, etc., to the line. The horse I was leading, and it was the first time I had a duty of this description to perform, had several cans of water balanced on each side. Spacing out about 25 feet, the party of about 12 to 15 men and horses moved up past Potize into the range of guns, which were firing adjacent to the road, not being able to move far from the road on account of the mud. While going up the Grafenstafel Ridge it was observed the enemy was sending over salvos every few minutes, and I expected we would have to halt and lay low until shelling ceased. However, the officer in charge, who was a new man, thought otherwise, and we proceeded up the dangerous spot. I was second from the end. The first lot passed safely, but the salvo came over with disastrous results when the final four entered the shelled area. The fellow behind me was killed, also his horse. The fellow ahead was also killed and his horse likewise. The fellow ahead of him was severely wounded and his horse killed. The shell burst threw my horse and myself from one side of the road to the other, my face being buried in the mud at the side of the road. I was completely dazed, and when I came to, trying to get up I found I was pinned down by the horse lying across my thighs. The horse was dead. Struggling to get free I finally squirmed from underneath and got up. How my legs were not damaged is a puzzle to me. I felt I was wounded but did not know where. My face burned as if hot wires were jammed into it. I was peppered in the face and hands with small pieces of shrapnel. Another salvo came over and the bursts this time so disturbed the air that I could hardly breathe. I quickly headed down the road and it was then that I noticed for the first time that my right arm, shattered at the shoulder, was dangling in front of me and twisted around. There were other injuries in addition.

From personal experience of shells exploding close to me, the concussion in some cases affected my breathing, which I presume means either a reaction on the lungs or heart or both. Others gave out a deafening report followed by no effect. The other explosion, as first mentioned, caused a tremendous outward pull of the tissues of the body, as if something was tearing me apart, and I have a feeling that this condition of aneurism was caused through that explosion, more so than when I was struck down and shoulder smashed.[3]

After he was wounded, Fraser was taken immediately to No. 3 Australian Casualty Clearing Station. Within two days he was en route to better care at the 1st Southern General Hospital in Birmingham and later at No. 5 Canadian General Hospital in Liverpool. He had received his "Blighty," and it was very apparent that his wounds were so severe that he would never be able to return to the front.

During the spring of 1918 Fraser was sent to Seaford as an invalid awaiting transfer to Canada. Whether he had the opportunity during this period to travel to Scotland to visit his sisters is not known, but probably he did. Early in June, Fraser left Liverpool for Halifax and finally arrived back in Calgary on June 22nd. His weight had dropped from 171 to 155 pounds, his wounds, especially in the shoulder, were still causing him some pain and indeed he was never to regain the full strength of his right arm. Following his discharge from the army on September 16, 1918, Fraser was granted a 30 per cent disability pension of $180 per annum. He was also granted a $35.00 clothing allowance and his application to take a six-month Civil Service Course was granted by the Disabled Soldiers Training Board. He completed his course at the Institute of Technology in Calgary in May 1919.

Fraser applied for a job within the federal civil service and was hired by the Department of National Revenue. He remained with

[3] Letter, Donald Fraser to Dr. Sheffield, 29 July 1939, in Department of Veterans' Affairs file 535-D-12. A xerox copy of this file is in the possession of Fraser's daughter, Miss D. L. Fraser, of Victoria, B.C.

this department for the next 26 years. He was instrumental in organizing the Calgary office of the Customs and Excise branch of this department and became the officer in charge of it until his retirement. He married Caroline Mackintosh on November 1, 1919, a young lady whom he had known in Scotland. Their first child, Hugh, was born in 1921 and a little over two years later a daughter, Deirdre, completed the family.

For the next quarter of a century the Fraser family lived happily and quietly in Calgary. As his daughter wrote later:

Dad was a kind and gentle man, quiet and modest, with a keen mind and a good sense of humour. Some said he was a "proud" man. This amused him no end. He possessed great determination and courage, and always welcomed a challenge. He was a very logical person, and at times it could take some doing for another to change his mind. Mother was the most successful at this. He was a wonderful father with infinite patience. His ideas and beliefs were definite—weakness of spirit had no place in his life. He was truly "one of the Old School." He loved his wife dearly, and she him, and they were great pals.

My mother said his war experiences took its toll. He lost quite a bit of his strength and vigour, and thus led a quieter life than he ordinarily would have. Also, he was unable to travel any great distance without feeling unwell. As a result his interest centered mainly on his home and garden, extensive reading and some writing.[4]

About a year before he was due to retire, Fraser became very ill. He went to Rochester, New York for a cancer operation but although the operation was a success, the strain on his heart, kidneys, etc. proved to be too great. "He was so determined to improve his condition," his daughter wrote, "that he, my mother and myself moved to Victoria as quickly as possible in April, 1946."[5] He died in Victoria on August 25th that year, aged 64 years. His wife, Caroline, continued to live in Victoria until her death in 1973.

Why did Donald Fraser decide to keep a record of his experiences in the trenches? The answer is best given by Fraser himself. At the beginning of the third section of his journal, he wrote:

Percy Craine was the source of inspiration that animated me to keep a diary during my sojourn in Belgium and France. On arrival at Kemmel, I saw him jot down particulars in a notebook and promptly thought that I would do likewise, notwithstanding that it was contrary to regulations. It coincided with the commencement of our campaign. Several months later, Craine lost interest in his diary; probably like most he thought it of more importance to devote his whole time to the art of keeping alive than looking for copy. Further on in the conflict he was, unfortunately, killed.

[4] Letter, Miss D. L. Fraser to editor, January 1983.
[5] *Ibid.*

I gathered most of the information contained in the following pages from personal observation and naturally it relates largely to the movements and doings of my associates and myself. It was impossible to follow the actions of others elsewhere as we were pinned down to our own narrow frontage. However, at various times I came into contact with members of other units who were quick to tell me of their experiences, and to relate incidents that they had heard. A number appear in this book. Of course, I have never been in a position to verify them. They are given, however, as part of trench gossip.

As it was impossible to be in every action my unit was engaged in, I made a point of eliciting as much information as possible from others; consequently, these actions are not fully covered. One time my unit might be slated to take the final objective, in another engagement it might be limited to the capture of the enemy front line, while again our particular duty might be confined to holding the support line in case of counter-attacks. Hence, this account is not intended to convey a full history of a major conflict my unit might be in.

In short, this diary is nothing more than a running story of our daily movements and observations, supplemented with accounts of happenings and sprinkled with comment and grousings. What is written here is more or less the common experience of thousands of soldiers.

This narrative is written very plainly without elaboration or embellishment, and is practically in the same words as expressed in the original diary. A lack of journalistic knowledge and patience is responsible for its weaknesses.

The reason for this typewritten volume was to obtain a permanent mememto of my wanderings and experiences in Belgium and France during the war between the periods September 1915 and November 1917.

Unfortunately, the original copy of his notes was either lost or destroyed. During the war, apparently he sent the detailed notes, or daily record, to his sister in Scotland for safekeeping. He did this for two years. The notes he made during the last several weeks in the trenches were lost when he was wounded and whisked to the hospital.

It was while he was recovering from his wounds during the Summer of 1918 that he decided to write an account of his experiences in the trenches.[6] With his diary notes at hand, and the memory of his experiences very fresh in his mind, Fraser wrote in long hand the first two parts of his journal. Apparently, from several references he makes in his text, he did not write the third part of his journal until either 1943 or 1944 when the Second World War was raging.[7] This portion was typed by his daughter, and fortunately all three parts of the journal were preserved by her.

When Deirdre Fraser brought her father's journal to my office about three years ago, it was several days before I had the opportunity to start reading it. I was intrigued at the outset because my own father had served with the 31st Battalion during the Great War before he

[6] See his diary entry for September 22, 1915.
[7] See his diary entries for October 16, 1916 and May 1, 1917.

transferred to the Royal Flying Corps in 1917. As a boy, I can remember him telling me something about life in the trenches. I also had in my library the regimental history of the 31st Battalion. Thus when I started to read Fraser's journal I anticipated a somewhat pedestrian account of the war in France and Flanders; what I read was one of the most fascinating eye-witness descriptions written by a Canadian soldier I have ever come across.

Fraser experienced just about every aspect of trench warfare during the two years he served at the front. He had a keen eye for detail, a warm respect for his comrades, a disdain for the useless "spit and polish" demands in the rear, and a sound appreciation for good leadership and planning in battle. He is caustic, at times, about staff officers when plans go awry, and not infrequently questions the granting of some awards and decorations which, he felt, were given too liberally. His attitude towards the enemy—"Fritzie," the "Hun," etc.—varies according to circumstances. Never, however, does he underrate them.

Fraser seems to have had an unquenchable curiosity and he comments on everything—weapons, shells, rifles, tactics, leadership, furlough, trench raids, rations, cooks, trench life, his superiors and comrades, the war in the air, No Man's Land, inspections, gas attacks, tanks, courage or the lack of it, spies, fatigues, souvenirs, Imperial troops, billets, snipers—the list is endless. Whenever the opportunity presented itself, he particularly enjoyed collecting souvenirs, especially buttons and badges or anything else that was small and easy to carry. Most of these he obtained from the enemy, either from prisoners or corpses. He called it his "weakness," but periodically, when he describes his wandering over an area which had been a battleground months earlier, one can easily imagine what it must have been like to have lived through the holocaust which raged over that particular part of the front.

Fraser was a hardened veteran when he wrote his journal. He was accustomed to death and bloodshed in all its forms. He writes about it without emotion, yet there is no doubting that he felt the loss of his close friends as one by one they were killed or wounded. He realized, as times goes on, that his own chances of becoming a casualty constantly narrowed. His transfer from the 31st Battalion to the 6th Brigade Machine-Gun Company probably increased his chances of survival to some extent, but even this would be limited. It is interesting to note, incidentally, that from the time the 31st Battalion was formed, 4,487 officers and men served with the unit. Of that number, 941 were killed and 2,312 were battle casualties. Considering that there were many transfers to other units and corps, taking into account attrition owing to other causes, and keeping in mind that an infantry battalion at full strength was a little over 900 all ranks, it is little wonder that the number of men still serving with the unit in 1918 who were among the "old originals" were very few indeed.

Despite the horrors and miseries of trench warfare, there is never any word of self-pity in Fraser's journal. He might rage at incompetence, criticize selfishness or be disdainful about those seeking soft jobs behind the lines, but he never questioned the righteousness of the Allied cause. His sense of duty never wavered, nor did he question the circumstances in which he found himself. Life was reduced to basics—survival, food, warmth, sleep. Comfort of any sort was an unexpected pleasure. Humour was an escape valve. Courage and loyalty were expected rather than demanded. Life in the trenches created a very tightly-knit group of men, and among them there grew a camaraderie which could rarely be shared by those who had not experienced it. It may have been a companionship of misery but it was shared by tens of thousands who knew that those at home could never comprehend what they were enduring. Only their comrades could understand and give their rough sympathy. Letters home describing actual conditions at the front would probably be censored, and even those which were not would only raise greater anxiety and fears among soldiers' families. Most soldiers, therefore, tended to pass over the actual conditions of life at the front when they wrote home.

Fraser, when he wrote his journal, was able to express his own feeling about the war with no such restrictions. His parents and his brother had died before the war. His sisters never saw the journal. He did show the early portions of it to some of his veteran comrades in 1919 and they tried to persuade him to have it published. Perhaps it was too soon after the war, or perhaps potential publishers felt the public would not accept such a vivid description of the horrors of war. In any event the journal remained in Fraser's possession.

Extremely few editorial changes have been made in the journal. The company, battalion and brigade war diaries have been used to support or correct any errors in personal and place names, but naturally no attempt has been made to alter Fraser's opinions of battle casualties or actions on his unit's flanks. Colonel G. W. L. Nicholson's official history of the Canadians in the Great War provides information about the battles on a large scale, and numerous regimental and corps histories are available for those seeking wider knowledge of events on a battalion level. Fraser writes about the war as he saw it—from the point of view of a private soldier.

University of Victoria, 1984   Reginald H. Roy, Ph.D.

CHAPTER I

In Flanders Fields

Friday, September 17, 1915

After a four months' training in Kent, England, where we had a very enjoyable time, first at Dibgate in the vicinity of Shorncliffe, then at Lydd where we had a rush shooting practice and finally at Otterpool where water was very scarce, we were considered fit and skilled in the art of warfare, ready to meet the hated Hun. When I think of it, our training was decidedly amateurish and impractical. It consisted mainly of route marches and alignment movements. Our musketry course amounted to nothing; we had only half an idea about the handling of bombs. We were perfectly ignorant regarding rifle grenades. But in due time we learned from Fritz what bombs, rifle grenades, trench mortars and machine-guns really were. The success his snipers had at our expense taught our command that sniping played a very important part in warfare. We, therefore, started out with inferior training to the German, squandering the many months over peace soldiering methods. I am afraid our wits were not well sharpened and we often displayed daring carelessness, call it what you will, which was a poor match for cunning and only meant playing into the enemy's hands.

Anyway, our training was at an end, word was passed round that we were leaving today for France. The camp was all excitement. At last we were to witness real fighting. It was almost too good to be true. Everyone was pleased at the idea though a bit dubious of the outcome. The consequences, however, were thrown to the winds, the only thing that mattered was we were bound for France. Orders to strike camp were given and in due time we were on the move, our packs choke full of clothing, etc. It was a memorable day as our brigade stepped out on the road and marched for Folkestone through Lympne, Hythe, Seabrook and Sandgate. The march was a gruelling one. Our packs were so heavy that the strappings almost cut into the flesh and there were many connivances employed to ease the aching back, and shoulders.[1] Near Folkestone at the Leas we halted and lay on the road. By this time the stragglers had caught up. It soon became evident there was something wrong and everyone was enquiring the reason for delay. The command rang out along the lines, "about turn," then we learned the reason — there were mines in the English Channel and we could not cross until the sweepers announced all clear. Our first battle, the retreat from Folkestone, commenced. Twos and threes were falling out by the roadside, the climb to the plains above Sandgate took the heart out of many, so they took up their abode for the night on the roadside, in gardens, in the fields, amidst bushes, and a few fortunate ones managed into houses. The Companies got badly mixed. By the time a halt was called the battalion was widely scattered. About a couple of dozen, including the writer, represented "A" Company. That night we slept on [Sir John Moore's] Plains under the canopy of heaven with only what we carried with us for covering. Next morning and forenoon the stragglers began to arrive from all directions and by the afternoon we were up to strength again. . . .[2]

Saturday, September 18, 1915

The channel was evidently clear for in the early evening we were on the road again. At Folkestone we embarked. The British Navy had its sentinels out, one particular vessel keeping a watchful eye on us. It darted hither and thither, racing alongside us or crossing our bow or stern. In the fading light England was soon lost to view—to many forever. Boulogne was reached about 9:15 p.m. and we filed out on to the wharf, where we remained in our fours.[3] After a spell we were on the move and passing through the town ascended in the darkness the steep slope leading to the hill camp beside the wireless station. This was the first camping ground of the original British Expeditionary Force. Women and children, dirty, sallow and unkempt, lined the

[1] According to the battalion's medical officer, the total weight carried by each soldier exceeded 70 pounds, which included 120 rounds of S.A.A. (small arms ammunition). "Too heavy," he thought. (War Diary, Medical Officer, 31st Battalion, C.E.F., 16 September 1915. This personal war diary is attached to the unit War Diary for the same month.)

[2] The strength of the battalion when it left camp was 29 officers and 890 other ranks.

[3] During the Great War platoons, companies, etc., marched in columns of fours, i.e., four files of men.

streets breaking the stillness of the night with their eerie voices uttering in broken English, "Beer, soldier, beer!" as they proffered plain unlabelled quart bottles. We were allotted to our various quarters, tents without floor boards and passed the night therein not too comfortably. We awoke next morning to find ourselves in France, in France at last.

Sunday, September 19, 1915

We were early astir and found the camp besieged by women and girls selling apples and pears and begging for souvenirs, the souvenirs they greatly coveted being tins of bully-beef, though one buxom damsel was bold enough to ask Mackie for a pair of boots he had still on his feet! At 10:15 a.m. we boarded the train. The train service did not compare favorably with that of Britain or Canada. The trains moved dreadfully slow. There was a half hour stop at St. Omer which was left at 1:30 p.m. It was generally mooted around that the Commander-in-chief of the British Armies had his Headquarters here. We soon reached Cassel our train terminus. This district is rather pretty. The country is more undulating than most of Flanders. The village itself is on the slope of one of the very few hills to be seen.

Once more we are on the march. It is a trying hike. Each man of the 29th Battalion was carrying an extra pair of boots, one slung on each side of the pack. The weight was beginning to tell on the men. One by one the unnecessary articles were flung to the side of the road, boots, shirts, underclothing, brushes, etc. being strewn along the roadside for several miles. It was a terrible waste. The French people in the neighbourhood must have garnered supplies of clothing for several years to come. We found out later that it was perfectly ridiculous issuing such clothing to us. Behind the firing line was a series of baths to which the soldiers go once a week or fortnight and exchange their dirty clothes for clean ones. A towel and two or three pairs of socks are all the clothing necessary to carry. By this time, however, we were accustomed to government waste. We remembered too well the waste of bread and butter in England. The former used to be dumped wholesale into the incinerator, the quartermaster ignoring the matter completely. Having no receptacles in the tents for rations, the butter or, rather, margarine, faded away with the heat.

Another huge farce was the entrenching tools of Col. Sam Hughes.[4]

---

[4] Colonel, later Major-General Sir Sam Hughes was the Minister of Militia and Defence at this time. The entrenching tool mentioned was the MacAdam shovel. Some 25,000 of these were purchased. It was designed both to act as a shield and a shovel, but was useless for either purpose. It was named after Hughes' secretary, who patented it.

Absolutely no person with a grain of sense would have passed these tools as practical. Their defects, their uselessness were obvious. Whoever was responsible for the issue must have had a childish idea of the requirements of the fighting man or he must have been financially interested in the matter. Most soldiers take the latter view. These tools were nothing more than small spades with a hole in them with metal shaft and handle. They were crudely made and blunt. How they ever expected an infantryman to pack such a heavy and unwieldy article around passes comprehension. Nevertheless they were issued to us in England and might have been seen stacked up in little piles outside the tents. They were never used. Every morning they had to be straightened out and dressed correctly so the the the O.C.[5] and his satellites could glance down the lines and with admiring looks give the password, "O.K."

Another perpetration and the most dangerous of the lot was the Ross Rifle. It has cost the 1st and 2nd Divisions many lives. Sam Hughes and his admirers defended this rifle persistently despite the wholesale condemnation by the men who used it and the musketry experts of the British Army. Its chief defects were it was too long and showed above the trenches. It was continually catching in the overhead trench signalling wire. It did not balance on the shoulder well and often tilted to the side, the muzzle catching in the mud. With so much open metal surface and mechanism it was difficult to keep clean and from rusting. But the principal objection was that it jammed. The least thing would jam it—a speck of just, a shower of rain, even a burst of rapid fire. Very often there was difficulty in loading. The Ross Rifle was a standing joke amongst the Imperial troops. It was a glad day when an exchange was made. In connection with this rifle there is one man the 6th Brigade would like to meet—a hireling of Sam Hughes. He was an officer, a musketry instructor and in England gave us a most eulogistic lecture on the Ross rifle. The Ross rifle is first and foremost a target rifle and in this capacity is hard to beat. Our snipers still retain it for sniping purposes; as a service rifle it is next to useless.[6]

Nearing St. Sylvestre Cappell, the brigade broke up into small units and our company took up its abode at a farm, the officers being billeted in the house and the men made themselves as comfortable as possible in the farm buildings, some sleeping in the barn, in sheds, in

---

[5] O.C.—Officer Commanding.

[6] The Ross rifle, Mk. III, was manufactured in Canada. Fraser expresses what most soldiers felt about this weapon, but it was another year before the Ross was abandoned in favour of the British Lee-Enfield.

carts. I passed the night on the grass. Excitement ran high when we ascertained that wine and beer could be obtained at the farm house. Thirsts developed suddenly and sampling was frequent. Beer, retailed ten centimes per glass, practically told the quality. Coloured water, medicinal flavour and a ghost of a froth that could only be produced by a three foot drop. This was to be one of our few beverages for the duration of our sojourn in Sunny France and Muddy Belgium. The others were wine and coffee. The wine, red or white, was weak, flat and sour. It would be a perfect delight to the temperance advocate. The other wines, grenadine and citron were very sweet. In its class, the coffee was the best and every soldier who has been in France has pleasant memories of those little bowls of coffee and slices of French bread. They proved so often a stopgap to hunger when our commissariat broke down. Before passing it may be well to mention the bread; we had so often to supplement our rations with it. It was practically tasteless and took many slices to ease that vacant feeling. It was conspicuous by its enormous size and in shape it was round or sausage. The cost ranged from 7½ d. to 1 s. according to size or place of purchase. This night was bitterly cold and I resolved that my next night would be spent indoors.

Monday, September 20, 1915

All day heavy gun fire was heard. We spent a considerable time watching aeroplanes. The enemy was using his anti-aircraft guns freely, the shells bursting in the air. No planes appeared to have been struck. I slept in the barn tonight.

Tuesday, September 21, 1915

Today the Brigade was reviewed by General Plumer,[7] the Army Commander, in a field near St. Sylvestre Cappell. He is an elderly man with white hair and moustache, heavy features and a weak mouth, the very opposite of what you would expect a soldier to be. Tonight I gave away my surplus kit to a French boy. My memory of the last march is still fresh in my mind and I am beginning to see the necessity of husbanding my strength.

---

[7] General Sir Henry Plumer commanded the British Second Army. About a week earlier, with the arrival of the 2nd Canadian Infantry Division, the two Canadian divisions had been grouped into the Canadian Corps under the command of Lt.-Gen. Sir E. A. H. Alderson who, until this time, commanded the 1st Canadian Infantry Division.

Wednesday, September 22, 1915

Left for Aldershot Camp reserve billets for Ploegstreert-Messines front, halting at Meteren for our midday meal. Reports were current that the Uhlans had been in this village and committed outrages there in the early months of the war. There was nothing to show that fighting had taken place so I presume what had occurred were cavalry skirmishes so prevalent in the early days. There was also a story going the rounds that the "Fishponds" were in the vicinity of St. Sylvestre Cappell. This was the place where the Highlanders drove the enemy into the marshes and ponds killing them in the water. I remember reading about the incident, and also saw a sketch depicting the scene in one of the London Illustrated papers. A mile beyond Meteren is the old French town of Bailleul, through which many a British and Colonial soldier has passed. (At the present time, July 1918, it is in possession of the Huns and is in ruins.) When we entered it, it was very busy. In the centre of the square was an interesting crowd of staff officers eagerly sizing up the Canadian Second Division and we tried to make a brave show as we almost ran through the town. Swinging into the Armentières Road we halted for a rest near the Catholic Home. The day was very hot and water bottles were empty so I got mine refilled at the Convent, the nun adding peppermint to make the water more palatable. Several miles along the road we turned to the left and soon reached the billets, wooden huts, situated in a sea of mud. Today's march was the most trying we have had and many were on the brink of exhaustion. Little judgment was exercised, the pace being too rapid for the hot day and heavy pack. No. 4 platoon was late in arriving having taken the Locre road by mistake. Blankets having gone astray we sleep in our sweater and overcoat.

Friday, September 24, 1915

Taking life easy. We are supposed to be in reserve. From the top of a hill we can see the shelled village of Neuve Église. We are now in Belgium. General Alderson of the First Division visited us and gave us some advice telling us on no account to look over the parapet in daytime and so forth.

Saturday, September 25, 1915

At 5:00 p.m. we get ready for a five mile walk to the trenches. Hitherto I have been assisting the Company Quartermaster. Finding we were making for the line the fighting spirit rose within me and I rudely severed my connection with him and went back to the Company much to the amusement of the platoon officer and sergeant and discomfiture of the Q.M.[8] who had to find a couple of men to take my place. The night was exceedingly dark and stormy and rain was falling steadily. After much delay we slowly moved away. Complete silence was enjoined and no smoking was allowed. We halted for a few minutes frequently. There was something peculiar and tragic in the march. Our utter ignorance of where we were coupled with this intense silence kept us in a pitch of suspense. What added to our amazement was the fact that we were passing soldiers in twos and threes smoking, humming, and acting with unconcern. Subsequently we learned that our extreme caution was unnecessary and we had many a laugh over it. We moved slowly along and saw much evidence of the war. We passed through Neuve Église, a gaunt skeleton village in ruins. There were great gaping holes in the buildings. Shell holes on either side of the road. Trenches running parallel and close to the road. Destruction was complete. It was decidedly eerie passing through this dead village and one felt a sense of insecurity till he got out of it. Away to the right and parallel to the road Fritz was sending up his starlights illuminating the country around and causing our prowlers in "No Man's Land" uneasiness for fear of detection.

Sunday, September 26, 1915

At 1:00 a.m. we arrived at our destination and in the darkness lay on the roadside to await further events. We were at the cross roads at Kemmel. The 29th Battalion went into the trenches named the Es and Fs on our right and the 28th Battalion into parts of the Fs and Gs on the left, the 5th and 4th Brigades occupying the adjoining trenches further north. Our frontage was the lower slope of the Wytschaete Ridge. The 27th Battalion proceeded to reserve billets at Locre and the bulk of the 31st to Kemmel Shelters. It was fortunate Fritz did not indulge in shelling for we were crowded on the road in a quarter which we subsequently learned was unhealthy and one which we used to pass quickly. Headquarters of the battalion to be relieved was busy giving out instructions and we found out later No. 3 and 4 platoons were bound for St. Germania's School at the eastern end of Kemmel on the La Clytte Road, their work being to carry rations, etc. during the night to the 28th Battalion. Our officers received their orders and we cut through the Kemmel Chateau grounds for the school. An officer of the relieved battalion in strident tones ordered us to halt asking where in the mischief we were going to, but

8 The Quartermaster was Captain J. C. Page.

only the last section heard him including our officer. He then directed us round the Kemmel Road and our first of many muddles started. We passed the rest of the battalion and in the dim light I could see the looks of bewilderment on the faces of a small group of our officers including the colonel. Our section of about ten including the writer passed on. Turning to the left we proceeded up the Locre Road when a figure sprang out from the darkness beside the Ypres Hotel with a bayonet pointing at us and in a menacing voice shouted: "Halt! Who goes there?" Our officer who was leading shook perceptibly, the unexpected suddenness giving him quite a start. The sentry being satisfied retired into the shadows once more. He belonged to the Canadian Scottish.[9] The next few minutes found us wandering about Kemmel. Rounding the church we struck the La Clytte Road, where we lay down disgusted, leaving the officer to find the place. A moment later the rest of the half company appeared so we tagged ourselves on to them and soon found the school. It consisted of two big rooms, most of the glass in the windows was gone also the doors. In the centre of the eastern room were several layers of sandbags beneath which was a damp cellar, a refuge from artillery fire. A trench led from this through the building to the outside. Being tired we soon began to make preparations for a sleep and lay on the tiles with a waterproof sheet beneath and an overcoat on top. About 5:00 a.m. we were rudely awakened by shells whizzing overhead. One struck the church tower near the clock, another demolished part of a house in which an old Belgian woman lay in bed sleeping. The greater part of the side of the house was blown out together with part of the floor, leaving the room which was on the second floor exposed. The woman, by a miracle, was unhurt. Three shells fell in the field adjoining. Inside of the school was a regular pandemonium. Everyone was chasing around gathering up their gear ready to flee. The place was in an uproar with fellows hurrying up to get out. Hastily chucking my kit into my pack including, I found out later, parts of my neighbour's kit, I got out of the room into the other but notwithstanding my desperate hurry, I was last. Making for the exit, I saw Capt. W. P.[10] at the corner of the building beside Doull, the sentry, and Lovell, my bedmate behind him. All of a sudden there was a whiz and the captain came chasing back overrunning the entrance in his hurry,

---

[9] This was the 16th Battalion (Canadian Scottish), a unit in the 3rd Brigade of the 1st Canadian Division.

[10] Throughout his journal, Fraser frequently mentions officers only by their initials. A list of the officers who served in his unit will be found in an appendix of the battalion's history: H. C. Singer and A. A. Peebles, *History of the Thirty-First Battalion, C.E.F.* Published by the 31st Battalion Assn., 1938.

with Lovell following. He sank on to the sandbags, buried his face in his hands, and appeared very much startled. Lt. H—— and he "were at a loss what to do," one suggesting to get the men out of the building and the other that they remain where they were. It was evident no instructions were given about what to do in the case of shell-fire. They were not even aware if we were within view of the enemy or not. We found out later we were not. Our estimation of our officers sank to zero and it was a lesson to us that in future it is best to rely on your own wits and do not expect too much from those senior to you. This was our baptism of fire and we emerged without casualites, but received a bit of a scare.

Monday, September 27, 1915

Rations arrive at night and are much welcomed.

Tuesday, September 28, 1915

The village was shelled slightly. We heard that several of the 28th fellows had been killed. Aircraft is very busy.

Wednesday September 29, 1915

We made our first trip to the firing line with rations, etc. for the 28th Battalion. The night is dark, wet and boisterous and we feel cold and shivery all over. Nevertheless we leave the school, pass the Chateau and halt beside H'Quarters, formerly the residence of the Belgian doctor. The house is in fairly good repair, only several panes of glass being broken and a few chips taken out of the building, whilst the garden possesses a souvenir or two in the shape of shell holes. We line up for our loads, my particular one being sandbags. Being a bit green and confident of my powers I tell the fellow who is loading to chuck some more on my shoulder. Frisk, a Swede, who was behind me, not to be outdone accepted a bigger pile. We had not gone very far when we were sorry we had spoken. We had to go about three hundred yards across the open before we struck the communication trench which rejoiced in the Latin appelation of "Via Gellia." The path was muddy and slippery which added to our trials. At the entrance to the trench a fellow ahead of me slipped and fell into a ditch. The air was blue with rich language for the next few moments. The trench led through a hedge then zigzagged for a few hundred yards. By this time it began to deepen and stray bullets were hitting earth especially near an old haystack close by. A little further on the trench was six to seven feet deep so we were fairly safe from rifle fire. Our loads were becoming troublesome, falling off our shoulders and the Ross rifle, inclining outwards, the muzzle now and then would catch on the side of the trench clogging up with mud. We had to rest frequently but not for long. Dead Cow Corner was passed and at Beaver Hat we entered the skeleton remains of a belt of wood.[11] Bullets were cracking in the trees. Strong Point 11 was soon passed. From here the trench began to wind up the base of the Wytschaete Ridge. On our right the support line branched off. A hundred and fifty yards further on we file into a trench without trench mats[12] near a couple of crosses denoting the graves of former occupants of the line.

We are now only a few hundred yards away from the enemy so we move quietly up to the appointed dump in the front line. There is a perfect hiss of bullets overhead and a peculiar hum from those that ricochet. Our own men are firing in return and every bay gives forth a crack, crack. It is the custom as soon as darkness sets in for both sides to keep up a more or less continuous fire at each other's trenches, to keep one another from attacking and also, to keep patrols from No Man's Land. It also shows that one is awake and there is not the same chance of being taken by surprise. The tendency when firing in the dark is to fire high with the result that the majority of the bullets go fringing over the trenches, maybe to find a victim two thousand yards behind; many men get killed in this fashion. It shows, therefore, how risky it is moving around in the open within rifle range.

Going up the trench, orders were passed down to keep low. The writer respected the command, so did those in front; but the fellow behind me in a spirit of bravado kept taunting me with the remarks, "What was I scared of." Being of puny dimensions it struck me he could ignore the order with impunity so I ignored him. However, he kept on ragging and I was forced to ejaculate, "Shut up you blethering idiot" but to no avail and my dander was beginning to rise. Whenever there is a hole in the trench mat, the warning is usually passed from man to man, the word "hole" being sufficient enlightenment to make one aware. It happened there was a hole and Buttress, who was in front of me, murmured "hole." My chance had come. I remained silent and stepped over it, the next moment my tormentor, K——, fell in a heap. He extricated himself muttering imprecations

[11] Trenches, as well as other key geographical points were usually given names which were often associated with the soldiers' home town (e.g., Regina Trench), with some peculiarity of the terrain, with an event which took place nearby, or for any variety of reasons which bubbled up in the fertile mind of Canadian, British, Australian and other soldiers. Sometimes they were called by letters of the alphabet ("G" Trench), or a combination of letters and numbers such as H4 or K3.

[12] A type of boardwalk made of wooden slats to keep the soldiers' feet from being constantly in mud and water.

on my head. The rest of the trip he was too busy watching his feet to annoy me.

At last we reached the dug-out where we dumped our loads. It was beside a long bay in which three 28th men were. They were on the firing step one at each corner and one in the middle. The fellow in the corner nearest me was peering cautiously into the darkness, his mate in the middle had worked himself into a fever heat with rage with, I expect, the idea of impressing me with his fighting importance. He was blazing away at the hostile trenches, cursing the Germans in unsavoury language and inviting them to come over to see what he would do to them. His rifle was troubling him. After firing he had to knock down the bolt with his foot before he could eject the shell and reload. It was a poor advertisement for the Ross rifle. In the midst of his tirade I asked him how far away Heiny[13] was. "75 yards," he uttered. I learned afterwards it was about 250 yards. Loads were all dumped so word was given to retire. We needed no further advice, but in good order beat it back quickly arriving at St. Germania's School about 1:00 a.m. after a good 5½ mile hike.

Thursday, September 30, 1915

Made the same trip tonight but got caught in the front line in a lively whiz-bang,[14] grenade bombardment. The enemy all of a sudden opened upon the front and support lines and for twenty minutes there was a regular display of fireworks. Our party hugged the trench mats closely with their hearts in their mouths. The shells were just skimming the parapet whizzing overhead with a roar. It was too dangerous to move so we lay crouched till some officer phoned to the artillery for assistance. It replied and evidently had a good line on the hostile trenches for Heiny quit shortly afterwards. We breathed a bit more freely and hurried out without much delay. On arriving at the school we found that the whiz-bang battery was not more than three hundred yards away.

Friday, October 1, 1915

At 2:00 p.m. we start for our six days in the trenches. The routine for the 6th Brigade is—two battalions in the front line, support line and strong points for six days, one battalion in and around Kemmel for six days and the remaining battalion in reserve at Locre, a village

[13] "Heiny," "the Hun," "Fritz," "Bosche," were terms commonly used by British and Canadian soldiers when referring to the German soldier.

[14] A "whiz-bang" was a high velocity shrapnel shell fired by the field artillery. See Fraser's comments for October 5, 1915.

several kilometers in the rear. The 28th and 29th have been in the line for their term so the 27th (Winnipeg) Battalion go in to relieve the 29th from Vancouver and the 31st take over the line from the 28th from the North West Provinces and my platoon goes into S.P. 9[15] which is about 800 yards behind the firing line. We start early. We had quite a long march through the trenches, the communication trench going under the name of Regent Street. S.P. 9 turned out to be a circular redoubt on slightly elevated ground, with a trench running round it and small trenches, covered in, radiating from the centre. At the eastern end a short trench branched off at the end of which was a machine-gun emplacement. Near it, on the left, a small trench ran out to the wire, the end of which was supposed to be a listening post. There were four guards in connection with this redoubt. One [was] beside the communication trench. The duty there was to challenge passersby at night time. One [was] at the listening post. This post was a huge joke for between it and the enemy lay our front and support lines. Nevertheless, a sentry was placed there and he could listen to the rats to his heart's content. The other two guards were in the redoubt.

I was posted as second relief on one of them. Asking Doull, the party I relieved, what the duties were, he replied, "You are supposed to stand on the firing step here and keep an eye on the country ahead!" But lowering his voice he said, sinisterlike, "Don't." His advice turned out to be good. An uncanny number of stray bullets were flying through the air and it was decidedly unhealthy keeping one's head above the parapet. There was quite an alarm caused when all round us we would hear now and then a crack, crack. We thought snipers were there and this was the report of their rifles. The officer and others planned to go out the next night and account for them. But instead of snipers it turned out to be stray bullets hitting the earth with a smack. Yes, we were dreadfully green! Our position, not being very important, we had fatigue duties to do such as taking up water and rations for the rest of the Company.

Tonight we had our introduction to dug-out life. The dug-outs were small, damp and cold and overrun with rats. It is needless to add once a fighting soldier leaves England he practically sleeps in his clothes till he gets back there again. Taking off our boots, there were three of us in the dug-out, we lay down between our waterproof sheet and overcoat and snatched as many winks as we could. There is a change of sentry every two hours, so the chances are you get

---

[15] S.P.—Strong Point. This was a particularly well dug in and defended part of the trench system, defended both by riflemen and machine-gunners.

wakened up between the shifts, either by your mate getting up or coming in or being wakened by mistake for guard. To interrupt your prospective slumbers, sometimes, the order to "stand to" for the night comes along which means you have to hold yourself in readiness for eventualities, in other words, you have to be wide awake with equipment on, etc.

And order to "stand to" is equivalent to expecting an attack. Many a time we wished those attacks would materialize so that we could get a half decent sleep afterwards. At sunrise and sunset there is a "stand to" every day, these being the times the enemy is liable to come over. When the order is given everyone is supposed to get out of his dug-out, get his equipment on and have his rifle handy. "Stand down" is usually passed along half an hour to an hour afterwards, when the day shifts start. In the daytime two or three guards are considered sufficient to keep watch.

A few of us went down to H'Qrs. which is about 400 yards away for our rations [and] whilst there we saw the 27th Battn. coming into the line. It was easily seen they were new for the officer in front did not slacken pace. When a large body of men is in single file and has difficult ground to cover, the pace has to be slow otherwise those in the rear will have to almost run to keep up. This is owing to fellows in the line losing distance a few yards then quickening their step to make up. This throws those in the rear behind. Again there is often delay in crossing a ticklish part of the trench or going under a traverse. This also strings the party out. The consequence is old timers like to be near the lead. It is easier on them. Anyway the 27th, with humped backs and bewildered looks, were hurrying past us till one poor fellow who was on the slow side failed to connect up and losing sight of his predecessor proceeded up a ditch about two feet deep and wide thinking it was the trench, much to our amusement. He went up about fifteen yards, his mates following, till we directed him.

We notice our rations are increased but there is no variety—tea, bread, hard biscuits, butter, jam, bacon, bully-beef, maconochie,[16] fresh meat, cheese, rice, dried vegetables. These are the supplies but they are not of daily occurrence. It may be tinned food one day and fresh meat the next and so on. It is general knowledge that rations are increased when we go into the line. The rum[17] we heard so much about came up tonight. We are given a tot—a few teaspoonsful either at night or early morning. It is much appreciated as it helps the circulation which gets very slow these cold nights for want of move-

---

[16] The trade name of a tin of meat and vegetable stew.
[17] Usually referred to as "SRD"—Service Rum, Diluted.

ment. Time and again it has come to the rescue and many owe their freedom from colds, rheumatism, and kindred troubles to the timely inward application of this liquor. The cigarette or fag is another lifesaver. The crave for cigarettes with many is irresistible. In the firing line it is almost their whole existence. It appears to soothe the jaded nerves and makes them tractable. Without fags I am sure many a soldier would soon go to pieces. One of the most noticeable things after a soldier is wounded is that he will call for a fag. When lying in hospital at Rouen wounded, a French-Canadian was taken to the bed next to me. He had been shot in the head regaining some consciousness in Rouen several days afterwards. Before he knew really where he was he called for a smoke. He was too weak to hold the cigarette so the nurse held it to his lips while he smoked.

The firing line is about 85 yds. from the enemy and the support line 150 yds. behind this. The trenches are old and evil smelling, in some places the stench being almost unbearable. This is usually caused by shells bringing refuse or dead bodies to the surface. Anyway chloride of lime or creosol is issued as a ration and the sanitary police attend to its distribution. Every company has its sanitary policeman whose duty it is to see to sanitation wherever the company may be placed.

Tuesday, October 5, 1915

The battalion has received its first casualty, a man named Nuttall being accidentally killed through a rifle going off. Lowe of my Company[18] was badly wounded today and has just passed out on a stretcher. He was in a dug-out when a whiz-bang came over and exploded above him lacerating his face and destroying his eyesight. The wounding of Lowe has caused quite an impression and judging by remarks and solemn expressions one would fancy it is the beginning of the end.

Several shells come over our redoubt, one bursting quite close sending several pieces of shrapnel into the trench. There was quite a bit of excitement towards the middle of the day over whiz-bangs. It was laughable seeing Major H—— and Asst. Adj. S—— making a bolt for cover on hearing one coming. We were kept busy lying low till the storm subsided. I found my first souvenir, a piece of newly fired whiz-bang. It included the nosecap and aluminum attachment. Whiz-bang is the name given to a light shell of high velocity and trajectory. It is practically on the top of you as soon as you hear the

---

[18] Fraser was in "A" Company at this time.

report of the gun. It is well termed. First you hear the whiz and almost simultaneously comes the bang, then a metallic singing in the air as the pieces of shrapnel fly through space.

Wednesday, October 6, 1915

About 8:00 p.m. we are relieved by the 28th. It took us till 1:00 a.m. to reach our reserve billets at Locre. After emerging from the trenches we go along the Vierstraat Road then turn to the left and pass through Kemmel, where we have an uphill climb over the right slope of Kemmel Hill, past the shelters on the left and thence on to Locre. Ranging along the Locre-Dranoutre Road are our billets, oblong huts sloping to about two feet from the ground. We sleep on the floor about ten to each side. Being dead tired most of us sleep soundly. So far we have not reached the stage where through excessive weariness and exhaustion, sleep becomes punctuated with groans and sighs and unconsciously one tosses from side to side as if racked with pain. Later on, when the campaign becomes more arduous and the strain more exacting, we experience this in full measure.

Friday, October 8, 1915

Another rest day. We have been up at the bath-house and have received clean underclothing which has freshened us up quite a bit. Our paymaster paid us the munificent sum of forty-five francs so we feel as if we are in clover. A franc is nominally rated at tenpence though I believe in Britain the exchange is eight pence half penny. Naturally, the boys roam the village to see what they can purchase. Army rations are neither too plentiful nor nourishing and if one depended wholly on them his strength would not hold out many months. Most fellows find this out and to keep them in shape make purchases of food as often as they can. Eatables, beverages, cigarettes and stationery account for the little pay given to the troops when in the field. Almost every house in Belgium will supply you with eggs, coffee and bread. On occasions you can get meat. The boys are so glad of a change that some of them consume as many as twenty eggs in a day. The order is usually three to six eggs per meal.

The village is dirty and the buildings seem old and unsanitary. The inside of the houses are bare and untidy. What pictures or ornaments there are, are usually emblematic of Catholicism. The people themselves are unkempt. Most of them have a smattering of English picked up from the soldiers and often use swear words not knowing what they mean. The troops air their French which usually amounts to madam, cafe, compres (*sic*), oui and a few other words. A conversation between a soldier and a Belgian is very amusing. Every third word is punctuated with "Compres (*sic*) and oui" with gesticulations. The majority of the Belgians speak Flemish and French. The women do all the trading with the soldiers whilst the men keep very much in the background. At times one is apt to think Belgians are more in sympathy with the enemy, they certainly do not show any gladness in seeing the British troops and seldom show animosity on hearing the name of the Hun. I once heard a Belgian in Antwerp speak disparagingly of the natives of Flanders, saying they were no good, they were half German. In my wanderings I only came across three houses in which the occupants were really frank and pleasant and showed a disposition towards friendliness. They were rabid anti-German and gave me an account of the happenings in the district in the earlier part of the war. Locre contains a few hundred inhabitants, many of whom are refugees from Ypres, Messines, Lille and the smaller villages in the fighting area. There is nothing of importance in the place. The usual ancient Catholic Church with its stained glass windows dominates the village. There is a large building, a Convent and Hospital, several hundred yards away. Every third shop is an "estaminet" which retails beer, wine, etc.

At 7:00 p.m. we receive orders to "stand to." Evidently a scare message has come from the line but nothing resulted.

Saturday, October 9, 1915

We leave Locre tonight on fatigue for the trenches. A few hundred yards up "Via Gellia," the communication trench, a stray bullet catches Big Woods, an Irishman, in the thigh creating a nasty wound and placing him *hors de combat* for the rest of the campaign. Skinner, a little Englishman, who was immediately in front of Woods, claimed in all seriousness that the bullet was meant for him. From this time onward his heart sunk to zero and he began to contract imaginary troubles, reporting sick so frequently that the doctor, Captain McGill, who subsequently earned the soubriquet "Iodine Pete," refused to have anything to do with him. As a useful force, Skinner was done and we were glad to see him shifted for good to the base. Several of our most enthusiastic members for things military whilst in Canada and England changed completely and before many trips were spent in the line, they were busy looking around for safety first jobs or trying their hardest to become sick or unfit so as to be removed from the fighting area.

It is astonishing the number of men who have disappeared to the base through sickness. In peace time, we draw our conclusions of fighting men from their physique and smartness when on the move. We find this is a poor criterion in war time. The best fighter of today may be summed up in the words "fearlessness" and "grit," two qualities that every husky [man] has not got and qualities that sometimes the weakest, the softest and apparently the most effeminate have. Time and again under trying conditions I have seen great, big, strong, noisy fellows absolutely appalled and dispirited with scarcely a sparkle of life in them and next to them little insignificant runts quite unconcerned and ready to give a good account of themselves. In soldier language "guts" is the best adjunct when in the line and it appears as if it is a lost quality with the expert in the barrack room training. On the whole those who have been well versed in military drill in our battalion have shown up very badly indeed when brought face to face with the realities of war.

The way our old soldiers, physical drill instructors, bayonet fighting instructors disappeared under the stress of battle to realms of easier work was a great disappointment to us. To instance a few cases. When the 31st became a battalion, the Regt. Sgt.-Maj. was a man named B——. He was one of the mainstays of the 103rd Calgary Rifles and naturally interested in military work. He was very insistent that we smarten up and be soldiers. His part of soldiering, however, was spent in England. He took good care to stay on the safe side of the Channel. As Sgt.-Maj. of our company—a hero of a hundred fights you would fancy him to be if you listened to his conversation—he wore four ribbons for service in Africa, Egypt and the Sudan and was a faddist on bayonet fighting. In England, he used to tap his side gently and remark that this, alluding to his revolver, was for N.C.O.s who refused to go over the top. I only saw this fire-eater pay a visit to the trenches once. I gave him the periscope to look through. He was very uneasy and had a halfhearted glance through it, slinking back to H'Qrs. a few minutes afterwards. This seasoned warrior obtained a commission and in addition managed [to get] back to Canada. I noticed his picture very nearly the central figure in a group of War Veterans, taken before their quarters on 9th Ave., Calgary.

Another hero was Major, or I think it is now, Lt.-Col. S——. He was an old regular and knew the manual of drill and regulations from A to Z. He started in as Colour-Sergeant and was a great stickler for red tape—a regular bully and worry to the men. He laboured trivial matters to a degree. This officer possessed the knack of turning sick when anything was doing. His actual experience of serious fighting was nil. These are only a few cases. In England there are numerous officers and men whose sojourn in the line has been that of Cook's tourists. When the war is over these are the men who will

39

come back as heroes, parade their length of service, and give the most vivid account of fighting. The army is jocularly classified by the actual scrapper into two groups, firstly the soldier who knows all and secondly the fighting man who does all.

Sunday, October 10, 1915

About 4:00 p.m. I am warned to proceed with several others to Poperinghe, a town about eight miles away. According to [the] Orderly Room the matter was so pressing that we could not wait to get something to eat. The Corporal in charge, Still, went to H'Qrs. for instructions. The Adjutant, Capt. Myatt, gave him a letter and showed him on the map what way to go. We were naturally very loath to be rushed away without a bite. Too often the important in the army is nothing at all and we suspected this.

The Cpl., who took his stripes seriously, marched us the whole distance as if on parade. Our route lay through Hyde Park Corner and Reninghelst, but the Cpl. insisted we include Westoutre as well because the Adj. said so. I happened to have a map and showed the distance that would be saved by taking the shorter route, but of no avail. We cursed under our breaths and wished Orderly Room would purchase shilling maps instead of six penny ones, they would get more details then. We reached Poperinghe about dusk and wondered very much what strange errand we were on, seeing we were several miles out of the Canadian area and amidst Imperial Troops.[19] We came across a remnant of the Royal Scots who had participated at the fight at Vermilles near La Bassce several days ago. The two I spoke to had not pleasant remarks to make regarding the way they were handled. They claimed they took three lines of trenches but were never backed up. No supports came to their assistance and they got badly cut up. As the Corporal could not find the party the letter was addressed to, he called at a certain unit's H'Qrs. Here he was advised that it was Croix de Poperingue and not Poperinghe we should have gone to. The former place is on the Bailleul Road in a different direction and only two miles from our starting point at Locre. Our adjutant came in for a volley of unparliamentary language and the whole Canadian army likewise. It was now dark and we were hungry and footsore so we dropped into an Estaminet and had the proverbial eggs and coffee served up in the usual Belgian fashion, plain and not too clean. We left one of our fellows—James—behind. He was too crippled to walk. He took up his abode at a church, but "Old Heiny"

[19] Imperial troops was a common term for British troops.

40

shelled Poperinghe that night and next morning James beat it back to healthier surroundings. It was nearly midnight when we got back to the camp at Locre.

Monday, October 11, 1915

We set out this morning for Croix de Poperingue and got directed wrongly once more. A motor transport picked us up and from the driver we learn what our mission is. It appears we have to shovel coal. The Canadian army has a coal yard at Bailleul station and our duty is to load the coal there on motor trucks which carry it to the Divisional dump at Croix de Poperingue. A supply is being stored up for the winter. We jump into the motor which is capable of carrying three tons and depart for Meteren, the mechanical transport's camping ground. Here we get rid of our arms and equipment and proceed back to Bailleul railway siding. We make four trips between Bailleul and Croix de Poperingue altogether and then return to camp. This work would engage us all winter but as our adjutant would not hear of us being kept from the line, those in charge of the transport had to seek assistance elsewhere. It was rather amusing; instead of taking the coal from the Canadian yard we took it from the British, the officer in charge went up in the air when he saw us coolly helping ourselves. An event of much importance happened, namely, that we dined on beef-steak instead of the everlasting mulligan and bully-beef. Naturally we voted the mechanical transport good fellows.

Tuesday, October 12, 1915

We leave for the trenches, this time by "Via Gellia." Our platoon is to be located in the front line at G3[20] about 250 yds. from the enemy. I was one of the advance party. The bay I took over was the scene of the death of one of the sentries of the 28th Battalion a couple of days previously. His fellow men appeared a bit unnerved over the incident and narrated the occurrence in subdued tones. It appears he was enfiladed from the left when peering over the parapet receiving a bullet in the head. The usual formalities were asked, namely distance to Fritz's line, strength of wire in front, thickness of top sandbags, any peculiarities of No Man's Land, any sniping and shelling on this particular spot, where and how far away is water, etc. A few hours later when it is dark, the battalion files in, three men dropping off at each bay. As soon as possible positions are taken up and the 28th Battalion departs, the relief being effected.

[20] That is, a section of trench designated "G3" on the trench map.

41

Reliefs are very often badly made and a general mixup ensues which riles the men badly. Often there is a block in the trench. A little attention to this by officers and sergeants beforehand would go a long way towards making a good relief. How to handle men going in and out of the trenches I think would be of more advantage than the usual field movements as practised in training. A jam in a trench for quite a long time is a common occurrence. We took some sort of a dug-out and decide on the relief. It is usually two hours on and four off. We consider ourselves lucky if we have no fatigues to do. Rations and water are almost certainties for the night.

During the day, if we are not on day duty, we are almost certain to be building dug-outs or fixing up the trenches, so our stretches of sleep even in the best and quietest of times is of short duration. If the line is quiet and the command does not anticipate trouble, two sentries can doze in their dug-out. The man on guard stands on the firing step and peers over the bags for any movement in No Man's Land at the same time listening intently for any sounds. The ears are more dependable when it is dark than the eyes. The touching of the wire, the stumbling against old tins, or the swishing noise of the grasses moving are apt to give a raider or patrol away. Unless on the skyline, it is difficult picking up anyone moving till they are almost on you. If you are suspicious, the usual thing is to get someone to fire a flare over the particular spot. A good sentry does not move much but keeps to a certain spot remaining mute for a considerable time and shows very little of his head. He is better able to detect and, what is of as much importance, he is less liable to be seen than a man who is moving around the bay. The majority of fellows, however, do not worry. They pass most of their time sitting on the firing step smoking the pipe of peace, with an occasional glance over the parapet. As a rule one can size up affairs pretty good. If Fritz is sending up star shells pretty frequently you can depend upon it his patrols or raiders are not out. If his riflemen are pinging bullets in our direction and they are low, you can rest easy in the belief that his men are behind his parapet. It is when his lights are not going up often or his shooting is nil or high, you should be suspicious and on the alert. It is then he is either up to mischief, making a relief or has fatigue parties out in front fixing up his wire.

When there are suspicions suggesting the possibility of an attack, no one is allowed into his dug-out at night. The men do not take very kindly to this and the ones not actually on sentry have the habit of sneaking back to the dug-out. As a rule, however, they doze with one eye open, though many are out and out careless. As time goes on one acquires a certain instinct that makes him move and act in a careful,

... [yet casual] sort of way. He takes in the lay of the country and senses the bad spots as it were. He is very observant and notices the slope of the parapet, the thickness of the top sandbags and whether they are ripped by fire or not. Certain corners look nervy to him; stumps of trees, any slight elevation or hollow or semblance of trench or shell holes in No Man's Land grips his attention. For long stretches he will gaze through the periscope for holes in the opponent's parapet, for sniping plates, looking intently at the base and corners of the bags. He looks well to his opponent's flanks as snipers have a habit of screening their position from the front by having it facing the flanks and firing across No Man's Land obliquely. It is this instinct of un-canny caution that makes a man, as soon as he gets into the line, become acquainted with the location of bombs. As a rule he keeps one or two very handy and does not wander away from his rifle. Unknowingly, one becomes wary and suspicious and the faculties become very alert. It does not take long when one can tell, when he hears the report of a rifle if the bullet is coming in his direction or not.

A dull pop from the opponent's lines and one immediately scans the horizon for a trench mortar.[21] In ordinary times such noises would escape one's attention. The German little fish tail bomb starts its course through the air with a swish, swish and makes a peculiar noise like wa-wa. Excepting high velocity shells, one has a fair indication of direction when he hears the report of the gun. Rifle grenades, when fired during shelling, are difficult to detect. I often wonder that when trench mortar companies [22] intend throwing over their shells, they do not get the artillery to kick up a noise so as their opponents will have to rely solely on their sight to pick up what is going to happen.

At this stage it may be well to mention what the ordinary infan-tryman in the firing line has to go through and what his nerves have to stand. Old No Man's Land had an average width of 150 to 250 yds.; in many parts of the line it would come as close as 35 to 75 yds. As a rule, the narrower No Man's Land, the weaker the wire. The distance between is so little that fixing up wire is impossible. Ready made

[21] Mortars, used since medieval times, were weapons designed to lob a shell or bomb a short distance but with a high trajectory. When trench warfare started late in 1914, a number of devices were created to throw a bomb or grenade, some of them made by the soldiers, across No Man's Land into the enemy's front, support or reserve lines. Sometimes crude catapults were used. By 1915, however, both sides were supplied with a number of trench mortars which threw bombs of various calibres. On the Canadian side the 3-inch Stokes mortar was the most common. Fraser, like other soldiers, frequently identifies the German mortar bombs by their shape as they fell towards the Canadian trenches. One especially, which he calls "a sausage," caused considerable damage owing to its size.

[22] Each brigade had a Trench Mortar Battery attached to it.

wiring obstacles have to be thrown over and, of course, they cannot be expected to be very effective. In fact, later on, Fritz had the audacity to fix on one of our wiring obstacles and pulled it on to his own side. Anyway, besides being liable to be shelled at any moment, the man in the firing line is liable to have bombs, grenades and trench mortar [bombs] thrown at him. Machine-guns may open up and rip the sand bags at pleasure. Clamped rifles go off every now and then, trained at likely spots the infantryman has to pass. Any moment a swarm of Huns may rush him. He is liable to be blown up by a mine tunnelled underneath [the trench]. On dark nights the enemy could crawl into his trench without being seen. It is the same when it is foggy. He exists under these conditions, wet or dry, often in mud and slush over the knees and almost frozen with the cold. Sometimes he sleeps on the firing step or in the bottom of the trench with practically no covering or protection. When he gets wet, his clothes have to dry on him—at times he is worked off his feet digging, draining, making dug-outs, carrying timber, corrugated iron, etc. and has to run the gauntlet of being sniped on many occasions. Knowing that any moment he may be hurled into oblivion, his nerves are keyed to a certain pitch and his existence is one of suspense. No wonder the average man's stay in the trenches is a few months. Unfortunately these men who brave such dangers daily, hourly, have nothing to show for it. A Canadian in England gets service stripes the same as he does, not so the British Tommy. A Brigade runner, who once in a while reaches the line, stands a better chance of a decoration. Hangers-on who are seldom within the fighting area and who sleep comfortably and soundly at night and can do their own cooking, get all the medals or clasps they are entitled to. It is high time some distinction was made between the actual fighting man and his numerous knockers in khaki who take practically no risk at all.

Wednesday, October 13, 1915

Before going into the trenches this trip we were informed that there was going to be something doing, that the artillery behind us was going to put up a bombardment. That there was something brooding was evident for at Locre, before leaving for the line, the Divisional Chaplain, Major Beattie, gave us a rather startling sermon, bluntly telling us that there might be dirty work at the cross roads, and many of us might not return. We did not quite relish his remarks. Any more addresses in a similar strain would not have helped the morale of the men. As it was, there was some serious thinking and most were inclined to think that it would have been better if we were left in blissful ignorance. However, in the forenoon word was passed round that at 2:00 o'clock our light artillery was going to open up for an hour and our heavies were to follow on for twenty minutes, after which we were to rush up to the firing line, throw our smoke bombs, then open up rapid fire, simulating an attack.[23]

A little before 2:00 o'clock, with the exception of one sentry to each bay, the rest of us withdrew to feather trenches between the firing line and supports. The reason was that we were not taking chances with shells that might fall short. In addition the feather trenches, being narrow, [gave] more protection. Before the bombardment, smoke bombs were sent up in a hurry and Cpl. Forbes came rushing along the bays instructing the fellows how to use them. They were after the jam tin fashion;[24] the fuse had to be lighted and then they were flung over the parapet when smoke belched forth from them. In my bay, Mackie was the sentry who was to stay behind. He seemed to be a little suspicious of these bombs and I figured he would not do very much with them when the time came. Presently, Lt. H——came along and told us to withdraw, that the racket was about to commence. The feather trenches being choke full, I withdrew to the supports along with D——l, E——s, and P——e. At 2:00 prompt, the artillery went off with a roar, the shells hissing over our heads at all angles. Presently Fritz returned the fire which added fuel to the tumult. We had no idea where the shells were bursting. The whole thing was a pandemonium of noise. Every other moment Fritz would land one with a crash which would almost take our breath away. There we lay huddled up whilst shells were hissing overhead, some perilously close that we thought we would be lifted out of the trench. There was no let up, not even a momentary lull, shell after shell followed in rapid succession; whiz-bangs came with the velocity of lightning; the heavier stuff tore through the upper air like the noise of a train. It was a nerve racking experience and the hour and twenty minutes appeared like half a day.

No sooner had the artillery ceased then there was a rush for the firing line, smoke bombs were lit and thrown over the parapet,

[23] This was part of a demonstration in which the entire brigade took part. It was designed to make the enemy think the brigade was about to attack and so prevent him from sending troops to reinforce his flank where the British were putting in an actual attack.

[24] Fraser is probably referring to "Tickler's Artillery." When empty, a tin of Tickler's plum and apple jam would be filled with bits of metal (used bullet casings, nails, etc.) around a core of high explosive. A fuse, cut so it would burn only a few seconds, would be lit and the "grenade" hurled or catapulted towards the German front line. If properly packed and sealed, it generally went off with a satisfactory bang and might cause some casualties in the enemy's lines.

enveloping No Man's Land in a shroud of fog. We then lined the parapet and blazed away in the direction of Fritz, resolved at least to scare him out of his wits. Luckily between our lines and his there was a ridge, otherwise his machine-gunners would have had a pcinic at our expense for we were all hanging over the bags blazing like fury with no protection whatsoever. The enemy reply was not very strong and when proceedings terminated, we found the only casualty in our Company was Sgt. Dunne, a New Zealander, who had his skull chipped by shrapnel. He did not think much of the wound at the time but it was severe enough to incapacitate him from further military service and in due time he was returned to Canada.

The casualties of the battalion numbered something like nine killed and sixteen wounded, "C" Company being struck the hardest. One of our officers, Lt. Tofft, a Dane, and a member of the R.N.W.M.P. was amongst the slain. It appears a shell landed in the midst of a small group and the lieutenant was blown to bits, part of one of his arms, with wrist watch attached, was found several days later quite a distance away. What remains there were, were collected and interred and at the spot between "F" front line and supports, a cross was erected to his memory and also [to] the others, their names, with the exception of McGinnis, I forget. Cpl. Fraser (Tiny), a native of my own district, and an old London Scottish man, was killed by a rifle grenade. A sentry in the same bay noticed it coming and warned him but it was too late. A curious incident happened, this sentry was wounded shortly afterwards and the nurse who attended him in hospital in Blighty turned out to be a sister of Fraser. I never found out whether the bombardment was intended as a "blind" to draw troops to our front and then attack elsewhere, or if our command tried it out with a view to creating casualties. It appears as if the latter idea is correct for later we were advised that an aeroplane was up and the observer stated that great execution was done, that he saw stretcher after stretcher being conveyed to the rear. He also mentioned that about 8,000 reserves were hurrying to the front, fearing we were going to attack, and that shells burst among them, creating much damage. This was our first bombardment and it was heard miles away. Curious to know how Mackie got on with the smoke bombs, I asked him what he did. "Catch me monkeying with those things," he said, "I did not do any lighting business—I just flung them as far over the parapet as I could."

Monday, October 18, 1915

We are relieved today and retire to reserve at Kemmel Shelters from which we do fatigues.

We have been out all day fixing up the communication trench which has collapsed owing to the recent rains. From now on "Via Gellia" keeps us busy when out on rest. The weather had changed completely, raining almost daily and the ground is in a sodden condition. For want of sunshine and wind, it is impossible for the ground to dry up and after a while we learn that it is useless trying to keep the trenches passable. The rain loosens the earth and the sides cave in. With additional rain the bottom of the trenches become liquid mud which defies all efforts at drainage. We shovel, shovel and keep on shovelling, but it is of no avail, the trench absolutely refuses to clean up. It is a hard proposition, the mud sticks to the shovel and after vigorous efforts to dislodge it, it only comes off to fall into the trench again. In time the bank becomes so high that we cannot fling the mud up so we have to get up on top and in a crouching attitude shove the mud further back, terracing it so as to ease the ground pressure and keep it from sliding down. In wet weather it is stupendous work and is about as hopeless as shovelling water. When a little progress is made posts are driven into the trench and are strengthened by being connected by wire with smaller posts on the parados. The sides are now revetted with corrugated iron which is placed behind the posts being kept in position by them and thus keep the sides from caving in. The pressure of earth, however, is often so great that it bulges the corrugated iron or snaps the posts. One can imagine, therefore, the enormous amount of revetting that is required and the immensity of work in connection with it.

The bottom of the trench has to have the trench boards raised above the water or mud so that one can move up and down quickly. These boards are roughly 1½ to 2 feet wide and from 5 to 8 feet long. They consist of a couple of deals with strips of wood laid crossways. These trench or duck boards are laid on a couple of supporting trestles. Through usage or faulty positioning, many fellows, in the dark, become croppers by stepping on the edge when the board tips or slips and down they go. Often some of the strips are missing or broken and down goes the unfortunate soldier. In some cases the trenches are wide and at night it takes some juggling keeping on the boards. Step to the side and down in the mud you go. On a dark night it is quite a problem manoeuvring along these boards. Without them it would be almost impossible to reach the front line. Later on, we spend about a couple of days trying to drain "Via Gellia" a few yards from the firing line. There was quite a slope and we thought the mud would run if we could only get it started. We had rubber boots on and were up to our thighs in the stuff. It was too soft to shovel out and yet the darned thing was not watery enough to flow. This part of the trench we gave up as hopeless. It was only in March, when the ground began to dry, that the trench became passable. What we failed to achieve Dame Nature did.

For four months we were continuously wrestling with trenches and dug-outs, shovelling, draining, ditching, digging, revetting, filling sandbags, carrying timber, corrugated iron, etc. When in reserve almost every night, as soon as darkness set in, we had to hike to the Engineer's dump at Kemmel and carry stuff up the line. We were usually too early at the dump and lay around in the mud and rain for half an hour to an hour waiting for the arrival of the Engineer. Orders called for our presence at a certain time and orders had to be obeyed. Meanwhile we would hang around, too often soaked to the skin and our clothes and equipment as heavy as lead, waiting at the side of the road for word to load up and move on. These working parties were a regular nightmare. Often when we were figuring on a fine rest, word would come along telling us to get ready for fatigue immediately. Wearily and with many complaints we would get up, get our goat skins on, equipment, rifle, and lastly our raincoat. If it drizzled the raincoat was admirable, but if it rained it soaked up the wet like blotting paper and sent a perfect stream of water down our thighs and legs. With a view to improving matters many fellows cut several inches off the coat but it did not help. Others substituted the water-proof sheet for it. Anyway, night after night in mud and rain saw us squatting around Kemmel, shivering to the bone, waiting to set out with our loads for the line.

During these unpleasant nights there was one bright spot, an estaminet below the Ypres Hotel. There were still in Kemmel a few Belgian civilians, who figured that the soldiers were a godsend to them and they could not withstand the temptation of braving shells for the sake of enriching their coffers. This estaminet was a perfect haven to us. It was barricaded in front with sandbags and inside, in a corner, were their stock in trade, a few tin goods of dubious age and other odds and ends and the usual Belgian beer and wines. About this time we found out that red wine and grenadine made a passable drink. To get out of the rain and cold, yes, and out of fatigue too, we used to slink in here, getting rooted out only to sneak back again. Many were the rushes in and out of this half-way house from which much fun and banter issued. Before moving off there was always a call to the recalcitrants who would chase out and fall into line, then like an African carrying party, we would proceed in single file, loaded with trench paraphernalia, arriving back in the "wee sma' hours" of the morning sadder and wetter men.

Kemmel, in peace time one of the loveliest and most frequented spots in Belgium, was, when we entered it, in a badly battered condition. Still there was quite a number of civilians and several stores were in operation. The town pump, situated in the centre of the square, was intact and from it we replenished our water supply. A fairly elaborate hostel, called the Maison Communale, was doing business as usual; a rather prepossessing young girl of about fifteen dispensing drinks to both soldiers and civilians. Lower down was the Ypres Hotel of doubtful repute. The Brewery, or Brasserie as it is locally called, seemed to be the outstanding industrial establishment though at this time it had ceased activities. Further up the hill were several stores and on the La Clytte Road were several more, including Marie's, which was well patronized by the troops. On this road was a barber shop occupied by a surly individual who was under suspicion as a spy. On the other side of the road was the Post Office; which was run by an old man, his wife and daughter. They likewise ran an eating house, and under war conditions, put up very creditable meals. The daughter was bright, intelligent, and a good linguist speaking English fluently. From her I gleaned a little of the history of the place. She informed me that thirty thousand Germans passed through Kemmel in retreat before the British, beginning on the 10th October, 1914. They were in batches and took seven days to pass. The British pursued them several miles beyond Messines, but were driven back by degrees to the front we now occupy. According to her, the British losses were severe for there was a constant stream of wounded through the village. A few of the German wounded were picked up by the British during the advance. One wounded German, who could go no further was abandoned by his brother soldiers, cried like a baby when he fell into our hands. Altogether thirty thousand British were driving one hundred and forty thousand of the enemy before them on the roads in the neighbourhood of Kemmel. Off the Kemmel-Messines road stood Kemmel Chateau, a magificent and imposing turreted building surrounded by a moat, crossed by a little suspension bridge. It lay in a pretty little wood and was a handsome residence, belonging to a son-in-law of Hennessy of brandy fame. His mother resided in a villa on the slope of Kemmel Hill. He was chief factotum of the village and was looked upon with awe by the villagers. He must have been a devout Catholic for at the western end of the grounds bordering the road was a beautiful little edifice built in the shape of a grotto, of stones of all sizes and shapes. It was a shrine and contained all the emblems of Catholicism, candelabra, case of beads, and a lovely statuette of the Virgin Mary. It was a most handsome and expensive piece of work, very artistically done and distinctly novel.

There seems to be a very strong strain of religion in the French and [we] were continually being reminded by the numerous shrines and crosses. At the entrance to many of the villages is a huge crucifix, usually erected on a knoll amidst a clump of trees. At many crossroads and field corners are little shrines whilst in recesses in the various buildings are figures of Christ or [the] Virgin Mary. The Chateau seemed to experience marvellous luck. The building was practically untouched whilst all around was in ruins. There were many conjectures why the building was in such good shape and the general opinion was, that Heiny was saving it, because the owner was a pro-German or supposed to be, also that the enemy perhaps figured retaking the village and the Chateau would be convenient for headquarters. None of us, however, dreamt that Heiny would be in this country again. We were confident in the assurance that having failed to drive back the little British army in 1914, there was not much chance of him driving us back now. But in his attack in 1918 he drove the British, and then the French who relieved them, from Kemmel and its almost impregnable hill to the outskirts of Locre. At the present time one can count Kemmel as no more for it is certain the village can be little less than a mass of rubble and the pretty little soldier cemetery started in 1914 unidentifiable.

The inside of the Chateau, especially the hallway and principal rooms, were tastefully constructed and arranged but upstairs its many rooms savoured more of a second class apartment house than a palatial residence. The rooms were even in size, cheaply painted and papered, with practically no cornice or tapestry work. There was full evidence that the occupants left in a hurry without salvaging much. Many of the pictures were still hanging on the walls. There were numerous ornaments: books and private papers and accounts were strewn about whilst much of the furniture and carpets were left as they were. Two of the principal bedrooms had gorgeous beds almost encased in curtains. I am afraid many things were stolen from this Chateau and more than the Germans were the guilty party. It is reported that Major Daly of "D" Coy (later Lt.-Col. of the 27th) stripped several pictures from their frames but was caught with them on board the boat for Blighty and was relieved of his souvenirs. Later on, when quartered here, I could not resist the temptation from cutting down a huge crystal drop from the immense and dazzling glass chandelier in the hallway. I also took possession of an ivory paper cutter.

My informant of the Post Office said she knew sixteen civilians of the village were killed by German shells, amongst them were two mothers with babies. The doctor's house on the Vierstraat Road, now headquarters, was the scene of one of Germany's atrocious crimes. When the Germans passed through this district, they shot the doctor in front of his two daughters, whilst standing on his doorstep. His daughters were afterwards outraged and killed.

Dominating Kemmel is Kemmel Hill surmounted by a Tower from which much of our observation of the enemy lines was obtained. This hill will be immortal in history for around it much severe fighting took place in 1918, the French dying to a man trying to withstand the enemy attacks. It is my belief a memorial will be erected here.

During our five months' stay on this front, Kemmel underwent many changes and when we left it was a deserted village, Marie and the Post Office occupants being the last to go. A number of Welsh miners were quartered in the village. They were engaged in sapping to the north of us. When in Kemmel a German band played in the bandstand in the square for a whole day. It is a pity Scotch Pipers could not have got in amongst them.

About this time there were strong rumours of spies being in the neighbourhood and pickets were sent out nightly on several occasions. There were suspicions in regard to the field workers and one could not help from scrutinizing these silent, innocent workers as they went about their avocations. On two occasions I heard reports of rifles from the direction of the Chateau Grounds, and twice bullets went whizzing overhead in an opposite direction from the firing line near the foot of Regent Street on the Lindenhoek Road. I heard that one fellow was struck here and that Lt. Martin had shot quite a youngster who was sniping at night from a tree. I cannot vouch for the accuracy of this, being hearsay. But in 1914 and 1915 it was a recognized fact that the enemy had many informants behind our lines. Notices were posted up in various places and orders were continually being issued warning us to be very careful in our conversation, especially in relation to movement of troops and expected happenings.

Sunday, October 24, 1915

We were back to the trenches once again, this time G2. The firing line at the southern end of G3 takes a sharp turn and penetrates straight to the German line, making the line almost conical in shape. Fritz's line is thrown out towards ours in similar fashion and at the apex, No Man's Land is scarcely more than 25 yards broad. The narrowest part is at G1. So close are the lines that bombs can be thrown into each other's trenches. You can imagine, therefore, that living in this quarter is decidedly unhealthy. It is almost impossible to take precautions, for there are bombs, rifle grenades and "sausages"[25] to contend with and one cannot be gazing skywards day and night. Luckily there is no artillery to trouble you, our line being too close for the enemy artillery to operate without endangering his own trenches. This desperate place has earned the soubriquet of "Glory Hole" and Glory Hole it certainly is. The trenches in this place are a perfect maze and rival the "Labryinth" near Ecurie, Arras. On account of being knocked about so much they are of a patched up character and there is absolutely no drainage, consequently they are muddy in the extreme. Looking through the periscope, and you had to be mighty careful in raising it, Fritzie's line seemed so near as to be almost startling. In moving around you could not get the idea out of your head that a bomb was coming and you would glance furtively for danger. Our Nos. 1 and 2 platoons had to bear the brunt of holding this part and moments were very anxious for them. There was always a sigh of relief when time was up. It can be said without contradiction that this particular spot is one of the worst on the whole front.

A little further south, on the 29th and 27th front, is a similar inferno, known as the "Bull Ring." A few days previously, when the 28th were in the line, the enemy exploded a mine beneath the better part of a Company and rushed to occupy the crater, but the 28th retaliated from the flanks and the enemy could not maintain a footing. The reports that reached me were that the 28th had about 20 killed, 30 missing, and many wounded. Later I heard that the total casualties were 78. I saw the remains of some of them. They were in pieces. It is said something like 1,500 men have met their death in this suicide place. Holding the line proved so hard that later our men were withdrawn and only a few running sentries occupied it. it was a wise move and should have been adopted earlier.

Tuesday, October 26, 1915

Two more of our fellows are wounded by shrapnel, Higgins and one of the 48th. Mackie helped to pack the former out. It was amusing listening to his experience as a stretcher bearer. According to him, Higgins was very refractory and they had a deuce of time with him. Mackie was all aflame when he returned from his trip and cursed every Higgins in creation loud and vehemently. Judging by his frame of mind, Higgins was lucky in not being dumped into an off trench.

---

[25] "Sausages"—a type of German trench mortar bomb ("minenwerfer") which was usually long and could be seen in flight coming towards the Canadian trenches. With the two front lines so close, both sides would use these close range weapons rather than artillery. See Fraser's comments on October 27, 1915.

I was watching Steele, of the sanitary police, repairing the side of a trench, when a pair of boots came into view. He stopped and looked curiously when someone came along and pulled one of the boots. It came away and with it the leg bone. Here lay the remains of a dead Frenchman. In a trice there was a terrific odour which just about flattened us. Steele, however, quickly plastered up the place and we moved a few yards away to fresher surroundings. This unfortunate individual was only buried about a foot underground. I heard that there used to be a cross but the troops, being short of kindling, thought they could put it to better use and promptly removed it.

Wednesday, October 27, 1915

I had scarcely got out of my dug-out when I saw something soaring through the air towards our lines dropping about thirty yards from me. At the moment I never dreamt what it was till I heard the most awful explosion, then all manner of debris went skywards. This was our introduction to aerial torpedoes, generally called trench mortars. At first I figured this missile was a bit alright. You could see it coming and consequently a decided improvement on artillery fire. Later on I changed my opinion. It can be safely said that trench mortars create more nerves than any other explosive. When it is fired you hear a dull pop from your opponents' lines. It goes a considerable height, turning end over end in its flight, like a rugby football, and one is kept guessing as to where it will fall. It is charged with a powerful explosive and fairly rends the heavens when it bursts. The hole it creates is of alarming proportions. It was not long before these missiles began to get our goat and gazing skywards rapidly became a steady occupation.

I went up to see the crater of the mine exploded by the Germans under the 28th several days ago. The hole is as big as a small quarry. A number of our men were blown to atoms. I saw several of the graves a little distance to the rear. The bodies, however, were exhumed the day before and buried elsewhere. One of the graves was left open. It contained a blanket, steeped in blood, with flesh adhering. Nearby was the grave of a French soldier.

Saturday, October 30, 1915

We leave the trenches for Locre in the evening. Finished our worst spell of trench life so far. Did not get much sleep, dug-outs being in poor condition.

I was rather amused, when on sentry, at remarks I overheard from a rat hole of a dug-out in which Doull and Clyne were trying to repose. This miserable hovel could only be got into on your hands and knees. You could neither sit upright nor be stretched out. Clyne, a veteran Scotsman, was six feet in height and as erect as a conifer, despite the fact that he was 56 years of age and a grandfather. He was a 21 year Naval Reserve man. To think that a man of his years was here in the front line trench is enough to make the blood of any righteous man boil with indignation; when over in Canada unashamed were men 22 to 28 years of age, single, without any family ties, in the pink of health, arrant cowards, afraid to match themselves against the Hun. Soaked to the skin and plastered with mud, he lay crouched and with groans was commiserating over his sorry plight, finishing up with the remark, "Oh, Geordie, what would Barbara say (Barbara was his wife) if she saw me now!" Geordie went into gasps of laughter, but old Clyne was feeling blue and did not appreciate Geordie's outburst.

Monday, November 1, 1915

Tonight we experienced our stiffest fatigue going from Locre to near the 29th firing line, a distance there and back of almost ten miles. For all the work we did it would not cover the wastage of shoe leather and on the face of it, one would call it a bad investment. We carried small timbers, dug-out supports, a considerable distance overland. The night was dark and the ground extremely slippery. Every several yards one or other of us would fall. For a time I enjoyed it, it was distinctly amusing seeing the fellows fall. There was much grousing and Flanders came in for unprintable language. No sooner did a man go down then several passed him and he lost his position in the line. For a time I was steering an even course, then my luck changed and thrice I came to earth beautifully, both feet going from under me. I had not even time to get rid of my load. it did a dance on my shoulder and almost broke it. I fell away to last place and by the time I reached the dump my thighs were positively aching through my endeavours to keep an even keel on the greasy mud. It was a relief when we reached the trench. I passed part of the trench where shortly before two of the 29th were killed when leaving for rest. The damage was not yet repaired.

Our rest camp is becoming a huge joke and if this continues it will be better in the firing line. These trips are beginning to feel a bit exhausting. When I arrived back I was literally covered with mud from head to foot.

We have practically had six days continuous rain and trenches are in a deplorable condition. We run great risks when on fatigue as parts of the communication trench are impassable and necessitates going overland. We receive reinforcements from the 48th and several of the sick we left in Blighty have come with them.

I forgot to mention an incident that occurred when we were in G3. About 7:00 a.m., when doing sentry, I was surprised to see a couple of fellows in No Man's Land about 50 yds. in, bending over something. It was foggy at the time and extreme vision was about 90 yds. At the moment I thought they were Germans and was just at the point of covering them when I saw they were our own men.

Being curious and my sentry period just up, I went over the parapet to see what was the matter. It was a dead Gordon Highlander and they were going through his clothes gingerly. A few yards away were some more dead. We found out later there was a fairly even line of dead three or four hundred yards long principally Gordon Highlanders, though there were a few evidently belonging to an English battalion. Most of the bodies were skeletons or partly mummified and fell to pieces when moved. Some were half buried. One Highlander was fairly intact. On two of them we found paybooks, a watch and some money. Their names were Robb and Anderson and they belonged to Aberdeen, Scotland. Robb was married and had several letters in his possession. There was one written by himself to his wife. Of course it was never posted. It was dated last December, namely, December 1914. He was very optimistic regarding the war, went even as far as to say it would be finished in a week or two, and expected to be home for Xmas. His paybook had only one entry, a payment made in October. He was clothed in winter garb and had his equipment over a light coloured goatskin. He was lying facing the German line and his rifle, with bayonet fixed, was laying about a foot to his right.

One could conjecture what had happened, seeing the bodies were in a row and equidistant. Roughly there were 250 of them. Piecing things together I came to the conclusion that they received an order to charge. Moving forward in extended order they only got about 50 yds. into No Man's Land when machine-gun or machine-guns opened up a traversing fire and they were killed on the run. I took a clip of shells out of the pouches of one of them and brought in his rifle and bayonet. The former I gave to Steeleand, the latter to Macnair, notwithstanding that the rifle had been lying there for ten months, in less than half an hour's cleaning still fired a shot through it. It was a marvellous exhibition of the serviceability of the little British rifle.[26] The 25th Battalion, which adjoined us, had in its ranks an old Gordon Highlander who told us that this Robb must have been a 12 yrs.' man and joined about the same time as he did for their numbers were very close. He said he could not have been long back from Egypt. A few weeks afterwards, glancing over the "Glasgow Herald" which was sent to me by my sister, I was surprised to see under the obituary announcements the names Robb and Anderson, "formerly missing now killed."

These bodies lying in No Man's Land made me interested in the history of this line and I made enquiries regarding the former occupants of this part, but strange nobody knew anything of the front, save that the 16th Battalion, Canadian Scottish, were here for a fortnight before us. A few months later, when further north in the M. and N. trenches, I came across a Jock[27] who was one of the sappers there and was busily engaged tunneling under Fritz's line. There was evidently a false alarm given to the sappers for this Jock emerged into the daylight near where I was, in hot haste with a rifle in his hand, very much excited, and working up a fearful temper, cursing aloud. He thought Fritz was coming over. It turned out he belonged to the battalion of Gordons, whose dead were strewn in front of G3. He told me they had about 250 killed there in an unsuccessful charge, being cleaned up by machine-gun fire.

I learned some more about this fight when I was in hospital in Birmingham. A convoy of wounded and sick arrived from the Salonica front and the fellow taken to the vacant bed on my left was a member of the Royal Scots. He was out in France at the beginning of the war, when only 15 years of age. His battalion, the 2nd Royal Scots, went over the top the same day as the Gordon Highlanders. He said the Highlanders were wiped out but the Royal Scots captured the German trenches. This was in December 1914. The facts are thus: On the 14th December, the 2nd Royal Scots on the left and 1st Gordon Highlanders on the right, co-operating with D'Urbal's Eighth French Army on the north, after considerable artillery pre-

---

[26] This was the British short Lee-Enfield. It is interesting to note that when the 31st Battalion took part in the "demonstration" or feint attack on October 13, the men were ordered to use rapid fire with their rifles against the enemy's trenches. As a result of this fire the Commanding Officer, Lt.-Col. A. H. Bell, reported that 138 of the Canadian Ross rifle had jammed. (War Diary, 31st (Alberta) Battalion, C.E.F., October 1915, Appendix No. 5, "Report of Operations...13th October, 1915.") Whenever a Canadian soldier had the opportunity to lay his hands on the British Lee-Enfield, he frequently took it. It was not until 1916 that the Ross rifles were replaced by the Lee-Enfields.

[27] "Jock"—a common nickname for a Scottish soldier.

paration, made an attack on Petit Bois at Wytschaete. The Royal
Scots under Major Duncan carried Petit Bois with a rush, taking 50
prisoners and 2 machine-guns, while the Germans fled out at the
other end of the wood. The Scots then entrenched themselves. The
Gordons, under Major Baird, advanced with a dash and gained some
ground, but were forced to fall back to their original position. Both
they and the 4th Middlesex, who supported them, lost considerably.
The casualties came to over 400, with 17 officers. These figures were
swollen later by the losses of the Suffolks and Irish Rifles who
continued to hold the captured position, in the face of continued
bombing. The Frenchmen were unsuccessful and lost 600 men. Five
days before the 1st Lincolns of the 9th Bde. made a futile attack,
having 47 men hit, including 3 officers. These, therefore, were the
actions that resulted in so many unburied dead, lying out in front of us
and which aroused our curiosity.

The next morning being misty, a number of the 25th Battalion,
with several of our men, including the writer, went over into No
Man's Land in quest of more bodies. Going further in we came across
some more Gordons, also I presume a Middlesex man. He had his
khaki overcoat on. None of them were in a good state of preservation,
skulls separate, bones broken and so forth. Several minutes after
coming in I heard three of the 25th fellows had been fired at, that two
were killed and one wounded, the wounded man managed to get
back. It was nearly a week before the bodies were recovered.

On three occasions, when going along the communication trench, I
came across stretcher bearers returning from the firing line with dead
or wounded. The worst case I saw was a 25th man with the top of his
skull almost blown off by machine-gun fire. I heard he died a few
minutes after passing us.

I have not elicited anything definite regarding the history of the
trenches we are in. Small funk holes were pointed out to me near Pall
Mall, Regent St.,[28] where the London Scottish were supposed to have
dug themselves in, preparatory to their famous charge to Messines
where street fighting ensued. I have noticed old French trenches,
almost covered in and overgrown with grasses. About 150 yds. from
where I now am, F supports, are the skeletons of French soldiers who
must have been killed in the early part of the war. They can hardly be
termed skeletons as the bones are detached, lying amidst their blue
clothing and equipment. Their clothing being dark blue tell us they
belonged to the old regular French army. I saw more than 20 of them.

[28] Names given to trenches on the battalion's front.

No doubt they were killed charging from their front line, which was only a few yards behind them.

There were names on the sand bags and woodwork of the dug-outs showing that several English regiments, a Welsh and a Canadian battalion, had been on this front but for definite particulars I had to go further afield and found them in the civilian and soldier cemeteries at Kemmel. From the inscription on the crosses, sufficient information was accorded me so that I could connect to a certain extent the movements of troops. In a field about a score of yards from the road opposite Kemmel Chateau is a solitary cross and inscribed thereon is the following: "Trooper F. Graham, 14th Hussars, killed in action Oct. 29, 1914." This is the earliest casualty I could find. In the civilian cemetery were crosses in memory of officers and men of the 5th, 12th and 16th Lancers, 2nd and 6th Dragoon Guards and the 129th Baluchis. There were killed in action in November 1914. These records showed that the cavalry were the first on this front. Visiting the soldier cemetery which is situated about two hundred yards north-west of the Chateau, I counted roughly six hundred graves. Therein sleep soldiers of fifty different units, including our own Canadians.

The older graves are well kept, some being planted with roses, ever-green bushes and box hedge. Each battalion has a distinctive cross. The Canadian crosses could have been improved upon. When I saw this cemetery first it was undisturbed by shell fire, later there were three shell holes. As this vicinity was the scene of hot fighting 2½ years afterwards and fell into possession of the Germans this graveyard must be now unrecognizable. In the civilian cemetery in the village were several shell holes and bones of long dead Belgians lay exhumed silent witnesses of the sacrilege of the Hun. There were a few solitary graves in the wood near the Chateau, one being that of an officer of the Liverpool Scottish.

In brief the incidents leading up to the formation of the line in front of us is thus: The Germans began to fall back from the Hazebrouck-Bailleul region about the 10th October 1914. A couple of days later Gen. Allenby, commanding the Lisle's First Cavalry Division and Gough's Second Cavalry Division, moved forward pushing back the enemy and having a skirmish at Mont des Cats, a small hill crowned by a monastery, where the body of a Prince of Hesse was picked up after the action. The killing of this German Prince has appealed much to the Belgian imagination. On several occasions the Belgians re-minded me of it, the last time being near Reninghelst when an old Belgian pointed to Mont des Cats in the distance and tried to explain that a German Prince was buried there. Still fighting its way, the cavalry moved forward to Berthen. Eventually they pushed on to beyond Messines where the Germans halted and thickened their line. On October 30th, the 24 German Corps and 2nd Bavarian Corps attacked our troopers and drove them back for half a mile, the 5th and 16th Lancers, suffering considerably. Three French battalions helped to reform the line. The 129th Baluchis, 7th (Ferozepone) Bde. had been helping the cavalry since October 23, but their ranks were decimated and they were fought to a standstill. The 1st Lincolns and 1st Northumberland Fusiliers of the 9th Bde. were sent to their assistance. They were surprised by the Germans on the road between Kemmel and Wytschaete on the night of the 31st and the Lincolns had a loss of 16 officers and 400 men. The Fusiliers were also hard hit. For a couple of days the battle swung backwards and forwards in front of Wytschaete and in the end the village was lost. The road leading from Kemmel to Wytschaete is known as Suicide Road. I heard it got this name owing to about sixty British soldiers being ambushed on this road and laid low by machine-gun fire. No doubt they were the Lincolns or Northumberlands. By November a second lot of French reinforcements appeared on the scene. On the right the London Scottish were hurried up from St. Eloi communications to the Messines front and though they maintained a hold on the village, the ridge gave way and the line was drawn. The First Cavalry Division lost fifty percent of its fighting strength within three days.

Paid a visit to Locre Chapel. It is much decorated and used as a school. Over one hundred and twenty British soldiers are buried in the chapel yard. They belonged to various regiments, the Sherwood Foresters predominating. A number of French soldiers are buried in one huge grave. A couple of our 28th are buried here. In this cemetery lie the remains of Major Redmond of the Irish who was killed at the taking of Wytschaete and Messines in 1917. The British papers paid him great tribute.

Friday, November 5, 1915

Left for the trenches. We are in supports. There is much shelling. Our portion, however, very quiet.

Thursday, November 11, 1915

Some excitement at Regent St. dug-outs. Two working parties were sniped at, a couple of Engineer Corporals being wounded. At Vigo St., a 27th man was shot through the abdomen. A couple who went to his assistance were also shot. All this happened within a few minutes. In the front line, Kerr, formerly of the 48th, was wounded. Above Regent St. dug-outs is another of those crosses to be seen, "Unknown

hero lies here." Those unknown heroes became so common that latterly two identification discs were given the soldiers instead of one, one being for official records, a voucher that so-and-so is dead, and the other for particulars for burial parties.

Sunday, November 14, 1915

During divine service Kemmel was shelled. We are out on fatique tonight. On the way home I came across a wounded 28th man. Lovely evening. Aerial activity considerable.

Monday, November 15, 1915

Fine dry, frosty weather. Kemmel was shelled and three were killed, Lt. Hughes of the Engineers, a nephew of Maj.-Gen. Sam Hughes and two 31st men. Most of the inhabitants have left the village. One of the 29th men, who was on listening post,[29] skipped across to the German lines. It is rumoured he was a German, enlisting as a Swede.

Wednesday, November 17, 1915

Back to the trenches once again. On fatigue at "Via Gellia" when passing a certain spot overland was sniped at, bullets passing very close. A moment later one of "B" Coy. is wounded in the leg and carried out in a stretcher. Kemmel is bombarded in the evening. Several natives are retiring towards Locre with their household effects. Received from Roberts, the Scout, a Gordon Highlander's shoulder badge. He took it off one of the Gordons when out patrolling in No Man's Land. He came across an officer lying beside his horse, fairly well in, between the lines. In No Man's Land is a couple of crosses. I could just make out the inscription "Unknown British Heroes" with the aid of glasses. Behind our front line is an old cross, half hidden amongst the chicory. If the land could only speak, what hidden tales it could reveal.

Thursday, November 18, 1915

A disagreeable wet day. Considerable aerial activity. A Sergeant in "D" Coy. was killed whilst out patrolling between the lines. He was shot in the stomach. When going on fatigue to the front line was sniped at.

---

[29] The listening post would be part way out into No Man's Land, connected by a trench to the front line. In this position it would be fairly easy for a deserter to crawl over to the enemy's trenches, especially at night.

Friday, November 19, 1915

A German aeroplane crossed our lines. It is very prettily built and proportioned. Our planes tried to engage it, but it was too fast and reached its lines in its own time. One of "B" Coy. was wounded in the face and shoulder. When strengthening Regent St. [trench] four French soldiers were unearthed. They were quickly covered and chloride of lime thrown over them. Near by was dug up several thousand French rifle shells.

Sunday, November 21, 1915

Left trenches for rest camp at Locre, via Lindenhoek and Dranoutre.

Thursday, November 25, 1915

We left for trenches once again. The communication trench being impossible, we go overland by Suicide Road till we strike the furthest up hedge when we cross through fields pitted by shell holes to the junction of G2 and G3 [trenches]. After leaving the road we have to be mighty careful as we are only a few hundred yards away from the enemy and if he suspected us, he could sweep our path with machine-gun fire. Several halts had to be made when starlights were flung up, the country around being illuminated, any movement could easily be detected. If we were not quick enough in getting down, we remained as we were, as mute as statues, till plunged into darkness again, when we would hurry on before the next starlight was thrown up. All the time we were in the line of stray bullets which would go whizzing past, making us uneasy. Walking was difficult owing to the slippery and boggy nature of the ground, the numerous shell holes and bits of trenches that had to be crossed. When trenches are broken down, getting into the line is a ticklish business. An alert enemy can discern your paths and prepare for you at night time. He may let off a burst of fire every now and then at a certain spot on the off chance that there are passers by. Coming up Suicide Road stray bullets were whizzing fairly thick and we were feeling decidedly uneasy. I remember our section officer was leading, the sergeant second, a Lance Corporal third, and I was fourth, when a bullet crashed through the hedge, a little beyond Ration Farm, and caught Jimmie Rodgers in the arm with a loud smack. He was about three yards behind me. The bullet came in a slanting direction and brought Rodgers to earth with a cry. Dunstall of our Company was wounded the same night, getting into the line. We heaved a sigh of relief when we reached G3 and had the friendly protection of the firing trench to keep the strays away.

We passed a quiet night. It was raining and snowing in turns and very uncomfortable.

One of "C" Company [was] wounded whilst on fatigue at communication trench. Two unburied dead Frenchmen found near a hedge between Suicide Road and "Via Gellia." The following day we had to leave the communication trench owing to enemy's shell fire. He evidently spotted us. His shells fell short but the nose caps came singing amongst us. We have no objections ceasing operations, it means more rest to us. I heard that a 27th sentry shot at and wounded one of the enemy's bombers. He yelled for help throughout the night. The following night he was found dead. A number of bombs were in his possession. He belonged to the 166th Bavarians.

Friday, November 26, 1915

Much aerial activity, principally British planes.

Saturday, November 27, 1915

The enemy snipers are very active. Collins of No. 4 platoon is shot through the head and has passed out unconscious.

In the parapet of the bay where I am sentry, I was surprised to see a human skull staring at me. It still had some hair on the scalp. I fancy a shell must have unearthed it. Thiebot buried it.

Under cover of darkness two of our scouts discovered a large German working party, repairing their trenches. A battery was immediately phoned to and in a few seconds several hurricane rounds of shrapnel was sent into their midst.

Sunday, November 28, 1915

It is very frosty today which is an improvement on the wet weather we have had. Many of us are suffering from half frozen feet.

During the day our artillery sent over quite a number of high explosives into the German lines.

One of "D" Company is wounded by a sniper. Roberts, the Scout who was out on patrol last night, was wounded by a shell at Kemmel. Adjutant M——t got scratched a little; some aver that is was not the shell that did it, that he hit himself against something in his hurry to get away. This officer, who never got further than H'Qrs., managed to get back to Canada. I noticed a reporter of a Calgary paper interviewed him and a romantic story was woven around this gallant hero. The adjutant kept up the deception playing his part well, but it created quite a furor amongst the 31st men in the trenches who felt they could have lynched him after reading such untruthful dope and knowing the calibre of the man.

Monday, November 29, 1915

Several trench mortars were sent over by the enemy, killing six and wounding one, a sergeant who is not expected to recover. Both his legs were broken.

When on sentry, a fellow stopped to tell me the wonderful escape he had a few minutes ago. There were five of them going along the trench, he being second. The first two got round a bend when a trench mortar came over bursting in the midst of the last three and killing them. The third fellow had his head blown off.

Opposite the "Glory Hole" several Germans with a white flag got up on their parapet and started talking to our men. Curious no one fired at them.

I was up in the "Glory Hole" seeing where trench mortars exploded. Some of "D" Coy. were digging out the remains of those killed. They had a few blankets into which pieces of flesh were being collected, all that could be found of the unfortunate men.

A dog came from the German trenches to our lines. It is the first capture we have made. I hear it is being named Fritz.

We are relieved. It is a disagreeable night and very dark. Practically everyone fell into ditches and shell holes on the way out. No sooner did I arrive at Kemmel Huts than I was detailed for Guard at Kemmel.

Tuesday, November 30, 1915

The Guard Room at Kemmel is in the basement of the Brewery. There are two posts, one in the square in the front of the Ypres Hotel and Maison Communale, and the other a considerable distance away in front of the Kemmel Chateau. There are the usual duties, halting everyone at night and seeing that vehicles are a considerable distance apart. Kemmel is in the shell zone and for protection parties are supposed to be strung out and wagons should be [at] about twenty-five yards interval. This is to keep down casualties. Guards are provided with a whistle which they have to blow as soon as they notice a plane coming toward the village. So many blasts are given for an enemy plane, so many if they are uncertain. When the coast is clear, if I remember aright, one blast is given. The idea is to warn everyone to get under cover. If a hostile plane noticed much movement, naturally it would communicate with the artillery, with, for us, disastrous results. Before going on guard we were informed that a spy, dressed in a Canadian officer's uniform and wearing a 1st C.M.R. badge, had been in Kemmel the day before. If we could capture him we were told it would mean a trip to Blighty. After we had gone on duty another message was delivered to us, namely that a spy, a cyclist, dressed in Belgian Police uniform, was in the neighbourhood a couple of days ago. These particulars brightened up our duties a bit and made us a little more keen than usual. We had an easy time of it, two hours on, and six hours off. The spare time of the first day was principally occupied in drying our clothes and scraping the mud off them. My first night's vigil or rather morning's, was between the hours of 1:00 a.m. and 3:00 a.m. I had only to challenge two parties, the first, a patrol on the search for the two spies and the second, some 26th Battalion men on the lookout for a prisoner.

Wednesday, December 1, 1915

As I was standing in front of the sentry box a couple of cyclists emerged out of the darkness from the shade of the trees. I did not notice them until they were within two or three yards from me, it being pitch dark. I challenged them at once and was surprised to hear a foreign voice. I noticed the Belgian uniform. The first fellow mumbled in broken English that he was a Belgian cyclist. It flashed across my mind at once that here, perhaps, were spies. Things looked fishy. I did not wish to give my suspicions away, so kept on plying them with questions; where did they come from; where were they going to? etc., all the time sizing them up. I did not get much satisfaction. There was no one about, the other sentry was in the village nearly a quarter of a mile away. The usual absurd and antiquated army orders stated that on no account was I to leave my post. Thank goodness I never took the army seriously. Pretending there was nothing the matter I walked to the village with them. Seeing they were bound for the La Clytte direction, I tried to persuade them to go up towards the guard room hinting that it was only a matter of form, to show their passports. They did not quite understand and looked at one another, the second fellow showing a little resentment and shoving his bicycle in the wrong direction. It dawned upon me if wits were no use, I would need to do the other thing. Luckily for them the latter was unnecessary. I heard the other sentry, Ben Stringer, coming down the way, and called to him, telling him to take them up to the guard room. Waiting to see that they went up, I then retraced my steps to my post, conscious that I had committed the awful crime of disregarding His Majesty's regulations. When I was relieved I heard the whole story.

The sergeant of the guard could make nothing of them, so called in the Military Police. They, in turn, were dubious and called in the Belgian gendarmes, who for a while were suspicious but ultimately let them go. The next morning the officer of the guard, who heard the story, was displeased and said they should have been detained. Their passports were signed by a lieutenant and he was under the impression that the latter had no authority to issue them. My vision of Blighty faded away. Some time after, I met one of the two in an Estaminet at Mont Noir. I went up to him and asked him how he got on that night, did he reach his destination? He was sore, but he did not blame the Canadian troops. He gave the Belgian gendarmes a roasting, making out that they should have known better. When I left him, he was singing Flemish and French songs and as happy as a lark.

Thursday, December 2, 1915

During the day, when on sentry and when I was looking in the opposite direction, a hare came down the road and ran past me crossing into the field opposite about sixty yards further on. The chief medical officer of the Division saw the whole performance and when passing me said—"Why didn't you catch it, that would make a fine dinner." Hares and pheasants appear fairly common. Troops, however, are forbidden to fire from behind the firing line.

Another fellow and I went on an exploration trip around the ruined buildings on the search for souvenirs. We went through the Maison Communale, which up till several days ago was doing business. Everything was topsy turvy. A well placed shell struck the building in the gable and very nearly demolished a quarter of the building. There was a considerable array of women's garments. I took several buttons off a French tunic and stamps off several envelopes. Many of these stamps have the postmark of Ypres, Lille, Messines, etc. and of course dates before the war.

Saturday, December 4, 1915

We are back to the trenches once again. Every trip we make we notice one or more of our number fails to return. The question usually goes through one's mind, who are to be the unfortunates this time.

Collins, who was wounded a few days ago, has since died.

Cpl. Haslam, our signalling corporal, who belongs to my section of about a dozen, is sniped, shot through the head, dying shortly afterwards. A fellow who was with him was wounded. We heard the latter's cries of pain and guessed some fatality occurred. Gerry

Morgan went to his assistance. Haslam, an Eastern man, was a fine type of Canadian, quiet, gentlemanly, genuine in all his doings.

Sunday, December 5, 1915

Toyne of No. 4 platoon is wounded heading for the trenches. We are located at G2. In front of us in "No Man's Land," about fifty yards in, is a belt of tall, shell-shriven trees. To show that our eye has not lost its cunning, several of us shot at small birds roosting on the branches. Bagging five out of six shots convinces me my rifle is well sighted.

Monday, December 6, 1915

For the next two days we are quartered in St. Germania's school, Kemmel. Our duties are carrying rations or fixing up the trenches. On the way back the Germans shelled us all the way to Kemmel. We had to do some hurrying. Perry was wounded in the back and partially paralyzed. He ultimately made Blighty; he forgot about the sterner works of war, and married his nurse instead.

Wednesday, December 8, 1915

Once more we move up to the trenches. On Suicide Road, near Ration Farm, we get quite a scare. Fritz sent over several shells. Some of our fellows threw themselves flat in the mud. We had quite a time getting to our quarters, Hl. It was raining heavily and we were soaked to the skin. To reach our position we had to wade through G4 and H1. There are not enough of dug-outs and they are soaking wet. For an hour or so we had to shovel back the earth from the top of the trench. It was tough work and to add to our troubles we were in the line of fire. Every few moments a bullet would go pinging past. We considered our chances of committing suicide were pretty good. The fellow next to me must have dug up a dead German for the smell was awful. You know German dead smell worse than other dead, so the soldiers say. Some of our fellows came across the remains of eight horses, harnessed up, evidently artillery horses, killed in the early part of the war. Two other fellows and I spent the night in a sitting position, cramped and half dead with the cold.

Thursday, December 9, 1915

Forty-eight hours is considered long enough to hold this part of the line, so we get orders to move. We reach a part of the trench where for sixty yards, it is practically impassable. Rather than force our way through the mud, the majority decide to make a bolt for it overland. I do not know how the others got on but Jerry had several shots at me and missed. But I did not get into the trench in the orthodox fashion, I simply threw myself in. I could not get down quick enough. As far as I can see, this is not the life for anyone suffering from a weak heart. It is one scare after another. We were back that night with rations. Spent the night in an old farm house, Parrane Farm, on Suicide Road. It was very filthy and unsanitary, a cesspool being at the western end.

Friday, December 10, 1915

Back once more to Locre. Our second batch of reinforcements has arrived.

Wednesday, December 15, 1915

On the road to the trenches once more. We are halted outside Kemmel till the enemy finish shelling the village. Our position is the northern end of the Hs. The firing trench is the worst we have struck yet. The parapet is low, hardly any dug-outs, and the water in the trench is in some places up to the thighs. All have to wear rubber boots. There is not such a thing as sleep. To see a sentry at his post is like a kingfisher perched on a stone above the water. We have our work cut out, keeping our rifles in shape. Mud is everywhere and on everything.

Saturday, December 18, 1915

Another shift, this time to S.P. 10, a welcome change. Dug-outs dry and first rate. We get good observation from here.

Buttress and I went overland in the day time to yesterday's trenches. We followed along the blind side of a little clump of wood and hedges. There was a trench from near Beaver Hat to S.P. 10 and a considerable stretch from S.P. 11 to G2, that was just completed and looked A-one, fine and straight, a model trench, yes, but we forgot about Flanders' rain. In a few days the sides caved in and it became waterlogged and useless. In digging trenches we learned that in future we would have to give the sides a considerable slope if they were to stand at all. On the way, we passed the skeleton of a horse lying beside Suicide Road. Further on we came across the remains of a French-man lying under a hedge. Close by were old French trenches, covered over in parts by straw matting. Near the top of the communication trench on the right side were a couple of dead men, a blanket covering each. They belonged to "C" Coy. We lifted the blankets to see if we knew them. We knew them by sight but not by name. Both were killed a few minutes previously, sniped by the same bullet. It went through one fellow's head and lodged in the upper part of the other's body. They were killed in the trench we occupied yesterday. We noticed the blood.

German sniping is much more effective than ours. They have the position being on the ridge and naturally command our back country.

On the way back a peculiar incident occurred which we could not make out. After crossing Suicide Road, I happened to look up the way and saw about three hundred yards away a fellow beckoning on us to get down. We doubled back over the road and lay down in a ditch wondering what was up. This fellow was peering very cautiously ahead of him. What struck us was there must be a Fritzie sniper behind our lines and this fellow had spotted him. The idea was possible but hardly probable. We waited several minutes till we got disgusted. Retiring alongside a hedge we crossed a small field into a clump of trees. From here we made for the road which we rapidly crossed to the cover side of another hedge. Hardly had we gone a few yards when ping, ping, ping came several bullets just missing us. In a trice we jumped into an old trench and lay there wondering. I was positive Fritz could not see us from his lines—and yet there was a German sniping from somewhere. Anyway, we could not remain in the trench all day, so we resolved to beat it once more, after yelling to three of our fellows who were looking for souvenirs about 150 yards away, to clear out that we were in view of the enemy. Buttress made a dash for it and the coast, appearing clear, I thought I would follow suit. I hardly got out of the trench when bullets came whizzing around. Continuing running I must have got out of the view for there was no more fire. When we got back to SP10 we puzzled our heads— figuring out how were we seen but could come to no conclusion.

Sunday, December 19, 1915

On guard between 3:00 and 6:00 a.m. About 3:30 I heard rapid fire coming somewhere between the Dickebusch-Ypres Front. Later bombardment commenced lasting several hours. In the forenoon our eyes began to smart owing to tear [gas] shells employed by the enemy.[30] We had to put on our goggles. We were very uncomfortable

---

[30] This was the first time the battalion had experienced gas of any form. Units in the 1st Canadian Division had been subjected to chlorine gas during the Spring. By this time crude gas masks (tube helmets they were called) or respirators had been issued to the troops. The tear gas experienced by Fraser and his comrades came from a German bombardment further north.

for about an hour during which time several hostile aeorplanes came over our lines. For a while they had it all their own way. According to reports the Germans made an attack but were repulsed. Several whiz-bangs came over our position but no one was hurt. I was sitting on the parados of the communication trench when a shell whizzed past me, for the moment bamboozling me that I fell in a heap in the trench. Curious, it burst beside three fellows and did not touch them, but they did some bolt.

Monday, December 20, 1915

For the first several months we felt Fritz had the upper hand; his positions were superior to ours; he had more variety of missiles; and he apparently had more shells and artillery. The artillery supporting us were either West Lancashires or Indian (Lahore) Batteries. There was a scarcity of shells and at times, when called upon to retaliate, our artillery could not do so, owing to shortage. The role they played, therefore, was mainly of a defensive character. From the Somme offensive onwards, shells were in plentitude and they were fired lavishly. For a time we relied on Imperial troops to fire trench mortars and rifle grenades in our sectors. The bombs around the trenches were of an old pattern, either expensive stick grenades or the spherical bombs that were ineffective and burst into the dust. We relied mainly on the Ross rifle. What machine-guns there were, were few and of American make, the Colt, a useless weapon that was discarded later. It was air cooled and heated up quickly. When a stoppage occurred, it had practically to be taken to pieces to have the stoppage rectified. For front line work it was superseded by the mobile Lewis gun and as a defensive weapon it gave way to the Vickers, a much more dependable gun.[31]

I forgot to mention that we are now wearing steel helmets. We started in with one to each bay, changing over from guard to guard. These helmets were treated as trench stores[32] and consequently were turned over to the relieving battalion. There was no ventilation in the

---

[31] This was a 1904 Maxim built in the U.S.A. by Colt. It fired a .303 round at 300 rounds per minute. It was replaced in the C.E.F. by the Vickers (450 to 500 rounds per minute) in the Summer of 1916. This water-cooled, 90-pound weapon remained in service for many years. The Lewis was a light machine-gun weighing 27 pounds. It was air-cooled, fitted with a 47-round drum magazine. The Lewis gun was introduced into the British Army in the Summer of 1915 as a company and platoon weapon.

[32] Trench stores included such items as Very Pistols, Hip Gum Boots, Vermoral Sprayers, S.A.A. (Small Arms Ammunition), machine-gun ammunition, gas alarms, and similar items needed in the front line which would be turned over by the unit being relieved to the unit coming into the line.

first issue and the head perspired freely. In time the helmet became part of a soldier's equipment and as soon as he came within range of shell fire he had to don it.

"C" Coy. had one man killed and another wounded by shrapnel.

Word has reached us that Roberts, the scout, has died from the effects of his wound.

Tuesday, December 21, 1915

There is a report current that our Colonel sent one of our Scouts over to the German lines with a message wishing them a Merry Xmas and asking them to come over and surrender.[33]

Thursday, December 23, 1915

On fatigue this morning at "Via Gellia." Enemy sent over several whiz-bangs and shrapnel. A party of the 28th happened to cross near a farm where the Huns had the range. All of a sudden they opened fire and two were wounded. We heard a cry for help. Our stretcher bearers went to their assistance. Our officer thinking we had remained long enough in the danger zone ordered us to go home. We had a little excitement getting out, having to run for it in the open. All got safely away.

Friday, December 24, 1915

It is Xmas Eve. A number of us have to go on duty tonight.

Saturday, December 25, 1915

We had a little more to eat today. The Government, exceedingly generous, gave us a tiny piece of plum duff.[34] We have a jovial time, the officers fraternizing with the men, the major carried shoulder high to his own quarters in the end. One or two small fights developed which some of our bright wits say, mean an additional bar to the medal. Engagement to be called "Estaminet." With several more, spent the evening at Mont Noir, on the France-Belgian frontier. We had supper there.

Sunday, December 26, 1915

Out on fatigue at "Dead Cow Corner." We saw a big shell that did not explode.

[33] Since Lt.-Col. Bell went to England on December 19 for a week's leave, this "report" is extremely unlikely.
[34] Plum pudding.

Monday, December 27, 1915

We left for Kemmel Chateau. I found a snug sleeping place in the basement under the stairs. A few of us were wakened at 1:00 a.m. to go in a hurry to the firing line to repair the parapet. The enemy had sent over several sausages,[35] wrecking the parapet and several dug-outs. Two men were killed. One was Sgt. Kemp. I was speaking to him a few days ago, in the shoemaker's tent. He told me he was the last of the original sergeants of "D" Coy. in the line. It was the other fellow's first day in the trenches. We buried the latter this morning in Kemmel cemetery.

Tuesday, December 28, 1915

A strange casualty. We heard yells and curses emanating from the Field Ambulance station, Kemmel. It turned out to be a 25th Battalion man suffering from "Delirious Tremens." The question now arises, "Who stole the rum?"

Wednesday, December 29, 1915

Four or five men were asked to volunteer for a burial party, the inducement being "no fatigues tonight." Needless to say, the burial party was more inviting than the fatigue and I clinched the matter. It turned out the dead man was Sgt. Kemp. He was wrapt (*sic*) up in a blanket, which was tied with signalling wire. We carried him to the cemetery on a stretcher. The minister officiating said a few words. The grave was a double one, the other fellow had already been buried, that is a few inches of earth were thrown over him. This had to suffice till Kemp was interred, when the grave would be filled in. When we arrived the grave contained several inches of water, coloured red by blood. Kemp was buried in this mess. As soon as the body stirred the liquid, it just about made us vomit, the effluvium being terrific. We found out later we were a bit previous in volunteering as no one went on fatigue that night.

Thursday, December 30, 1915

Up to the firing line once more. I am one of the advance party. Our position is G4. Whilst taking over the posts, Heiny sent three trench

---

[35] Mortar bombs, or as they were sometimes called, aerial or trench torpedoes, which from their shape were called "sausages." They carried a fuse in their tail. Early in January 1916, one landed in the trench and a soldier quickly withdrew the burning fuse, thus saving many lives. He was recommended for the Victoria Cross, but was awarded the Distinguished Conduct Medal (W.D., 31st Battalion, C.E.F., 30 January 1916).

mortars over, one with disastrous effects. A dug-out and emplacement, much envied because it was constructed of bricks, received the force of the explosion. Two were killed, I think, one died of wounds, and several were injured, the majority being machine-gunners. Webb (Commodore), an American, passed out wounded leaning on his friends, so did Harvey who was very talkative going out. Beach, who died of wounds later, was in dire agony, his face being distorted with pain. Bennett, belonging to my platoon, saw the "sausage" coming but the trench was so crowded he could not get away in time and was partially buried. He was shell shocked and was no longer fit for the line. Being tried out a few weeks later, his nerves could not stand it. He was afraid to go into a dug-out and shivered in the trench. He had to be taken out and got work to do as a groom, remaining behind at the transport lines. Loucks, of our Company, had a remarkable escape. We thought he was blown to atoms as there was not a vestige of him to be seen; about three hours later, as I was passing the place, I heard a groan. Several who had been digging, but were resting, also heard it. Immediately they buckled to their work and in twenty minutes they had him out. Outside of bruises he was uninjured and at the moment appeared alright. But he was shell shocked and no longer of use as a fighting man. He had a miraculous escape. For three hours we were going backwards and forwards over him unaware of his presence. The trench mat saved him. He was below it. It kept back the earth from his face and left a small passage through which the air filtered. Loucks made England of it later and I hear obtained a commission and married an English girl. It appears "wounded, Blighty, marriage" is becoming a popular pass time with our fellows.

Friday, December 31, 1915

Our artillery opened fire on the German lines continuing for quite a time. After a pause the enemy, thinking we had finished, started the music by sending over whiz-bangs in rapid succession to the left "H" trenches. A little later I was looking along the trench towards Major S—— and Sgt. P——n. All of a sudden P——n caught a glimpse of a sausage in the air and shouted, "look out—a sausage." He evidently startled the Major, for he turned ghastly white and horror stricken, and like a shot about turned and bolted towards G3. Looking up, I caught sight of the sausage and following the rest, like a streak of lightning, made towards the right. One of the other company fellows, evidently a batman with a couple of sandbags across his shoulder, came into the firing line from the communication trench unconcerned—at peace with the world. He was in my path. I made a rush to get past him, but the trench was too narrow. I tried to push him ahead in my desperate hurry to get away from the trench mortar. He turned sharply round, in anger, then an awful look of fear came into his face as he saw the "sausage." Throwing down the sandbags he flew. His sandbags tripped me up and down I went. I threw myself into a dug-out at the moment the "sausage" exploded. At the instant I saw Thomas scooting round into the communication trench with a huge stride. It was a tragic event but most amusing.

A few moments afterwards we began to return to our posts. I went back with Cpl. Still who was breathing heavily and just about pumped for want of breath. Between his gasps, he said, "Heiny is finished now," with the authority as if he was one who knew, when another came wobbling over. I saw it first, shouted and bolted. I thought Still would have died, he made such a violent effort to pull himself together and get away. Once again Thomas gets round the corner into his communication trench last. Supper was ready when they first came over. Thiebot, the cook, got quite a scare, in fact he had a narrow squeak. His dixie lid of cheese was thrown in the mud. We had a half-hearted meal and changed over to SP11. I remember asking P——n if he saw Still. "Yes," he said, "I met him down the communication trench. He was gazing skywards looking for trench mortars." I said to him, "Supper is ready up there." But Still, without taking his eyes off the heavens, replied disgustingly, "To H--- with supper."

Quite a number of shells dropped in the vicinity of SP11. It is the first time I have seen Fritz reply with vigour. The West Lancashire artillery, who have left, always kept him well in hand.

MacKay, a six footer, is the character of our Company. He is most amusing and possesses a fund of dry humour. His one great fault is, he is infernally lazy, but in MacKay laziness is excusable and we never complain. He is an awful man to waken for guard, always late on duty. It does not matter what is happening, if not on sentry MacKay makes for his dug-out. If his own is full, he goes into someone else's. I remember him telling me that he was going down to the next bay to see the fellows there. In a few minutes he returned disgusted, and in his broad dialect said, "If you want to go down to see those chaps, you better take off your boots and crawl down on your hands and knees, Powell is like a Red Indian, lying on his stomach on the trench mat, with his ear to the ground saying there are Heinies on the other side of the parapet." Powell was of high strung temperament and ultimately went semi-insane.

A number of us spent a day in an estaminet at Mont Noir, celebrating the festive season. We were given sixty-five francs in addition to the thirty per month so decided to break the monotony and have a jovial time. As I was the only one who knew where the place was, I was guide: not much guidance was required going, but it was very much needed coming back. Our number consisted of MacKay, Buttress, Swinton, Evans, Tardell, Duncan, Kelter, a friend of Kelter's and myself. The first four have made the extreme sacrifice, whilst others bear scars from wounds.

The party who looked after the estaminet was Madame Beck assisted by her daughters, Marie and Alice. Alice had been betrothed to a Frenchman across the border, who was killed at Souchez, a few months ago; Lora, a pretty little child, with a wonderful memory, was a grand-daughter. She could talk English splendidly. The daughters had a fair knowledge of it also. They ushered us into a back room. Pork chops were obtained from the neighbouring butcher's shop, and under war conditions, a fine meal was laid before us, certainly a treat compared to army food. Champagne was ordered and we had a great time. Singing, then speeches. Swinton sang his favourite "There's a wee hoose 'amongst the heather'." MacKay, feeling the pace was too much for him, stole softly away. A few were a little touched up and for twenty minutes Fardell, Duncan and myself were doing nothing but taking the others out. No sooner had we one out than another would go in, as he said, to bring some one out. It was most amusing.

Looking into another estaminet, I spied MacKay seated at a small table trying to argue with a Belgian civilian. I am afraid I was a bit of a mischief. Going in, I ordered a drink for MacKay, then another, and when I mentioned a third MacKay burst out laughing and fled out. In going home a few were seeing three moons in the sky. Near Mont Rouge, we decided on a deuch an dorris,[36] at an estaminet with an unpronounceable name. Warning the rest to square up I went in and ordered the drinks. The Belgian scrutinized us carefully, then poured out the beverage. There was silence as the Imperial artillery-men stopped conversing to gaze on the newcomers. The strain, however, was too much for Buttress, who subsided into a chair, knocking over a glass. There was a shake of the head and we filed out, vanquished. Being up to tricks, I led them short cuts through fields and along the muddiest paths I could find. Going through a wire fence, a bottle of champagne fell out of Evan's pocket and broke. At the cross-roads, Buttress got stuck in the mud and fell flat in it. The next day MacKay would look over his eyebrows at Fardell and I and mutter to those around, it is the last time I am going out with teetotallers. We were supposed to be free from guile. Needless to say

[36] A Gaelic phrase meaning a drink at the door, or more popularily, "one for the road."

the day passed off good-naturedly and months afterwards we looked back on it with amusement and pleasure. Poor MacKay fell at Ypres, Buttress died of wounds after a raid at St. Eloi, Swinton obtained a commission and was killed on Vimy Ridge, whilst little Evans paid the penalty at Ypres. Fardell was shot through the lung at the Somme, Kelter hovered between life and death for a while. He was twice wounded by our own men, firstly by a bullet ricochet from a sniper, and secondly from a splinter of a shell that fell short. Duncan, who put in strenuous work for over two years, also bears honourable scars.

The majority of soldiers look with contempt on senior officers, simply because the firing line does not require their presence and I fancy also owing to their activities in worrying the men when out on rest. One officer I can single out as a decided exception. He is General Turner, V.C.,[37] in command of the Second Division. I saw him several times in our sector and twice by himself. With another fellow I had been up in the "Glory Hole," where our "D" Coy. was located. Fritz had a white flag up and was showing himself above the trench. Our men were so flabbergasted and curious that no one fired. Going back we were commenting on the incident disgustingly when we met the General, whom we did not know and who was minus staff colours. He overheard us and asked us what was the matter. Rather heatedly we explained affairs. He told us of a German white flag incident and then finished up his remarks with "Never trust a German, shoot them every time." Turner, who is mild featured and wears glasses, looks the reverse of a soldier. The frequency with which he visited the trenches stamps him as not deficient in moral courage.

One night we wondered what was the matter with the fellows in the adjoining bay. Whenever a shot was fired, it just about deafened us. Thinking I would find out, I stole round the corner and watched. Instead of Doull getting on to the firing step and firing in the direction of Fritzie, he thought it would serve as well, to stand in the bay and blaze into the sky. It would save trouble and the result would be much about the same. But the worst of it [was] we got all the report. Clyne, Doull and Rooth were afterwards styled the "Doull Battery."

One of the most disagreeable duties is "Listening Post." Listening Post is in No Man's Land as far forward as is deemed safe. It is either a shell hole position or the end of a small trench running out from the firing line. The idea is to detect an enemy movement and nip an

[37] Major-General R. E. W. Turner, V.C., a veteran of the South African war, had originally commanded the 3rd Brigade of the 1st Canadian Division at the outset of the war. Turner was promoted to command the 2nd Canadian Division in August 1915, just prior to the division's move to France.

attack by stealth in the bud. From the post to the firing line there is connection by cord or telephone wire. The sentry at "listening post" pulls the cord; according to the number of pulls one, two, or three, the fellow at the other end is made aware of happenings and ready to warn the Company. The signals are few, usually all clear, or small or large hostile parties approaching. The enemy is often aware of these "listening posts" and makes a point of capturing them or bombs the sentry. In consequence, one has to be all alive when he takes on such work.

To show the diversity of army orders we were, for a time, not allowed to remove our boots when off duty in the firing line. Being soaked through and through with ice cold water, our feet were numbed and we could not sleep. Naturally we disobeyed these orders for our own health and comfort, taking chances on Heiny surprising us. This order was in vogue for a while till another came out, the very reverse, warning us against trench feet, and telling us to remove our boots when not on duty. Goose fat, an antidote or rather a preventative for trench feet, was issued and we were supposed to smear our feet with it. I never heard that it did much good and most fellows ignored it.

One night when on sentry, Clyne rushed into my post, with the alarming news, that the 5th Bde. passed down word that the enemy were advancing on the left. I hurried to the adjacent bay and communicated the news to the sentry there, who sent the fiery cross further down the line. Rushing to the dug-out, I shouted and pulled at Buttress and MacKay telling them to hurry out, then jumped on the firing step with bayonet bristling and scanned No Man's Land for the foe. With no artillery preparation, what a glorious opportunity it would be for us. Buttress arrived out in double quick time; but had to chase back several times to get MacKay out and when the latter did come, it was only to give us a round of abuse for not warning him sooner. We hung around the bay with bayonets gleaming ready for eventualities, which did not arrive. Sauntering round the bay we gave vent to our wrath on our next door neighbours for getting us into such an uproar. When the alarm was sounded there was a call for starlights and Lt. Hartt was chasing around excitedly. Nobody knew who had them or even the pistol.[38] Anyway our lights were very feeble, about as bright as five cent squibs, and a quarter of them never went off when fired. Fritz must have been amused at them.

[38] Lt. Hartt was looking for the Very pistol and the cartridges for it. The pistol threw up flares—Fraser calls them "starlights"—of various colours. The white flare gave only modest illumination. Lt. Hartt, incidentally, had been posted to the battalion only two days previously.

About the end of the year an order came out warning us that when peace was declared, we were not to cheer if in the trenches. Surely headquarters must have been drinking.

Saturday, January 8, 1916

Whilst at Locre I saw a number of troops returning from the Ypres front and other troops going up to take their places. The bulk of those returning were north of England regiments. The Liverpool Scottish, one of the earliest territorial battalions, was amongst the number. We leave for the trenches tonight.

Monday, January 10, 1916

Artillery and aeroplanes fairly active.

CHAPTER II

Behind the Lines

Tuesday, January 11, 1916

A heavy bombardment is heard on the left. The 28th Battalion had a quiet six days in the trenches—only one man killed and another wounded by the same bullet.

I was talking to an officer of the 28th Battalion whilst sheltering from the rain in a ruined house at the crossroads at Kemmel, beside Suicide Road. He was very sore because the communication trench was not open yet and he was losing men going over the open. He lost one of his best men a few days ago on the SP11 path whilst carrying rations. A stray bullet struck him in the ribs. A few minutes afterwards he died after saying "Goodbye boys, my time is up."

At "Tete Jaune Cache" between Kemmel and Locre I passed a monster of a gun, a 12-in., drawn by a caterpillar. The weight of the shell it fires is 750 lbs. Not a very pleasant thing to burst in your ear. We are still depending on the British artillery. Last night I passed another.

Whilst in England I attended to the Company's stores, but ran away from the work the night we made for the line. Much to my surprise, whilst on sentry, the Q.M. asked me to go back and assist him. Thinking the matter over I came to the conclusion that it would be a decided improvement on the work I am at, which largely consists of working around the trenches, interspersed with shivering spells on the firing step, waiting for Fritz to come over, so I accepted the offer.

The work I would have to do would be to draw rations from the Regimental store for the Company and divide them according to platoons. The usual procedure is to lay out the rations, then bag them into sandbags, tying the sandbags together securely. By tying sandbags together they can be easily carried by slinging them over the shoulder, one in front and one behind. A small wooden tag is affixed to each sandbag with one, two, three or four notches on it, thus stating which platoon it is for. Our work is semi-safety first. We stay in a tent at Locre several kilometres in the rear. When it begins to get dark, we load up the rations on the limbers and hike for Ration Farm, halfway up Suicide Road, several hundred yards behind the line. This is the furthest we can go. Any further and the noise of the limbers on the road would give us away. Two or three men come down from the firing line, support line or strong points, from each platoon to the ration dump. They are usually waiting there when the limbers arrive. As a rule it does not do to hang around the spot long, so we unload as quickly as possible. The fellow in charge of the party has the two most important things handed to him, namely the mail and the rum. There are always strong enquiries after the rum and it generally takes the form of "Did the rum come up tonight." Smiles of gladness creep over their faces when the answer is affirmative. The features expand still further when they are told there is an extra jar.

In the dark we feel for the notches. If there is only one, we call quietly for [the] carrier for No. 1 platoon and hand him the sandbags; if there are two notches we call for [the] carrier for No. 2 platoon and so on till the rations are handed out, then we are given outgoing mail and maybe a list of orders. After this we return, generally having to walk it the whole way back. Occasionally we manage a lift. Our transport will not stay a second longer than they have to. There is always a chance of Fritz opening up, with artillery or machine-guns, so those trips are done by stealth and in a hurry—a get up and a get away.

Meanwhile the carrying party make for their respective positions in the line. They turn over their loads to the N.C.O. who looks after the rations. Articles requiring cooking are handed to the cooks. Where cooking is done, the front is looked upon as a quiet one. Other goods such as bread, butter, jam, etc. are divided up amongst the fellows. Bread usually runs three to four men per small loaf, for one day. Occasionally, when supplies are scarce, it may run six to seven to one loaf and that loaf may be almost in crumbs. The difference is made up of huge hard biscuits, not unlike dog biscuits. There are times when both bread and biscuits are scarce and for a few days it spells starvation. Rations, therefore, are up and down. At the best they are never too plentiful. The tendency is to be on the scrimp side. A small tin of jam is made to suffice five or six men and a tin of butter is issued bi-weekly between eight to ten men.

For a long time the brand of preserves was marmalade and

everyone was heartily sick of it. Later on Australian and New Zealand produce came to the fore, "XL" and "Cockatoo" being very prominent trade marks. I often wondered why Ontario and B.C. did not take advantage of the war situation and turn out tons and tons of preserves. There is no doubt in this respect Australasia was more alive to her opportunity, for before the war she never exported a tin of jam to Europe.

Maybe once or twice a week we would go up to the front line to hear how things were going on. There is an understood order that at night no man can go in or out of the trenches without a comrade. When the battalion is back at rest billets, pickles is an occasional ration, one bottle going to about sixteen men. You can guess rations is a source of much trouble and a difficult matter to divide equitably. The platoon ration man has quite a handful satisfying each individual. We arrive back at our quarters between 12:30 and 2:30 a.m. The danger attached to this work is not great. At times you may run the gauntlet of shells, machine-gun fire or stray rifle bullets, but this is temporary when you are going up and coming back. The work is easy but there is a considerable amount of tramping. It was a nice change though. I figured after a spell I would get tired and go back to the scrapping which I ultimately did.

During the battalion's last stay at Locre, two of the 29th men were buried in the cemetery there. One of the 24th Battalion was killed tonight coming out of the line.

During a spell in the "Glory Hole," when Fritz was particularly active with his trench mortars, one of our fellows, Butson, lost his nerve and went semi-insane. After the fireworks quieted down a bit Butson was found crawling around the trench on his hands and knees quite demented. He was taken out. Returning to the Company a few months later, when word was announced that the Company was leaving Scottish Wood for the line, Butson became unnerved again and threatened to shoot himself. He said he could not face the music. To keep him from going into hysterics, he was taken out and returned to the base.

Another incident happened when we were in the "Glory Hole." My platoon was in G2, adjoining the rest of the Company, whose bombers were the principal occupiers of the most dangerous posts. When we were in the trench a few shells were coming over, but nothing to alarm us. Lt. Eccles, formerly a ranker in my section, came rushing down very much excited, exclaiming, "save the poor boys up there," "get up on the firing step," and "give them rapid fire." He was quivering with excitement. Our platoon officer, Lt. Wooley-Dod, who was behind him, was also agitated but had nothing to say. I

80

wondered what was the matter. I saw nothing much out of the ordinary, and naturally, felt reluctant to fire, when there was nothing to fire at. However, I got up on the firing step, being almost pushed by Eccles, who with Wooley-Dod beat it down the trench moving towards the exit. Sergeant Barrons was a few yards away and I bluntly remarked to him, "What in the world is the matter with Eccles trying to work the men into such a panic. He should be with his bombers instead of around our line." Barrons had his mind made up before I spoke. He was also dumbfounded at the sudden unnecessary outburst and promptly reported the matter to the Major. Shortly after this, Eccles received a safety first job with the Brigade as bombing instructor, but owing to the battalion having had almost all their officers casualties in our first trip in the Somme, Eccles was returned to the battalion only to be killed when we went over the bags[1] the next day.

When in G3 some of our fellows were renovating the Major's dugout. Part of the work was knocking in posts and, of course, was done at night so Fritz could not detect the noise and consequently imagine a working party about. The sentry in my post, being nearest, had to fire a round every time the mall descended on the post thereby deadening the sound. We shot away about four belts (bandoliers) and thought we were making rather peculiar use of our rifles.

About this time we received in a draft an officer of the 50th, Lt. Robertson. At first he was looked upon with amusement, being very particular about his food. He remarked in my presence one night to Lt. Pouncey, in a very effeminate manner, that he had only one cup of tea, he always had two cups of tea, and he must, he must have his tea. We thought him a regular Johnnie. But before many months had passed the men thought the world of him. He was absolutely fearless notwithstanding his effeminate ways. This is a war in which blood counts, not bone; nerve is the test and not strength.

Robertson was wounded later. Returning from Blighty he was killed further on in the campaign. I remember talking to a First Division man in hospital at Buxton. He said one of the biggest surprises they had was a dude officer, an out and out "haw haw" Englishman. You would think he had not the strength or grit of a fly, nevertheless this officer would tackle any dangerous work, was about the most daring man they had. He always carried a cane which he twirled incessantly.

There was one British airman whom we all recognized. He was the

[1] "Over the bags" or, more usually, "over the top" into no man's land. The parapet of the trench was lined with sandbags.

coolest and most audacious on our front. He was known amongst us as the "Mad Major." Seldom a day passed but he was up all on his lonesome. He flew slow and very low. Fritzie riflemen in the trenches would fire at him, round after round, but he would never turn a hair. Back and forward he went as if on a beat. He appeared to bear a charmed life. There were strange rumours regarding him, one that he was an artillery officer, an eccentric individual who owned a private plane, and relied on his own observations for his batteries, ignoring the aerial service completely. I often wondered what became of him.

One of our officers, Lt. Whitehead, though quiet and not very approachable, was well liked and a good man. He left us for the Flying Corps. In his first trip he was reported missing.

Scotty Mearns was one of our characters. When leaning against the parapet one day, a rifle grenade burst on the other side, and part of the sandbag hit Scotty with considerable force. Scotty danced around the bay, holding his arm almost sure that he was wounded, and already saw visions of Blighty. But when he removed his tunic there was only a bruise mark. Scotty was horribly disgusted and showed it on his face, much to our amusement. Several months late at Hooge on the Ypres front, he was wounded and carried his machine-gun, which was damaged, all the way with him to Poperinghe several miles away. It was left at the Hospital there. Nearly a year later Mearns returned to the firing line from Blighty and was killed at the Battle of Fresnoy.

On the Kemmel front, amongst trench stores, was a safety device for firing during the day. This device had a periscope attached. The rifle was clamped into it and the trigger was gripped by a sort of clasp which was connected with the trigger of the device. I do not think it was much good for accuracy. No one made much use of it.

When the night was quiet we often had much amusement over rats either firing at them or getting after them with sticks.

During winter a few sandbags of coke and charcoal were sent up the line nightly to burn in the braziers and help keep us warm. It was quite a job keeping the braziers going; fuel was so scarce and so quickly eaten up. We were continually making uncomfortable trips to ruined buildings close by, stripping them of their timbers and lugging them to our positions, where we would chop them into bits with our entrenching tools. I soon tired of this game preferring the cold to the trouble and smoke. In the "F" supports, as ill luck would have it, I was in a tiny dug-out with Rooth and Powell. We could only be on our sides and even then it was a tight fit. The others were determined to have a fire whilst I voted against it. This fire was nursed inside the dug-out for about three hours. We never received a particle of heat. My eyes were watering and I was almost choked with smoke, whilst my head ached with the stuffiness. I resolved that in future I would keep away from these fire fiends and partner with some cold blooded men.

Our first trip in the line was the occasion of one or two amusing incidents. Naturally we were green and imaginative. Lovell, whilst on sentry, reported that he saw Germans up a certain tree. It turned out the tree was no bigger than a bush. He was relieved for the night till he regained his natural senses. Lovell was a pretty good sticker and lasted till he met his death on the old battling ground of the Bluff.

When out for rations to near the middle of Regent St., an enemy machine-gun opened up and just about caught Rooth, the bullets hitting earth beside him. At the time I was about to get out of the trench but the swish of the bullets above my head made me change my mind. Rooth dropped into the trench in a hurry.

At this time we were rather low in spirits, being completely fed up with Flanders' mud and rain and the amount of carrying we had to do. Returning to Regent St. Dug-Outs one night laden, as usual, the sentry challenged us "Who goes there!" One of our number out of sheer weariness and disgust shouted out "pack mules." The adjutant heard him, stopped the crowd and gave us an awful slating. He was very regimental and figured the answer was lowering the dignity of the army. But soldiers are only human.

One of our number, Skinner, a little Englishman, a useless sort of fellow, got stuck in the mud. First, a Swede was ordered to go to his assistance. He was sore at Skinner and grabbed him roughly, giving a tug he pulled him completely out of his rubber boots. There was much laughter over the incident.

On another occasion the sergeant was giving out the rum at SP 9. A shell came over, bursting close by, sending everyone to cover. A few minutes later the men reassembled. MacKay took advantage of the situation to get in line for a second supply. Barrons, forgetting in the scrimmage for cover whom he had served, gave MacKay a second tot, much to our amusement.

So much for a few of the incidents that happened to keep us in good humour.

Friday, January 14, 1916

We are out of the trenches once more. A few hours before leaving there was some excitement. The enemy opened up rather violently with coal boxes,[2] whiz-bangs and aerial torpedoes. The latter kept us

---

[2] A heavy calibre German shell which, on exploding, sent up a cloud of black smoke— hence the term "coal box."

very busy, several of the fellows having narrow escapes. The 25th Battalion on the left had a sergeant and sergeant-major killed. Our artillery retaliated strongly and gave the Huns a merry time of it.

Monday, January 17, 1916

The report that the 29th man who was on listening post and went amissing sometime ago was a spy was found to be incorrect. He mistook his direction and went over the German parapet thinking it was the Canadian line when he was seized by several Germans and sent inland as a prisoner. This fellow escaped a number of months afterwards and made Blighty, where he met several men of his old battalion.

Thursday, January 20, 1916

I have noticed in orders that two of the 27th Battalion and two of the 29th Battalion have received the D.C.M.[3] Sometime ago a 28th man received the same honour. He helped to dig out several of the men who were buried when Heiny exploded the mine beneath the 28th in the "Glory Hole." The military medal had not come into being yet. There are many anomalies in this war. The public still conceive the old fashioned idea that, because a soldier receives commissioned rank when in the field, he has done exceptional work and the advancement is an award for his gallantry. This is a fallacy that needs exposing. The facts are: the ambitious soldier merely puts in his application, which being earmarked by his colonel or someone of like authority, receives in due course, in nineteen times out of twenty, official sanction. In ninety per cent of decorations a similar anomaly exists. It has been often remarked that officers spend a considerable time recommending each other for honours. There is no question of doubt but D.S.O.s and M.C.s[4] have been sprinkled around like water, the vast majority of recipients doing absolutely nothing out of the common to earn these awards. I know personally of several, one or two of which have hardly seen the front lines. Many who are not even members of fighting forces, earn these decorations, miles behind the fighting area, simply on the strength of doing good work in their particular sphere.

[3] D.C.M.—Distinguished Conduct Medal, an award for bravery given to those who did not hold an officer's commission. The Military Medal, somewhat less prestigous, was later awarded "for bravery in the field."

[4] The D.S.O. (Distinguished Service Order) and M.C. (Military Cross) were awards granted only to officers. Fraser's bitterness here is only partly justified, although the editor's father remarked that once, when offered either a bar to his military medal or a week's leave, he took the latter!

The remarks apply also to the men, though I think in a lesser degree. After an engagement, decorations are sure to follow whether there is any outstanding work done or not. As a rule it means the O.C. gets the D.S.O. or M.C., likewise one or two of the officers. The sergeants are next in line for the D.C.M. or M.M., that is, providing nothing of importance was done by anyone else. If any of the fellows showed up well and his gallantry was noticed, naturally he would get recognition, but in the vast majority of cases the decorations are merely awarded for nothing in particluar. Those who are in close touch with the staff or officers or in charge of units have the first call.

This indiscriminate trafficking in decorations is a crying disgrace. It is a pity these honours were not retained solely for men who have done deeds of bravery. Amongst the crowd it is difficult to pick out the real man. One has to enquire through his fellow men in his unit to ascertain if he earned the honour or not. Any eulogy from them can be taken as a sure sign that he deserved the award and full credit should be accorded him. Decorations have become so much of a joke that the recipient, conscious that he has done nothing, often remarks when questioned by his "pals" what did he do: "Oh, I guess I was first at the rations!" as if to signify that the Quartermaster dealt them out. Failing which he may answer quizzically, after pondering the matter over, "Blest if I know." There have been many jests made over the "Iron Cross" owing to their lavish distribution, but our Military Cross and Military Medal could stand as much banter. Comment is unnecessary when in 1916 the Prince of Wales had the Military Cross conferred upon him.

Friday, January 21, 1916

Many of the fellows are busy gathering souvenirs, mainly nosecaps.[5] SP 10 is the happy hunting ground. Fritz peppers this place freely, knowing considerable observation is obtained from it.

Yesterday a German plane came over our lines. We eagerly watched our anti-aircraft guns shooting at it. Their aim was very inaccurate, the shells bursting hundreds of yards away. All of a sudden a battery opened up behind us and shell after shell just about got it. Turning to the north it was soon out of range. A British machine was cautiously making for Heiny, when the latter made a dart, banged a burst of machine-gun fire, sending the British plane to earth near Locre, at the back of our rest billets. It was not badly damaged. Our plane was a very late type and considered a splendid machine. According to one of our flying men, the enemy has at the

[5] Shell nosecaps tended to remain in one piece when the rest of the shell fragmented.

85

present time particulary good planes and it is risky work encountering them. He intimated, however, that a new machine is being perfected and when it comes into use will give Heiny a fright.

There has been considerable talk about supremacy of the air. Up to the Somme the enemy has had more that the edge on us and many of our most daring and courageous men have been killed in aerial combat through waging an unequal war in inferior machines. Like the "Contemptible Little Army"[6] they have been sacrificed. At the Somme the Germans completely lost the upper hand and scarcely a plane was able to show itself on the horizon. Their aerial observation was practically at a standstill, not even their "sausage" balloons[7] were safe. The Allies were king of the skies. In the beginning of 1917 the Germans were in the ascendancy once more. Between Arras and Lens, from February to June, our machines were pickings for them, the "Travelling Circus"[8] under Baron Von Richtofen having the time of their lives at our expense to the chagrin of the men in the trenches, who were witnesses of many of the duels. Supremacy was changing from one side to the other according to improvements made. Every few months saw an increase in speed, an ability to rise and swoop quickly, and an improvement in speedy manoeuvre. The old straight-laced machine which could only turn in a wide circle was displaced and the later machines performed such antics that not even the birds could emulate them.

A French Canadian of the 22nd Battalion, who are on our left, informed me that one of their number received the D.C.M. A working party of the enemy, about two hundred, were out working in front of the parapet in view of our lines unknown to them. An officer asked for a volunteer to snipe them. A machine-gunner mounted his gun on the parapet and let go, dropping quite a number. He also caught a string of them on the run. Just as he completed his work, a rifle grenade came whizzing through the air, damaging the gun and breaking his arm.

The reason for the aerial activity lately on the part of the enemy is ascribed to the light railway that is being constructed at the rear of our lines. He is trying to locate its position with a view to shelling it.

La Clytte was shelled a few days ago.

[6] The term used by the Kaiser to describe the small regular British Army available for service in 1914.

[7] Observation balloons, which looked a bit like a rather fat sausage, used primarily to assist artillery batteries firing into enemy territory.

[8] Baron Von Richtofen, the famous German ace, had the aircraft in his squadron painted in a variety of bright colours, hence the common term "Flying Circus." Richtofen's own plane was painted a bright red.

Saturday, January 22, 1916

Rifle firing is a little more active than usual. Had a narrow shave from machine-gun strays near Ration Farm.

Sunday, January 23, 1916

Enemy planes are very active over our lines. Anti-aircraft guns are busy, but as usual the range is inaccurate. A few days ago five German prisoners passed through Locre. I understand a sentry of the 22nd Battalion, whilst on listening post, captured them. There could not have been much fight in them.

Monday, January 24, 1916

Whilst a party of the 27th Battalion were out wiring in front of their parapet the other day, Jerry opened up with a machine-gun, killing four and wounding eight.

Our Q.M. had to turn back twice last night near H'Qrs. owing to high velocity shells bursting in his path.

Thursday, January 27, 1916

The battalion is relieved once again. It has had a lucky spell, not a single casualty occurring. Some of the 27th Battalion were killed by our own artillery firing short. One fellow had his head knocked off. It is rather strange—his chum was killed a few hours before. Both crossed to Canada from the Old Country together. They enlisted together and are now killed about the same time.

Old Dad Cameron, a Boer War veteran, and a hardy customer of uncertain age, a native of Eastern Canada of Scotch parentage, with a great gift for fun, was quite a character amongst us. We had many amusing times in his company. I referred to him as the "half Hieland Irishman from Quebec." This always brought forth a rejoinder, usually in scathing terms of everything Scotch—but whisky. Cameron was a scout and gave me a couple of clips of German bullets he had taken off a Hun corpse when out on patrol in front of Heiny's wire. He obtained one or two souvenirs, including a sort of pole-axe.

Saturday, January 29, 1916

Almost all the battalion was out on fatigue last night laying a cable. They came dribbling back at all hours.

To the left of our line a Lieutenant with a small party, under cover of darkness, went over to the German lines and after throwing forty-four bombs returned unhurt. For a while the enemy were very nervous.

Sunday, January 30, 1916

We were all lined up in a park near Locre, to hear the recommendation read out by Major-Gen. Turner, V.C. of the 2nd Division, for a V.C. for Pte. Jackson of our battalion. The Rt. Hon. Andrew Bonar Law, Brigadier Gen. Ketchen,[9] Col. Bell, and several staff officers were present. Bonar Law made a speech. The deed for which Jackson was recommended was—whilst a party was busy working in the trench, Heiny sent over a minnewerfer[10] shell which landed beside them. Jackson at once pounced upon it, snuffing out the fuse, thus rendering it harmless, thereby saving the lives of his comrades. These were the facts as related to me though there appears to be a conflict of opinion regarding the whole matter. The V.C., however, never came through, but instead a D.C.M. was awarded and tacked on to it was the Russian Order of St. George. Several weeks later Jackson was severely wounded in the leg and returned to Canada.

The 28th and 29th Battalions made a bombing attack on the enemy last night. The former in front of the Gs and the latter in front of the Fs. The 28th is the battalion which relieves us. Eighteen of the 28th took part in the attack. They crept out over "No Man's Land" in the dark, minus all identifications, equipped with bombs, revolvers, knobkerries,[11] all the paraphernalia necessary for raiders who have desperation written over their features. Reaching the wire, they had to cut a passage, right under the nose of the German sentries, who were only a few yards away. The wire clippers were set to work but it was a slow process as the clippers could only be brought into action once in a few minutes and then quietness till another favourable opportunity presented itself. Flarelights were being thrown up and our men had to lie immovable during the illumination. After a couple of hours a passage was eventually made. The bayonet men hopped over into the trench and landed beside a sentry. Flashing a small lamp that was attached to the rifle in his face, one of them made a lunge at him, catching him in the side of the neck. Immediately he let out a yell

---

[9] Bonar Law was the British Secretary of State for the Colonies at this time. Brigadier General H. D. B. Ketchen commanded the 6th Canadian Brigade, of which the 31st Battalion formed part.

[10] The Canadian soldier's slang for the German term minenwerfer.

[11] A type of short club.

and up went his hands, but the rifle was discharged almost blowing his head off. The bombers at once ran along the trench, throwing their bombs into the dug-outs, executing considerable damage. The Captain of the Brigade bombers, who was to a large extent responsible for the plans, was in command. He carried a revolver and bayonet, and was bent on blood. Whilst hiding behind a corner he bayoneted one man, then another as he came along the trench, a third man following got stabbed in the vitals, but unfortunately he could not withdraw the bayonet. A Hun, who was behind, shot at him with a revolver but it did not go off. He then flung it at Captain Taylor's face, damaging his nose. Whipping out his revolver, the gallant Captain emptied its contents into No. 4's stomach. Another man was shot before the officer beat a hasty retreat. He received several wounds but they were of a slight character. This fighting officer was killed on the Somme a few days before the attack, whilst on duty, holding the line with the 29th Battalion. I saw his body as it lay on a stretcher awaiting burial in an improvised Australian cemetery, near the almost obliterated village of Pozieres. The 28th made the mistake of overstaying their time, remaining twenty-five minutes and in coming back, shrapnel and machine-gun fire were turned on them, killing three and wounding eight, only six getting back unhurt. One of their number was left on the wire entanglements, either dead or wounded. They were rustling a couple of prisoners before them, when one was killed by shrapnel from one of his own guns and the other, unwilling to move quick enough, was killed. The only clue the enemy got of the raiders was from a revolver lent to the fellow who was hung up on the entanglements. The name of D. McGill, with his battalion, the 31st, was on it.

Twenty-nine men took part in the 29th bombing attack which turned out highly successful, only one man being wounded. Like the 28th, they had their faces blackened. They remained in the German trenches for only four minutes, returning with three prisoners, one a warrant officer. They bayoneted several and threw bombs into the dug-outs. The enemy was taken completely by surprise and received a great scare. They were chased out minus tunics, equipment, and were wholly unprepared. The head bayonet man bayoneted one man, shot another, and a third Hun fled from him. On the way out the warrant officer received a nasty jab in the regions from an over zealous 29th man, who could not resist the temptation.

The prisoner seemed elated on being taken captive. He remarked that he was never so surprised in all his life. He had been in twenty-two engagements in the East and had only arrived on the Western Front for a rest two days ago. He was spick and span, the very embodiment of German military culture. A tall, dark-haired man of fine physique and appearance. He was said to be one of the Prussian Guards, but this was contradicted, as it was Silesian troops that opposed the 29th, the Prussian Guards opposing the 28th. When in hospital at Locre, some one removed a couple of buttons from his tunic, which exasperated him greatly. I paid the hospital a visit in order that I might get a glimpse of this Kaiser warrior, but there was a guard on to keep intruders away.

You must remember up till this time a Hun was a curiosity to us. Later on we saw the men in field grey[12] in plenty. Many Canadian soldiers, however, have spent several months in France and gone back to Canada without catching even a fleeting glimpse of the enemy. Since the attacks Jerry has been extremely nervous, indulging in rifle fire and flinging up star shells intermittently, a sure indication that his nerves are on edge. It is reported that Saxon troops have relieved the Prussians. They cried over to our battalion that they would not strafe us, if we would not strafe them. They are not as bellicose as their domineering brethren. The men who took part in the raids are to be given a pass to England. In connection with these exploits the following decorations were awarded: three D.S.O.s, one to the 28th, one to the 29th, and one to an attached man. Three Military Crosses —two to the 29th and one to an attached man. Four D.C.M.s, three to the 28th and one to the 29th. These were the first raids carried out by the Canadian forces.

A few days ago Madame Beck of Mont Noir, informed me that in 1914 the Germans took all the young civilian men in the Westoutre district prisoners. At Neuve Eglise a civilian was shot and the gendarmes at Westoutre were killed.

Both Kelter and Campbell were wounded today by the same bullet, supposed to be a ricochet from a shot fired by one of our snipers.

Three of the 27th were wounded.

Twenty men from the 56th Battalion have reinforced us.

Coming back from the Ration Farm several stray bullets whizzed past us, quite a distance behind the line. Kemmel was shelled a short time before we passed through, one shell landing on the roadway.

Saturday, February 5, 1916

A German plane dropped a bomb over Kemmel killing six horses. There was considerable aerial activity today. Both British and Ger-

---

[12] The colour of the German soldier's uniform.

man planes kept manoeuvring for position for attack, but did not engage each other.

I have just heard that seven of our sappers were struck by splinters from a rifle grenade in the "Glory Hole," one being killed.

Sunday, February 6, 1916

The enemy retaliated for our bombing attacks with everything at his command, coal boxes, aerial torpedoes, minnewerfers, etc., sending several over at one time. Our men had to retire behind for three hours till the storm subsided. Part of our trenches, particularly supports, were blown to pieces. Rifles, equipment, etc., were lost in the explosions. Strange, no one was killed. Many had narrow escapes. Buttress and Gordon were slightly scratched.

After handing rations over to the ration party at Ration Farm, I crossed over to the communication trench with them intending to go up the line for an hour or two to ascertain what was going on. On going up the trench a little way I suddenly remembered that I had left my rifle against the hedge at Suicide Road. Retracing my steps over the open I had scarcely gone a hundred yards when a bullet crashed through the hedge and with a wicked swish just missed catching me in the side. For the moment I held my breath, thinking it had gone through me, it was so perilously close. A few yards further on several whizzed around but they were a considerable distance away. I did not dally on the way, but made a bee line for my rifle. Coming back I was hoping that particular Heiny would be quiet when I was passing that uncanny spot. You can guess I hopped over to the trench gingerly, my ears straining for a rifle report but nothing came so I strolled up the trench overtaking the party near Beaver Hat.

On my return, whilst proceeding on my lonesome down Suicide Road, the nails on my boots, sparked against the cobbles and in a few seconds three bullets passed overhead a little in front of me. Whether the sparks were observed by an alert German sentry or not I cannot say, but it impressed upon me the necessity of safely walking on the cobbles.

Monday, February 7, 1916

Our brigade is taken out of the trenches for a rest, the 7th Brigade[13] relieving us. The latter comprises the Princess Pats, the Royal Canadian Regiment, the 42nd [Canadian Black Watch] and the

[13] The 7th Canadian Brigade, commanded by Brig.-Gen. A. C. Macdonnell, was part of the recently formed 3rd Canadian Division, commanded by Maj.-Gen. M. S. Mercer. Of its four battalions, only the Princess Patricia's Canadian Light Infantry had

49th, an Edmonton battalion. It was only lately that they were brigaded. The Princess Pats was formerly attached to the Imperial division. This battalion relieved the 31st after a spell as a labour and guard battalion. Our company spent the night at Kemmel Shelters. The R.C.R.s had one man shot dead going into the line and the 27th Battalion one man shot on listening post.

During our stay on this front, from September till February, our casualties were about two hundred, sixty being killed. Discomfort owing to the rigours of the season was the greatest thing we suffered, the enemy being of secondary consideration. Exposure sent many of our men to the base with sickness, rheumatism, and kindred troubles. Though our sector was a quiet one, the complexion of our battalion was altering; the 31st was beginning to give way to other units.[14] As time wore on, the 56th became the predominant unit. Casualties tore their ranks, then the 82nd took prominence. They soon gave way to the 89th, then as Vimy approached, the 137th came to the front, and so on till Passchendaele, when the 202nd had perhaps the majority. When the armistice was declared a considerable number of conscripts must have been in our original ranks, a sad take down to those who had gone before.

Tuesday, February 8, 1916

We are on the hike to our rest camp.[15] Emma, a Belgian girl, who stayed at the chicory mill, came down to us with a jug of home-made beer a few minutes before we left. She was a refugee from Passchendaele, leaving it in 1914 for Ypres, which, in turn, became too hot for her, so she turned her eyes to Locre. In 1918, Heiny took possession of this village, and I guess poor Emma would be adrift once more and would have to seek safety in France, at Cassell or perhaps further back. There must be thousands of Belgians and French in the same plight as this girl; the majority will never obtain the same comforts as they enjoyed before the war. To the older folk the outlook must

---

experience in the line. This unit had been formed at the beginning of the war and had been serving with the British 27th Division prior to being moved to the Canadian Corps. The Royal Canadian Regiment, at that time Canada's only Permanent Force unit, had spent the first eleven months of the war on garrison duty in Bermuda. It arrived in France in November 1915. The 31st Battalion does not return to front line duties until 13th March.

14 Fraser here describes the impact of a constant stream of casualties and reinforcements from other Canadian battalions on the original 850 officers and men who went into action with the 31st Battalion. Reinforcements were sent from other battalions which were drawn upon to send drafts to the front rather than go to the front as battalions.

15 At this point the battalion goes well behind the front line.

92

indeed be gloomy. I remember being in a house at Mont Noir; in the room I was ushered into were three women between eighty and ninety years of age, refugees from Neuvre Eglise. They were sisters; the daughters of one of them contributed to their support by taking photos of the soldiers. There they sat in this little room, crowded together, silent, with listless, hopeless looks on their faces, gazing into the unknown.

Our route from Kemmel Shelter lay by Locre, near which we passed the 49th, one of the huskiest of Canada's battalions, then Hyde Park Corner, Westoutre, and finally our Company camped at a farm overlooking Boescheppe about a kilometre away. We were on rising ground and had a splendid view of Flanders. The billets, farm buildings, had daylight streaming through multitudinous holes and crevices, so we were bitterly cold and slept huddled together for warmth. During the day we lay in our billets covered up in our blankets, it was the only way we could keep half warm. For a winter billet it was a crying scandal. Instead of a rest camp, it was torture. Snow lay on the ground and the air had a decided bite in it. We washed in a slough of ice, very evil smelling and had shivering fits during the operation. Housing soldiers under these conditions, miles behind the firing line, is very poor policy. It only helps to undermine their constitution and sows seeds of discord in the ranks. There is absolutely no reason, when there is a stationary front, why suitable reserve billets are not found.

Wednesday, February 9, 1916

Paid a visit to Boescheppe, a sleepy little French village near the border.

Thursday, February 10, 1916

It is a stormy, wintry day. Poperinghe and Elverdinghe are shelled.

Friday, February 11, 1916

Thirty shells were sent over Kemmel in quest of our 12-inch gun near Tete Jaune Cache.

Saturday, February 12, 1916

There was bombardment almost all day in the vicinity of Ypres. During the previous night our lines were subjected to heavy shelling. Apparently this is a precursor to an attack.

We passed Berthen, Schaexken on the road to the baths near Meteren.

Sixteen of our planes returned from the direction of Armentieres after doing a raid, I presume.

We had some amusement over Skinner, the smallest man in the company. The line did not appeal very strongly to him so he lost no opportunity in endeavouring to develop trouble. At Boescheppe he found that there was something the matter with his knee—the ligaments were on the bum was his plea. His weakness of heart was very apparent so he obtained no sympathy from anyone. We collected several of the biggest men we could find and had him hoisted on to a stretcher. They carried him very reverently to the medical officer's quarters, a retinue following him ready to relieve should his bulky form of ninety pounds prove too heavy for them. There was much laughter as the procession moved off. Ushered into the doctor's presence he refused to have anything to do with him, threatening him with the guard room for malingering. Skinner arrived back on foot. A few days later he was sent to the base and ultimately to Blighty to swell Canada's mighty army of misfits.

Monday, February 14, 1916

All last night there was a heavy bombardment on the Ypres front; apparently the enemy is preparing to attack. Our artillery retaliated and from our vantage point, we witnessed the flashes from the guns, spitting out fire every second. It was a beautiful sight. Amidst the incessant roar of the guns came gleam after gleam, first from one spot then from another, darkness and light strangely intermingled. The flashes from the heavy guns showed up most vividly. Our artillery appeared to be working at high pressure, pouring out destruction to save our men. What a night for a fight, snow and wind and sleet, a perisher for the wounded. Smothered by a deluge of fire or frozen to the bone must have been the unhappy lot of those unfortunates who were bearing the brunt of the attack. Speculation was rife as to the exact spot and also the outcome. Somewhere between St. Eloi and Hill 60 was the consensus of opinion. We greedily awaited news. Rumours began to filter through. The first report was that our trenches to the north of St. Eloi were obliterated, the Germans taking one thousand yards of the front line, advancing in mass formation; coming in thousands according to one who had been through it. Our casualties for the day were two thousand, this being the number that passed through the clearing station at Poperinghe. Later on, a further

94

thousand was added to the number. A little to the north the Sherwood Foresters lost a stretch of trenches. So far have heard no official news. The current report is that the Lancs, Yorks, Dorsets, Staffords, and Sherwood Foresters have suffered badly.

The following is a correct version of the fight that has been raging. The centre of the attack was the well-known elevation called the "Bluff." It is a very important point for artillery observation. The front line having changed hands so often [it] has been named the International Trench. The enemy bombarded our front for a distance of several miles creating heavy losses. Our right was held by the 17th Div., the centre by the 50th and the left by the 24th. After many of the trenches were reduced to mud heaps, five mines were sprung under our lines, followed by a rush of the enemy infantry. The 10th Lancashire Fusiliers were nearly all killed or buried. To the north the 10th Sherwood Foresters and 8th South Staffords tried to hang on, but their positions were practically untenable owing to an enfilade fire that was being poured into them. The Colonel of the latter battalion who directed the defence was wounded four times. The Foresters had to withdraw after losing 12 officers and several hundred men. A counter-attack was engineered by the 7th Lincolns, 7th Borders and survivors of the Lancashire Fusiliers, who gained some success at a heavy cost, but six hundred yards still remained with the enemy. A lieutenant with 40 bombers of the Lincolns, 38 of whom fell, were said to have performed deeds of valour. The attack extended to the north but was repulsed by the 24th Division. A company of the 9th Sussex who held the extreme left had a mine exploded beneath them, burying forty. In the general mix up which ensued, the officer in charge, Lt. Macnair with a handful of men, held the enemy from the crater. The officer was awarded the Victoria Cross.

There is a report going the rounds that our Brigadier thrice offered the services of the Brigade to retake lost trenches, but the general commanding declined. It was very kind of the Brigadier, but we are not looking for suicide jobs quite yet. A few months later, we were in this spot and lost a couple of officers killed and about two dozen other casualties, when we were only holding the line. The writer and four others were almost snuffed out when a shell just missed landing on top of us. It managed to wound three slightly. This place certainly belies its name. It is no bluff—it is the real thing.

Wednesday, February 16, 1916

Obtaining a pass I made a trip to Bailleul passing through Berthen, Schaexken, and St. Jans Coppell. I noticed very pretty lace and silk goods in a store in the latter village. Talking to a young Frenchman I was told that the Germans, when they occupied Bailleul, spent most of their time drinking. In fact it has often been said that it is the wine vaults of France that saved Paris. One civilian, a Belgian, was killed by the enemy in Bailleul. He mentioned that a number of the womenfolk were outraged. His elder brother was killed at Souchez last September. He himself was due to be called up in October. Being deformed he expected to be exempted.

Friday, February 18, 1916

This morning, a little to the north of us, not far from Boescheppe, German planes dropped several bombs, killing three horses and injuring several men. They came over our line under cover of fog. One of our planes which went up after them, on returning came to ground suddenly, burying the nose of the machine.

The day the Princess Pats relieved us they had to vacate H1 trench and retire to the rear owing to the enemy sending over about fifty "sausages."

The Brigadier of the 7th Brigade, whilst going through our trenches to make himself familiar, thought he would peep over the parapet, with the result that he was shot through the shoulder.

Sunday, February 20, 1916

The German airmen are displaying great activity, dropping bombs in the rear of our lines. This afternoon there was an aerial battle in process. We heard the rattle of the machine-guns in the clouds. The Huns who usually fly very high seem to be playing with our men. Their planes travel faster and often, when they are pursued, make for the clouds evading our planes with apparent ease. This is the first time I have seen them so daring. Previously they returned to their own lines on approach of our airmen, but now they are on raiding expeditions every day. They dropped bombs in the square at Bailleul accounting for five people.

We had a tramp today to Mont Noir near the Belgian-Franco border via Berthen and Schaexken for the purpose of going through poison gas for practice. The smoke helmets are not very comfortable and require a little practice to inhale and exhale properly. Owing to leaky helmets a few of our fellows got slightly gassed.

Tuesday, February 22, 1916

There was a heavy bombardment in the vicinity of Armentières yesterday.

Wednesday, February 23, 1916

Throughout the day there was lively shelling on the Ypres front and an alarm of gas was sent to us necessitating us having our gas helmets in readiness.

It was very wintry today, snowing for several hours. In addition it was dark and foggy.

Thursday, February 24, 1916

The enemy dropped several bombs in the vicinity of Poperinghe.

Friday, February 25, 1916

Our rest has been cut short and we are ordered to the line once more. Saying goodbye to Boescheppe we head for the huts near La Clytte, passing over the border, Westoutre, and Hyde Park Corner, en route. It is some place "A" Coy. Q.M. has struck. We have no cooking utensils or brazier and we are existing on bread and marmalade. Once again I am in revolt and figure going back to the Company. The battalion stayed here overnight and next evening made for the trenches, H and Ks.

Saturday, February 26, 1916

Tonight we leave with rations for the firing line.[16] They were loaded on mules, a novelty to us. It appears the V.C. road, which leads from the Vierstraat Road to the trenches, is in bad condition, and owing to the noise made by limbers on the cobbles, it is risky going close up. Mules, therefore, are handier in this respect. They also help out the ration parties who will not have to travel as far. The road is open and elevated, an ideal spot for machine-gunners to play on. A few bullets passed us but they were high. As there was very little firing indulged in we could not say if the road would be a hot one. Passing along the La Clytte-Kemmel Road in the dusk, I observed on the right three graves, then further along another three, and on the left a single one. The latter was the grave of an artillery man, killed in November 1914, and the others were "Unknown British Heroes" killed about the same time.

---

[16] On its return to the front, the battalion takes over a section of trenches on the immediate left of those it had been defending prior to going into Corps and then Brigade Reserve.

Approaching a sentry of the Princess Pats, who was doing duty at the side of the road, I asked him how their battalion fared after taking over our old trenches. He replied that there were three killed by snipers.

It is difficult keeping note of what is occurring on the battalion front, so one has to be content recording the incidents of the company. Casualties occur in our other companies which we never hear about. Much that is interesting, therefore, escapes our notice. We are restricted to the narrow outlook of our small frontage and consequently are unable to give more than a garbled version of any conflict which embroils several units. In consequence these notes are only authoritative in what I myself or those with me have seen.

We relieved the 24th Battalion from Montreal, which had in its ranks a considerable quota of French Canadians. For physique they cannot compare with our lot. The cooks of one of their companies, who stayed with us overnight, thought we were on the big side for their trenches and prophesied that many of our men would be shot through the head. They figured their casualties for the five months were about 300. Of the division the 5th Brigade, I think, had up till this time more losses than either the 4th or 6th. In their last trip to the line the 24th Battalion lost three Macs, one after another.

When they were changing sentries on one of the listening posts a few nights ago, they captured a Hun on patrol. He was about 20, stood 6 ft. 2 ins. and was a finely built man. He was well dressed, and equipped with a knife, axe, revolver, and bombs, fully prepared for the warpath. According to his story he watched our sentries changing guards since the last three nights. When he was caught he was preparing to fling a bomb. He remarked that we should have waited a few minutes longer and we could have had a couple of his companions. They were more afraid than he was and were following in his wake, letting him do the scouting. He belonged to one of the Prussian Guard battalions. It appears the German trenches are in much better shape than ours. Judging by the clothes and equipment he was wearing, their dug-outs must be dry and roomy.

The distance we have to go with rations must be close to six miles, making the double journey almost a dozen miles.

La Clytte, which is a small place, between Locre and Dickebusch, is uninteresting. It possesses an old church with sun dials on two sides, and a crucifix on another. The attached graveyard is in a wretched condition. Near La Clytte is a little elevation, with a windmill on top, called Scherpenberg.

Sunday, February 27, 1916

There has been much aerial bombing activity on the part of the enemy. Bombs were dropped behind our billets at Locre, but did no damage.

Monday, February 28, 1916

Campbell, one of our new men, has been wounded in the arm.

Tuesday, February 29, 1916

One of the "D" Coy. has had his head blown off by the explosion of a shell. There have been two or three casualties in the other companies.

The 49th Battalion lost a man going into our old trenches today, whilst the 27th had Capt. M——s shot dead by a sniper.

There has been much shifting around lately which does not conduce to the vitality or comfort of the men. Our battalion tramped several miles to billets near La Clytte, stayed there overnight, and the following evening were on the hike for the line. The 24th took possession of their billets, leaving the subsequent day, when the 19th arrived. They disappeared almost as soon and the 27th arrived on the scene. Last night the 29th took their place. I presume when we arrive back in the early morning after delivering rations that some other battalion men will be sharing the billet with us.

It appears as if there is some mix up for a Staff Officer stopped near the Q'Master's store and asked a couple of fellows what battalion was here. On being told he explained that they were in the wrong area and would have to move.

The fellow in "D" Coy who was killed the other day was a new man and had only been a day in the trenches.

Wednesday, March 1, 1916

There was a fairly heavy bombardment this afternoon.

When going for the rum near Vierstratt a bullet ricochetted somewhere and whizzed past us. I hardly expected a bullet to come so far from the firing line.

Thursday, March 2, 1916

In the early hours of the morning there was a severe bombardment on our left by our own artillery. A report has reached us that the International Trench has been retaken and several hundred yards besides. This means that the recent German advance has been nullified. The Gordons and Lincolns are reported to have been the attacking parties and that 200 prisoners were taken. Another rumour, as persistent as the last, states a further batch of 500 have been captured. One of the 29th who was in Reninghelst when the prisoners passed through said they were a poor lot physically, being young, small, pale and puny. They were dressed in uniforms of various hues. The only good thing about them was their boots. They complained of being half starved and looked it. Our men were giving them cigarettes for buttons. For the sake of getting information, I understand rum was distributed freely to them. I have garnered additional and more authentic news. A couple of brigades of artillery were brought up and a withering fire was poured into the enemy in the early hours of the morning. Our infantry leaving their trenches in the dark, crept forward, and in the first streaks of dawn dashed into the enemy's lines. The 1st Gordon Highlanders, the regiment that made a plucky but disastrous charge on our old front last December, was the assaulting party on the left. They had the most difficult work of all to do and were hung up in their first rush. Nothing daunting they attacked again and again and with the assistance of the supporting battalion, the 7th Lincolns, carried their line forward. The battalion in the centre, the 8th Royal Lancasters, overran the German line and suffered severely in the process. The 2nd Suffolks on the right rushed the opposing trenches with great gusto. It was a sorry morning for Fritz and he lay down in defeat. Several counterattacks and bombardments came as an aftermath but our line remained inviolate. The 9th West Ridings on the northern flank nipped a flanking counterattack in the bud. Two companies of sappers, the 10th Welsh Fusiliers and 12th West Yorks, did yeoman service consolidating. The prisoners taken numbered 254 including 5 officers. Thus ended a small but severe engagement involving altogether several thousand casualties and the net result was a slight loss of territory to the aggressors.

Our battalion had eight casualties today, three of them severely wounded.

Saturday, March 4, 1916

We are back again to our former billets near (Corps Reserve) Boescheppe. The roads are very muddy and the weather is decidedly wintry, snow being on the ground. A few days later Major Dawson left the unit owing to severe illness, and did not rejoin.

Sunday, March 5, 1916

Whilst out on patrol opposite F trenches, one of the 42nd scouts was killed.

100

Tuesday, March 7, 1916

It is reported by the signallers that G3, a portion of trench formerly held by us and considered the safest part of our line, has been mined by the enemy and that the troops have been withdrawn from it. Considering that it is 250 yds. from the German front line, the news is a surprise to us. I have my doubts regarding the matter.

Wednesday, March 8, 1916

The latest news is that two spies were caught a few days ago at Locre. One was dressed in British uniform and was collared by the Military Police at Locre Hospital.

The other was found in the clock of Locre Church. The hands of the clock were observed to be moving rather mysteriously one day and on being investigated a German in priest's clothing was found secreted therein.

By this time these two will be in regions where espionage is unknown.

The 49th, who relieved the Princess Pats in our old trenches, has been kept pretty busy by shell fire from an armoured train. At Kemmel Quarters a couple of shells landed amidst them wounding eleven, one of which was my informant. The first shell exploded on the crest of the hill and each succeeding shell dropped about forty yards lower down till it reached their quarters. When firing started, it was noticed that the windmill close by was revolving. There were suspicions regarding it and the matter, I understand, was investigated. It is presumed it was signalling the range.

Part of the 60th Battalion, which spent a day in our last trenches for the sake of being broken in, had one man killed and two wounded. I passed a company at the side of the road. They were in good spirits and cried over to us that the war would soon be over, that the 60th had arrived. We hardly dared to ask them if they were down-hearted, for our response to their vociferous, "No" would undoubtedly be, "Well, you will soon be."

A portion of the 52nd Battalion, sponsored by a battalion of the 7th Brigade, likewise received their baptism of fire opposite Kemmel. They were more fortunate coming out the next day without loss.

Thursday, March 9, 1916

We left again for Locre, our old quarters, to relieve the 42nd. Last night the road between Locre and Dranoutre was shelled, the result being eleven casualties. According to a Belgian whose house is about forty yards from our tent, one civilian was killed whilst going to the aid of the soldiers. One of the killed, an engineer, was buried today. His remains were taken from Locre Hospital. There was a big gathering at the cemetery.

The Belgian who informed us of last night's occurrence invited us into his house for a cup of coffee. He told us that he was a refugee from Neuve Eglise, and that his brother and baby daughter were killed by a shell at La Clytte two months ago. This village was shelled yesterday.

Saturday, March 11, 1916

Another funeral today, this time an officer of the 27th Battalion. He was buried at Locre Cemetery.

Quite a number of troops passed our billets today—the Yorks, 9th Northumberland Fusiliers and 12th Manchesters. They were very small men, but sturdily built.

A young Belgian, a refugee from near Ypres, was lodged in the Westoutre guardroom. It appears one of our despatch riders collided with him at Locre and the latter claimed that he tried to take his papers from him. Knowing the Belgian I can hardly credit this. Belgian friends who he worked for gave me the story.

We were inoculated today in the breast. It appears that as Fritz cannot get a stab at us, our own doctors must.

A battalion of the Lancashire Fusiliers went through Locre today. The four battalions comprise the 17th Brigade.

Sunday, March 12, 1916

Quite a lot of machine-gun fire was heard tonight on our front whilst to the right there was a considerable bombardment.

Monday, March 13, 1916

Our men leave for our old front once again to relieve the 28th Battalion. They all got in and out without a casualty. Every night one of the ration party has to go to the firing line to hand over the rum to the Company Officer and get a receipt. I observed that G4 supports were blown to bits.

The sergeant of the scouts of the 28th Battalion was killed last night beside the German wire while out on patrol. The Germans took him in. He held the D.C.M. and was a most useful man. Whilst returning to quarters the motor ambulance passed with a 25th Battalion man. He was wounded by shrapnel.

There was a heavy bombardment all through the night away to the right, evidently south of Armentières.

Tuesday, March 14, 1916

A beautiful morning. The bombardment is being continued. In the evening the enemy dropped "coal boxes" a couple of hundred yards to the right of the Grenade School, evidently trying to damage the railway. The explosions were terrific.

Bennett of our platoon had to be sent to H.Qrs., his nerves giving out. Several weeks ago he was buried by a "sausage" and since then he has been unfit for the firing line.

We witnessed an aerial fight today. One of our planes tackled three of the enemy's. He was slightly higher than theirs when we heard the report of a machine-gun going. Immediately the nearest German machine let out a trail of smoke and made for his lines. We figured the petrol tank must have been struck. At the same time our own machine flew in the direction of La Clytte making for land. Later in the day we heard our machine-gunner was mortally wounded, dying a few minutes after reaching earth.

Wednesday, March 15, 1916

Our artillery got busy and strafed Fritz unmercifully, who replied with "sausages" over G3. Whiz-bangs and shrapnel, however, quickly quietened him. This day was ours without doubt.

When going up "Via Gellia" the enemy was sweeping overland with machine-gun fire in a semi-circle finishing between Ration and Parrain Farms. His fire appeared to come from the direction of the Ks. The bursts passed over our heads.

Thursday, March 16, 1916

Kemmel Huts were shelled tonight a few minutes before we passed with rations. Two of the 28th were wounded.

A couple of our men were wounded by one of our own grenades going off.

One of the ration party, whilst returning to billets, was wounded by machine-gun fire. The enemy played on Suicide Road whilst we were going down. If this continues, I see where things will be lively for us.

Headquarters was shelled tonight, the roof of the guard room being almost lifted off.

Another burial at Locre.

Friday, March 17, 1916

An officer of the 28th Battalion, who was killed by a bomb exploding at the Grenade School, was buried today. There has been a funeral from the hospital practically every day this week.

Kemmel is fast disappearing. The village pump is smashed. The Bandstand in the square is wrecked. Shell holes gape in the streets. The houses and stores are being levelled. Our engineers and artillery are helping in the destruction by removing the brick work from the buildings for their own use. The Engineers' dump is gone. Kemmel has become a dead and deserted village.

Saturday, March 18, 1916

A lovely morning.

I watched three of our planes chasing a German. Our leading plane opened fire at long range, but it had no effect. It was galling to see the German fly away with apparent ease and not in the direction of his own lines either. If we are to be a match for the enemy it is obvious we will require speedier machines.

I have just heard that the First Division on our right has been knocked about a little, one battalion losing sixty men.

Monday, March 20, 1916

We have been reinforced once more, "A" Coy. receiving 12 men from the 50th and 56th Battalions.

Tuesday, March 21, 1916

A considerable number are on fatigue near Dickebusch. Motor buses took them there and back. One of the "C" Company was wounded.

Wednesday, March 22, 1916

The Lahore (Indian) Battery, which was stationed throughout the winter behind us and which lately removed to the salient, had seven killed and eight wounded recently.

I was informed that the 28th came upon a German patrol of about a dozen and took them prisoners.

Our snipers have been having quite a bit of luck lately. According to orders they are bagging Huns daily.

We tried a ruse the last time we were in the trenches but nothing came of it. A dummy was rigged up and left in No Man's Land near the German wire. It was expected that as soon as darkness set in the Germans would go over and inspect it. Our men were there waiting but Heiny was too wary and kept away.

The enemy also tried a ruse. At night they threw up new lights, which when alighting on the ground, kept aglow for a long time. The idea was to get our men to look over the parapet when their machine-guns would play along it. Fortunately our men did not expose themselves and the rain of bullets on the sandbags did no harm.

Thursday, March 23, 1916

Quite a lot of rifle fire is indulged in tonight but artillery is very quiet.

Periodically pamphlets in German are thrown into the German trenches or left where they can be seen, exhorting the enemy to surrender in small numbers and that they will be well treated. Reasons are given, showing that they are fighting a losing battle. In many cases prisoners have given themselves up without the pretence of a struggle.

Friday, March 24, 1916

There are several inches of snow on the ground this morning. I heard, from one of our men, who has just arrived from hospital, that a French plane engaged a German one with disastrous effects to the latter. He happened to see the fight. The German airman dropped a couple of bombs on Hazebrouck, two on some other place, and four on St. Omer, when the French airman was sent after him. The German crashed to earth, both occupants being killed. Unfortunately the French observer was shot.

Saturday, March 25, 1916

We are back to the trenches once more. I asked a 28th man how did they get on during their last spell. In his company there was only one killed. He was struck by a shell in the communication trench. Several shells were sent into Kemmel Huts as we were leaving. One of the 27th was wounded. He belonged to an advance party.

We have some fun over fifty new troops, belonging to the 2nd Pioneers, who have joined us for the purpose of becoming acquainted with the line. It appears their rations were sent up to us without notice being given. Our cooks got possession and dished them out to our own fellows, thinking the quartermaster was a little more generous than usual. Next evening the officer of the Pioneers in blissful ignorance, enquired after feeding arrangements. He mentioned that his men had nothing to eat all day save what they had carried in with them the night before. The matter dawned upon us, we were dining at the expense of the Pioneers.

It was amusing to watch how cautious they were. Two were in the bay I was in, doing sentry, whilst our boys lay back watching them. It was dark. One mentioned that he was going to fire a shot at Fritz's line, which greatly excited the other. Twice or thrice, the first fumbled with his rifle, raised it towards his shoulder, and straightened himself on the firing step, but his heart failed him, and he would get down. They would then engage in whispered conversation and once again would engineer another trial. At last, cowering behind the parapet, with the rifle pointing at a ridiculous angle, a shot was fired, and at the sound of the report, they almost fell in a heap in the trench. The second fellow was so elated over their triumph that he ran to the next bay and informed his associates of the marvellous feat.

Going down Kemmel Hill, the connecting pole broke, precipitating the hind limber into the ditch and upsetting rations. It was nearly 2 a.m. before we got back to Locre.

Sunday, March 26, 1916

One of the Pioneers is shot through the head near the "Glory Hole," their first man to be killed.

We were informed that something was going to happen on the following morning. Mines were to be exploded on the right and left, gas was to be used followed by a bombardment and an attack. I am afraid, like many of these events, it did not come off. Anyway, we did not see or hear much more than usual.

When going down the communication trench, I came across a French Canadian, drafted from the 78th to the 24th. He lost his way, and being unable to speak proper English could only tell us he was sapping, where—he did not know and where he was going to, he was uncertain. We took him out. Further on he recognized his bearings and with delight pursued his way.

Headquarters was very nearly struck today by a shell. It passed a little to the south, exploding at the hedge across the road, sending the nosecap through a window into the chateau.

We have had another draft today.

Monday, March 27, 1916

As predicted, something did happen but it was further away than expected, and the reports that filtered through gave credit to the 4th and 5th Brigades, who had nothing to do whatsoever with the attacks. Dame Rumour, however, is always vague and cannot be depended upon. This attack developed into the Battle of St. Eloi with, for us, disastrous results. Meanwhile we were carrying on in our trenches unaware of the horrors we would be launched into in a week's time.

Today all along the line there was considerable strafing and much shrapnel was singing through the air. Fortunately no one was hurt, but one fellow had a narrow shave, shrapnel passing through his tunic. "B" Company had one killed and three wounded.

The other evening we noticed an observation balloon behind Wystchaete, being driven eastwards by the wind. At first we [were] under the impression that it was one of ours that had broken loose, but according to others it turned out to be an enemy balloon.

One of the 28th men shot an officer whilst a 27th man accounted for another Hun.

Tuesday, March 28, 1916

Some activity on the Locre road, the West Surreys and North Staffords going south, whilst the 3rd Canadian Brigade goes north. The 4th Cameron Highlanders, who were badly cut up at Festubert, and lost their colonel, Colonel Al Fraser of my home town, are doing duty as a labour battalion on our frontage.

One of the 24th scouts who was killed in No Man's Land the other night has been found and brought in.

Thursday, March 30, 1916

It is a lovely morning. There is considerable aerial activity. One of "B" Coy., the last time we were in the trenches, had a marvellous escape. A shell buried him. A few moments afterwards another came along and unburied him. Troops have been busy passing and re-passing. The 4th East Yorks who, I understand, relieve us arrived today.

Friday, March 31, 1916

One of "D" Company was wounded by a "sausage"; Fritz sending eighteen into the "Glory Hole."

We come out of the trenches today and tomorrow make for new quarters near Bailleul.

107

Saturday, April 1, 1916

Wearing steel helmets for the first time, we leave for new billets, Corps reserve, between St. Jans Cappell and Bailleul.

One of the girls in the Convent was buried this morning in Locre Cemetery. The nearest mourners, some of them little girls, were wearing black veils. The priest officiating was in white, whilst most of the mourners had pale blue ribbons around their necks. Little boys with sceptres and other Catholic emblems preceded the funeral, the whole party chanting the while.

The Sgt.-Maj.'s dug-out, where we used to spend an hour or two after taking up rations, was blown to atoms by a "sausage."

Sunday, April 2, 1916

We were surprised to receive orders about 5:30 a.m. to get ready to trek for new quarters near Dickebusch about eight miles away. The day was very hot and the march, especially up Mt. Noir, was a trying one. Several fellows fainted on the way. Our route lay by St. Jans Cappell, Mt. Noir, Westoutre, Reninghelst and Ouderdom. The billets were situated a few yards off the Ouderdom-Hallebast road at "A" camp, which was latterly changed to Micmac camp.

CHAPTER III

The Battle of St. Eloi

Monday, April 3, 1916

It is a lovely day, the sun shining in all its glory. The roads are crowded with troops, passing and repassing.

Yesterday there was a bombardment by us lasting almost all the day. There appears to be great activity on this front and from what I hear, it is a murder hole. Dead are said to be all over the place. The trenches can hardly be termed trenches, they are so much flattened and disfigured by shell fire. Dead horses lie along the roadside, killed whilst carrying up munitions and rations. Regiments from all quarters appear to be in this part of the line—Durhams, Yorks, Northumberlands, Suffolks, etc.

A few moments ago word was passed along that German prisoners were coming down the road. We immediately made a chase to the roadside. Presently they came into view, a few members of a Welsh regiment escorting them. There appeared to be one or two officers or non-commissioned officers, it was difficult to distinguish. They were of a good physique and intelligent looking, but the rank and file were nothing special. Big MacNair, who was beside me, was scrutinizing them closely and finally in disgust remarked, he would take on twenty of them himself. Anyway we felt that we need not be afraid of them in a rough and tumble bayonet scrap. On their shoulder straps were the number 211 or 216,[1] I could not make out exactly which. Their uniforms were a slaty blue colour, inclined through usage to a coffee colour. They sadly required a shave and were pretty worn out with

---

[1] This indicated the prisoners' regiment.

the exception of the leaders who showed a semblance of defiance. The others were meek and cringing.

I was very much disappointed to see some of our fellows giving them cigarettes, etc. A little reflection concerning their actions and one would be forced to concede that in being taken prisoner and kept as they will be, is more than they deserve. Within the course of a few days many of our fellows were laid low by the comrades of these self-same prisoners and it is perfectly nauseating to think that any of our men would show any camaraderie towards such despicable humanity. As they passed along I counted them; there were sixty-one. In the afternoon another batch of sixteen passed. This lot appeared a little more pleased to be captured. Anyway when one of our fellows shouted, "Fritz, you will get three square meals now," [he] smiled as if to say that will be so. There were several fairly young looking fellows, but on the whole their average age would be slightly higher than ours. It was quite a pleasure besides a novelty to see a German, for up till now very few saw more than a momentary glance of one.

The 150th Imperial Brigade took over our trenches at Kemmel coming from the Ypres Salient to do so. It was composed of the 4th East Yorks, 4th Yorks, 5th Yorks and the 5th Durhams. Their strength was very much reduced. It is always the case on the Ypres Front.

Our next episode deals with the tragic Battle of St. Eloi, which proved so fatal to our division. It practically covered the battle ground of nearly a year ago, when the Princess Pats made a desperate stand.

A little to the east of the obliterated village of St. Eloi is a small elevation about thirty feet high, called the Mound. Around here our front line turns and twists, forming one of those many small salients throughout the line. This rising was of great importance to the enemy for artillery observation, so our command considered there should be a change in ownership. The sappers were set to work and after several weeks of energy the work was completed; galleries were run underneath the German trenches and 30,000 pounds of ammonal[2] were laid. The 3rd Imperial Division of regulars that recaptured the Bluff a few weeks previously, were told off to perform the desperate deed.

The enterprise was known to be a precarious and risky one. The assaulting battalions chosen were the 1st Northumberland Fusiliers who were to sweep round on the right and the 4th Royal Fusiliers who were to take the left, a frontal attack being considered impossible; the remaining battalions of the 9th Brigade, the 1st Scots Fusiliers and

---

[2] A high explosive.

12th West Yorks, were to be close up in support in the centre. The five mines were exploded with telling effect, blowing the German garrisons into the air. At 4:15 in the darkness of a misty, rainy morning, the British troops sprang forward capturing 5 officers and 193 dazed and affrighted men belonging to the 18th Reserve Jaegers. The Northumberlands gallantly worked their way round to the rear of the craters formed, but the Royals could only manage part of their objective. The left centre was in the air and the line was ragged and irregular. The attack being on a small frontage, the enemy now finding how affairs stood, had every battery within range, concentrated on the captured positions and on the two battalions in support, creating heavy casualties and confusion. The same night the 9th Brigade was withdrawn and in the darkness, the 8th took over the new line.

The situation, however, was complicated. Contact to the rear of the craters was not properly established, and the Germans were in possession of the northernmost crater, No. 5. On the 30th, the 76th Brigade relieved the 8th. The veteran 1st Gordons, who have left an indelible mark on Belgium, were now in the line, holding on with grim vigour in drizzling weather. It was apparent a further effort was required—push forward, join up and consolidate the line, and wipe up the German detachments in the crater and vicinity. The 8th Royal Lancasters were detailed for the work and they responded gallantly, sweeping over the contested ground and gathering in 4 officers and 30 men. These were the prisoners we saw coming down the Hallebast-Ouderdom Road.

During these trying days the enemy was raining shells continually; the trenches were in a quagmire and unconnected; communications were entirely broken down; there was not such a thing as a firing trench; the enemy gave us no peace to consolidate; neither could materials be brought up; our men, battered and weary had all their work cut out to shelter themselves from the devastation that was happening around. Casualties were heavy and the men so completely worn out that reliefs were frequent and each change found the situation more obscure; the whereabouts of the enemy unknown, our own bearings in the air. Under this cloud of darkness and uncertainty on the night of April 3rd, our 2nd Canadian Division took over the line, a line completely new to us, not even its communications being familiar. The battalions to relieve the Imperials were the 27th Battalion from Winnipeg who took up the right, and our own, the 31st from Alberta, who took the left, whilst the 28th and 29th went into support. Our old front line trenches, covering the debatable ground, were known as the Is and stretched from I14 to I19, trench 19 to 28, 1500 yards.

111

On the afternoon of April 3rd it was announced that we were to relieve the Imperials at St. Eloi: the 27th were to take over the right flank of the line, and the 31st the left; whilst the 28th and 29th were to be in support, and the 4th and 5th Brigades in reserve.

As the light began to wane we moved out of camp and proceeded up the Ouderdom Road to Hallebast, where we met the Bailleul-Ypres Road. Turning to the left we passed through Dickebusch, a long straggling village, then on to Vijverhoek, and at Cafe Belge, which was in ruins, we turned to the right and proceeding up a slope and along a moor, headed for Vooremezeele. This was the starting point of our troubles, and being within machine-gun range, the entrance to the danger zone proper.

As the skeleton buildings of the village loomed up in the darkness, it seemed to bespeak war with its attendant horrors and death. A few weird figures flitted out of the gloom and took possession of us; they were the guides to lead us to our hell.

By this time the battalion had dispersed into Companies and was in the process of further disintegration into platoons. The safety that comes from numbers was vanishing and loneliness began to grip the individual as he realized that everything now depended on a clear eye and steady nerve. He forgot about the battalion and from now on his vision became limited to his platoon and its official commander. The lieutenant became the general; the sergeant the colonel. The higher command faded away to pleasant surroundings somewhere in the far, far rear. By this time no smoking was allowed, not a match to be struck, and silence fell like a pall over all. Lassitude arising from their late exertions had overtaken the gunners and as we filed along the Convent wall, the line was in comparative quietude.

A few hundred yards overland and then we stepped down into the communication trench and slowly moved forward. Soon shell holes appeared in our path; many direct hits had been made on the trench, and walking became difficult. British Tommies, in the throes of exhaustion, were slowly and laboriously bringing down their human freight of suffering. Still figures in stretchers commanded the passage and we had to make way. Anon a wounded man in agony writhed and moaned. At various intervals along the trench our dead lay waiting for an opportune time to be taken out for internment. Onwards we go through Shelley Lane, down into shell holes, clambering up on the other side, into the trenches again, down once more into a hollow, slipping, falling, we curse our way forward, whither we know not, and neither do we care. Striving to keep up we struggle desperately in the mire. At last, when nearly exhausted, we reach the front line. No. 3 platoon passes along a small trench about twenty yards long which

112

runs out from the left junction of the old British line with the new, into an old crater No. 6, under the impression they were in No. 5, which was recently formed. From here a short, shallow shell-wrecked trench leads to crater 7, which our bombers take over. The latter is about forty yards across and very shallow, affording little or no protection, and overlooked by the country ahead. Our crater is about the same size but deeper, and some semblance of digging is shown. In the centre is a slimy pool of rotten, stagnant water. This is the bed of thorns we stepped into about 12:30 in the morning of April 4th.

The English Tommies we relieved could furnish us with no information regarding the whereabouts of the enemy or our immediate connections. We could only look into an impenetrable darkness and conceive in our minds the general situation surrounding us. The whole place was wrapt in gloomy mystery; all sense of direction was lost; around was a chaos of shell holes and mud heaps.

When passing out one young Imperial showed visible signs of distress. "What's the matter?" said Andy Dearden, "Cheer up! Don't be downhearted!" "You'll be downhearted," whispered the Tommy, "when you see what's up there; I have lost my best chums." He was overcome by grief for his fallen comrades. Another stocky Englishman about middle age, feeling contented with himself, no doubt on account of being relieved, could not refrain from saying, "We gave them hell, boys." A number of the battalion had their faces blackened and their bayonets red, showing they were storming troops, and lately made an assault. It is presumed they were the 8th Royal Lancasters.

It was fortunate the night was quiet, though it lulled us into a sense of false security, for the silence was only an ominous hint of the impending storm. Sitting down, Buttress placed his hand on something clammy and jumped up with a start. Questioned what was the matter, he said, "You sit there." He had touched the face of a corpse.

When day broke, the sights that met our gaze were so horrible and ghastly that they beggar description. Heads, arms and legs were protruding from the mud at every yard and dear knows how many bodies the earth swallowed. Thirty corpses were at least showing in the crater and beneath its clayey waters other victims must be lying killed and drowned. A young, tall, slim English lieutenant lay stretched in death with a pleasant, peaceful look on his boyish face. Some mother's son gone to glory. He was wearing a gold signet ring, having an eagle with outstretched wings engraved thereon. It was removed by Munro, who thinking it of no value, handed it to Doull, who has it in his possession today. It was so narrow it could fit very few fingers. Another English second lieutenant was lying at the edge of the crater, huddled up, with his legs uppermost. One of the most

113

saddening cases was a stretcher bearer near half a dozen dead Tommies, a little to the right of the trench—leading to crater 7. He was sitting with a bandage between his hands in the very act of bandaging his leg, when his life gave out, and his head fell back, his mouth open, and his eyes gazing up to heaven, as if in piteous appeal. There he sat in a natural posture as if in life, the bandage in his hands, and the Red Cross bag by his side. Lovett was his name, and he belonged to the King's Liverpool. Another strange, appalling spectacle was a couple of Tommies sitting on the firing step; the head of one had fallen forward on his chest, and between his fingers he still held a cigarette. There he was as if asleep, yes, but in a sleep that knows no awakening. His comrade beside him was in a sitting position but inclining sideways. Both were unmarked and must have met their doom by concussion.

In the support line an Imperial with a Balaclava cap on was lying on a stretcher, dead. Eight bodies of British soldiers were collected in the crater for burial, when a shell came over and burst amongst them, plastering Webber and Doull with gangrened flesh. At daybreak one of the bombers was shocked to find himself standing between a dead German and English officer, whilst close by was a German private and English Tommy. What trench mats there were seemed to rest on bodies. One could not dig anywhere without coming across a human corpse. Huddled together amongst the dead our men passed their lonely vigil in the early hours of April 4th. "Amidst life is death" was indelibly printed on the minds of everyone present on that fateful morning.

When daylight set in, the first thought was to evacuate the wounded and clean up and consolidate the line. We had scarcely taken over the positions, when Burney of the bombers, who was busy digging in the craters, received a stray bullet in the head, killing him almost instantly. He was carried out to the junction of the old and new firing line.

Most of the men got busy digging out additional cover, or improving the passage way. Ritchie and Dearden dug up four sandbags of bombs which had been buried by shell fire. Sergeant Barrons who had collected in a sandbag, identification discs, paybooks, money, photos, all personal matter, from the dead in the crater, laid the sandbag on the side, when a shell came over and it vanished. Unless survivors of the respective battalions can supply the necessary information, these unfortunate victims will be listed amongst the missing. Jimmie Miller helped to throw three dead Germans over the parapet.

There was an ever flowing stream of wounded to be taken out, and this proved a serious burden on our men. Movement in daylight was well nigh impossible and great risks were undertaken when anyone attempted to make his way in or out. The communication trench was pulverized and mired beyond description so that, in attempting to traverse it, one was as often within view of the enemy as not. Frisk and Thiebot in packing out an Imperial were all in and begged succour from Dearden. Andy, ever ready to assist, carried him a considerable distance, till he got stuck in a shell hole in mud over the knees, and his strength eked out. Another had to come to his assistance, but he came unwillingly. Being a new man he had not yet become accustomed to ground hog life. This slimy shell hole, though innocent looking, was a veritable trap, and almost every fellow fell into it. It was a perfect graveyard of Ross rifles. Rescuing a rifle from this jackpot was not worth the candle. It was better taking a casualty's rifle than waste valuable time over it. In coming out Munro, who was in a desperate hurry in his rush down the trench, saw a trench mat in the middle of the hole. He made one leap, alighted on the mat, which turned over and down he went. He crawled out the other side like a drowned rat, and bolted down the trench to the supports minus his "Maggie Ross."[3] When called later to go up again with the rest he was purposely missing. He had had enough of St. Eloi. For a few days he was looked upon as a casualty, the officer and sergeant being unable to find any trace of him.

One of our sergeants, with a couple of men, set out to find ammunition. On the way, the latter were ordered to carry out a wounded Hun. They were exceedingly wrathful as our own wounded were still lying around. When they got out, no ammunition was to be found. Realizing the work they had undertaken, Teddy Miller upbraided everything in general. Fritzie was lucky in not being despatched. Two months later Miller died of wounds, killed by high explosive fire by a Hun.

A wounded Royal Scot, who was found beside a dead German, was also taken out. In simple language he told us that the German tried to knife him, but he got there first and Fritizie paid the penalty for his crime.

A Gordon Highlander and Scots Fusilier, lying wounded in a dugout, were also conveyed to the rear.

Almost everyone did stretcher work and quite a few got hit whilst thus employed. It is one of the most exhausting duties a soldier can undertake. In the mud, under shell fire, carrying a dead weight is almost heartbreaking especially to the man behind. It took hours to reach the dressing station at Vooremezeele, and the stretcher bearers

[3] Evidently a term used to describe the Ross rifle.

115

were so done up that they could scarcely drag themselves back to the lines again.

Lt. Robertson early showed good sense by sending half of 3 platoon to the supports for a rest, one half for part of the day, the other half for the other. During the night the whole platoon manned the crater. Lt. Arbuckle, formerly a ranker in my platoon, with six scouts went out to reconnoitre, one failing to return. He went a considerable distance over till he struck a trench, which did not contain a living soul. All along was a line of German dead.

About 6:00 o'clock in the evening of the 4th, as Lt. Robertson and Cpl. Still with a small party of six or seven were preparing to move up from the supports to the crater, Sgt. West came rushing down exclaiming that the enemy had occupied the crater. One of two Imperial machine-gun sergeants, belonging to the Shropshires, not much more than eighteen years of age, overhearing these remarks, at once turned to his companion and ejaculated, "Gor blimey, the Canadians have lost our trenches, let's go up and shift the Bosches." Promptly shouldering their half-clogged gun and all their ammunition, an odd drum or two, straightway made for the front. It was only by the expostulations of our men, who calmed them by saying the ground was not lost, that they retraced their steps. These earnest, gallant fellows, put in sixteen days without relief. One was said to have received the D.C.M. but was killed afterwards.

Captain MacPherson who had also heard the rumour regarding the craters being lost, rushed up to Dearden's post and asked him where No. 1 and No. 3 platoons were. He repeated his query twice being under the impression that they had been forced back. Dearden, who was hopelessly trying to clean his rifle with his handkerchief, and at the moment speculating that his only chance lay in bombs and the bayonet, reassured the captain that the platoons were still in the same positions.

One of the things that impressed us very badly was several of the 27th in rubber boots, beating it through our lines, completely demoralized.

At the break of day, Gen. Turner, the commander of the 2nd Division, came down the line from the 27th direction and stopped to question Sgt. Boyd regarding the units on his flanks. He also enquired if the boys had their rations and rum. He was up looking over the line with a view to consolidating the position. Whatever plans he had formulated were never properly executed for Fritz shortly afterwards started shelling; the fire intensifying later and developing as the time went on, so that no opportunity was given for trench work. At 9:30 a.m. prompt the hostile artillery began to speak and by noon it was raging in all its fury. Shrapnel came pouring over the lines in a ceaseless whine, interrupted only by the crumps of 4.3s and 5.9s [shells]. From every direction this fire storm was turned upon us. Every gun within range seemed to have cut loose and the very gates of hell let open. Overhead bursts, then deadly sprays of shrapnel, were showered into our midst. Heavy shells rocked the earthworks and buried their occupants. The artillery concentration was tremendous and the range was painfully accurate. Imperials, who had been at Loos and previous battles, never experienced such a concentrated fire on so small a frontage. There seemed to be a nest of batteries on the northern flank. Men were digging in feverishly to escape this blast of iron, but of no avail. The bombers were the first to suffer and before long half of them were casualties. Crater 7 quickly became untenable and the survivors stole along to crater 6 for protection, but it was only going from the frying pan to the fire.

Sgt. Wilson of the bombers, one of our Company, was struck down early in the day. He lay there till darkness set in before he could be got at and removed. His injuries were fearful yet no one could succour him, his arm being almost blown off and bodily wounds besides. He was ultimately removed but succumbed later. The Cpl. of the bombers, George, who had found a German rifle and had taken it to the supports for safe-keeping intending to take it out as a souvenir, was returning to his post when a shell burst almost upon him, mortally wounding him and injuring an officer, who fled out to the dressing station. George, when dying, requested the boys to tell his parents "that he had died like a soldier." He left a widow and a child he had never seen. The second sergeant, with three or four bombers, was sent up to reinforce his badly stricken comrades, bursting into the crater in the face of heavy fire. But they could not stick it, they soon began to fall. Before being relieved the enemy had taken its toll. Tom Smith going to the assistance of a wounded man was sniped at, receiving an explosive bullet in the arm and shattering it completely, returning to Calgary several months later, an amputation case. Blackie Sayce had his arm almost torn off and is disabled for life. Hannan was also wounded and both bombing officers were casualties. L/Cpl. Dalziel, 6 ft. 2 ins. of humanity, finally came out of the shambles, leading the remaining bombers with an enhanced reputation. For his gallant work he was awarded the D.C.M., but never knew of the honour, for the day it appeared in orders, he was killed in the Canadian Battle of Ypres. Meanwhile the company was gradually being wiped out as shell after shell burst burying and unburying dead and living. The fire was so murderous that it was impossible to live under it. It was a miracle that anyone emerged alive. Sgt.

Crossland was instantly killed by a shell exploding beside the parapet half burying him and breaking his back. When last seen he was lying in two beside the communication trench. It was a sad blow to the company for he was one of the best and cheeriest of fellows. Rowley, who was literally blown to bits, had only been married a few months. Steeles, a new man, was also slain. Sandy Moncrieff, who had been remarking how sorry he was over Crossland's death, was following in the wake of McNair and little Dan MacLeod, when a shell burst beside him, sending him fifteen to twenty yards away and nearly knocking MacLeod out as it shot him through the air. At first they did not know where he went, but hearing groans they found him. He died three hours later, blood pouring from his ears. The concussion practically shattered his whole system. Both he and Wilson hailed from the same quarter, a shire that has produced the leading lights of the Army, Navy and Air Service—Sir Douglas Haig, Rear Admiral Sir Rosslyn Wemyss and Lord Weir. Currie, who was severely wounded and ultimately succumbed, lay unattended too for a long time. He came of a fighting stock, having one brother killed, and two prisoners of war in Germany.

Teddy O'Brien was sitting in a corner in the support trench, cleaning his rifle when a 5.9 [shell] struck the parados burying him. He was dazed when dug out, but still retained [a] grasp on his rifle, which had the barrel twisted and butt smashed to smithereens.

L/Cpl. Kerr, who received a shrapnel wound in the neck, thought his end had come. Jimmie Miller took a hold of him by the shoulders and asked Dearden to hold his chest up, whilst Kerr remarked, "Carry on, I am finished, take care of yourselves." The stretcher bearer tried to render first aid but he would not wait, but struggled out. After a long spell in Blighty he returned to the line only to be wounded once more, returning to Canada with the Military Medal ribbon adorning his breast.

Cpl. Johnson passed out badly wounded. L/Cpl. Lilywhite received shrapnel in the face and lost sight of an eye. Ritchie, one of our snipers, was wounded in the arm, returning to the Company from Blighty during the Battle of the Somme when he was killed. Williamson, who was also struck, like Ritchie, returned to be killed at the Somme. Musgrave had his foot badly injured, his heel being almost blown off. With the aid of silver supports, he made a splendid recovery. Like many of our finest soldiers, he could not stand the red tape and humiliation at the base, and managed, though palpably unfit, to get drafted to France. At Lens he received his quietus: he was a volunteer of the finest calibre.

Dan MacPhee, another wounded man, in due time returned to the line, only to be once again on the casualty list, wounded and gassed, and returned a war wreck to Canada. Sgt. Clements was missing for a while, but was ultimately found half-buried in a dug-out. One of our officers was accidentally wounded by a bomb, whilst the nerves of another played out and he was sent elsewhere for a rest. Our stretcher bearers behaved magnificently and praise was lavished on them from all quarters. Young Avery worked valiantly going from wounded to wounded, ignoring shell fire, attending to the injured for 48 hours without rest. Both he and his partner, Northard, were wounded. A few months later he was awarded the M.M. for his gallantry and self sacrifice.

Our cooks were not even immune from danger, both Barringham and Hall being on the casualty list. Three of our fellows almost lost their reason owing to the terrific fire and murder. They were all a-quiver and became as little children. St. Eloi put the finishing touch to their military career and in due time they retired to quieter surroundings. During the height of the shambles one of our scouts started crying but later controlled himself. Several men were reported missing but most of them turned up later.

Cpl. Hunter, one of our finest men, was twice buried. L/Cpl. Wood had four rifles, three having been buried or smashed.

Notwithstanding that stretchers, ammunition, every requisite disappeared under an avalanche of shells, our men never flinched, but hung to the crater for 48 hours, despite the fact that they were melting away, and the position intolerable and untenable. These were the times that tried men's souls.

Other casualties in our Company were Allen, Falk, White, Orr, A. Smith, Copeland, Cutmore, Desmond, Biggin, Bell, Dunlop, Jones, Stewart, etc., the majority being slightly wounded.

Several men were reported missing but they practically all turned up later on.

No. 4 platoon relieved us on the night of the 5th, stuck to their guns, then turned the crater over to "D" Company on the night of the 6th. No. 1 platoon's position was on our left and adjoining them was "C" Company, "B" and "D" Companies being in support at Spoilbank and Voormezeele.

Coming out of the crater the survivors of No. 3 retired to White Horse Cellar and its environs, odd stretches of battered trenches connected by shell holes. They took up their positions in the most habitable portions in small groups of twos and threes. White Horse Cellar, a cellar in a building in St. Eloi, was about the only indication that the village ever existed. This identical ground has been contested from 1914 till 1918 and is reckoned one of the hot spots of the war. The village is just in the rear of our firing line and in consequence vanished under the influence of artillery fire into thin air early in the war.

Our men, feeling fairly good on the next morning after the resuscitating effects of rum and a breakfast of cooked meat sent up from the transport lines the night before, were astonished as they foregathered, to see a hostile observation balloon high up above the lines. We were seen, for in half an hour afterwards the enemy started shelling. As luck would have it, the shells either fell short or went over. Fortunately when the range was found and he levelled the positions to the ground, we had departed, having been relieved.

After the harassing and nerve wracking experience in the crater we were all highly strung, and woe to the man who took liberties of even permitting a glimpse of himself to the enemy. The slightest exposure would be the occasion of a violent outburst by his comrades and for minutes afterwards there would be angry mutterings about "giving the position away." We saw several Huns, most inviting targets they were, but orders had been given that we were not to shoot, in case positions might be spotted.

When "D" Company took over the forward positions we retired to the supports at Spoilbank, spending a long uncomfortable time trying to find them. No. 3 [platoon] was isolated during the day at an old farm house. Crouching in front in an old musty trench in mud and water, packed like herrings, was our unhappy experience for twenty-four hours.

During No. 3's occupation of the crater, the enemy bombarded our new positions with fire of various degrees of intensity, paying especial attention to the stretch from Bathurst Butts to beyone Campbelltown Corner. There was practically no cover when we took over this portion owing to the severe shelling it had undergone. The line was held by very few men, a few groups of gunners and bombers and roving sentries, and it scarcely afforded shelter even for these few. This gap, so sparsely and insecurely held by the left and right flanks of the 27th and 31st Battalions respectively, faded away under the devastating fire of the enemy. The men were either buried by the deluge of shells or blown out by the explosions, and the remnants recoiled to the flanks to escape complete annihilation. The ground was churned beyond recognition and no living thing could stay upon it. About 3:00 a.m. on the 6th, before the 27th were properly relieved, the enemy sent over a hurricane bombardment which destroyed almost every vestige of the line from Sackville Centre to the extreme left and within it perished the remaining sentries, for when the enemy advanced in parties down the Wytschaete Road scarcely a rifle shot was to be heard. About 250 penetrated to craters 2 and 3 and by night they were in possession of craters 4 and 5. The latter were those the 31st were to occupy when all the time they were hanging on to two old craters 6 and 7. The existence of the larger craters they were unaware of. It was owing to this confusion that the enemy were able to get the footing they did. It was only on the 16th, when the sky cleared, that our airmen were able to detect the disastrous error. During this time the Germans in craters 4 and 5 were left in absolute peace by our artillery and consequently were able to concentrate their efforts on further aggression.

About 4:30 a.m., on April 6, after the attack on the 27th, a large body of the enemy, about 150, were seen advancing towards our line in the direction of crater 6. Rifle fire was brought to bear on them and many were killed and wounded, whilst the remainder fled or took refuge in shell holes. Towards evening a batch of about twenty or so advanced in single file, each man with his hands on his neighbour's shoulders. Fire was opened up on them and only a few regained their lines. There is some division of opinion as to whether they intended to attack or surrender. Some aver they were bombers for they noticed bomber aprons on them. At dawn the next morning a small party, presumably the survivors, came over opposite "D" Company. Firing at them, 7 were killed, 1 wounded and four, including the wounded man, were taken prisoners. They intended surrendering for it was found they had no arms. They declared our artillery fire was terrific and they had at least two thousand casualties. One remarked that 7 of the 27th were taken captive, having mistaken their way.

Counter-attacks were organized by the bombers of each battalion in the Brigade and they were futile, the bombers being either cut to pieces, lost their way, or through sheer exhaustion were unable to push forward through the mud. A number of those on the left managed to force their way to craters 6 and 7 and found the 31st in possession, so retired as there appeared to be confusion as to what further was to be done. They only repeated the former mistake by occupying the wrong craters. A call came from Major Daly to "A" Company for bombers and Cpl. Hunter, with a small party consisting of Doull, Thomas, Rogers, Plummer, etc. of 3 platoon, proceeded to the fray. The Cpl. on the way showed those who were uncertain about the handling of the Mills bomb,[4] how the deed was done. It was quite a picture—these few moments' exhibition of how to grasp the bomb

---

[4] The Mills bomb, or No. 5 pattern grenade, was issued during the war. About the size of an orange, and filled with explosive, it had a fuse which burned several seconds after the grenade left the thrower's hand. Its metal casing then burst to give a shrapnel-like effect. A modified version, known as the No. 36 grenade, was widely used in the Second World War.

above the lever; pull the pin; then the throw. Some of them reached the crater where "D" Company was, but, on account of some reason or other, they were not required, so retired picking their way across the open in the face of much danger.

On the night of the 8th, the 19th Battalion of the 4th Bde. relieved our sorely tried battalion. Our company trudged its way out to rest billets by the Lille-Ypres road, very weary and sad at heart for the loss of so many gallant fellows.

The battalion casualties were about 180, out of this "A" Coy. had 5 killed, 45 wounded, 2 suffering from shock and 1 missing. "D" Company, who occupied the crater last, was struck the hardest. The 27th, who bore the brunt of the fighting, had a casualty roll of 217, whilst the 29th had 117, and the 28th, 101.

A 28th man went out of his mind and had to be held down by his comrades. One of our men noticed three of the 28th standing together: A shell came over and when he looked again they were no more. Sgt. Proven, a younger brother of one of our Coy. sergeants, died of wounds, so did a co-worker in civilian life of the writer's, Lt. A. B. Irvine of the 27th.

Let us now review what is happening in the rear. About 7:00 p.m. on the night of the 5th we set out with rations for the Company and arrived back at midnight. In due time we reach Vooremezeele and unload rations at the western end under the shelter of the wrecked corner building, beside the cemetery. We were only there a few minutes when a machine-gun opened up and began knocking sparks off the building beside us. The bullets were reaching earth not far away. After waiting for an hour without any signs of the carrier party appearing and being unable to obtain any information from stragglers, we were glad when our transport hove in sight and ordered us to load up and make for another dump on the Ypres-Lille Road. Whilst we were waiting, one of our men arrived from the line, evidently dazed for he was acting very peculiar. He had no idea of going back again. I tried to keep him in sight to see what he was up to, but he disappeared in amongst the wreckage of a building, and when I hunted for him, he was nowhere to be seen.

Quickly loading we turn back to Lankhof Farm, turn to the right, cross the Ypres-Comines Canal, and a few yards beyond the railway strike the Lille Road, which we follow for about a mile and a half, to where the dump is situated. From Dickebusch onwards, practically every building had been shelled. It was uncanny the way each building had been located and razed to the ground. Solitary farm houses nestling amongst trees or hidden in hollows, one would have expected to see intact, but no—the hostile artillery had searched them out and left nothing but crumbling walls. After leaving Lankhof Farm we scarcely met a soul, till we struck the Lille Road, three quarters of a mile south of Ypres. The Ypres-Comines Canal was narrow and overgrown with weeds and resembled a huge furrow, devoid of water, except what had collected at the bottom. Our route seemed puzzling to us. We appeared to be surrounded by the enemy. Behind us on our right, star shells thrown up by the Hun seemed but a few hundred yards away. It was the same in front, whilst behind on the left the flarelights were so near as to be positively startling. We were in the Ypres salient. During the day it appeared wide enough, but at night the flarelights showed up so vividly and so close that one truthfully imagined the flanks were separated by only a few hundred yards. A burst of light in the darkness apparently plays riot with one's ideas of distance. The shattered trees, upturned wagons, and dead horses at the side of the road made us sit up and take notice.

CHAPTER IV

Routine Life in the Trenches

Monday, April 10, 1916

There are several German observation balloons up today. A number of Scottish yeomanry, the Border and Lothian Horse, are busy in our vicinity, constructing a railway line for an armoured train. Beside the road a dummy house is being erected to house the gun. The rails run right in, so the gun can be pulled out when necessary. The camouflage is so good that one would actually pass the house without noticing anything peculiar. The gable facing the line has the top part removed when firing commences. The track is covered over here and there with divots,[1] etc., so that airmen will have difficulty in tracing its outline. The gun is a 12-inch and fires a shell weighing 750 lbs. and has an effective range of six miles.[2] I see where we will not have much peace when it commences firing. If observed, ten to one our camp will come for a dickens of a shelling.

Last night there was an exceedingly heavy bombardment.

One of our fellows, Evans, who had newly returned from hospital, told us that there was a Russian in the hospital with him. He was taken prisoner on the Eastern front and was shipped to the Western front to do fatigues. Then another Russian went over the parapet to our lines. His friend was killed in No Man's Land and he himself spent two days there.

Today a German plane was shot down a little to the south of St. Eloi by one of our anti-aircraft guns. It crashed to earth and was a total wreck.

[1] Pieces of turf or sod.

[2] This must have been a howitzer, since the ordinary 12-inch gun had a range four times that mentioned by Fraser. (See Fraser's entry for 29 June 1916.)

At night I sauntered along the road to Ouderdom and from there to Reninghelst. Both places are small and uninteresting. On the Vlamertinghe Road near Ouderdom, beside the garden of a house were four graves of British soldiers, one belonged to the Scots Fusiliers and another to the Duke of Wellington's. In Reninghelst Church yard were buried upwards of a hundred French soldiers besides a considerable number of British.

Tuesday, April 11, 1916

The 18th Battalion transports were unfortunate the other night on the road to Voormezeele, two of their number being killed and one wounded.

A heavy bombardment on our left tonight. As I write it is quietening down. We had to "stand-to."

One of our guns, a short distance away was put out of action, the enemy registering a direct hit.

Wednesday, April 12, 1916

Currie of No. 1 platoon has died of wounds. He lay unattended to for a long time. He had a brother killed and another two prisoners of war in Germany. They belonged to Imperial troops. Unfortunately, he leaves a widow and several children.

Late at night one of the ration party of the 18th Battalion came into our quarters in great excitement and covered with blood. He met a civilian carrying a soldier's pack and questioned him, asking who he was. Three nights in succession he came across this fellow. The fellow replied saying he stayed down the way, which was not far from our billets, and that he had his passport in the house. After giving four loud taps the door was opened and immediately three men set upon him beating him unmercifully. The Military Police were apprised of the affair but I have heard nothing further regarding the matter.

Unfortunately the civil population is allowed too much rope and it is common knowledge that there are a number of Germans or German sympathizers amongst them. Anyway the British or Canadian soldiers do not receive the attention one would expect from the civilians, who seem to look upon them as a means for making money, too often charging exorbitant prices.

It is not every Belgian householder or farmer who will permit the soldiers the use of their pump. As often as not the plunger is taken out and the soldiers have to seek elsewhere for water. The men folk, on the whole, are very reticent and somewhat sinister, and in most cases you wonder if he is friend or foe. The women folk are more open and in many cases sympathetic towards us, but on the whole are not as glad at our coming, or our struggles on their behalf as one would suppose.

Since the German entry into France or rather since the evacuation of Antwerp, the Belgian soldier has done practically no fighting. He has merely lain low between Dimude and the Coast and owing to this is looked upon by our troops as a nonentity, relying on the laurels gained by him in the first several weeks of the war. He is going to come out of the war with a small proportionate death rate, compared with other troops. Still their army will hold the public imagination for all time on account of holding up the German hosts in the dark days.

Thursday, April 13, 1916

One of the transport horses died today, It is thought to be the result of our last trip to the line with rations. The other one of the pair received a piece of whiz-bang in the knee, but is about all right again.

The battalion was out on fatigue tonight, arriving back about 2:00 a.m. It appears the fatigue was a farce. All the work could have been done by a sixth of the number.

A 49th man visiting us said that seven of their battalion were captured at Hooge. Their total casualties were 60. The spell before that cost them 50.

Friday, April 14, 1916

Four of our fellows were wounded when out on fatigue tonight.

Monday, April 17, 1916

Our battalion was out on fatigue last night, digging a communication trench at the back of T16,[3] near Shelley Lane. Unfortunately, the enemy got wind of us and opened up with shells and machine-gun fire. Being in the open a few of our number got caught. Miller, a Scot from Wick, had his arm almost blown off, his legs broken, and other injuries, and died on the way out. He was buried at Voormezeele, to the south of the road. The two of us were together, immediately before he left for the line. Grimes and Sharp were also wounded, whilst Webber is missing. It is presumed he was blown to bits or has been buried by a shell.

There has been quite a stir over our last spell in the trenches. I understand we had everyone standing to between here and St. Omer

---

[3] T16—The name of a trench.

126

and that General Haig, also Generals Alderson and Turner,[4] were phoning what was the matter.

"B" Coy., which left a few days ago for reserve duty at Dickebusch, had a casualty yesterday. One of their draft and two Belgians were killed by a shell.

It is reported that one of our guns in the neighbourhood was put out of action and that a spy residing in the vicinity of a battery was taken prisoner. It is time the civil population was scrutinized more closely. It would be an advantage if they were shipped at least half a dozen miles from the firing line.

A brother of Rowley, who was killed at St. Eloi, was here making enquiries. He was quite a youngster and belonged to an English battalion. He appeared down in the mouth over his errand.

Poor Miller, amongst his personal effects was his pocket book, with on one side an identification card, stating his next of kin, and on the other side a photo of his girl in the north of Scotland. His experiences in the Battle of St. Eloi impressed him deeply.

A search party had been organized to look for Webber.

Tuesday, April 18, 1916

Webber has been found. He was half buried by a shell, and lay in the shell hole. He was in pieces, even his badges and knife being bent or broken. His tunic was in threads. Being torn to ribbons, he had to be left where he was. His personal effects and identification disc were removed. An Englishman, a minister's son, he was farming near Langdon, Alta.

Wednesday, April 19, 1916

Our battalion left for supports last night, relieving the 25th who had lost 80 men, the 24th losing 120. "A" Company took up their position in Old Frenchmen's trench, mere water holes. Being only 24 hours here they should survive the ordeal, though they won't have a very pleasant time of it. We arrived at Voormezeele without incident but had a long cold wait before the carriers put in an appearance. Where our Company was located no fires could be lit, not even at night, so bacon, tea, sugar, etc. was no use to them. We arrived back at 1:15 a.m.

We went up with rations tonight. Receiving orders that our Company would be relieving "D" Coy. at Dickebusch we were up there shortly after dinner. After a long wait, orders reached us that we

---

[4] Haig, Alderson and Turner, that is, the army, corps and division commanders.

127

had to go to Voormezeele. At 7:00 p.m. there was nothing else for us to do but to load up again and get on the trek. At Vijverhoek a bombardment commenced. Immediately transports became choc-a-bloc and in the melee orders went out to return to our lines pending further instructions. We had quite a time getting back. Motor buses with troops were being rushed up, and they kept us busy jumping back and forward in the mud. We are back again at our quarters wondering when we will have to move. The battalion is without rations and we have a long journey ahead of us. Whilst in Dickebusch I paid a visit to the soldier's cemetery. About 450 British troops are buried here, some of the earliest being the Princess Pats. A namesake, a Captain N. Fraser, 2nd Cameron Highlanders, D.S.O., is interred here.

Dickebusch Church spire has been knocked off, showing two church bells. The church itself has also suffered.

The ambulances appeared very busy.

At 11:30 p.m. we are ordered to move off again and arrived at Voormezeele without incident. Several new shell holes appeared in the road and a few wrecked limbers strewed the way. As usual there is the same excitement in unloading; a few of the transport party being inclined to be panic-stricken can hardly wait for the rations to be taken off in fear that a shell may come over.

There is always a number ready to work themselves into a state of excitement when there is nothing to warrant it. We settle down for a long wait till the carriers appear. At last they come and are in a hurry to get back before daylight sets in. Our company has had a rough time of it and are pretty well all in. No sleep and no resting place. They are huddled in a broken down communication trench and it has been raining more or less constantly since the last week. About 4:00 a.m. we depart, arriving back at 5:30 when we immediately repair to our beds.

Thursday, April 20, 1916

Up once more with rations, this time to Scottish Wood, a wood which is named after the London Scottish, who, as I mentioned in the earlier part of this narrative, were rushed from the St. Eloi communications to stem the German rush at Messines in 1914. The quarters here are dug-outs and covered huts. Our company came down in the early morning to Dickebusch and at night had to go on fatigue to the firing line to erect wire entanglements.

There has been considerable murder work near the crater once

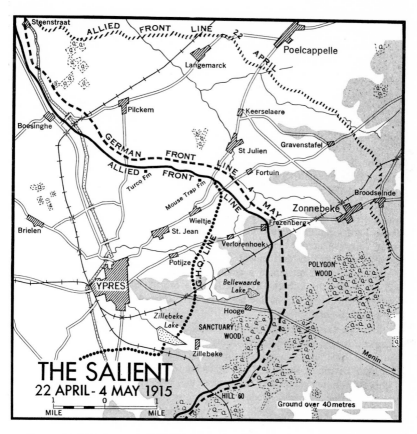

Steenstraat
ALLIED FRONT LINE
Poelcappelle
Langemarck
Pilckem
Keerselaere
Boesinghe
GERMAN FRONT
St Julien
Gravenstafel
ALLIED FRONT
Turco Fm
Fortuin
LINE
Mouse Trap Fm
Broodseinde
LINE
Zonnebeke
Wieltje
Frezenberg
Brielen
St. Jean
Verlorenhoek
Potijze
POLYGON WOOD
YPRES
Bellewaarde Lake
Hooge
Zillebeke Lake
SANCTUARY WOOD
Zillebeke
Menin

THE SALIENT
22 APRIL- 4 MAY 1915

1   0   1
MILE   MILE

HILL 60

Ground over 40 metres

Maps reprinted with the permission of the Directorate of History, Department of National Defence

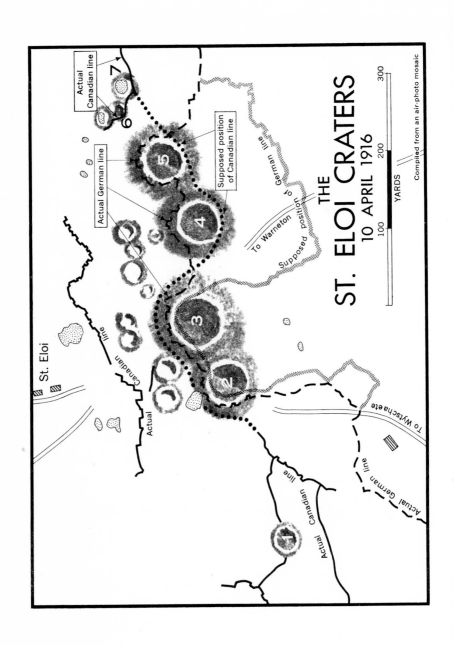

THE
ST. ELOI CRATERS
10 APRIL 1916

Actual Canadian line

Supposed position of Canadian line

Actual German line

To Warneton

Supposed position of German line

St. Eloi

Actual Canadian line

To Wytschaete

Actual German line

Actual Canadian line

YARDS

100   200   300

Compiled from an air-photo mosaic

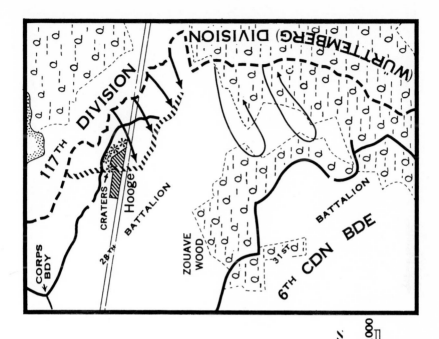

THE
ATTACK
ON
HOOGE

6 JUNE 1916

German front line after attack ---///////////

100   500   1000
YARDS

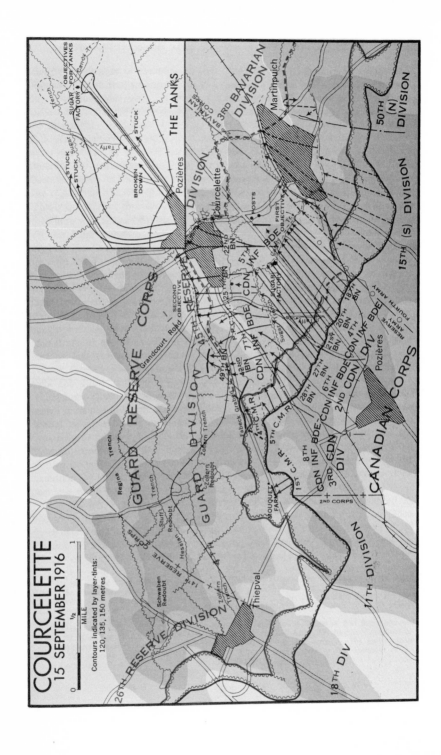

COURCELETTE
15 SEPTEMBER 1916

Contours indicated by layer-tints: 120, 135, 150 metres

0   ½   1
MILE

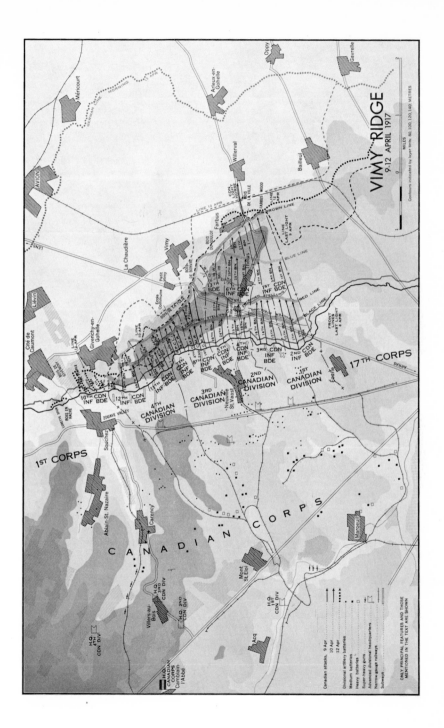

VIMY RIDGE
9-12 APRIL 1917

MILES
0   2

Contours indicated by layer tints: 80, 100, 120, 140 METRES

Mericourt

Avion

Lévin

Cité de Caumont

Givenchy-en-Gohelle

10TH CDN INF BDE

12TH CDN INF BDE

11TH CDN INF BDE

4TH CANADIAN DIVISION

Souchez

Zouave Valley

1ST CORPS

Ablain-St. Nazaire

Carency

CANADIAN CORPS

Villers au Bois

H.Q. 3RD CDN DIV

H.Q. 2ND CDN DIV

H.Q. 4TH CDN DIV

H.Q. CANADIAN CORPS Camblain l'Abbé

Mont St. Eloi

H.Q. 1ST CDN DIV

Acq

Marceuil

Arleux-en-Gohelle

Willerval

La Chaudière

Vimy

Farbus

BROWN LINE

BLUE LINE

RED LINE

BLACK LINE

3RD CANADIAN DIVISION

9TH CDN INF BDE

8TH CDN INF BDE

7TH CDN INF BDE

6TH CDN INF BDE

5TH CDN INF BDE

4TH CDN INF BDE

3RD CDN INF BDE

2ND CANADIAN DIVISION

2ND CDN INF BDE

1ST CANADIAN DIVISION

1ST CDN INF BDE

FRONT LINES LAST LIGHT 8 APR

17TH CORPS

Oppy

Gavrelle

Bailleul

ARRAS

Canadian attacks, 9 Apr
                        10 Apr
                        12 Apr
Divisional artillery batteries
Medium batteries
Heavy batteries
Super-heavy guns
Advanced divisional headquarters
Narrow-gauge railways
Subways

ONLY PRINCIPAL FEATURES AND THOSE
MENTIONED IN THE TEXT ARE SHOWN

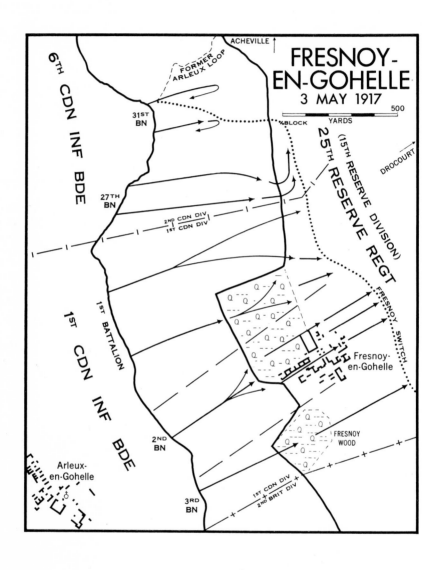

ACHEVILLE ↑

FRESNOY-
EN-GOHELLE
3 MAY 1917

500

BLOCK   YARDS

6TH CDN INF BDE

FORMER ARLEUX LOOP

31ST BN

27TH BN

2ND CDN DIV
1ST CDN DIV

1ST BATTALION

1ST CDN INF BDE

Arleux-en-Gohelle

2ND BN

3RD BN

(15TH RESERVE DIVISION)
25TH RESERVE REGT

DROCOURT →

FRESNOY SWITCH

Fresnoy-en-Gohelle

FRESNOY WOOD

1ST CDN DIV
2ND BRIT DIV

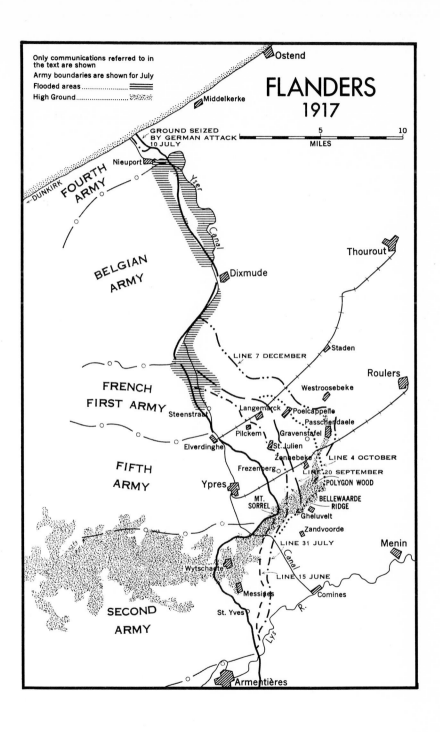

Only communications referred to in
the text are shown
Army boundaries are shown for July
Flooded areas.........................≡≡≡
High Ground...........................

Ostend

FLANDERS
1917

GROUND SEIZED
BY GERMAN ATTACK
10 JULY

5   10

MILES

Middelkerke

DUNKIRK

FOURTH ARMY

Nieuport

Yser

Canal

Thourout

BELGIAN ARMY

Dixmude

LINE 7 DECEMBER

Staden

Roulers

FRENCH FIRST ARMY

Westroosebeke

Steenstraat

Langemarck

Poelcappelle

Passchendaele

Pilckem

Gravenstafel

Elverdinghe

St. Julien

Zonnebeke

LINE 4 OCTOBER

FIFTH ARMY

Frezenberg

LINE 20 SEPTEMBER

POLYGON WOOD

Ypres

BELLEWAARDE RIDGE

MT. SORREL

Gheluvelt

Zandvoorde

LINE 31 JULY

Menin

Canal

Wytschaete

LINE 15 JUNE

SECOND ARMY

Messines

Comines

St. Yves

R.

Lys

Armentières

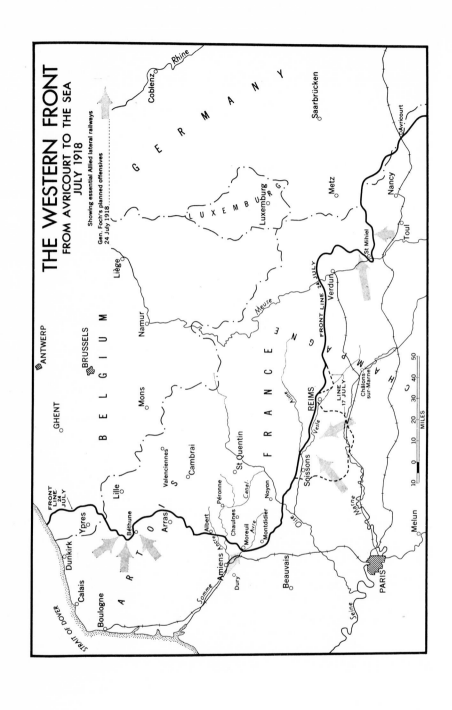

THE WESTERN FRONT
FROM AVRICOURT TO THE SEA
JULY 1918

Showing essential Allied lateral railways

Gen. Foch's planned offensives
24 July 1918

FRONT LINE 24 JULY

LINE 17 JULY

FRONT LINE 24 JULY

MILES
10 0 10 20 30 40 50

G E R M A N Y

Rhine

Coblenz

Saarbrücken

Avricourt

L U X E M B U R G

Luxemburg

Metz

Nancy

Toul

St Mihiel

Verdun

Liège

Namur

Meuse

B E L G I U M

GHENT

ANTWERP

BRUSSELS

Mons

Cambrai

Valenciennes

Lille

Béthune

Ypres

Dunkirk

Calais

Boulogne

STRAITS OF DOVER

A R T O I S

Arras

Albert

Ancre

Somme

Amiens

Dury

Beauvais

Moreuil

Avre

Montdidier

Noyon

Chaulnes

Péronne

Canal

St Quentin

Soissons

Oise

REIMS

Vesle

Aisne

Marne

Châlons-
sur-Marne

Seine

Melun

PARIS

C H A M P A G N E

F R A N C E

A post in a quiet sector of the Canadian front, probably in the reserve trenches since one soldier appears untroubled about enemy snipers.

Canadian Pioneers laying trench mats over mud. Battle of Passchendaele. November 1917.

St. Eloi Craters. Kemmel in background.

16th C.M.G. Co. holding the line in shell holes. Battle of Passchendaele.

A Canadian Battalion going over the top. October 1916.

As the Canadians advanced, German prisoners were happy to surrender during the Battle of Vimy Ridge, April 1917.

A British tank bogged down in No-Man's-Land. These heavy slow vehicles needed firm ground for maximum efficiency.

more and the 29th have suffered badly.[5] Reports are confusing, but what information has leaked out is, that the enemy made an attack in daylight, took the crater and our front line and captured 40 of our men. The shelling is so severe that no one knows if the crater is occupied by either side or not. Our company being in support escapes the carnage this time, only four casualties occurring, Doyle, Orr, O'Brien and Hutton, the first three being Irishmen.

Friday, April 21, 1916

The weather has changed for the better, the sun shining brightly this morning. Kelter who was slightly wounded sometime ago has returned to duty. He was at Boulogne and Rouen and saw a number of bodies that were washed ashore after the disaster to the *Sussex*,[6] and obtained a souvenir in the shape of a French necklace from one of the bodies.

One of the Durhams told me that they have been having a deuce of a time in our old trenches at Kemmel and have had many casualties.

A few bombs were dropped by hostile aeroplanes this morning, but they were not sufficiently close enough to make us get up and see.

Another change; we came out of reserve tonight and go to "I" Camp, between Westoutre and Reninghelst. It has been one continuous downpour of rain tonight and I was soaked to the skin, getting back to "A" Camp after delivering rations. I am becoming quite a night bird these days, travelling Belgium at all hours of the night and early morning. On the way back I passed our Company and directed them to the Camp. They were very wet, footsore and weary.

Saturday, April 22, 1916

A further four of our men are on the casualty list. Calkins and Wildish are suffering from shock. The latter had to be taken out; he was crying like a baby. Still was slightly wounded and Watson was injured by bricks falling on him at Voorzemeele.

There are many conflicting reports regarding the 29th. Out of one platoon only an officer and five men returned from the crater and out of another only three men. One of our machine-gunners claims that

---

[5] The six large craters blown in front of St. Eloi on the 6th Canadian Infantry Brigade's sector resulted in bitter but confused fighting. Owing to poor communication, poor weather which prevented aerial photography, and poor intelligence, the Canadians' positions at the front were not where they were thought to be, and a German counterattack succeeded in regaining part of the ground won earlier. (See Appendix to War Diary, 31st Battalion, CEF, April 1916.)

[6] On 24 March 1916, a German submarine torpedoed, near Dieppe, the cross-channel steamer *Sussex*.

he saw several of them going over and surrendering to the Huns. According to rumours it appears that the Germans bombarded the crater, then stopped, makings signs for our men to go over and surrender. Not paying any attention to them the bombardment would be resumed for another while, till they were glad to give themselves up. The men were dazed by the shelling and I am sure did not know what to do or where to go.

Monday, April 24, 1916

A fine day. In the early morning aeroplanes were astir dropping bombs behind our lines. At the dump midway between Ouderdom and Reninghelst, I noticed captured rolling stock, a couple of red painted wagons, belonging to a German Railway Company. Frankfort-on-Main was marked on one of them.

I have just heard that Sgt. Provan's brother, Jim, belonging to "C" Company has died of wounds. He succumbed after having a leg amputated.

Tuesday, April 25, 1916

Bombs were dropped at L'Abeele today, but no damage was done. Last night our battalion went to the trenches on fatigue duty—wiring. Five were wounded, one belonging to our Company, Packford, a bullet badly damaging his leg.

Bell, who was missing, has been located in a convalescent home.

Out of 99 [men] who went into the crater [of the 29th] only 8 returned.

Wednesday, April 26, 1916

Our artillery bombarded the enemy heavily tonight.

Dickebusch residents are flitting with their worldly possessions. It looks as if the civilian population will be a thing of the past shortly.

Early this evening the enemy sent over very heavy stuff, which dropped a few hundred yards away: many shell pieces went singing over our heads, one piece landing quite close.

There is considerable activity on the Wytschaete front, the Northumberland Fusiliers losing, since they relieved the Canadians, about five hundred men.

Thursday, April 27, 1916

We left for Dickebusch. There is a usual mix up, no proper arrangements being made. Men in very bad humour over handling. Orders are late; no blanket guards; no proper guides. Men raking over the village for their billets. No one to direct them. At last our lot take up their abode in a ruined building near the windmill. System is becoming worse as time proceeds. Much time and labour lost. As the vitality of our men is not of the best, those responsible should harrass them as little as possible. Nonsensical parades and fatigues of the fool's-errand type are occurring too often. This is seriously impairing the strength of our men and what is worse, [it means] losing confidence in those in charge.

Friday, April 28, 1916

It is a lovely morning. We had a fine view of a couple of our aeroplanes hard on the track of a Hun plane, but they were unable to overtake it and it reached its lines in safety.

Saturday, April 29, 1916

Another warm, sunny day. Country beginning to look pretty. Quite a number of shells falling to the right of us. Aeroplanes fairly busy. Hostile planes are keeping up high.

Sunday, April 30, 1916

When going up with rations last night, several shells went over our heads at Dickebusch exploding in a field one to two hundred yards away. It is reported eleven horses belonging to the Engineers were killed.

We were awakened early this morning by our guns opening up simultaneously from all corners, especially opposite Wytschaete. The gas alarm was sounded and we lost no time getting up and investigating our gas helmets, to see they were in order, in case we might have to use them. The guns poured out their shells at a terrific rate. For a while I stood and watched the firing line. Red lights were thrown up and the sky was ablaze with the ordinary flarelights. The whole line appeared a bit nervy. Being a bit chilly, I retired to my bunk and read the "London Magazine" till our guns quietened. Expecting the attack to be over I went to sleep again. The first report that has reached us is that a couple of German deserters reached our lines, informing us that a gas attack was planned for midnight. Owing to this we were ready. It is rumoured the Derbyshires lost 400 men. Further details are that two attacks were made, one opposite Kemmel in the "Bull Ring" and the other near St. Eloi-Boesinghe. The enemy came over as usual in large numbers. Many of them were killed. A few got into the "Bull Ring" but were shortly afterwards bombed out again, seventy prisoners being taken. A mine was sprung by the enemy but we were first to occupy it.

It appears that in the gas attack the other day near Kemmel the gas went back on the enemy and for 24 hours their ambulances were busy taking the gassed and wounded away.

It is rumoured that the Burgomaster of Dickebusch has been arrested. He was caught with a telephone in his cellar.

Yesterday the 5th Brigade had three casualties near Dickebusch which compelled them to shift their quarters. Their new quarters were shelled today, one shell killing twelve and wounding one. They had thirteen killed and sixteen wounded. They are now quartered beside us at Canada Huts "A" Camp. The total casualties around Dickebusch today were thirty-five. Most soldiers are under the impression there are spies around this quarter.

Yesterday I took up a couple of crosses for Miller and Webber's graves.

Monday, May 1, 1916

Another "stand-to" early this morning, the gas alarm being sounded.

A lovely day, planes busy as usual. Germans out very early.

I met a Royal Scot in Ouderdam who told me Poperinghe was bombed this morning. He was there with a view to purchasing whisky for his officers, when the bombs were dropped, 35 in all, several horses were killed, but no people. They dropped beside a church. He never bought the whisky but retreated from the town as fast as his legs could carry him. The natives were very much alarmed and sought safety in all directions. Yesterday he was in Dickebusch when it was shelled. Five were killed beside the church.

He told me of an affair that happened a few days ago in the "M" trenches, where the Royal Scots are. The Germans started to come over No Man's Land in small numbers when an order not to fire was given. Three of them, with their hands up came into their lines where the parapet was blown down. The sentry carelessly left his rifle on the firing step and was going to a dug-out to get assistance when they grabbed his rifle and clubbed him to death. Fraser Brown was his name. It appears a German officer in disguise got into the trench and gave the order not to fire. Realizing what had happened, the enemy were treated to a small bombardment.

A shell came through the house our officers were billeted in and wonderful to relate although the place was wrecked no one was hurt.

Tuesday, May 2, 1916

A horse having a big wound in the jaw came into our camp. The groom who was leading it was on the lookout for a veterinary surgeon. It received shrapnel at Dickebusch.

The water tank at the side of the road near Dickebusch Lake was put out of commission today by a shell landing in front of it on the roadway. Hundreds of soldiers every night refreshed themselves at this well. Every fatigue party from the line halted here for a few minutes. It is one of those spots that lives long in the memory, especially of those half dead with thirst.

Wednesday, May 3 to Monday, May 8, 1916

The battalion went into the firing line last night. We were up at Voormezeele with rations. The building we stopped at before was almost levelled to the ground. The Engineers removed their dump from the vicinity. We were compelled to find another dump which we did on the Voormezeele-Wytschaete Road at the head of Elzenwalle communication trench. Coming back we got into a wagon and, going down the brae towards Cafe Belge, it went into a shell hole, pitching us into the ditch at the side of the road and almost turning turtle. Three of the 2nd Battalion jumped in alongside of us. They were coming out after a spell in the trenches opposite Hill 60. They had a lively time of it. The Germans sprang a mine, rushed their trenches, but only got a footing in one bay for a couple of minutes.

Omens of ill fortune burned into us the seriousness of the situation and showed that Heiny had the range of the road. Would he open up and make things unpleasant or would he keep quiet and let us through? We seemed to sneak along furtively despite the fact we were quite a distance from the line. To many, the approaches are the worst part of the job. How often has one given a sigh of relief when he has struck the friendly protection of the trench!

No sooner did we leave St. Hubertushoek and strike the Hallebast corner than our artillery commenced to roar. The bombardment was terrific. It opened up suddenly and we figured our boys in the craters sent up the "S.O.S." After passing through Dickebusch we literally threaded our way through a maze of batteries. On either side of us came blinding flashes from the guns and report following report seemed to rend the heavens. The noise was that of a hundred thunder claps. The air was seething with the whiz of shells. Every portion of our vicinity was enveloped in momentary flames and when a salvo went off, it almost burst our ear drums. As we passed the pump station, a wicked set of batteries on the embankment on our right beside Dickebusch Lake, went bang. We stared hard in the direction watching for further flashes, so that we could brace ourselves for the report, when all of a sudden a heavy gun on our left under the shadow of the windmill, scarcely ten yards away, fired just as we were passing in front. The flash almost blinded us and the air went warm, whilst the report nearly made us fall off the limber—and the earth trembled. A little further on, to the right of the crossroads, another noisy battery seemed to be firing like fury. A regular stream of metal went roaring through the air up from Cafe Belge; on the left, we stepped into a battery that was tearing the air asunder. In a wood on the upper left heavies were barking out wicked stuff, whilst in Scottish Wood and vicinity the blaze and noise was bedlam. From Dickebusch to Lankhof Farm was like a hideous nightmare. We could scarcely hear ourselves speaking and our eyes were blinking owing to the dazzling flashes. It was an awesome and weird spectacle. The thunderous bangs from the guns, the incessant roar of the shells above, the fire gleaming and flashing from every corner, showing up the muzzles of the guns through the darkness, whilst overhead, shells from a certain battery could be seen describing a semi-circle in the air. It was a marvellous sight. One could see what appeared like a red hot shell shoot up from the ground, climb up the arc of the sky and disappear after it had gone slightly more than half the distance. We were facinated by the phenomenon and wondered what kind of shell it was.

Our men were being snowed under in front of St. Eloi by the hostile artillery, but anyone who passed up the Dickebusch Road on the night of [May] 5th during our bombardment must have felt convinced that some ungodly work was happening around the German supports and that many a Heiny must have bit the dust.

The latter part of our journey was quieter than the beginning. We had only to wait a short time for the ration party and returned when the bombardment was simmering. We passed several ambulances coming and going.

We are up once more with rations to the same dump, arriving about 10:00 p.m., having walked about seven miles. It was 4:00 a.m. before we got away, sleeping or half dozing on the roadside, whilst waiting for the ration party. Twice I was awakened out of semi-slumber by rats running over me. Two or three times a few shells and stray bullets came in our direction sending us in a hurry into the ditch for cover. Case after case was being carried out to the dressing station, and those who could walk staggered along as best they could. A racket started on our right and we got up and watched spellbound the biggest fusillade we have seen in our lives. For a space of a few hundred yards, shrapnel, sausages, etc. were bursting every second.

134

The whole line was illumniated practically all the time and soon became a screeching inferno. Amidst the blaze of red resounded ear splitting explosions. The 27th at the time were finishing their relief, and upon it and the 29th came the full shock of the bombardment. Following this iron storm came the attack, and as already narrated, we lost craters 2 and 3. From our position it looked like sheer slaughter trying to stand up against such a fire. About 4:00 a.m. the carriers arrived at the dump, and were in a desperate hurry to get back again before daylight would appear with its certain chances of detection. They were nervy and ill at ease—the last few days of murder changing their whole attitude. The cries and groans of the dying and wounded had visibly affected them and they were very solemn and contemplative. We ourselves were beginning to feel anxious about getting away. Being unfamiliar with the area we were not sure if we could be seen in daylight or not. Retracing our steps we hugged the shadiest part of the road as much as possible. There was not a soul to be seen. A noticeboard stuck up on a tree, on the right, warned us not to proceed along the road in daylight unless necessity compelled us to. Not far away were a few graves of soldiers, badly needing attention. The crosses were about rotten and the graves overgrown with vegetation. Before reaching Shrapnel Corner the enemy started bombarding in the Dickebusch direction, setting a couple of houses or farms on fire. We had to keep our wits about us and once or twice had to take shelter owing to shells bursting ahead in our path. On the other side of Shrapnel Corner a horse, recently killed, was passed. It blocked part of the road. We halted at the crossroads at Lankhof Farm and waited for a quarter of an hour till Fritz stopped shelling the road ahead of us with light stuff. Making another dash we came across a couple of artillery officers near Cafe Belge and beside them was a notice stating that there was no foot or wagon passage this way during the day. Pointing to the notice I asked if it was obsolete. The reply came back, "Nothing is supposed to be alive in this area," which was very encouraging. At the corner we had left was another batch of soldiers' graves. Further down on the Dickebusch Road on the right were several more, well attended to, one having a rifle butt uppermost, serving as a gravestone.

On the road tonight with rations. A shell landing on the right beside the windmill, up from St. Hubertushoek was the signal for a bolt. Luckily I was sitting on a limber. The transports flew along the road and it was with difficulty I stuck on. My steel hat had slipped down over my eyes. My left hand grasping the rifle and the right hanging on to the rations, the limber bumped along the road and about shook the life out of me. We cut Hallebast corner at a lick and did not stop until the outskirts of Dickebusch were reached. When we arrived at Voormezeele we found we had to go to White Horse Cellars, where the Major and No. 3 platoon were. The carriers were loaded up, each being told to what platoon the rations he was carrying belonged. I had the rum, a couple of jars in separate sandbags, which were tied together and slung over my shoulder. The fighting had far from subsided and no one seemed to relish having to roam over the open. Proceeding on our way, a machine-gun opened up, making a wide traverse. Fortunately the gunner had given too much elevation and the bullets swished harmlessly overhead. A number of rifle bullets pinged around, but they did not find a human mark. Nearing St. Eloi, whiz-bangs started to come over. We struck the Ypres-St. Eloi-Lille road and slowly crept along it. It was full of shell holes, whilst fallen trees had fallen across it. Fritzie was extremely watchful, throwing up flarelights almost every second, lighting up the landscape like daylight, and giving us little chance to make progress. The going was desperately slow. We could only manage a few yards, when up went a starshell and down we crouched. Sneaking along in this fashion, with shells coming over at intervals was far from pleasant. We had to move very warily and when a shell just skimmed over our heads, but luckily did not explode, we began to get fidgety. After what seemed a long time of stooping and creeping, and inwardly cursing those jars of rum I was carrying for they proved a disagreeable load for this bobbing up and down progress, we reached White Horse Cellars. Many of the fellows during the crawl had changed places and when we tried to sort them out, it was found that owing to the state of their nerves, some had forgotten to what platoon the rations they were carrying belonged. Others, not being very partial to the spot, quietly beat it away to their positions with whatever they were carrying. It was no place to loiter so each dispersed and the rations were left to be sorted out as best as possible. A little bunch got down into the cellar and the rum was uncorked and Major Millington totted it around. What satisfaction seemed to pervade the little assembly after they had partaken. Once more they were normal and steadied. A few minutes later we stole away, several shells helping us on our journey.

Last night the enemy shelled the huts to the left of us, about three hundred yards away, killing and disabling ten horses, killing two men and wounding about seventeen. I saw one shell land amongst a couple of lines of horses and another crash into a hut. All the soldiers in the neighbourhood fled to the flanks, a considerable number coming to where we were. When Fritzie gave over shelling they returned in ones and twos, hoping that old Heiny would not return to the attack.

About midnight we came across a small group of soldiers carrying a dead man on a stretcher, which I presume was one of the victims.

Tuesday, May 9, 1916

After thinking our men were coming out tonight we were surprised to receive a hurry call for rations. We made them up quickly, loaded them on the transports and hiked for the dump on the Lille Road. Nearing Shrapnel Corner we heard shrapnel whistling through the air, bursting over the road with a ping. We were told to sit tight as we were going to run the gauntlet. Away we flew at breakneck speed, crossed the railway, swung round the corner at the gallop and did not slow down till we got out of the hot stretch. Whilst on the move a couple of shells came flying over, but luckily we escaped. Half a mile further on we came across our company, or rather the remnants, on their way to camp. There was nothing for us to do but to turn and go back. We had to face the music once more and as we neared this infamous spot off we flew again. Another couple of shells came over but fortunately no one was struck. On the way we scattered a bunch of troops who scurried into the ditches. Our men were footsore and weary and at Dickebusch motor buses were waiting to take them as far as Hallebast. Thus ended the second phase of the Battle of St. Eloi.

[At about this time Private Fraser was granted furlough to Scotland—what follows below is his account and reflection on what occurred during the St. Eloi battle as well as an outline of events relating to his battalion while he was away. He continues his daily journal on May 20th. The 31st Battalion went into divisional reserve on May 9th, but almost every day it had to provide a working party for the front line trenches. While repairing barbed wire, strengthening trenches, etc., at the front, there was a steady drain of casualties. Usually the working parties would leave at 7:00 p.m. and return about 3:30 a.m. to take advantage of the darkness. On May 22nd, "after a rest of 16 days," as the unit war diarist wrote, the battalion left Reninghelst, about five miles southwest of Ypres, and began its move closer to the front. Private Fraser had rejoined the unit by this time, as we shall see. Ed.]

The British troops were in possession of seven craters and a line forward to them. When we relieved them, all that we could turn over to our 4th Brigade from the East were the two ancient craters 6 and 7. Though we did not maintain our ground, it is doubtful if any other troops could have done better. It is true the Imperial 3rd Division carried their attacks forward in face of heavy shell fire and over boggy ground, but we had even greater troubles than they to contend with.

137

It rained practically all the time we were there, making movement almost impossible. The artillery concentration was too much for us and what attacks were engineered on our side were on a ridiculously small scale. There was not much display of generalship. Affairs ran themselves. Our men hung on till they were completely wiped out by shell fire. Unfortunately, though the opposing artillery held us, ours could not restrain them from attacking. Those who were in the centre of the conflict quickly realized that the positions were impossible, that they were untenable, and casualties would have been saved by withdrawing, but the command only realized this several days later when the whole line was lost, and then they ceased aggressive action.

St. Eloi taught us a lesson, a lesson the ordinary soldier through bitter experience quickly learned; namely, that it spells disaster to attack over a small frontage, for it allows the enemy artillery to concentrate its fire. The Canadian command, however, failed to grasp this significance and the same errors were repeated at Fresnoy and Lens. Objectives at those places were taken but we had to retire shortly afterwards, after suffering heavy losses. As usual the command to bolster up their cause would give out the usual announcement that we inflicted heavy casualties on the enemy, when all the time the engagements were rank failures.

These brigade or battalion movements never find much favour with the fighting man. It is invidious to compare one set of troops with another, for the simple reason so many things have to be taken into account, and the conditions are never alike. Weather, artillery support, defences to be overcome, infantry, strength of opposing artillery, etc. are to be taken into consideration. It is amusing, therefore, and almost childish, to pick on any set battalion or army. The Glory goes to the battalions that have seen the most and hardest service. At Vimy, our Division had a walk over, thanks mainly to the artillery, whilst the 4th had considerable difficulty in overcoming the enemy. Therefore, no comparison can rightly be made between our Division and the veteran Imperial 3rd Division, which captured the mound, though losing trenches is always a sore point to the loser, and a mark of elation for the gainer.

On the night of the 8th, the 19th Battalion relieved us. No sooner did the 18th and 21st get into the line than they made an endeavour to retake craters 3 and 2, but did not succeed; instead [they] piled up heavy casualties. Further attacks were undertaken, but they were futile owing to the severe shelling and impassable nature of the ground. Shelter was of the most casual kind and many lost their way in the dark. A private of the 29th Battalion lived for nine days in a shell hole, subsisting on the rations and water bottles taken from the bodies of the men of the 3rd British Division killed in the fighting of the last days of March. The 4th Brigade took their gruelling, suffering 403 casualties, and were succeeded on the 11th and 12th by the 5th Brigade. The enemy made several bombing attacks on craters 6 and 7 on the night of the 14th but were repulsed by the 25th Battalion. In the darkness of the 18th, our Brigade once more stepped into the line; this time, the crucial positions, the small craters, were taken over by the 29th Battalion. The following night saw the craters pass out of our hands and our troops back once more into the old British positions.

About 2:00 p.m. of the 19th the enemy started shelling, principally with light stuff. After a pause he reopened with heavies creating a number of casualties. Later on a bombardment of terrific intensity commenced and heavy casualties were created, many of the wounded were killed, and shelters smashed in. The gunfire switched to Crater 7 and shortly afterwards rifle fire opened up from the opposing craters and when it died down fifty to sixty Germans started across. It was raining and our men were glued in the mud. The survivors were in no condition to offer fight being dazed and shell shocked. The rifles were clogged and useless, only two or three being capable of firing. These commenced but the feeble fire soon died away. By this time the enemy were into Crater 7 and our men had their hands up surrendering. The order was given to those in Crater 6 to retire if they wished but only five did so, the rest being disinclined to take the risk. Out of this number, two were wounded. Along with a wounded officer they regained their lines, but only one man got back untouched. Thus ended the closing tragedy of the craters whose garrison of ninety men were practically all killed or taken prisoners. The Germans did not occupy the ground but left it to the dead.

During this second trip our battalion was in supports. "A" Company took up their position in Old Frenchman's Trench which was nothing more than a straggling ditch, relieving the 25th Battalion. We were ordered up to attack with bombs but owing to the barrage could not make our way through. The following twenty-four hours saw us manning the communication trench and the rest of the spell was spent at Voormezeel School along with a number of the 2nd Pioneers. This battalion did yeoman service consolidating around St. Eloi in face of extreme danger and suffered heavily. Rush work at all times is exhausting, but under shell and machine-gun fire with death in the offing is enough to paralyse physical effort. St. Eloi should be written in large letters on the honour scroll of the Pioneers.

A peculiar occurrence happened, namely, the sounding of the gas alert when the wind was in our favour. It appears our artillery at Ridge Wood hit a gas cylinder in Fritz's lines liberating the gas, hence the alarm.

139

Tom Helliwell had a spent bullet hit him in the shoulder but did not pierce him.

Last December our company drew lots for leave. Out of a strength of 224, I drew 41st place. An odd one or two have been going away since January. At last my time had come and with Cpl. Hunter, I set out for Poperinghe to entrain for Blighty—Blighty the dream of every British and Canadian soldier. Arriving in Poperinghe from Micmac Camp after a six mile hike we strolled around the town till evening. At Poperinghe several hundred French soldiers in their invisible blue uniforms got into a train and pulled out. They were all ages and sizes and wore an assortment of whiskers. They harangued each other freely, gesticulating the while. Shortly afterwards a battalion of the Grenadier Guards marched to the station in fours. They were undoubtedly the finest body of men I had ever seen and they carried themselves magnificently. Splendidly built men, everyone of them— erect and broad shouldered with finely cut features. They commanded my admiration. A Corporal, several inches over six feet, was following in the rear. They quickly boarded a train, which sped quietly out to Ypres, the most dreaded front on the whole Western line. Retiring to the Y.M.C.A., we lay and dozed on a form till about 2:00 - 3:00 a.m. when a cry went up that the Blighty train had pulled in, when there was a rush for arms and equipment and a bolt across the way to the station. After sitting in the carriage for an hour and a half, the train moved off, and in due time we reach Boulogne. Then over the Channel to Folkestone and London and a few hours later we are on our way to the Highlands of Scotland, our Mecca. But good times must always come to an end and within a fortnight we are back again to take our lives in our hands once more.

During our absence Kelter, Brett and Lawson have been wounded, the former dangerously, being pierced in the lung by shrapnel from one of our own shells.

CHAPTER V

The Third Battle of Ypres

Saturday, May 20, 1916

A sentry awakened us early this morning with the news that a zepplin was about. Away to the north in the vicinity of the channel searchlights were searching the heavens and shrapnel was bursting in the air. There was a considerable bombardment all through the night and periodically shells came over our heads. Quite a number of Dickebusch civilians are leaving the town.

Sunday, May 21, 1916

Dickebusch was shelled today and one of the 28th was killed.

Friday, May 25, 1916

Our Company is located in support at Scottish Wood which has been shelled since the last few days. The nerves of one of our fellows gave out and he had to be removed.

Saturday, May 26, 1916

In the afternoon, hearing machine-gun fire overhead, I looked up and saw a running air fight. A German plane was making for its lines as fast as it could travel, and a considerable distance behind were three of our planes about equidistant in a straight line trying to overhaul it. Our leading machine gave out several bursts of fire but the distance was too great and they had no effect. This machine and the one behind were too slow and could not catch up. The last, the smallest of the lot and the highest in the air, was travelling at a lick and quickly shot ahead. It caught up on Heiny well over the German line, but the gunner must have been a poor shot for he could not bring the hostile plane to earth. The enemy anti-aircraft guns opened up in strength, forcing our plane to retire. The other two, finding they could not overhaul their opponent, gave up the chase. It was most gratifying to see that at last we had a plane that could show signs of speed.

At night our men moved into the front line, after receiving forty-eight hours rations. They are occupying a very bad portion of the line, T15, 16 and 17 and R2.[1] Before leaving Scottish Wood, Monck was severely injured. He picked up the nosecap of a German shell. Strange to say it exploded blowing off his right hand and injuring him in the face and leg. It also slightly wounded Hemmings.

Eleven fellows in "C" Company located near Convent Wall had a shell burst amongst them killing one and wounding the rest. The fellow killed was wounded in our first [action] in St. Eloi trenches.

Sunday, May 27, 1916

James was killed by a sausage. He was [a] runner. Several sausages had been sent over and he was advised not to go down the trench for a few minutes. He ignored the advice and started on his way, but a sausage coming over him got him, tearing him in the middle. The following night he was taken out to Voormezeele, where the ration limber picked him up and took him down to the transport line. In the morning he was taken to Reninghelst where our band attended to the burial.

Monday, May 28, 1916

There were several air fights today. It is claimed we brought a couple down. One of our patrols, a single seater, was shot down near Voormezeele, making a head-long flight to earth. The Germans opened fire on the vicinity, expecting to catch a rescue party.

The enemy is pretty active sweeping the back country with machine-gun fire.

Poperinghe is getting considerable attention paid to it by an armoured train, which is dropping shells regularly, accounting for a number of the population.

Wednesday, May 30, 1916

The Engineers quarters near Cafe Belge were shelled today.

---

[1] In this case Fraser, when referring to "our men," is writing about those men in "A" Company.

Thursday, June 1, 1916

Another batch of twenty has been drafted to our battalion.

Friday, June 2, 1916

A further draft has arrived. This makes thirty new men for our Company.

[At this point Fraser, rather than give a daily account, describes the events of the next five days. It is usually termed "The Battle for Mount Sorrel," a name which his battalion still carries as one of its battle honours.]

We now enter into another conflict which is soon to embroil the whole Canadian Force, consisting of the First, Second and Third Divisions, the Fourth Division not being a fighting unit yet. This time the aggressors were the Germans and the attack developed into the Third Battle of Ypres or designated later the Canadian Battle of Ypres. All previous engagements, Ypres, Festubert, Givenchy, St. Eloi, affected only several battalions or at the most a division, but before this battle was brought to a close, operations were carried on a more stupendous scale and the resultant casualties more numerous than heretofore.

The line attacked stretched from the north of the village of Hooge to Mount Sorrel in the south, the distance along the trenches being three to four miles. It followed a series of ridges, backed by shattered woods, Zouave Wood, Sanctuary Wood, Maple Copse and Armagh Woods. Between Sanctuary and Armagh Woods, a long stretch of high ground, Observatory Ridge, ran back from the line towards the village of Zillebeke. From the right of Hooge to Sanctuary Wood was a gap through which the enemy could look down to our trenches in the plain. Their positions slightly dominated ours and in consequence were more favourably situated for attack. To be pushed off the plateau would place us in a precarious position and furnish the enemy with complete observation. They could register on our trenches and fortifications to a nicety. It was absolutely essential, therefore, that we retain our positions and thus blind his observation as much as possible.[2]

No doubt smarting under the punishment inflicted at the Bluff and St. Eloi and conscious of our coming operations on the Somme, the Hun command resolved to disarrange our plans and sought out the

---

[2] This part of the Canadian line formed the most easterly projection of the Ypres salient. Although, as Fraser writes, the enemy controlled certain advantageous ground, the Canadians did also, especially Observatory Ridge, which gave them a good view over part of the German trenches.

weakest spot in the line, namely the Ypres salient. The attempt was not considered to endanger the Channel ports, otherwise the aggregate behind the attack would have been more formidable and the frontage covered of greater magnitude. Apart from interrupting our plans in the south, the attack was intended to straighten the salient and enable the enemy to occupy an even greater strategical position.

We were not without warning for it was known that hostile troops had been massing in villages in the rear. It was also observed that "T" saps were being driven out into No Man's Land with a view to being linked up and forming a new line. These warnings, however, went unheeded. Not only the command but the rank and file were very optimistic regarding their defensive powers. Massed artillery fire as it is now known, was a negligible quantity up till lately. On account of this, the ordinary infantryman looked upon defence as much more inviting than attack. Since then, this opinion has been altered.

On the first of June the respective battalions in the firing and support lines were, from the right, between Mount Sorrel and Hill 60, the 4th Canadian Mounted Rifles; from here to the Dip [sic], the 1st Canadian Mounted Rifles; continuing to the Gap were the Princess Pats and onwards over the Menin Road to Bellewaarde Beek was the Royal Canadian Regiment. The other battalions of the 8th and 7th Brigades were in second support and reserve. On the right the line was held by our First Division, whilst the men of the Imperial 60th Brigade looked after the left.

For the last few days, shelling was more constant than usual but no prominence was given to this for the Ypres salient is at all times stormy and every battalion that takes up its abode in this stricken field usually returns to a more peaceful front very much attenuated in numbers. In these days it was a byword amongst the men that one was not a soldier unless he had served on the Ypres front. Since the fall of 1914 till armistice was declared this countryside has been bathed in blood. Here have fallen thousands of our best manhood. Many a soldier grievously wounded has staggered back plastered with mud and blood from head to foot and dazed almost beyond reckoning. The traffic in human flesh in this region is scandalous. Thousands pass up to the line, returning shortly afterwards completely shattered. It will always be a debatable point—was the salient worth holding? The Germans themselves had a dread of this front. The mention of Ypres conveyed a sort of horror to them. It had always sinister forebodings of death. I remember when I was on my second leave in October 1917, in the Highlands of Scotland, my brother-in-law shuddered, when in answer to his query, what part of the front I was returning to, I replied Ypres. His premonition turned out too true, for within a fortnight, I was smashed up and out of the Great Adventure for good, disabled for life. But everyone gets it at Ypres.

In preparation for the attack on the Somme, the several fronts were stripped of as much artillery and reserves as was safe and sent south, so Fritzie in timing his attack, timed it well, just when our artillery was in a state of flux.

It is customary, if things are quiet, for senior officers to make a tour of the trenches in the morning, for the purpose of acquiring first hand knowledge of the peculiarities of their front. Tommy is always a great supporter of any Colonel or Brigadier who exhibits any fondness for roaming around the firing line, and he is lovingly referred to as having "guts," a much more acceptable name than "dug-outs," an epithet commonly applied to those officers whose chief concern is the depth of their trench abode.

About 6:00 a.m. of June 2, General Mercer, the 3rd Divisional General and Brigadier Williams of the 8th Brigade, with a few of their staff set out for battalion headquarters, which they reached about 8:00 o'clock.[3] A few minutes later they started for the line and on the way up the comparative stillness of the morning was broken by a crash from the enemy's guns as a torrent of metal came streaming down on our trenches. The success at St. Eloi had taught the Hun the advantages of intensive fire and he prepared himself accordingly. His plans were laid; our trenches had been registered upon with an artillery accumulation and he simply sailed into us and we soon foundered amidst the wreckage of obliterated trenches, smashed dug-outs and torn sandbags. Our men simply melted away under this tornado. In less than no time the ground was strewn with the remains of the mangled—and the dying. The survivors, few in number, tried to creep away. It was in this inferno that the Generals were caught. Enveloped in shell fire, the Brigadier was wounded and when the enemy came over, captured. General Mercer tried to win his way back, but he never got further than Armagh Wood for there his body was found several days later with three wounds in it. He was buried at Poperinghe, a village where, in the old cemetery on the western side of the Reninghelst-Poperinghe Road, lie the mortal remains of Colonels Hart-Machary and Boyle of the 7th and 10th Battalions respectively, killed more than a year previously in the Second Battle of Ypres.

The fire continued for about four hours and when resistance was considered broken the Germans emerged from their trenches in the southwest carrying packs and overcoat, and advanced in several

[3] Mercer and Williams had come forward to reconnoitre the Mount Sorrel area. It was Williams' brigade which was responsible for defending the threatened area around Observatory Ridge.

145

waves. After pulverizing our front line the artillery lifted and barraged the supports and approaches, creating heavy casualties in the Communications. Our supports held but if the enemy had never made the common error of easing up when the road was clear and the line confused, they could have advanced much further. As it was they threw away their opportunity and gave us time to rush up reserves. It is said some of their patrol penetrated as far as Zillebeke, but were beaten back in skirmishes, paying the penalty in full for their rashness.

Though the attack started on the right it gradually worked its way north and soon the 7th Brigade were in desperate straits. Both C.M.R. battalions had been snowed under and in consequence resistance was weak. The 4th C.M.R.'s had 640 casualties[4] and the 1st fared little better, their trenches being completely flattened and casualty roll 367. The Princess Pats now came in for a gruelling. They resisted valiantly, fighting rearguard bombing actions. Being surrounded, the remnants had to retire to the supports early next morning.

During the retirement two eighteen pounders,[5] sacrifice guns, were lost in Sanctuary Wood. Sacrifice guns are placed in advanced positions to be utilized in case of emergency either for attack or defence. Consequently they are silent, till the moment arrives for special action. It is essential that they refrain from shooting if they wish to escape detection. Being so close up, an imprudent shot would be at once observed and woe to the unfortunate gunners. These guns opened up when the attack started and kept on firing till the enemy appeared over Observatory Ridge. Practically all the gunners were killed.

The attack still continued northward but came to a halt opposite the R.C.R.'s. Instead of pushing against a weak line, the enemy made the fatal error of digging in in Armagh and Sanctuary Woods. The Engineers who followed up the infantry quickly had suitable trenches dug.

A counter-attack was planned but it had to be postponed several times because certain units did not reach their jumping off positions. When it was ultimately launched, there was no co-ordinated effort and it failed, nevertheless a few patrols were brushed away and we established ourselves nearer the German line. The members of the battalions participating belonged to the 7th, 10th, 15th, 14th, 52nd, 60th and 49th. The casualties were heavy, the 14th losing nearly 390

[4] The 4th Canadian Mounted Rifles suffered 89 per cent casualties by the time this battle was over. Their roll of killed, wounded and prisoners was actually 626.

[5] The 18-pounder gun was the normal field piece in close support of the infantry. Both guns were recaptured later.

146

men. The attack should never have been delivered. The artillery preparation was poor; the exact positions of the enemy uncertain; and the time was daylight. In addition there was no cohesion or definite understanding. Our men were met by a withering fire and did the best they could in digging in. The 52nd and 60th were badly cut up in the communication trench having been caught in barrages. The 49th had also a disastrous time getting in.

It is estimated over eight thousand took part in the assault. The troops were the Wurttemburg,[6] under the command of the Duke of Wurttemberg and the furthest point they reached was seven hundred yards in the direction of Zillebeke. They captured besides General Williams, Colonel Usher, thirteen officers, 518 non-commissioned officers and men, 168 of whom were wounded.

The enemy was now in possession of the Ridge and our left flank was in the air. Up to this period our losses were about 80 officers and 2,000 men.[7]

When the 3rd Division was attacked our battalion was resting for a few days in (Divisional Reserve at "G" Camp) Reninghelst, and rumours soon spread about the disaster. We saw artillery and regiments being rushed up to the front, and the 31st Battalion received orders to stand to. I had to make a hurry call from "A" Camp with smoke helmets.[8] Having a bicycle enabled me to get there quicker. At night we watched red rockets, the ominous signal for help being sent up along the salient. No sooner did they go up then everyone focused their attention on the line. If persisted in, we knew that there was something desperate going on and expected to be drawn into the vortex before long. Little serious groups of us gazed intently towards the Ridges, meditating on the happenings and eager for news. The following evening we witnessed our batteries raining shells on the enemy. The wind blowing across their lines deadened the sound of the gun fire but we could see flashes spurting out from every clump of trees.

A certain battalion was reported to have shown very little fight. Such reports, however, cannot be relied upon. But these things stick in the minds of our men later when questioned on the march by any

---

[6] The main attack was made by the 26th and 27th (Wurttemberg) Divisions of the 13th Wurttemberg Corps.

[7] It should be kept in mind that Fraser is writing this account in the summer of 1918. Even by this time exact casualty figures had not been compiled, and he would not have access to official figures. Generally speaking, his estimates tend to be on the conservative side.

[8] Presumably gas helmets.

passersby what battalion we belonged to would laughingly reply the battalion in question.

The tragic but expected orders have arrived warning us to prepare to move towards the line as our brigade is to relieve the sorely beset 7th in the Hooge or northern sector. Once again we are on the hike but this time along the Reninghelst-Vlamertinghe Road. Passing Ouderdam we halt at the huts beside the line (Camp E) on the left of the road, spending the night therein. Our abode is only temporary and soon we are heading for the stricken field, whilst the transport move their quarters to near Busseboom, collecting unoccupied camouflaged tents on the way, and re-erecting them on a grassy sward further on. The battalion marches onward taking short cuts across the fields and keeping in the shadows as much as possible. Everyone is loaded with extra ammunition and a couple of bombs and this exasperates our men greatly. The weight that is piled on to an infantrymen is always a serious burden and handicaps him very much. The small boy who said a soldier was a person to hang things on did not deviate much from the truth.

At this time the 45th Battalion, a Manitoba regiment, was broken up and drafted to Belgium, reinforcing the 6th Brigade. A considerable quota was sent to us and their entrance to the battle zone was a disastrous one, for within a few days they were nearly all on the casualty list. Quite a number that were attached to my company had their surnames beginning with "B," plainly showing that the alphabet played a considerable part in the drafting. Austin, one of the most reliable of them, killed at the Somme, always maintained that we received the small men of his battalion. But big or small, each goes into the melting pot. Unfortunately several of the recent drafts did not appear to have much knowledge of the Mills bomb. One fellow complained bitterly to his comrades for being furnished with bombs as he did not know the first thing about them. Being dissatisfied and absolutely fed up on the way to the line, he remarked that he hoped the bombs would blow him to hell and added that he would get a wooden or a Victoria Cross. A pal, an old timer, chirped in that he would get the former, and sure enough, before many hours had elapsed, he did. A cross, however, was never erected for his body was scattered to the winds.

It is the night of [June] 5th and the 28th Battalion takes over the R.C.R.'s positions on the left, one and a half companies occupying the firing line and bombing posts. The remaining two platoons [are] in close support and the balance of the battalion [is] in a support line running from the Menin Road to Zouave Wood. Here it met our companies which manned the left arc of a semi-circular line, south of

Zouave Wood, the right being now held by the 43rd. The better part of a company of the 60th were occupying a trench, running at almost right angles to the enemy. The remaining battalions of the brigade, the 27th and 29th, were in reserve. The 28th on our left front stepped into most precarious positions for its right flank was gone and in its stead was the enemy. There was no connection between it and our battalion which was several hundred yards behind on the right in the old support line but now the firing line. The R.C.R.'s pulled out with a loss of about 400, the 42nd and 49th with about 450 each, and the Princess Pats who were most heavily hit, suffered to the number of 680. The 7th and 8th Brigades had between them over 3,000 casualties. The 9th and 1st Brigades relieved the right centre and the right, letting out part of the 7th Brigade and the 2nd and 3rd Brigades. The front line is held in turn from north to south by the 28th, 31st, 43rd, 2nd and 1st Battalions, with a portion of the 60th wedged in in the centre.

Our men, as usual, thin out and file into the communication trench which is badly wrecked. There was intermittent shelling of a wicked and accurate kind creating quite a disturbance and scattering or bunching the men, making contact irregular, and giving the sergeants some trouble trying to hold their platoons together. Having a number of fresh men in our ranks who scarcely realized the necessity of keeping in touch, our seasoned warriors gave vent to vehement remarks regarding them. Experience teaches the value of cohesion and the veteran dogs his platoon, being determined that he will not be separated from it at any cost, in consequence any momentary setback only makes him redouble his efforts to catch up. No so the new man, who is liable to wander and be easily lost. The embryo soldier realizes what a casualty is in a vague sort of way. Though he expects to see men get killed and wounded, that vision is of an entirely different sort from witnessing a shell burst and one of his comrades, alive a moment ago, now dismembered, bleeding, dead. One has therefore no conception of the horrors of war until he is in the midst of it.

It was not unnatural that many of our newcomers were unnerved and sickened at the sights, and apt to be panic stricken by the gunfire which helped to create this trouble. At the very threshold of getting in was a shrapnel burst over the communication trench which got eight men including one of our officers, Lt. Wolley-Dod. A number of the men were newcomers, and I believe they all made "Blighty."[9] Cpl. Angus, Ptes. Atkinson, A. Smith, and I. Williams were among the number hit.

[9] Blighty, an army slang term for England. To get a "Blighty" was to receive a wound which would ensure a return to England for treatment in hospital.

The communication trench was not deep enough and in many places it was impassable. The 48th Battalion, a Pioneer regiment, was busy building a new trench towards Armagh Wood. Along China Wall we go, continuing to Yeomanry Post, which is about three-quarters of a mile from the front line. The approaches from Zillebeke were lined with Canadian dead and further up we encountered the bodies of German skirmishers.

We sneak into the firing trench which in many parts is shallow and blown down, on account of which the troops cram themselves into isolated spots. The 42nd Battalion, whom we relieved, beat it out quickly. "A" and "B" companies, together with machine-gunners, both battalion and brigade, take over the firing line for the first three days and "C" and "D" companies and the bombers remaining in support.

A number of shells were coming over which made us anxious. When red flares appeared on our right and gunfire increased, several of the new draft lost their heads and either scattered wildly or got jumbled up in the trench. Regan got struck in the neck, blood streaming from the wound. Hellawell was hit in the forehead and lay unconscious. Several hours later as he was lying on a stretcher, the death rattle sounding in his throat, a shell burst on top of him and blew him to atoms. Cpl. Steel tried to pacify the half a dozen men whose wind was up and they ultimately calmed down. A young fellow cowering in the trench tried to hide himself behind the firing step.

A marvellous discovery was made—a jar containing rum. As there were no prohibition measures embodied in orders, Dearden, Steel, Buttress and Jack Macartney nursed the foundling. To be left in the trench by such a Scottish element as the 42nd under existing climatic conditions is enough to upset all current theories regarding Scotsmen and the drink question.[10]

Artillery fire was fairly heavy during the early morning of [June] 6th. About 7:00 o'clock a bombardment of unprecedented ferocity began and the range was of uncanny accuracy. The shells were bursting in or near the trench and the gunfire would run from end to end. It played along the line as if worked by a hose. Gunfire so precise and methodical in its execution strikes terror, even into the bravest hearts. Stuck in a trench, with shells creeping gradually nearer and nearer to you from the right, and through a piece of good fortune you escape, only to go through the same ordeal as the fire sweeps back from the left, is unnerving to the last degree. All the time you hear the

[10] The 42nd Battalion was raised and recruited in Montreal from Scots Canadians. Its sub-title was "Royal Highlanders," and today it is perpetuated by the Black Watch of Canada.

noise from the guns and brace yourself for the burst, which you expect every moment on top of you. Such was the situation we had to face until 2:00 p.m. when the assault came. This systematic shellfire, which aims at complete destruction of a helpless foe, has swelled our hospitals and asylums to the brim. No fighting is so tense as at these moments and never has the reason hung on so fine a thread. To get up over the parapet and rush to certain death at the hands of machine-gunners or riflemen would be a welcome mental relief to remaining stoically in a trench with an avalanche of shells smashing and burying everything before it. Standing up to shellfire of such method and accuracy is the hardest part by far of a soldier's trials.

It was raining continuously and where my unit lay, contained only one dug-out, which sheltered an officer. The trench by this time was filling up with water, there being over a foot, and behind was a swamp. Everything became saturated with the wet, the bread in the ration bags went into a pulp, all eatables, excepting canned goods, were completely destroyed. Clothes and equipment weighed as heavy as lead. Shells were exploding all around, sending up showers of mud and water. The wounded lay where they fell on the poisonous ground of Flanders.

Our men were harassed by the fire and kept constantly moving from spot to spot according to the fierceness of the shelling. A few of our men were sniping at Germans whom they detected on a ridge about five hundred yards away. One of our fellows who was lately in the band foolishly kept steady at this job until he was observed. Eventually a bullet went straight through his steel hat, grazing his head and causing him to cease further action.

A shell which burst close to Buttress and Dearden made them separate, the former making tracks as quickly as possible for another spot, was overtaken by another shell, which almost knocked him out. Recoiling from the place, he staggered back to his old position, pale and almost fainting.

This gunfire was a prelude to the assault, which was ushered in by the springing of four mines silmultaneously, engulfing one whole company of the 28th almost to a man. The remaining forward platoons were involved in the catastrophe. The survivors, scarcely more than a score, tried to steal back over the open. How many escaped it was difficult to learn. One fellow, who reached our lines, said that two who were with him were shot down. It was rainy and misty at the time; and though we saw figures flitting about ahead, we could not shoot as we were uncertain whether they were the enemy or our own men.

After the mines went up the enemy came over with full accoutrements evidently expecting a walk over. The infantry attack started on the left, opposite the Imperial 60th Brigade, who easily repulsed it. They then moved south and came over on the 28th, who in the front line were wallowing in death. Quickly overcoming this line they headed for the remaining Companies of the 28th in support, but were repulsed. Their next assault between 3:00 and 4:00 p.m. was delivered opposite our two companies. Attacking in waves of several hundred men, they came across, but notwithstanding the difficulties we were in, encumbered with the dead and wounded; the firing step smashed in many places; in mud and wet; rifles half clogged; and though dazed and crazed we pull ourselves together, line the serviceable parts of the parapet and blaze into the advancing enemy, who recoil in confusion. All they could accomplish was to penetrate down our old communication trench into Zouave Wood.

Our machine-gunners got in some very useful work, equalizing matters a bit. The infantry also figured largely in the repulse, each having his individual tale to tell. Cpl. Hunter got a bead on a Hun and dropped him. Macdougall accounted for an officer who was waving his men forward. A Hun going to his assistance got a renewal of the dose and dropped to the ground. Unfortunately, Mac's own existence was of a short duration for three months later he was listed with the missing on the Somme.

The casualties, however, had been mounting up. A heavy [shell] came over and got eight, killing Simpson and J. W. Clarke, and almost dismembering Teddy Miller, whose leg was fearfully shattered. He was carried out by Doull and Plummer, who had just arrived back from leave, and lingered on till the following day when death claimed him. It was Clarke's first trip to the line.

Lt. Robertson was wounded and among the others were Lambert and Thomas. The toll was augmented still more, Rogers being killed and about a couple of bays away, Cpl. Cox and little Diffey met instantaneous death from a shell burst, being flung clean out of the trench over the parapet into No Man's Land.

Just as "B" Company Sergeant Major had left his company clerk Imrie and Dalziel, sergeant of the bombers, a shell alighted and both were hurled into oblivion. Imrie was up in Scotland on leave with me a few weeks before. J. Langlands was killed and his brother wounded, both recent arrivals. Steeds and Holland of the machine-gun section were reported dangerously wounded and later dead. Lt. Downie, formerly machine-gun sergeant, was wounded while going in on inspection. Another of our company officers to be wounded was Lt. Hartt. Lt. Batemen was killed and Capt. Tucker wounded. Among the rank and file of the company who suffered wounds, some grievously, were Hopkins, Sexsmith, Swann, Sherrett, Brown R., Burbon, Ball, Banks, Batemen, Desmond, Bellegrass, Bignell, Bowles, Broadfoot, Bradford, Sgt. Barrons, Cameron, Bodkin, Godfrey, Cutmore, Chard R., Donaldson, St. Jacques, Wills, Rowbottom, Turner, H. M. Williams, Charbonneau, etc. A considerable number were new men and several were back in the ranks after a few days lay up.

Mackie, another of No. 3 platoon, who had lately been transferred to the 2nd Tunnelling Coy., was sapping when the Bosche attack started. It is believed that he got out of the sap and mixed with the infantry, for the account that reached us several days later was that he had been found dead in a shell hole with several dead Huns around him. He was one of the characters of the battalion.

Mearns was wounded on the way out near the dressing station. He was another of our characters and was killed further on in the campaign.

A whole gun crew, No. 14, of the 6th Machine-Gun Coy. was wiped out. A year and a half later, the crew of the same gun, of which the writer was No. 1, were casualties not far from the same location on the Ypres front.

Gazing through the periscopes, the enemy were observed consolidating their positions. A plan taken from a dead Hun officer revealed the fact that they had seventeen machine-guns in No Man's Land. We therefore ran risks in firing and had to content ourselves by watching the enemy.

When we went into the line, there were half a dozen wounded Germans in our dressing station having been captured after our counter-attack. They were great big fellows, quite young. One hung on to his cap like grim death, frightened it would be taken from him.

Wednesday, June 7, 1916

It may now be well to narrate what is happening in the rear. We left the transport lines about 8:00 p.m. with rations, and had a seven mile journey ahead of us. The road was in bad repair and exceedingly bumpy. Gangs of men were working on a side road and in [the] course of time ours, I presume, would receive next attention. At Vlamertinghe we turn sharply to the left, beside a brick house, which has a hole a yard in diameter through the eastern gable. Passing over the railway we were confronted by one long line of transports along the Poperinghe-Ypres road. They had been held up until darkness would set in and for the sake of position had collected early. Those in the van are naturally the quickest back. This column in close formation stretched as far as the eye could see. At last we got behind and moved on with the throng. The amount of money that passes along this road at night in the shape of horses, wagons, ammunition and rations, must be immense. At this time, the light railways were not thought of and to keep up with the demands of the firing line, the roads congested with traffic. It required an army in itself to bring up munitions and as the hours of work were dependent on darkness, a hum of activity developed as the shadows fell in striking contrast to the stillness and loneliness of the road during the day.

The Poperinghe-Ypres road is one of the finest in Belgium, straight and broad, and fringed on either side by stately trees. As one proceeded he could tell by the rugged nature of the road, the increasing number of shell holes and the shattered trees, that he was quickly approaching the seat of war. Slowly we moved along, passing Vlamertinghe dressing station on the right. There was very little destruction to be observed until we came upon the church and turned the corner. From here onwards every building was completely or partially destroyed. Strange, the western end seemed to be immune while the opposite end was practically demolished. The church, a huge imposing edifice was bereft of the roof, and the spire was gone. A jumbled mass of masonry blocked the entrance. The sides and gables were still standing, though the structure itself was little more than a skeleton. We pursue our way for a couple of miles to Ypres. For part of the distance the railway is on our right, then crosses the road to the left, not far from a pretty Chateau. Batteries near the road occur at intervals. Huge grassy mounds attract our attention. Beneath them are the quarters of the gunners. Presently we leave the shade of the trees and at the cross roads we view the approach to Ypres. On the right the fields give a sense of openness and we miss the friendly protection of the trees. On our left is a huge building, encircled in parts by a wall. A number of gaping holes in the latter forcibly tell us to hurry on. The building on the whole is not nearly as badly damaged as those we have already passed. Being isolated on the outskirts of the town it has a commanding appearance and readily arrests our attention as a landmark beyond the ordinary. It is the Seminary.

Further along on the right side of the road is a stretch of houses completely destroyed. Continuing on we enter the town passing over both the railway and canal. The former is still used at night to transport troops between the town and Poperinghe, but the latter is dry for the locks and banks have been smashed by shell fire.

Ypres, strangely silent, with its gaunt, skeleton buildings, frowning down upon you, is a dead city and the city of the dead. Beneath its crumbling walls and accumulated debris, many bodies of soldiers and civilians lie entombed. The noxious and peculiar odours emanating from the buried cellars arise from the dead. Words fail to express the destruction of this city. When halted less than three miles aways, the Bosche gave vent to his spleen by pouring thousands of shells on this helpless city. Never an hour passed without it being strafed. At every period of the day the explosion of shells reverberated through the silent streets. The square was studiously avoided and little bunches travelled through the narrowest streets on their journey through the Lille or Menin gate. Perhaps this was the best time to view Ypres in its ruined splendour, if such a term can be applied, for as months rolled on shelling continued, buildings rapidly disappeared into dust, settling down till in many places scarcely the outline could be discernible.

We leave Ypres by the Lille road. Three-quarters of a mile further on we pass Shrapnel Corner. Another hundred yards or so we take a road that branches off to the left. The going here was heavy. Small shell holes, and ruts caused by the traffic over a sodden surface, tried the horses to the limit. The road was more undulating than usual and this added to the strain. A few shells came over our heads on the way to Shrapnel Corner. We zig-zag our way along a sheltered road, till we debouch on the open. On the right we can make out a long ridge, the southernmost part of which is Hill 60. For the first time I observe a communication trench below us, at the right side of the road, and soldiers passing along it. The truth dawned upon me that we were within range and view of the enemy, so I changed my position by getting on the sheltered side of the limber. Shortly after this stray bullets whistled around causing us to emit muffled oaths. On reaching Zillebeke, instead of turning to the left, we continue on, pausing where a road led up to the ridge on our right. The party in charge seemed undecided, but eventually we move forward over an open road, on which the limbers were kicking up a deuce of a row, advertising our approach to Fritz in no uncertain fashion. Bullets were whistling around but they were very high. All of a sudden we were confronted by a barricade of sandbags across the road, and a sentry stepped out from nowhere and asked us what in the devil we were up to. "Good God," he uttered, "the line is only a few hundred yards away, this is no place for a dump." There was a quick about turn, and we hurried back, to Zillebeke, muttering all sorts of nasty things about incompetent transport officers and sergeants. All of a sudden a machine-gun opened up and considerably startled us, the report sounded so close. Turning to the right we pass through Zillebeke to the dump and dispose of our rations. We return by the

Menin Road. Nearing Hell Fire Corner, the driver lashes the horses like fury and we plunge headlong towards Ypres.

The next night we were on the road again. For a distance of a mile on, before coming to the Seminary, smashed limbers, shells and shell cases, lay scattered along the right of the road. Some artillery transports had come to grief, and at the Seminary four dead horses lay at the side of the road, with ghastly wounds, two of them disembowelled. The following night everything was cleared away, the shell holes filled in, and the road as innocent looking as before.

Sunday, June 11, 1916

Owing to the Ypres Road being so much used, and it is well into the morning before we arrive back at camp, we take a new route by cutting down to the Vlamertinghe-Reninghelst Road, which we follow to near Vlamertinghe, then turning to the right we continue till we meet the Dickebusch-Ypres Road which takes us into Ypres near the station. We noticed on our way an observation post on a high tree beside a chateau. Several graves were also passed. A solitary grave was seen in Ypres in the rear of the Infantry barracks.

Monday, June 12, 1916

Our company is being relieved tonight and will retire to the barracks at Ypres for several hours rest. We left with rations in daylight and at Vlamertinghe the traffic control made each limber string out several yards distance. We arrived in Ypres without mishap, but Fritzie was sending over lachrymose shells somewhere for our eyes were smarting.

Our men were late in arriving and trudged it back in groups, stragglers following on. Some had difficulty in finding the billet. They were encased in mud and the weariest and most haggard looking aggregate imaginable. Some dropped on the floor and went to sleep immediately, being even too exhausted to eat. Others clamoured for the rum and food, whilst a few on whom the hardships seemed to fall lightly laughed through their grime and spent the time recounting happenings. Many had sore feet and removed their boots as quickly as possible.

Tuesday, June 13, 1916

On the next night, notwithstanding the punishment the battalion endured, it was called upon for further sacrifice, and once again our Company was sent along the road to the melting pot. No excuses are permitted in the army, tiredness, shattered nerved, semi-starvation goes for nothing and once again the music is faced, but even with officer and all details scratched from the transport lines, all our Company could muster was eighty men. At this stage the original members of the battalion gave way to draft units, though they still held the reins of government as commissioned and non-commissioned officers.[11]

Kemmel, St. Eloi and Ypres blotted out the old 31st. Theirs was a defensive force with the odds against them. They missed the satisfaction and glory that goes to storming troops. Nevertheless a considerable number managed to hold out until the Somme and paid off old scores for their former comrades, but beyond that not much more than a score took an active part in hostilities, while a few casualties came back for each battle to the very end. In my platoon only six originals went in for the second trip at Hooge.

It is raining heavily and the trenches are in a fearful mess. Again we set out with rations, through silent Ypres and out by the Menin Gate we pursue our way. One of our fellows, after crossing the railway, was slightly wounded by a splinter from a shell. The shock was sufficient to knock him down. Nearing the Seminary we observed a ruined building in flames, no doubt set ablaze by shellfire. A couple of shells come over in front of us and burst beside the building. Near Shrapnel Corner, at the junction of the Menin Road with the St. Jean-Zillebeke road, the road became rugged and the trees shattered and branchless betokening much strafing. The enemy in the Ypres salient had the cross roads well marked and it was the petty hobby of his artilleryman to belabour these parts. These were the spots where we held our breath as we hurried along. If held up—the time was carefully gauged, and as soon as a shell had exploded, we rushed forward and out of danger, before the next one came over. Fritz, however, was not always so thoughtful and at times our men were caught by a follow on. At last we reached Zillebeke and the new dump. Headquarters had removed from the rear of the firing line and established itself in the basement of a ruined house. The place where we used to dump the rations went up in the air a few days ago and with it went a pile of ammunition. As we were not expected we had to wait quite a while until arrangements were made regarding the disposal of the rations. While there stretcher after stretcher on wheels passed along the road to the dressing station demonstrating what slaughter was going on. We ascertained that in the last 24 hours our

[11] Fraser notes that although reinforcements are coming to the 31st Battalion, and although the "old originals" of the unit become scarcer owing to casualties, there are still many of the "old originals" who are now officers and N.C.Os. These hold "the reins of government" or command in the battalion.

Company had 18 casualties, reducing its usefulness to 62. A heavy came through the parapet and killed Dad Allen, chewing up almost his whole side. C. A. Owen, one of the draft, was another to receive his quietus. Sgt. Downie was wounded in the legs. Sgt. Clements was slightly wounded for the second time. Sgt. Graham severely wounded, rushed past, hurrying to get out. His arm was completely smashed, was amputated later. He was one of a number whose duties did not require his presence in the line, but owing to the weakness of the battalion, and the strenuous time expected, all details were collected and sent up the line. Cpl. Lilywhite received wounds in the face, losing the sight of an eye. Davenport, likewise, received it in the face. L/Cpl. Jull, Cpl. Foley and Cpl. Green are other wounded non-coms. Hardy Salter and D. Robertson were also casualties. E. C. Godfrey was severely wounded, while Geordie Evans, of my platoon, who was transferred to the Machine-Gun Section, was killed. Being a genial little fellow he was sadly missed. Others on the casualty list were Kilford, Harris, Macdonald, Larson, Ross, Christie, Beattie, etc., some of them being only slightly wounded. A considerable number were fortunate after their recovery in being able to stay in England on staff work.

Sgt. Beaton, late of the Transport, was killed on his second trip to the line.

At night when the fight quietened down a bit, the dead were buried in the vicinity of the trench. A grave was dug and one of our dead was put into it, but it was too small and he was pulled out again. Some more digging and the process was repeated until finally the dimensions were made. The work was dangerous and the diggers anxious to complete their work in the shortest time and with the least labour, hence the gruesome job of fitting the grave to the corpse.

The casualties created in the battalion for its participation in the Canadian Battle of Ypres were estimated at 217, made up as follows: 150 for the first trip and 67 for the second.

1st Trip

	K	W	M	Total
A Coy.	9	47	1	57
B Coy.	3	16	1	20
C Coy.	4	18	—	22
D Coy.	16	35	—	51
	32	116	2	150

	K	W	M	Total
A Coy.	4	14	—	18
B Coy.	7	14	—	21
C Coy.	5	19	—	24
D Coy.	—	4	—	4
	16	51	—	67

We had a good seven mile walk back to the transport lines and started at a brisk pace. At Ypres I fell behind with the intention of catching a returning wagon. Luckily I managed to jump on an artillery limber, but had great difficulty sticking on. The horses galloped and the limber danced merrily along. A riderless horse from the direction of the line flew past us.

Wednesday, June 14-20, 1916

Our men were relieved tonight and arrived in Ypres about midnight where they will be quartered for 24 hours. They were in a wretched state when they reached billets, being covered with mud up to the thighs. Several had trench feet in its early stages. We have just received word that Armstrong, a new man, has died from wounds. So far Heiny had inflicted severe punishment on our Corps besides capturing valuable ground. He quickly dug in without much molestation. Knowing the temper of British troops it was natural for him to expect counter attacks. Our hastily arranged and feeble assaults of the 3rd came to naught. The situation was too critical to be allowed to remain. The salient, at all times a purgatory, was rendered more so by the latest menace.

Plans for recapture were accordingly laid with studied care. Aircraft, the eyes of the service, was to be the advisor; artillery, the backbone of the army, was to have the major say, and the infantry were to be the moppers up. There was to be no hurry, indeed, hurry was useless, for Heiny had already entrenched himself, having built no less than eight communication trenches and a strong support line.

The first thing was to mass artillery behind the line. The neighbouring batteries were borrowed while reserve guns volunteered. I wonder how many Canadians are aware that in no small degree they owe their success to the surplus British artillery that supported them

159

in their chief engagements. The Somme, Vimy, and many other battles saw the men of the R.F.A. and R.G.A.[12] pounding the way for us to victory.

If any country should be grateful for honours that have gone to them it is the United States. During their short term of fighting and the few engagements they have been in, they have depended to a great degree on allied artillery and aircraft. These branches of the service are very much slower[13] to train than the infantry. Without that allied backing, their success would have been negligible.

When the sky cleared our airmen were up surveying the landscape, photographing the hostile line, and trying to locate artillery and machine-gun emplacements. In addition they were notifying our gunners regarding the range, who, firing at intervals to allay suspicion, became silent when they found their targets.

The artillery being satisfied, all was in readiness. The infantry received their orders, though not as explicit as Vimy and other engagements they were sufficient, for the country to be taken was of no great depth and was known to a number of the troops taking part.

While our Division was in the line, the 1st Division was in the rear preparing for the assault. They relieved us on the nights of the 11th-12th. On the night of the 12th the German trenches were subjected to a tremendous bombardment, which was repeated at intervals. Belgian Field Artillery assisted in the operations and Tommie seemed to get it into his head that the shells that fell short were from the Belgian Batteries. Whether by wrong report or otherwise, he was suspicious of their gunners and blamed all shorts on them. At 1:30 a.m. the barrage lifted and the 3rd Battalion went over in drenching weather penetrating Armagh Wood and regaining Mt. Sorrel. The 16th Battalion in the centre, to escape the counter artillery, crept out of the firing line, and took up their jumping off positions in an old unmarked trench about one hundred yards forward. At zero hour they were off and shortly afterwards they signalled by throwing up red flares that the objective was obtained. The 13th, which had been shelled considerably before mounting the parapet, met with more opposition —from machine-gun fire, but it ultimately surmounted the obstacles and swept forward. The new German line was carried and a second heave lifted the troops into the old British trenches. Demonstrations were made on the flanks so as to keep down machine-gun fire and they proved successful. Smoke from over 200 bombs screened the ad-

---

[12] R.F.A.—Royal Field Artillery; R.G.A.—Royal Garrison Artillery. In brief, Fraser praises the gunners manning the field, medium and heavy guns.

[13] Fraser really means that it takes *longer* to train airmen and gunners than it does to train infantrymen. The greater the skills, the longer the training period required.

vancing infantry. 150 prisoners belonging to the 119th, 120th, 125th and 127th Wurttemberg Regiments were captured, and in addition nine machine-guns. The total operation cost the Canadians about 7,000 men. The net result was severe losses on both sides, with the Hun in possession of the ruins of Hooge. Once again we let go a small strip of ground which the Imperials had contested bitterly. On June 16th, 1915, the veteran Imperial 3rd Division, always in the van, took the Hooge Sector. A section was lost on the following July 30 by a brigade of the 14th Light Infantry Division, but was subsequently regained by the 6th Division on August 9th.

Judging by results, therefore, the British Tommies had good cause to grouch because we did not hold the ground turned over to us and it ill befits those patriots to talk so loosely and loudly about the Canadians never losing a trench. The Canadian soldier is well content to rest on his just laurels, without untruths being brought in, for the sake of placing him on a higher plane than other soldiers. These methods should be left to others who have more need to bolster up their war record.

Thursday, June 15, 1916

I arrived back at Camp at 5:30 this morning and a few hours later left for "H" Camp, Reninghelst, passing three graves near a shrine. The battalion should leave Ypres tonight.

Friday, June 16, 1916

At Reninghelst once more. Passed en route on the mud road a solitary cross. The battalion received a fresh draft today, our company getting six. They belong to the 45th Battalion.

Tuesday, June 20, 1916

Near the R.E. Dump, beyond Ouderdom passed a solitary grave, not far from it, near a farm (on the north), four graves were seen. The grave seen a few days ago was that of a soldier, named Thomson, of the Royal Scots. He was killed in March 1915. We have received another draft of eleven men, but are still much below strength. I left tonight for Voormezeele with rations, our Company being stationed at Convent Lane. The front here is quiet. Machine-guns are, however, very busy. It is rather dangerous and one has to stalk around the ruined buildings as the main street is swept by machine-gun fire very regularly. Quite a number of bullets strike the road at the entrance to the village. The cross on Jimmie Miller's grave which is situated between Elzenwale Trench and the main street has a rifle bullet through it. We came home a new way, via Cafe Belge and debouching on the Ouderdom-Vlameringhe Road, near Vlameringhe, arriving back about 2:30 a.m.

Wednesday, June 21, 1916

We have shifted our transport lines once more. This time we are back to "A" Camp or as it is now known, "Micmac Camp." Our Company has moved to Scottish Wood so we went there with rations tonight. We managed to get a lift going back so got home in good time. Since our trip to Hooge, Dickebusch has received considerable shelling, the buildings evidencing this fact.

Thursday, June 22, 1916

The weather since the last few days has been sunny and warm, though at nights it is cold. Today we witnessed another air duel and saw one of the planes fall. After an exchange of shots, one of them, whether British or German I could not say, like a huge bird began to fall, turning over and over before crashing to earth. It must have dropped somewhere between the Ypres-Poperinghe Road and Brielen or Elverdinghe. I am rather of the opinion that it was a British monoplane.

The big gun, a 12-inch, at the side of the Ouderdom Road, hidden in a camouflaged house, began to talk this afternoon. The first shot gave us all a start. It was impossible to keep one's eyes off the gun for one had to be braced up and ready for the report, otherwise his nerves would suffer considerably. The Belgian women in the house adjoining had to get out, the vibration loosening the plaster off the ceiling and walls. After firing about twenty rounds, much to our relief it stopped. We watched the shells leave the gun. Although weighing 750 lbs., they shot up towards the heavens almost perpendicular and appeared from behind like cricket balls. The trajectory was a fearful curve, and the shells were soon lost to view in the clouds, when they were still in their upward course. It was almost unbelievable that a shell standing about three feet in height, and weighing almost five times the average weight of a man, could be hurled into the skies out of sight only to drop in hostile territory several miles away.

It was rather amusing, as soon as the first shell was fired, a small dog bolted out of a nearby house and flew down the road terror-stricken towards Ouderdom, followed by its owner, a woman, who was calling it but it was deaf to all entreaties, judging by its desperate hurry to put kilometers between it and the gun, I was doubtful if it will ever return again.

During one of its brief firing spells an aged Belgian couple was passing in the vicinity of the gun when it went off, and it was pitiful to see the woman totter and stagger for several yards, due to sheer shock and fright, before she could compose herself. An experience of this description is enough to kill anyone suffering from a weak heart.

Saturday, June 24, 1916

Up last night with rations. Weddell, a younger brother of our Sergeant Shoemaker was killed by machine-gun fire when out on fatigue. He had only been transferred to our battalion from the C.M.R.s two days previously and had not yet been in the firing line with us.

An aeroplane dropped a bomb over our lines near Dickebusch yesterday afternoon. The 20th Battalion pulled out for the Bluff.

There was a considerable bombardment on the left tonight, somewhere between Ypres and Boesinghe, but it did not last long. Later in the evening it started down the line in the region of Armentières.

Monday, June 26, 1916

This afternoon the rumblings of a bombardment could be heard in the south pretty far down the line.

The casualties of the battalion are reported to be over 700 up to date.

Wednesday, June 28, 1916

It was fearfully wet going up with rations last night; a regular deluge came down and we were soaked to the skin. I heard this morning that our airmen went over the German lines and destroyed three of their observation balloons.

Thursday, June 29, 1916

The battalion came out of the line tonight. There was quite a bombardment in the early morning and an alarm of gas was sent out.

The big gun beside us demolished a chateau behind the German lines the other day. One of the gun crew informed me that its effective range was seven miles. It took part in the Hooge bombardment when our lines were regained.

Saturday, July 1, 1916

Today, Dominion Day, is our gala day. We were reviewed by Maj.-Gen. Turner, commanding the 2nd Division and by Maj.-Gen. [*sic*] Byng's Chief of Staff.[14] In the afternoon we had sports, the 27th and 29th Battalions taking premier honours. The chief item on the programme was the tug-of-war and the huskies from Vancouver won.[15]

Further down the line, however, in the vicinity of the Somme, there was more serious work, for today ushered in the Somme offensive, in which over twenty divisions took part, or more than six times the number of Canada's troops. This may be termed the beginning of the British offensive, which ultimately culminated in victory.

Previous to this we felt we were fighting with our backs to the wall, on account of lack of artillery support, and all we could do was to hold our own on the defensive, but from the first of July onward, we were Heiny's masters, and could wage war on even terms. In fact when we saw the way our artillery was pounding his lines we congratulated ourselves on being on this side of No Man's Land.

Sunday, July 2, 1916

Our transport lines are shifted from MicMac Camp to near the Windmill above Reninghelst. The brigade appears very hard up for reinforcements, and to increase its fighting strength is taking details it would not dream of before. If this is more than temporary it will be a mistake to run a third division. Our Company is very much under strength. A lot of crocks have been sent to us from the base.

Monday, July 3, 1916

The enemy dropped bombs in our vicinity early this morning.

[14] Here Fraser is referring to the commander of the Canadian Corps, Lt.-Gen. the Hon. Sir J. H. G. Byng, later Governor General of Canada. Byng's Chief of Staff at this time was Brigadier P. P. de B. Radcliffe.

[15] "The huskies from Vancouver" Fraser refers to were "Tobin's Tigers," the 29th Battalion, which was part of the 6th Brigade.

CHAPTER VI

The Somme Offensive

[During the past several months Fraser has been working for the Quartermaster, engaged primarily in bringing rations and supplies up to a point close to the front line where they would be picked up by men and carried by them for distribution in the front and support trenches. Although not in the front line himself, Fraser was rarely if ever out of range of the enemy's artillery, and frequently within range of German medium machine-gun fire. He would be in constant touch with men from his company and with those from other companies as well. When they came out of the line for a rest Fraser would be able to catch up with the news, and even when delivering the rations each night he was able to find out what was going on in the trenches from his comrades.

Aside from saying that he was tired of being a "packer," there is no indication why he decided to rejoin his platoon and go back into the routine of trench life. He takes this step just before the Battle of Somme, one of the bloodiest periods of fighting during the entire war on the Western Front. As usual his keen eye for detail captures life in the trenches as experienced by thousands of Canadian soldiers who were there.]

Tuesday, July 4, 1916

I have tired of my job of "packer" and have returned to the Company to engage in more serious work once again. As the evening shadows fell we quietly move out of Reninghelst along the road to Dickebusch, and onwards over the Ypres-Lille Road, and up by the left of the

165

banks, which we hug closely, as bullets come skimming over the brim, not many inches above our heads. On our right are many dug-outs and funk holes,[1] carved into the side of the bank among brushwood, with their human inmates busy stalking in and out, bent on some business or other. As usual the dumps are much in evidence, and one anticipates having to make midnight trips to them for material and hopes within his heart that the line is not far away, for long distance fatigues are a source of much annoyance and anxiety, especially when one has a perpetual longing for sleep and more sleep, and knows that such cannot be obtained until fatigue duty is over. Gradually the battalion separates. My platoon starts on an upward climb over rugged surface, interspersed with small trees and brushwood. The enemy is very active with machine-gun fire, which sweeps the ground ahead of us. The sharp, staccato sound tells us that he is not far away. We crouch as soon as firing commences, and feel confused as to whereabouts the bullets are striking. There is always an amazed, lost feeling when one goes into a line he is unfamiliar with, and especially when he is hustled by fire. We are up and on again, in a hurry; nearing the crest another burst of machine-gun fire comes tearing about us, which sends us down on our hands in an instant. Feeling this is a hot spot we are not anxious to tarry, so up we rush as soon as firing ceases, and cutting to the left, proceed down a pathway, where we breathe a little easier, slowing up until we are all in close single file again. Turning to the right, a short distance further on, we enter the communication trench, and pursue our way through the scarred remnants of a wood, dropping off the platoon cooks who take up their abode a short distance up a trench on the right, in a semi-covered enclosure of tree trunks, etc., more representative of a location for a private still than for anything else. The rest of us gradually fade away into surface dug-outs and funk holes, in ones, twos and threes, in the communication trench, support and front lines shifting places later on, as each section is called upon to relieve each other in the more forward positions. It took us about four hours steady plugging to reach the line from Reninghelst. Our Company took over T32 and T32 supports from the 18th Battalion, while the 28th Battalion partnered us on the north. Geordie Doull and I tumbled into a dug-out on the left side of the communication trench and promptly tried to sleep, huddled up in an area hardly big enough for a good sized dog.

The trenches were in good shape and there were plenty dug-outs of a kind. The front and support lines were abominably evil smelling. At

---

[1] Generally speaking, a dug-out was a shaft going down to an underground shell-proof shelter; a funk hole was similar to a slit-trench, in brief a hole dug in the ground or in the side of a trench capable of holding one or two men.

the back of the support line on the right was a morass of stagnant, stinking water and the ground was rotten with filth and semi-buried dead, while the front line, especially the near rear, was about as bad. There was much evidence of the fight that took place last February, when the enemy captured the International Trench, but were driven back a few weeks later. In the counter-attack, the British entrenched themselves in a new line about fifty yards ahead of the International Trench, which received its name on account of it having changed hands so often. The International Trench was almost levelled to the ground. In parts it appeared to have been blown in on the German occupants. The ground in the vicinity was pitted with shell holes, betokening much strife, while graves in ones and twos dotted the landscape. The crosses were, however, almost rotten, and the inscriptions scarcely legible. It is one place the Graves Commission should visit, if they want to keep the graves from being lost sight of. At the back of the front line, within two yards of a dug-out, was a wooden cross with the inscription thereon: "James Young, 1st Gordon Highlanders, Mar. 3/16, killed in action." The Gordons, as usual, seem to be in every fight that is happening, and their slain always appear in the van. Another Gordon, Glen Dey by name, is buried in the parapet of "Lover's Lane"[2] the communication trench between the front and support lines. G. Dunne, a third Gordon Highlander, is interred at the bottom of "The Drive." Behind a sentry post, near the southern end of the support line, were a couple of crosses in memory of L/Cpl. Etheridge and Pte. Deverall of the 13th Canadian Battalion. Behind the supports were numerous graves. One contained the bodies of 18 soldiers. Several had the familiar notice "Unknown British Soldier" buried here.

Wednesday, July 5, 1916

With several more [we] have moved up to the supports line about 80 yards from Lover's Lane. It is [a] fairly good trench, especially near the north end, and it is well manned, but further south it is rotten and stinking, and is held by a smaller garrison. Close to my position was a Stokes gun, the crew of which, Imperials I think, were fairly active throwing bombs over. I figured they were taking great risks, for Heiny could hardly have missed observing their fire; the enemy sent over a number of whiz-bangs, several coming fairly close, but still Heiny could not quieten them. However, we did not relish being in so close proximity to the gun, for in trying to shell it, we ran the risk of being

---

[2] Another of the numerous names given to a trench, especially to one that has been in place and occupied for some time.

shelled also. The firing line is roughly about 150 yards in front of the supports. Word came down to us that two of our men ahead were wounded early this morning. Rowbottom got it at Listening Post, and Brisson received it from a small hand bomb which the enemy flung into the bay, in which he was doing guard.

Towards evening S.M. [Sergeant-Major] Lawson came along the supports and in an anxious manner ordered me to the firing line to take up the post where Brisson was wounded. He also ordered another man for a similar duty. I followed him along the supports, then turned into Lover's Lane, glancing around trying to take in the lay of the trenches. Soon we struck the firing line and turned to the right. The trench was fairly deep, but it was so tortuous that it seemed nothing but a mass of corners. The Sgt.-Maj. pushed ahead very hurriedly and never spoke a word. As we only met a single sentry about every fourth or fifth bay, and not the usual three men to a bay, I began to think the matter rather strange. Wondering if this was really the firing line I started plying questions, but obtained no response, which made me suspicious. Dropping the other man at a bay the two of us went forward through what appeared to me a deserted line. At last we halted, then the Sgt.-Maj. spoke for the first time, and in rapid succession said: This is your post—you won't be relieved until 8:00 in the morning—there is nobody with you—watch yourself. Brisson was bombed here—keep a sharp look out, Heiny is only 40 yards away—the line is held by a few sentries and is believed to be mined. Then, before I had time to say a word, he about turned and shot round a traverse and was gone. For the moment I was nonplussed and scratching my head muttered to myself this is a fine pickle to be in. Trench mined—Fritzie only a hop, step and leap away—the line held by a few sentries—we are sacrifice men. Huh! Huh! Well, this is blamed cool. After getting over the shock of being stuck here for a whole night with the Hun over the way your nearest neighbour, I began to figure it was about time I got acquainted. It was now dark and later developed into inky darkness. I moved along the trench to the left and after passing several bays came across my next door comrade. He seemed to be just about as lost as I was. I spoke a few words and then went to see who was on my right. There happened to be a bay or two nearer. Going back to my post which was in a very forward bay, I peered over the bags and saw the Hun parapet looming up high in front of me and most uncomfortably close. There was no wire to speak of—only a few jumbled pieces of old rusted material lying here and there. As I was glancing down the left a shot struck the parapet just below where I was looking over. If caution counted for anything, I knew Fritz would not catch me giving him an

168

easy mark to hit. I always prided myself on being pretty canny in this respect. At once I saw how futile it was to keep watch by looking over the bags. It was so dark that a patrol could crawl over into your trench a few yards to the right and left and get around into your bay from behind. On account of this I took up a position in the trench itself, at a corner of a traverse, from where I could see on the skyline any object coming over the parapet several bays on either side. Collecting several bombs, and our line here was full of them, they were lying around in all nooks and crevices in the parapet and parados, I took up my lonely vigil for the night. The time passed uneventful; a few shells came over, and bombs burst a fair distance away on either side, while rifle and machine-gun fire played around a bit, but there was nothing disturbing except the rats, who every now and then would bring me up with a jerk and make me doubly alert. In the morning I was relieved and retired to supports for a good old trench sleep.

Three weeks later the trench I had left went up in the air, but by this time, our battalion was relieved and we were holding the line a few miles south. The sufferers were the 7th Battalion and their casualties numbered about 50.

Thursday, July 6, 1916

We were advised that a bombardment and an attack was coming off on our left by a battalion of the 1st Division. At the appointed time our guns opened up with shells of all calibres; soon Fritz sent up red rockets followed a while later by green ones. Flarelights were kept going up all the time. Unfortunately the attack proved a fiasco and we had our [work] cut out to quieten Fritz's artillery, which responded in force shortly afterwards. The following day the enemy tried to attack us but he came off about as successful as ourselves. No sooner did our attack die down than bombing attacks started on our right.

Friday, July 7, 1916

Lt. Richards, formerly Sgt.-Maj.,[3] was killed, shot through the head. The day is very hot and noxious smells abound. I had a look over the ground to find traces of German occupancy. Found coils of enemy barbed wire, German bombs, spades, etc. Parts of the Hun trenches remaining have small sandbags, made of various materials, resem-

[3] During the first part of 1916, the 31st Battalion had a constant stream of non-commissioned officers and men being promoted to commissioned ranks. Some go to an officers' training school for one or two months, others are literally "commissioned in the field" and assume their rank and responsibilities immediately. The rate of casualties among officers was very high.

bling small flour bags. I came across one of their dug-outs, all concrete. Going up the International Trench in the early morning, on my hands and knees for most of the way I noticed that every few yards there were facing the supports, iron plates with peep and firing holes, which the enemy used to obviate the necessity of shooting over the parapets. I came across a German overcoat; further along encountered the bodies of a couple of Huns in an advanced state of decomposition and nearing Lover's Lane came upon part of the kilt of a Gordon Highlander caught on some barbed wire.

Sunday, July 9, 1916

Today Doull, Dearden and self are on duty at the extreme south of the supports, where it adjoins the communication trench, and in closest touch with the firing line. Fritz was shelling one of our other Company's supports, their line being several yards to the right rear of us. The shells, fired from the direction of Hill 60, were passing directly over our post, bursting about 250 yards further on. They came over, a single at a time, every few minutes and we got so used to them that we ceased paying any attention. Scarcely had Jack Macartney and Plummer joined our little bunch when a report from the Hun gun instinctively told us that the shell was going to fall short, and we immediately scattered, Plummer running up the communication trench towards the firing line, Jack Macartney proceeding north along the supports, while Doull and Dearden flung themselves into a dug-out close at hand, both sticking in the entrance, and the last thing I saw was their nether regions showing on the outside. I rounded the end of a two foot wall of sandbags and threw myself flat on the ground. I was scarcely down when a 4.3 [shell] passed over me by a matter of inches and exploded not two yards away throwing all sorts of debris sky high. The explosion, besides deafening me for a while, about knocked me out and I felt as if I was burst asunder. The question surged through my mind, am I killed, but clods of earth coming down on my back and shoulders, soon brought me to my senses, and I braced myself for something worse. A sudden burning nip behind the left ear made me put up my hand to my head where I found a small trickle of blood. I was stung by a tiny piece of shrapnel which for a few minutes burnt into me like a hot wire. Thinking that the shell had exploded about fifteen yards away, I was amazed to see the hole right at the junction of the trenches, almost below my feet. One glance showed I was saved by the force of the explosion going forward. It blew out a big chunk of the parapet of the communication trench and threw about a dozen picks and spades several yards away, while the

170

little wall of sandbags I was hiding behind, was riddled with scrap iron. Doull, Dearden and Macartney, wonderful to relate, miraculously escaped with slight wounds on the back, arm and leg respectively. Macartney managed to put a fair distance between him and the shell when it exploded. Plummer escaped altogether. A mess tin, which was lying on the top of the dug-out into which Doull and Dearden scrambled, had a big hole through it, and my overcoat which lay beside it was cut in three places by small pieces of the shell. It was a wonderful escape. The rest of the fellows thought we were done for, but we quickly reassured them by skedaddling along the supports in their direction and stuck there until we considered Heiny's fire had blown over, when we repaired to our post again, but with our ears cocked for further trouble. The post was originally a machine-gun emplacement, but had been put out of commission some time ago by explosives.

In the evening while we were on duty a fatigue party belonging to the 18th Battalion filed up past us evidently intent on patching up the trenches, laying a cable or performing similar work. A few yards from our post we noticed in the shadows several figures moving in the open, and a moment or two later, a faint cry told the tragic tale that someone was hit. Shortly afterwards the party retired. Asking what occurred, I was told that one of their members was struck by a stray bullet and had passed away a few minutes before. It was the old, old story—killed on fatigue. On many occasions more excitement was created during a fatigue than when participating in actual fighting.

Monday, July 10, 1916

We are up to the firing line again, this time at the extreme right of our line. It is more a bombing post than anything else. Andy, Buttress, Plummer, Kelly and self look after a couple of posts. One of the dug-outs had about six inches in depth of rotten, mouldy sandbags, which I started to throw out. The sandbags created such a stench that we considered it would have been better if we left them where they lay. We were certain some human remains must have been mixed up in the soil.

As soon as the day began to break I went along to the adjoining bay on the left and was surprised to see the sentry, a new man, Martin, sitting on the firing step, with his head thrown back, his mouth open and sleeping—dead to the world. Imagine a sentry in the firing line asleep—and the enemy less than seventy yards away. An "Old School" Army Major would have almost sprung a fit to see such dereliction of duty but the fellow was a youngster. Although most

171

youngsters are active, better conditioned and the best sort of men to employ in any rush work, I noticed they could not stand the long, steady plugging on scanty food and indifferent weather that those between 28 and 40 were capable of. They also seemed to require more sleep than the older men.

The enemy appeared to have had a crack regiment of riflemen opposed to us. It was rumoured that they were the Jagers.[4] Right along this front they had "shooting plates" in the parapet. A small peep hole to look through and a hole through which to fire. The latter was closed by a shutter when not in use. We were informed that their shooting was deadly, and later we found that the periscope we were using was the only one that was untouched by their fire. Being very cautious we moved the periscope very gradually upwards between the sandbags, allowing hardly more than an inch above the parapet, just sufficient to see and no more. Old Heiny was cracking away through his iron plates at the periscopes to the left, but ours, which was much nearer, escaped detection. I spent quite a time examining his line and noted some suspicious looking holes at the base of his parapet. I could see the rifles sticking out of the firing holes a few inches. Presently a thumping noise was heard and when I looked in the direction from which it came, a big yellow coloured mallet was seen above the parapet every time it was raised and fell on a post that was evidently being driven in, in the trench. To my amazement the top of a Heiny's head appeared, and with every blow he unconsciously straightened himself out bit by bit until his whole head came into view. He was wearing the usual Heiny bonnet with a thin white band around it. I was furious to fire, the target was so easy, but my better judgment said, "No," remember these snipers behind the plates; show yourself above the parapet for a second and you're a goner. It was exasperating. If we had only shooting plates in our parapet, what a snap. This was one of the phases of battle in which Heiny had the advantage over us.

It was about this time that a certain officer belonging to the 50th Battalion was drafted to us. While I was looking through the periscope he suddenly appeared behind me, coming from the right. I had never seen him before and was surprised to hear a would-be American cowboy's blustering voice vehemently informing me that the —— Germans had chased him along the trench with bombs and shells and just as he poured this torrent of exaggeration and invective into my ears, a faint noise of gunfire was heard, and he immediately beat it further along the trench. This man was without exception the

4 Jager—a rifleman or sharpshooter.

windiest and biggest funk of an officer I ever came across. A few months put the kibosh on him. Going into the Somme he accidentally (without much emphasis on the accidentally) slipped and was supposed to have strained his ankle. He backed out of it and another officer had to take his place and was killed. This officer was the object of contempt by every man in the Company. It is needless to state the firing line saw him no more. He became another of the useless, expensive parasites living on the Treasury of the country, without giving five cents adequate fighting service in return.

Tuesday, July 11, 1916

Just when daylight was setting in, word was passed along the trench that Lovell, who was on guard a few bays on my left was killed. When talking to Sgt. Barrons, a flarelight was sent up, and he jumped on the firing step to look over, when a bullet came across catching him in the head, splashing his brains on the parados and sending him reeling on the top of the sergeant, stone dead. He had been firing pretty steadily throughout the night from the same spot, and it happened Fritz had noticed his fire, with the result that each engaged in a duel, shooting at each other's gun flashes, with the above ending. Poor Lovell was taken out and interred at Reninghelst. He was one of those who, on account of family connection, could have obtained a commission without much trouble and led an easier military life, but he preferred to be one of the boys and serve in a simpler way. A couple of the fellows at our post were indulging in the same practice, but when they learned of Lovell's fate, they became more cautious. One of them, who was feeling rather active, thought he would bore a small hole through the parapet and then try his hand at sniping. The rest of us were not in favour of this, for we were sure Fritz would observe fresh ground on the other side. He, however, persisted and made a mess of things by making the hole too big. Seeing this, he left it. To blind observation, I stuck a spade over the place. At this time Sgt. Barrons came along, and seeing me rather interested eyeing the Hun line through the periscope, asked me what was I seeing. I told him I was watching a Fritzie, opening the shutter of the iron plate, thrusting his rifle through and shooting at something to the left of us. He wanted to see, so I handed him the periscope and told him where to look. It was most amusing, after watching for a minute or two, he said, "Here he is, he is pointing his rifle through the hole"; and the next second—bang, and a rifle bullet went through our periscope, but luckily below the glass. The Sgt. never suspected that the Hun was going to aim for him. Just as we stood together thinking over the matter, the spade which

173

covered the hole (the Sgt. was not aware of this hole) was sent dancing on to the trench mat. Fritz had fired into the hole. The Sgt., figuring our bay was uncanny, shoved the periscope into my hand, and promptly went along the trench the same way he came in, no doubt wondering if he stuck around longer what else would happen.

Shortly after this the Colonel and Medical Officer came along the trench. When I saw them it at once flashed across my mind, what if Fritzie shoots through the hole when they pass. I at once beckoned them to get down, intending that they pass the spot in a crouching position so that if a shot was fired it would go over their heads. They, however, appeared to think there was something desperate about and with anxious, puzzled and half-scared looks, hurried past me without murmuring a word. I will never forget the expression of bewilderment and fear on their faces, and I bet they wondered for a long time afterwards what the whole matter was about.

Lt. Campbell, who was [the] officer of the Scouts, attached to our Company, was killed in No Man's Land by a rifle bullet. The casualties for the battalion for the trip were 25, five killed and twenty wounded. The sergeant of the machine-gunners was wounded by shrapnel for the second time. On the whole our spell was quiet. Still we had to be on the alert as fishtail bombs, rifle grenades and "sausages" were sent over frequently, while snipers were showing much activity.

Saturday, July 15, 1916

Along with Cpl. Woods, L.Cpl. Recknall and Austin, all three killed two months later on the Somme, I went on pass to Poperinghe. We were, however, held up on the outside of the town owing to hostile shelling. We were informed that there were two hundred casualties in the town yesterday, and eighty the day before. At the side of the road were two dead horses. We visited the Old Military Cemetery and saw the graves of Lt.-Cols. Hart MacHarg and Boyle of the 7th and 10th Battalions. Most of the crosses showed peculiar inscriptions and probably were the graves of French Colonials, who suffered severely by gas in the second battle of Ypres.

Being forbidden to enter the town we retraced our steps to Reninghelst and then to Ouderdom. Quite a number of troops were leaving the town for safer billets.

Tuesday, July 18, 1916

Several days ago we received reinforcements from the 56th Battalion,[5] 54 being the quota for our Company. This number altered the complexion of our unit considerably. A number of our 31st fellows were hardened cases, and no inducements could prevail to make them accept promotion. Though promised full Corporalship, they refused to stir from the ranks, with the result that a number of the newcomers retained their rank of Sergeants and Corporals and several of the old timers were detailed to act as guides and teachers when they made their first few trips to the line. The new rankers felt rather shaky trusting themselves to green non-commissioned officers, and gave vent to expression that they should be led by those who had experience of the line.

We were out on fatigue tonight digging a trench for a cable. The line marked out for this work lay along the northside of a hedge, then over the Dickebusch-Ypres Road, near the Windmill, and onwards in a slanting direction, towards the road running from near Vijverhoek to Elzenwalle. We string out, each having about six feet of a trench to dig and the same in depth. Quickly we buckle to our work, for the sooner it is finished, the quicker we will be back to our billets. Our motley crowd of labourers, farmers, artisans, storekeepers, office men, etc. wire into the job in hand as if they were life long navvies. It was fairly bright when operations started. Once we had to cease work when a Heiny plane, high up, passed overhead. Apparently we were unseen for the hostile artillery left us severely alone.

Wednesday, July 19, 1916

The village of Dickebusch was shelled today and several were killed and wounded.

Thursday, July 20, 1916

On the road once more bound for a further spell of fatigue. Near the windmill on the Ouderdom-Hallebast Road we take a short cut across the fields for the southeastern end of Dickebusch. Lt. Foster, who was in charge of our platoon, formerly Q.M.S.[6] for "B" Coy., received a sudden shock on entering his duties as a commissioned officer, and doubtless for the moment, wished he was attending to

---

[5] The 56th Battalion was raised in Calgary, Alberta. It provided reinforcements for other units in the corps and was absorbed by the 9th Battalion, C.E.F.

[6] Q.M.S.—Quartermaster Sergeant.

175

rations again. It was bright when we crossed through the fields, and as an enemy "sausage" balloon[7] was up, we were evidently observed, for when we were on the point of stepping on to the Dickebusch Road, a dull report from the line promptly told us a shell was coming our way, and the next moment it exploded fair and square on the road, at the corner, not thirty yards away. We took cover on the other side of the road in a ditch expecting every second to hear a salvo come thundering down on the top of us. As a few minutes passed and nothing happened, up we got and hurried past the line of fire.

The trench we are to dig is a continuation of the one we were digging the other evening. The line marked out runs up towards Scottish Wood. It had been raining and parts of the ground were very wet. Taking my cue from the lay of the land and composition of the ground, I took care to pick a nice easy part to dig, where the soil was soft and dry. Quite a long time was taken over the job. A few of the fellows were unlucky, being up against stony ground or they struck water. We had several laughs at their expense, though they had the satisfaction of holding us up until the work was completed. Cable laying is usually done quickly, a whole battalion being on the job at one time. The trench has to be filled in and smoothed over, so that hostile vermin will not be able to discover what has occurred. This is the only way to maintain proper communication. Wires laid along the surface are not much use, for in a scrap, they are soon destroyed by shellfire.

Friday, July 21, 1916

This afternoon we left for a camp near La Clytte, where a number of Imperial troops are stationed—Devons, Durhams and Northumberland Fusiliers. It is a fairly good camp with Y.M.C.A. Baths, etc. Apparently we had made a mistake for a few hours later we hike for the M & N trenches. We are, however, used to rambling around Belgium taking the longest routes, all for nothing, much to the amusement of the Belgian people. Two of our cooks were wounded near Hallebast Corner. So many roads converge here that it is an ideal spot to shell, and Fritzie sends over an occasional burst so as to keep us moving. From here we work our way up towards Vierstraat, in a slightly brushy country, turn to the left, then after going several hundred yards, take a sharp turn to the right and head for Brasserie, where we loiter around for a time. There was the usual hubbub of

---

[7] An observation balloon which resembled a sausage. Both sides used them to observe activity on the other side of the front and to direct and correct artillery fire. They were a favourite target for aircraft.

176

transports and carriers each in a hurry to complete his work and get back to his quarters. Occasionally an anxious enquirer would ask for some platoon or company and curse because he could not find it. Carriers would rush to each limber hoping to recognize their transport. It was in this melee that we reached La Brasserie. To the ordinary infantryman, who is never informed of anything, but has to content himself with the bald intimation of "stay here" while the sergeant or a similar personage goes away, on what mission sometimes it is puzzling to know, perhaps to a comfortable billet for a quiet talk and a drink of rum in the offing, but the platoon, when it has to hang around near cross corners, in the shadows of shelled buildings, within gun range, always fidgets to get going on, and meditates on the inefficiency of the service. At last some one says "move on" and soon we are in to the communication trench, after passing on our left erections to blind observation. A number of bullets were swishing around in this part. Presently the trench zigzags through a wood, where dim lights from dug-outs cast a gleam here and there, creating a weird-like effect. Being one of a small party who stayed behind to carry in rations, we go quietly along the trench, which at first seemed puzzling on account of so many trenches branching off, but by questioning a sentry or passers-by, we find we are on the right track and continue on our way. When a shell crashed into the wood on our right it was thought we may be due for a bad time in getting in. The trench became very narrow and at this point we met a unit coming out and had to stand for about half an hour in various parts to let them pass. It was a tight squeeze and there were many humorous remarks when it required a struggle to pass. Near the firing line a well placed shell landed in the trench blowing out both sides and leaving it exposed. Striking the line, which was built on a slight slope, we turn to the right and move along to our positions, passing first one of our Companies and then our right half. Seeing someone lying dead on a stretcher at the side of the trench, I enquired of the nearest sentry, "who got it" and was told Dean Douglas. He was killed a few minutes before by a rifle bullet. The news did not surprise me for Douglas was an active man with his rifle, ever on the lookout to get a pot at something, and this class of man usually gets it sooner or later. We are, however, familiar with death and the transition into the next world of one of our number is merely a phase in our existence.

Saturday, July 22, 1916

The trench we are occupying is in good shape and there are plenty of dug-outs. Shell fire has not troubled it much but it is beginning to crumble with age and the dug-outs are rather musty. The bays are regular and the field of fire good. There are a few shooting plates; this innovation our men welcome. There was one, at the back of which one could be comfortable—and there was overhead cover. Cpl. Hunter, who was an enthusiastic soldier, and at the termination of hostilities commanded the Company, was busy trying to rig up a sniper's post; but as little encouragement was given to any form of individual aggression, and work requiring much labour did not appeal to us, scanty fare and still scantier sleep not being conducive to an over-supply of energy, he ceased operations as no backing was given him.

We were pleased to find in the dug-outs tins of jam and an odd tin of butter, left by the Imperials whom we relieved.

Early in the morning Giles, one of our latest draft, had a couple of fingers broken; while resting his hand on the parapet a bullet came along and got them. In the afternoon the enemy were busy flinging over "rum jars" and "minnies" interspersed with whiz-bangs, we retaliating with shell fire and Stokes [mortar bomb]. On our right in No Man's Land was a crater, which Fritz was said to occupy at night. Andy Dearden claimed to have dropped a couple of Huns while they were leaving the crater at daybreak. Imperial sappers were hard at work tunnelling under the German lines beside us. A series of mines were being laid from Hill 60 to near Kemmel and were ultimately blown when Messines Ridge was taken in June 1917.

To the casual observer our line appeared very weak. One communication trench served for a longer stretch of front than is customary. We had no immediate support line. Behind was a flat expanse which ran back to a grove of trees. Between 100 and 200 yards in front was the enemy line. The slope being in his favour it would take a minimum of time to sweep down on us. To all appearances our men would have been trapped if anything savouring a formidable attack was engineered.

Having a telescope, I took up a position behind a firing plate and spent many hours waiting patiently for the Hun, but he appeared to be asleep for not a soul would venture to expose himself even for a moment. I watched keenly for the opening of the shutter on a shooting plate on my left flank, the telescope showing up clearly every little detail on the enemy parapet, but nothing moved. Towards evening, to try out my rifle, I aimed at the shutter and struck it with a ringing note. A Fritz, standing about a couple of yards away, must have been peeved, for a few moments later the barrel of a rifle was shoved up above the parapet and a shot fired wildly into the air.

178

Sunday, July 23, 1916

We spent a very quiet time in the trenches. Cpl. Matthews of the Scouts was wounded. Don McLeod, who transferred to the Stokes Gun, was severely wounded, and I heard died later in Blighty. It was reported that a curious mix-up resulted in his burial. We had two Donald Macleods in the Company, the other Macleod being a native of one of the islands of Uist in the Outer Hebrides. His body was forwarded to this out-of-the-way island for internment in the local churchyard and advice sent to his supposed relations. The body arrived, but apparently the relatives had recent word from Donald Macleod No. 2 and so refused to take charge of the remains. The lid was unscrewed and the mistake found out. After lying around for about a week "Big Don" was lulled to sleep in the island within roar of the mighty Atlantic. Though he spent practically all his life time in Canada, his birth place was the island of Lewis, so his final resting place was fitting for a scion of the race of Torquil.

Wakelyn, a new man, received slight injury. Jack McCartney, when going out, was sniped at in the exposed part of the communication trench; the bullet hitting his bayonet, and glancing off, grazed him. Later on in the war he had a bullet trace a nasty wound across his head, one of the closest shaves from death it was possible to experience. Strange things, however, have happened in this war, and every battalion can point to two or three men, who seemed to be bullet proof.

I saw several graves, almost covered over, at the back of our trench. Two were in memory of soldiers of the Royal Scots, killed last January, a Strathcona's Horseman killed the previous November, and a German soldier who died last May. Some joker, almost certainly a Cockney, had erected a cross and inserted on it—"To a dud."

Sunday, July 30, 1916

Another draft arrived today, some being former casualties.

Tuesday, August 1, 1916

Early this morning we reach St. Eloi trenches, "A" Coy. going into the "Switch." I was in charge of an advance party, having under much compulsion blossomed out into the much abused position of "Lance Jack."[8] On arrival I was buttonholed by a similar individual,

---

[8] "Lance Jack"—Lance Corporal, the most junior rank among non-commissioned officers.

179

with a sheet of paper in duplicate, on which was written an inventory of trench stores, comprising gas alarms, small arms ammunition, bombs, spades, etc., the location of which I had to familiarize myself with, and if satisfied with the correctness of figures, sign. Notwithstanding that the object of our mission is scrapping with the incidentals thereto, there still was carried out some semblance of business when taking over and leaving positions.

Behind our lines were four crosses with the familiar inscriptions "Unknown British heroes buried here." The 20th Battalion, whom we relieved, attended to the graves passing word on to us to look after them likewise. Wonderful to relate the 20th were reported to have had a quiet time, only 1 killed and 1 wounded. The "Switch" branches off the communication trench to the south and extended over the St. Eloi-Voormezeele Road. The southern end, on account of paucity of dug-outs, was thinly manned! A few hundred yards in front of us was Bus House Trench, a support line, and a similar distance beyond that the firing line of the infamous memory. I was informed that one of the 20th had a narrow escape, a bullet passing through his helmet and grazing his scalp. Machine-gun fire is active at night and as the enemy are firing low our men have to be careful at certain spots, especially near the road beside the Gas Alarm post.

Wednesday, August 2, 1916

Word has reached us that Sgt.-Maj. Coulson of "C" Coy. has been killed. In the early morning he observed a couple of the enemy, dropping one. In the evening, along with a Corporal, he sallied out into No Man's Land to locate his victim. Coming back they came upon a patrol of five men. On challenging them they opened fire. A short skirmish took place, revolvers being fired and bombs thrown, and the Sgt.-Maj. received a bullet in the head during the scuffle. The enemy retired.

There were four other casualties during "C" Coy.'s two days' spell.

Thursday, August 3, 1916

Today we relieved "C" Company in the front line. So far, things have been quiet, but both the enemy and ourselves are very much on the alert, the tension being quite acute at times. The memory of previous attacks is very green in our minds, and as the trenches are much smashed about, with little or no parados, coupled with the fact that we have quite a number of new men in our ranks, who appear eerie over the business, a peculiar sense of expectancy pervades the air. One of our new sergeants, Sgt. Moore, became quite anxious when darkness set in. In a constant fidget he kept stealing along the trench from bay to bay, enquiring in quiet tones if everything was all right and always hastening back to a point in the trench connecting with [the] Listening Post. As I had a wandering commission, most of my time was spent moving from bay to bay along the Company front, and I was continually being challenged by the sgt. who, in whispers, would mutter quickly, "Who's there, who's there, who's there?" He seemed to be deadly serious from his attitude one would almost imagine that Heinie was stealing under our wire. Sneaking along in the inky darkness he came round a bend in the line, where I was on the parapet gazing at the skyline in Fritz's direction and listening hard. This aroused his curiousity and he eagerly enquired if anything was the matter. Answering that Heinie had not sent up any flarelights for quite a time, he suggested that a flarelight be sent up. Having the pistol I said, "Here you are!" But he replied, "Fire it yourself." I was going to do this when he became quite excited and asked me to move to some other bay and fire it from there. He appeared to take the army and the enemy very seriously. Six weeks later his life's mission was ended. Fritzie got him on the Somme.

The ground in front of our line is pitted with shell holes and craters. Our trench is ragged, narrow in parts, and on the point of collapse. A considerable portion is absolutely useless for firing purposes. Dugouts are few and of no consequence.

However, our men are pretty well strung out so there is no crowding. One of our officers is a recent arrival, a Calgary man, well up in years and formerly a major of a draft battalion. He came to us in the capacity of platoon officer. It showed a good spirit on the old chap's part but poor fellow he was palpably useless in the line and seemed sadly out of place. Seeing him scrambling backways out of a dug-out and trying to maneouvre along the trench was painful; he appeared all in, a tottering old man. His place was the barrack square, with its attendant ceremonies—not with the firing line. This trip practically finished him, for a short time later I heard he obtained a job of Town Major or billeting officer. He, however, is one of those army diehards for when hostilities were concluded, he next appears as Commanding Officer of a Mounted Unit back in Canada. In this capacity he will loom up large in front of his men, but in war, how small, how feeble, how pitiful he seemed to be. Strange when realities are encountered how very, very often, the man who feels strong and reliant is the common soldier.

The Scout Officer, Lt. Sara, was severely wounded today, a bullet smashing his jaw and cheek bones; the following day it was reported that he had died. Dunlop, one of our Scouts, was wounded early this morning when out on patrol in No Man's Land. He received a bullet in the foot. As daylight was setting in, Benwell observed a couple of Huns and on taking aim was shot dead by a sniper. This happened on my left in Trench 18. The Company is looking after the firing line from the top of the communication trench at 14, and north to 19.

While looking through the firing hole of an iron plate near where new Shelly Lane debouched on the firing line, just when the first glimmer of daylight began to appear, I noticed something about 200 yards in front of me move. It was a Hun cautiously raising his head above the parapet. He was extremely careful, raising his head gradually inch by inch, and then peering over a corner of the parapet. Looking from side to side he slowly lowered his head again. There was no mistaking the fact that he was a good sentry and knew how to handle himself. I was somewhat puzzled to know what he was wearing on his head. It was a Trench helmet, but up to this time I had never seen one, nor even heard that they were being used. He came up several times for a few moments and I was raking my wits about how to stalk him. It was impossible to see him with the naked eye, and as there were no distinctive landmarks on either side, I could not get a direct line on the exact spot. If I did, I knew it might be possible, if I concentrated hard enough, to detect his movements. As he was looking mostly to right front I had a good idea that this was the Hun that shot Benwell. It was extremely interesting watching how warily he moved. He was in no hurry, yet he was keen to get a snipe at one of us. Little did he know that he was being watched. Every time I got a glimpse of him through the telescope, I tried the moment afterwards to locate him with the naked eye, for if I managed this the shooting would be dead easy. The fates, however, were kind to him, for he did not show himself again, much to my annoyance, as the light was improving. However, I made up my mind that I would be around the spot again within twenty-four hours.

One of the Machine-Gun Section was killed this morning. Yesterday afternoon Fritz did considerable shelling and sent several shells into "Voozmezeele Switch." One of them struck the edge of our cook's dug-out and exploded in the slough nearby sending up a column of rotten stagnant water and slime. One of the cook's equipment was badly torn and the bayonet was bent almost double. A 4.3 [shell] failed to go off. Artillery men took it to bits for inspection. I observed through the telescope Germans passing to and fro in the rear of their front line trench. They were wearing blue uniforms. Owing to the fading light they could not be made out by the naked eye and so could not be fired at. A little excitement was caused among our new men, a sentry claiming a Fritz was trying to shoot him from the rear of our trenches.

McKay, who was reported missing after the Hooge-Zillebeke fighting, has been found. It appears he must have got out of the sap and fought with the infantry. His body was found in a shell hole in Sanctuary Wood with several dead Germans around him. Sgt. Hunter received a few of his belongings, his ring and lucky charm, which he used to boast of, the latter a pebble with a hole through it.

The 27th Battalion pulled off a raid last night. About 30 of them went over No Man's Land and got into the enemy trench unobserved. They came across a working party. After bombing them they retired with two prisoners, one wounded who was carried by the Scout Officer. Unfortunately Fritz sent over some parting bombs, killing the unwounded prisoner, further wounding the injured man, and wounding the officer in three places.

The supply of bombs being exhausted, our men retired. Our casualties were fifteen wounded. The enemy was supposed to have had fifty casualties. This is the version of a couple of 27th men who connect with our support line. Another version is that we found Fritz alert and too strong so had to retire.

Going in to the firing line tonight by way of R6 we passed some of "D" Company coming out. A wounded man, I think it was Swift, was being dressed in Shelly Lane Trench. He received a rifle bullet in the arm. Further up a dead man, a draft from the 45th Battalion, was being taken down for burial. He was sewn in a blanket and slung to a pole, two of his comrades carrying him out.

Monday, August 7, 1916

Was on duty in the firing line in trenches 17, 18 and 19 behind the craters where most of our men got cut up at the St. Eloi scrap. Nothing of much importance happened. Fritz was quiet but on the alert. He had working parties out in front of his line. The scouts of the 29th Battalion noticed them and sent word back. A bombing party, headed by an officer who obtained a Lewis machine-gun, sallied into No Man's Land and drove them in. A few hours later, one of our listening posts came in with the news that a German wiring party was out and moving towards the left. Along with another fellow, we notified the machine-gun men on our right and left and they dispersed them.

In the morning, just as it was turning daylight, I moved along to the iron plate in the parapet to the point where I saw the Heinie sniper a few days ago on the expectation of sending him into eternity. Getting out the telescope I peeped through the firing hole and sure enough in a few minutes he made his appearance above the sandbags and fired several shots. As before, he moved his head upwards very slowly, looked to the right and left and then lowered his head gradually. His rifle lay on the parapet. Now and then he would pick it up as if he saw something. With considerable difficulty I was at last able to distinguish his movements with the naked eye, and a feeling of exhilaration came over me as I now felt he was within my grasp. Knowing his position to a nicety, I got my rifle ready, thrust it into the firing hole and tried to align it, but found the plate was at such an angle that it was useless for firing purposes. It was most galling for I felt it was impossible to miss. I then noticed, on account of the firing hole being small, the plate has practically to be embedded upright in the parapet to enable you to sight your object. It was most aggravating to see the Hun and yet not being able to fire with safety.

There has been considerable artillery fire by our gunners this morning, attention being largely centered on the area around the craters and enemy wire.

Tuesday, August 8, 1916

A few days ago, when down in the "Switch," near Voormezeele, the N.C.Os. of the Company were gathered together by Major Splane, in a hollow in front of the trench, beside the road to discuss the question of a raid on the enemy line. At this time, the Somme offensive was in full swing and the British command was anxious to know what effect their drive was having on the enemy. To stem the onslaught the Germans were stripping their lines and sending the troops to the Somme area, replacing the vacated sectors with the worn-out and sorely betried battalions which had been bearing the British attack. Interesting and valuable information could be obtained from such men as to the German morale and also what havoc was being executed on their lines and to what extent they were being pushed to hold their front. Raids were therefore being carried out at this time against various parts of the German line and the major explained that the sole idea of the raid was to obtain prisoners for information purposes. He was enthusiastic over the matter and thought if "A"

Company could carry it out without assistance from the rest of the battalion it would redound to their credit. No plan had been formulated but he mentioned we would have the co-operation of the artillery. The idea was well received and we felt a sense of pride surging through us as we pictured ourselves the bloody participants of the fray. On parting we set our wits agoing as to what would be the best course to pursue to achieve our object. Success at the expense of a minimum of risk appeared to be the cardinal point to work on. I expected the most feasible scheme would be to throw out a few small parties into No Man's Land at dusk each taking care of a certain frontage and lie in wait for a hostile patrol. If this was too slow a proposition, as there was no guarantee that Fritzie would risk his skin out in front of his line while we were in this part, then the alternative seemed to be that our Scouts should ascertain the easiest course to his trench, and by stealth we would take him by surprise, rushing back with the necessary prisoners. This plan would entail a considerable amount of luck and dexterity to be pulled off successfully. Any other scheme with a limited number of men appeared hopeless and suicidal.

The matter was gripping and interesting and I was thirsting for news. Any scheme that afforded us a fighting chance made me desirous of being counted in on it. Little information could be gathered as to how the raid was to be carried out, and a certain indefiniteness and lukewarmness developed as none of the officers appeared to be taking an active interest in the matter. Sgt. Hunter came along the trench where I happened to be taking things easy, and enquired if I would volunteer for the job, to which a reply was given in the affirmative, provided the scheme proposed carried hopes of success. From him I learned for the first time how the raid was to be carried out. I was badly disappointed when he mentioned that the artillery would be employed to break up the enemy wire and make the pathway easier for our men. The idea flashed through my mind that making use of the artillery meant advertising the raid to the enemy and allowing him to prepare plans to counter it. If that was the final plan I intimated that I declined to participate in it as it spelt absolute failure. Geordie Doull was apparently of the same mind and declined more bluntly prefacing him remarks with, "You know, Pat, I'm not scairt." Buttress of our Section volunteered without asking any questions, and when I talked over the matter with him he had a novel and original reason for volunteering. He knew our Company would be in the front line when the raid was pulled off and after it was over the raiders would retire to Headquarters and possibly the transport lines. Having been through the St. Eloi scrap and knowing

185

that Fritz had our line well registered, he said our trenches would be subjected to particular H--l after the raid was over, consequently he reasoned he was taking the lesser risk if he volunteered. Little Sgt. Torrens probably exemplified the best soldier spirit, though possibly lacking in business acumen, when he dramatically said he would take part in any raid originated by the Company.

Tonight was set for the raid. Being engaged in the southern part of our front, I asked the Sgt.-Maj. to let me shift to the north end, from where the raid was to take place. There were about thirty raiders, including Capt. Jewett of another Company, who was a last minute entrant. They were armed to the teeth with bombs, revolvers and knobkerries. Their faces were blackened, badges removed and all correspondence left behind. A considerable amount of banter was indulged in as they lay in the trench, big MacNair being particularly jubilant. (Towards the end of the war MacNair, a 6 ft. 2 ins. Highlander, was killed in a raid, reported to be shot by one of our conscripts, when returning to our lines.)

A wire was connected up with the artillery in No Man's Land, the signallers having a buzzer with them. There was the right, left and middle party, with the scouts, signallers and machine-gunners ranging across No Man's Land. As zero approached we shook hands all around and the raiders silently climbed over the parapet and crouching stole softly into the darkness on their desperate mission to the Hun. I stood on the firing step for a few moments until the blackness swallowed them up, then ran south along the trench to a bay where it was arranged the prisoners would be rushed to by Sgt. Hunter. Expecting that he would be pretty well exhausted, I was to grab them at this point and rush them along the front line and down the communication trench to Headquarters.

A round of two by four[9] was let out over No Man's Land to assist the raiding party to find their back. The route taken was by crater 7 and 6 to crater 5. Everything was quiet as the raiders stalked into the darkness and as I stood on the firing step waiting to hear the report of bombs, showing that they were in contact with the Hun, I began to wonder what was the matter, they had ample time to reach their objective, surely something was holding them up. Presently the darkness was lit up as bang, bang went some bombs, and a little distance away further explosions took place a few moments later. In a

[9] In the butt of the infantryman's rifle there was a place where he kept a small brass bottle of oil, a pull-through and a "two-by-four," a piece of cloth measuring two by four inches, used to oil the rifle barrel. Fraser's "round of two by four" refers to a reel of this cloth which, light gray in colour, would assist the raiders to find their way back in the dark through the barbed wire.

trice Heiny shot up his flarelights along two or three hundred yards of his front and I could see several of our men scurrying back, bent double. It was seen at once that the raid was a fiasco. A moment later our men came tumbling into the trench. Lambert coming into my bay in great state, holding his shoulder from which blood was streaming and apparently in great pain. A hurry call was made for stretchers, for it was quickly seen a number were wounded. Word was passed along the line enquiring if they were all in. Buttress and Holmes seemed to be uncertainties. Dearden was practically riddled with scrap. He was in a bad way for a long time, but ultimately recovered and was returned to Canada for discharge, being too badly disabled for further service. Andy was one of the stalwarts of our company and a first class line man. Buttress was another who got badly injured and succumed later. It was believed he could have pulled through but the strain of the campaign marked its effect on him long before the raid and he was not physically the man he once was. Frank was the "Adonis" of the platoon, six feet with thick, curly, black hair, quiet and uncomplaining, a very pleasant comrade. In his genial moments he used to hum "Sunny Alberta for Mine" but he was destined never to see Sunny Alberta again.

Apparently, when about twenty yards from the enemy wire, a German sentry called out according to the interpreter, "Here they are, about twenty of them." A second later and seven or eight bombs were thrown in our midst. Immediately our men returned post haste only to receive a few moments later a couple more bombs from further to the left to speed them on their way. Fritz was prepared and waiting for the raid. He had men out in front of his wire. Luckily the raid was not persisted in. About sixteen out of the thirty were wounded, including Taylor, the interpreter, Capt. Jewett, Lambert, Dearden, Buttress, Worsley, Rumford, MacNair, Parsons, Holmes, French, Burton, Bowles, and Burley.

Fritz took the raid quite quietly. He threw up a considerable number of flarelights, but indulged in no shooting or artillery fire and the rest of the night passed uneventful. There is absolutely no doubt but that the preliminary artillery fire gave the cue to what was to follow with ignominious failure for us. From "Bus House Trench," I observed through my telescope several Fritzes passing through a gap in the parapet of their front line. They were big fellows and were wearing bluish gray uniforms. One of our snipers was keeping an eye on this gap and claimed he had shot three of them.

Thursday, August 10, 1916

A party from the 28th Battalion raided the enemy tonight, obtaining one prisoner, a sentry, catching them napping. The officer in charge of the party, Lt. Williams, was wounded.

Saturday, August 12, 1916

It was reported that the enemy made a gas attack on the last night of our previous trip in, in the vicinity of the trenches to the left of Ypres in a part of the line held by Imperial troops. It is understood between 600 and 700 were gassed, including a working party of about 100 men who were caught unawares a considerable distance away from their gas helmets.

The enemy have been getting working parties of late. A report reached us that a hostile machine-gun obtained forty of our men with one sweep.

We are bound for Voormezeele today, relieving "C" Company, for a four days spell.

There is a considerable aerial activity tonight. In the afternoon "Big Lizzie" sent over several rounds.

Much valuable information is being obtained from prisoners captured during recent raids. Our command now know who are their opponents, where the enemy billets are, what mining is going on, etc. Confirmation is being obtained from photographs taken from aeroplanes. To extract information from the prisoners the common mode is to have a fluent German talker dressed in a German uniform, mingle with them. He overhears their conversation and with this knowledge can question shrewdly.

Monday, August 14, 1916

There was quite a bombardment for a short spell, during the early morning and afternoon today, the enemy opening up in the morning and we in the afternoon. The King [and] Sir Douglas Haig were reported to be in the neighbourhood and the firing was for their benefit. Our artillery in Scottish Wood certainly rattled the stuff out.

Tuesday, August 15, 1916

We were relieved tonight by the 25th Battalion, and arrived in Reninghelst shortly after midnight. This was our best spell so far, no casualties and very few fatigues.

I heard the 27th Battalion made another raid, disguising themselves this time with grass coverings. They were more fortunate than before, obtaining one prisoner who showed much fight. One of our men was wounded while the invaded trench suffered severely.

There have been many rumours regarding the result of the gas attack on our north some time ago. It is claimed that the enemy used a new and more deadly gas. The victims were reported to be part of the 29th Division, who were cut up badly at the Somme a month previous and recently sent to the Ypres front.

Friday, August 18, 1916

General Sir Sam Hughes along with General Turner reviewed the 6th Brigade in a field between Reninghelst and Ouderdom. As usual with inspections our command was all worked up. I never saw so much excitement and hullabaloo as took place several days previous to the review. We were continually being pulled out of our billets to go through all sorts of parade drill as if this was the chief mission of our lives and war of secondary importance. Officers, [and the] R.S.M. and C.S.M.'s, were jumping about and Orderly Room giving out confusing instructions; one day it was pack dress, another day it was skeleton order, ultimately it became drill order. We were subjected to no end of button polishing and inspections, twice daily, until we were heartily sick of the whole affair, and felt disgusted that so much attention was being bestowed on things of little account when a plethora of real work was to be done in the firing line. There is no mistaking the fact the business end of military life does not appeal very strongly to the barrack-room class of officer; on the parade ground he is in his element and as far as he is concerned it is there that all battles are won. Right turn and left turn are a delight to him, forming fours and "on the left form platoon" send him into ecstasy.

We marched on to the review ground, a huge field on the north-west side of the Reninghelst-Ouderdom Road and quickly fell into our respective positions. The General, when passing my section, enquired who the men were on our left front. When informed that they were the machine-gunners—"Worth their weight in gold" was the reply. On being told to close up, with officers in front, he addressed the assembly, turning first of all to the officer at his side and enquired what Brigade this was, to the merriment of those in front, who overheard him.

The address was very disappointing. He seemed to lack all knowledge of the brigade's activities and achievements and when he concluded, Major Daly of "D" Company broke into cheers with so much exuberance that when General Hughes stepped down, he went straight over to him and shook his hand first. It was significant to note that the Major got the Colonelcy of the 27th Battalion shortly afterwards.

Sunday, August 20, 1916

We left Reninghelst early this morning for France[10] for the purpose of undergoing training for offensive work which we conjecture will be in the Somme region. After a few miles marching the battalion enters France, passing through L'Abelle then on to Steenvorde. Passing through Steenvorde we proceed south for a mile or two, then double back on a parallel road, and camp for the night at a farm a few hundred yards from Steenvorde. Apparently somebody had a vague idea of the location of our billets, when we had to take such a circuitous route to reach it.

Monday, August 21, 1916

Next morning saw us on the move again. The march took us through Steenvorde, Oxelaire, Bavinchove, Noodpeene, to Bollezeele, where we halted and camped in farm buildings. A considerable stretch of country was covered and a number fell out by the way, particularly on the last stretch, but they were picked up by limbers and reached Bollezeele later. The marching was pretty stiff owing to the hot weather and heavy packs. Bollezeele, although quiet, is a rather pleasant little town. The French people appear more frank and kinder than the Belgians. The country is prettier and more undulating. The roads are in good condition and the villages are cleaner and better built. Prices of articles are lower and the range greater than we have been accustomed to, possibly owing to being further away from the fighting area. I have seen several French soldiers; one young fellow, a Despatch Rider, whom I was talking to, had been wounded at Verdun and was home convalescent. It was curious seeing so many women in proportion to men. One would think all the able-bodied men had vanished, the only men to be seen being elderly, hunchbacks or cripples.

An incident occurred in our Company which caused considerable merriment. In the early hours of the morning, when the best part of the company was asleep on the floor of a barn, which served as a billet, Powell of my section rose up and in serious tones began addressing us,

[10] Reninghelst was in Belgium; the Somme, further south, was in France.

saying, "Boys, I am saved; I have been commanded to go home to my wife and children; I have had a terrible night, but I have won out." Upon hearing Powell talking in this strain, one by one of our fellows woke up and in amazement glanced over at him wondering if he had gone mad. Sgt. Barrons finally told him to lie down and go to sleep, which brought forth the rejoinder, "Sergeant, I am no longer afraid of you, I am under a higher command." Someone shouted, "You are crazy, Jack," to which Powell replied, "We'll see if I am crazy," and then began crying out, "Dr. McGill, the fellows are saying I am crazy. Am I crazy, Dr. McGill, am I crazy?" He then commenced saying, "Never mind, boys, the war will go on all the same and we will dine at the same old cook kitchen," proceeding in this strain until Jack Macartney interjected, "What about those ten francs you are owing me, Jack?" A smile flitted over Powell's face and he remarked, "Me owing you ten francs, Jack Macartney, you forget, Jack Powell died last night. I am a new man." In the morning Powell was out on the green gambolling and smiling to himself like a five year old youngster. Dr. McGill and several officers called at the billet and after watching him for some time, had him removed for further observation. He never came back to the company. Returning to Canada he soon became as rational as anyone of us. After a few weeks in the line it was noticed Powell was becoming highly sensitive and fast losing a grip of himself.

Wednesday, August 23, 1916

Wednesday was the market day and the square was full of improvised tents and stalls. Most of the articles for sale were dry goods in the shape of ginghams, prints and calicoes.

Sunday, August 27, 1916

Today divine service was held in the open in the rain near the station at Bollezeele, the whole Brigade being present together with Engineers, Red Cross and other units. The Brigadier and staff were also there.

The following poetry in honour of the 6th Brigade—27th, 28th, 29th, and 31st Battalions, is reported to have been composed on June 12, 1916 by a member of the 1st Division belonging to the 7th Battalion, Walter T. H. Cripps, on account of the strong defence put up by the 6th Brigade at the engagements of St. Eloi and Ypres, which earned it the name of "The Iron Sixth":

191

"The Iron Sixth"

Canada's 'Golden Gateway' sent forth her gallant sons,
Who proudly march with smile and song to face the German guns.
Where their duty called them 'twas there they won their fame,
And on the scroll of honour is the 27th name.

Yet farther west, and still her sons is Canada sending out.
The 28th Battalion fights with never a fear or doubt.
From the head of Lake Superior and the Province of 'Golden Wheat',
The boys are marching 'gainst the foe with never faltering feet.

B.C. has sent her quota and the 29th is there
Broad chested, stalward manhood, but just to do and dare,
Vancouver's boys are marching with steady step and true,
Determined all to 'Play the game' and see the whole thing through.

A breath from Calgary's City, flung where the fight is worst,
Still more of Canada's manhood is the gallant thirty-first.
From prairie land and city, they've answered to the call
And bravely shouldered rifle lest their Empire's honour fall.

From Winnipeg's Golden Gateway to Vancouver's rainy shore
Come Canada's men to keep the flag of the Empire to the fore,
From Kemmel down to Ypres, go when and where you will,
The "Iron Sixth" have paid their toll, and are bravely paying still.

Monday, August 28, 1916

We left this morning for another camp about three miles beyond
Watten, a railroad and Canal town. There was no town or village of
any consequence seen en route. A French sentry was on guard beside
the waterworks above Watten. Watten is a fair sized country town
and possesses a jute mill, employing several hundred women and
girls. No. 3 platoon was billeted at a farm, the N.C.O's. occupying the
byre.

Tuesday, August 29, 1916

Today, we went to our training ground, three or four miles away,
passing through Moulle. A milestone on the Calais-St. Omer Road
showed that we were 31 kilometres from the former town. The
training did not impress me. It consisted of the usual sectional drill
with a little extended order and advance work. By this time, it became
known our destination was the Somme. The major informed us that
we would have a pretty easy time as our artillery had Fritz well
in hand, pulverizing his line so completely, that the advance was

192

practically a walk-over, and the wounds were nice little Blighties. He seemed to believe this story himself, but it turned out quite different, the Major himself being one of the first to fall.

Thursday, August 31, 1916

Out again for instruction to the training ground. This time we take a different route, passing Epilecques, which possesses a quaint old church. Two of our men were accidentally shot. When orders were given to fire, some apparently had their rifles loaded. The village we are quartered at is called Ganspette. We had a pretty good time and a fair amount of leisure, enough to enable us to engage in jumping and putting the stone, with occasional rambles along the road to estaminets for beer or coffee.

Monday, September 4, 1916

We left Ganspette for St. Omer late at night, passing through Watten, and proceeding alongside the Yser Canal. At 5:00 a.m. on the fifth we entrained, being packed like sardines in a tin. Cpl. Ricknall and the writer climbed up into a sort of lookout tower on the top of the rear end of a coach and about froze therein. Candas, our train terminus, was reached on Tuesday afternoon at 3:30 p.m. Some places passed were Wimereux, Calais, Boulogne and Abbeville. The Royal Flying Corps was in strength around Candas. A couple of miles further on we halted for the night at a very poor billet (Val de maison).

Wednesday, September 6, 1916

On the road once again heading for the Somme. The Australians passed us on the way to the Ypres front with sadly depleted forces after their spell around Mouquet Farm and Pozières. The platoons looked like sections while the companies resembled platoons. Neither fronts would pass for health resorts. We exchanged humorous remarks in passing, the Australians hinting that their handful represented a Brigade. Their appearance bore out that they had undergone terrific hardships, their faces being wan, eyes weak and watery, shoulders drooping and marching irregular.

We travelled a flat prairie-like country for several miles, ultimately striking the hills. As we proceeded the booming of guns became louder and louder. Passing Vadenvourt, Herissart, we ultimately bivouacked for the night in a field overlooking Contay, sleeping on the ground with nothing but waterproof and overcoat. Expecting to be cold I dug out a grave-like oblong in the ground about seven feet long by two feet wide and two feet deep. Going to a wood adjoining I cut several branches of laurel trees. Placing my waterproof beneath me, overcoat above, pack and equipment for a pillow and pulling the branches across the trench, buried myself beneath, like the babes in the woods. Being sunk in the ground, the cold winds passed harmlessly above and I slept a little more comfortably than those lying on the top of the ground.

The booming of the guns has been incessant today.

Thursday, September 7, 1916

We were up early this morning and on the road immediately after breakfast. The sun came out strong and marching became hot and trying. Warloy-Baillon and Bouzincourt were passed on the way. The farming villages passed through are not as prosperous looking as those encountered in the mining areas. We came upon over two hundred German prisoners working on the road, guarded by "Scotties." Four or five of them sported the black and white Iron Cross ribbon. On the whole they were a miserable looking outfit though there were a few huskies among them. Nearing Albert, seventeen observation balloons were counted above the Somme salient. Outside of Albert at the Brickfields, on the east side of the road, the Brigade bivouacked, crowded into small, sloping oblong tents. I paid a visit to an overflow of the River Ancre about a mile away for the purpose of getting a wash, water being scarce in the immediate neighbourhood. Close by was a chimney stack which I started to climb to see if observation could be obtained of the German lines. After ascending about forty feet, I deemed it better to return as the going was dirty and I would resemble a sweep before I could get back. Our bivouac tonight was extremely cold and very few slept. Many more nights of this and our usefulness will be on the ebb.

Friday, September 8, 1916

Up again at a ridiculously early hour. Shelling is still going on. Fritz has sent a few over our quarters. Albert, which is not much more than a mile away, has received to date a fair amount of shelling. The crucifix on the top of the Cathedral resting on a block of stone connected by an iron bar to the remainder of the spire, is hanging over and swaying with the wind. The French claim that when it drops the war will be finished. Towards the end of the war, Albert was razed to the ground.

Saturday, September 9, 1916

I visited Albert today. It is one of the major places on the western front. Judging by the number of chimney stacks, it must have been of fair commercial importance. Identification patches were issued to the corps.[11]

Roads converge on Albert from all directions and it is served by two railroads. The buildings are crowded with troops. Scottish regiments, Irish Guards, West Indian Rifles, Indian Cavalry, and many Imperial units are quartered in the vicinity.

Sunday, September 10, 1916

Instructions have been received that we are to move today to the slaughter grounds of the Somme or, as the Germans have expressed it, the blood baths of the Somme. A cousin whom I had not seen for several years turned up in the morning, he belonged to the 16th Battalion, the Canadian Scottish. Several months after cessation of hostilities he died in Eastern Canada from the result of wounds. George Brown, an Edinburgh boy, formerly teller in the Quebec Bank, Calgary, and who enlisted at London, England, with the 16th Royal Fusiliers, also looked me up about an hour before we left the Brickfields. Within a week he was killed, information reaching me through the Edinburgh Weekly Scotsman.

It was with no regrets that we left the Brickfields, for the camping ground was windswept and towards evening bitterly cold. Leaving in platoons we soon passed over the railway and through Albert coming out on the Bapaume Road. The day was hot and we sweltered as we crept up the hilly road, bordered for the first stretch by brick buildings, until a cemetery was reached on the right, where the burial of an officer of the First Division was taking place. A little further on we passed the "Stragglers Post" where stragglers and prisoners were sorted out. At the top of the ridge quite a panorama enfolded itself. On the left could be discerned the valley through which the River Ancre flowed, and on the right small woods in the vicinity of Becourt and Tricourt broke the bareness of the landscape. The old British and German trenches could be traced up and down the ridges, by the chalkiness of their outline. Down in the dip near the junction of the

---

[11] These were small (3 inch by 2 inch) pieces of coloured cloth worn on the upper sleeve of the tunic. Each division, for example, wore a different colour. Fraser would have worn a dark blue patch surmounted by a smaller patch of similar colour. The latter (blue on blue) denoted the 6th Brigade; as the smaller patch was square rather than a circle, semi-circle or triangle, it identified the wearer as belonging to the highest numbered battalion of that brigade. There were variations of shapes, sizes and colours for the cavalry, corps troops, etc.

195

Pozières and Contalmaison Roads lay all that was left of the village of la Boisselle. Near the entrance on the right was an ammunition dump, which went skywards a few days later. We threaded our way through a regular nest of batteries on the left in la Boisselle and saw closely an enormous crater formed by the explosion of a mine under the German line on July 1st.

One was amazed at the German entrenchments in this sector. The ground was honeycombed with deep dug-outs and machine-gun emplacements, and wiring entanglements crossed and recrossed the front of their trenches. It was difficult to realize how the men of the 34th and 19th British Divisions managed to over-run and capture this line. It seemed a hotbed of trouble and must have been a hard nut to crack. It was at la Boisselle that the Somme advance really took place. Though the attack commenced north of Hébuterne, the northern army of the 7th, 8th and 10th Corps, advanced a little here and there, piled up enormous casualties and fell back on their old line. It was left to the southern army to make an impression on the German lines and it was at la Boisselle that the indent on the line started and quickly widened during the subsequent months. Trenches branched in and around the buildings at all angles, giving full scope to the enemy to hide himself and forcing our men to dig him out with bomb and bayonet, a risky job in an irregular line, where the enemy could pop out of one hole and snipe while our men were endeavouring to clean up one another. Further on, the remains of a German cemetery were seen; big, blue-gray coloured crosses, dull and depressing looking, marked the graves. All around were shell holes scarcely a yard apart. Soldiers were busy repairing the road and gun emplacements were rapidly being constructed. Cubby holes in the banks along the road were observed, obviously occupied by the advancing soldiers, who at this point had the double role of not only pushing forward but watching their left flank also. Near Contalmaison was another German stronghold, which proved, I should think, pretty stiff work to take. Scattered throughout the battlefields were many isolated graves. On the road to Contalmaison I stepped on the body of a Hun, embedded in the soil. Where the road goes down to the junction of the Contalmaison and Pozières roads, the right was fringed with several deep dug-outs. The Germans appear to be very partial to sunken roads. In fact the very first thing that appears to strike the enemy is to construct a deep dug-out, a contrast to our men who evince no desire to do so, being quite content to grovel around the surface and take chances. At this spot the Y.M.C.A. had a dug-out on the left side of the road where troops returning from the line could obtain coffee or cocoa, served out by a kiltie in various tin canisters. Further on near the remains of a wood lay the ruins of Cantalmaison, levelled to the ground, the nearest buildings showing up skeleton-like from our point of view. Turning to the left we proceed up a valley towards Pozières. On our right is seen a couple of German guns captured by the Black Watch, 1st Battalion, 1st Division, last July. The guns were old and useless looking, the dates shown thereon being 1874 and 1875. On the slopes were batteries of French 75's.[12] manned by Frenchmen who were firing when we moved forward. Further on we passed a couple of little cemeteries, also a dump containing guns and equipment. We relieved the 19th Battalion and went into reserve, the line taken over being roughly constructed in the face of a small bank ridged up a few feet and consisting of a stretch of surface dug-outs and cubby holes, with galvanized iron, old blankets and waterproof sheets for coverings. Australian overcoats and equipment littered the place. The Australians apparently did most of the fighting in this area. About eighty yards behind my dug-out was a cemetery, lately started, consisting of about forty graves, occupied mostly by Australian dead, though there were a few crosses erected to the memory of Canadians of the 1st and 4th Battalions. I counted nine dead lying around waiting for burial. A few days later the number of graves grew to one hundred and twenty.

Monday, September 11, 1916

Today a few of the Company had to go up to the front line for the purpose of getting acquainted with the trenches and obtaining information as to how the German line lay, so that there would be as little confusion as possible when the attack would be pulled off during the next few days, it being understood that these men could act as guides and mentors to their comrades. If I remember rightly, Sgt. Hunter, Cpl. Steele and myself were the chosen for this work. We had a pretty rough time getting in. We went over the open for the first three hundred yards, then entered the communication trench and zigzagged upwards. All the way up, in fact, during the short spell we spent in the line, Fritz was shelling incessantly, apparently nervous of an attack, and the men of the 29th Battalion, who were bearing the brunt of their fire, were very anxious and ill at ease in their positions, and showed animosity when seeing us crawling around, lest we should draw fire to their direction. The trenches in the vicinity were named after cities in Australia, Sydney Street, I think, being the name of the communication trench. On the way up a couple of dead Canadians

---

[12] The famous 75-mm artillery piece was an excellent field gun. It fired six rounds per minute, each shell weighing 16 pounds (shrapnel) at a range of 7,500 yards. The comparable British and Canadian Field gun was the 18-pounder.

were passed, lying on the parapet awaiting a suitable moment to be taken down for interment. Further on was seen a big, fat, fresh complexioned fellow.

Glancing here and there over the parapet could be observed the dead bodies of Germans and Australians lying in all directions, some dismembered while the ground was pocked with shell holes. Indications showed every evidence of severe fighting. The village of Pozières was completely wrecked, shelled no doubt by the British in the first instance and later by the Germans in their efforts to stem the onslaught. Pozières will be forever linked with the Australians for they were instrumental in taking it. On reaching the front line we had to crawl through a narrow, shallow, hastily dug trench, with at intervals a 29th Battalion man crouching and looking decidedly uncomfortable. After obtaining a few peeps through periscopes we returned, picking our way back gingerly, as shells were whizzing and bursting all around. Anxiety was plainly written on the faces of the sentries we passed and spoke to.

Every hour of the day a steady stream of troops were passing between la Boiselle and Pozières, bringing up rations, material and munitions. A continuous queue of wounded were being brought down to the dressing stations and the pioneers were busy burying the dead in the new cemeteries springing up. A few hundred yards away lay a wrecked British aeroplane.

Tuesday, September 12, 1916

Today we witnessed a fine though unequal aerial combat. A daring German airman was patrolling above the battle lines while several of our planes were engaged in similar work not far away. Fritz's wits, however, were not well sharpened and our airmen were out to snare him. By clever manoeuvring a British airman got within tactical distance forcing him towards our line; another flew towards him, and in a matter of moments about five planes rushed him from various directions, the first two firing and driving him towards earth. The whole lot were on top of him, circling around and around so that Fritz was hopelessly enmeshed before he knew where he was. A few seconds and a shot ignited the petrol tank, the plane falling to earth in flames, near our quarters, and the sole occupant burned to death. A rousing cheer went up from our lines when we observed it falling. Foolishness on Fritz's part and fine tactics by our airmen were responsible for enveigling him to death. It was an exciting encounter while it lasted.

Today Moore had a narrow escape when wounded by shrapnel.

A German surrendered to the 19th Battalion. He had been on the firing line since six days, the last two in a shell hole in No Man's Land. He belonged to the 216th Regiment and had been on the Messines front. A six-footer he was trembling all over apparently afraid of the reception he would get. When an officer gave him a drink of water and a cigarette, he took off his ring and presented it to him.

Wednesday, September 13, 1916

We went out tonight to dig assembly trenches for the attack. Ruff, a new man drafted from the 82nd Battalion, was killed. It was his first trip to the trenches. Sexton, who had been previously wounded, and returned to the Company, was again wounded. Austin and Sewell were slightly wounded, also Cpl. Stringer. Captain Taylor, D.S.O. of the 29th Battalion, who led the raid at Wytschaete, was killed. He was buried in the improvised cemetery behind our line.

Thursday, September 14, 1916

Cpl. Steel was badly wounded today while working on Major Splane's dug-out. He received shrapnel in the face, disfiguring him badly, and was returned to Canada. Hannah, a new man, was also placed "Hors de Combat."

A number of us were detailed to carry Stokes bombs[13] up the line to a dump for tomorrow's attack. I was in charge of a small party. A guide had been allotted to direct us to the required dump newly constructed off the front line. Scrambling along we piloted ourselves with our precious and dangerous cargo up the communications a considerable distance until the guide acknowledged that he had lost his bearings. Deciding to remain where we were until he found the route to the dump, we stuck around the trench while he went forward. Minutes passed and he did not return. The men became impatient and anxious so I decided to push on and find the dump myself, the others following. Getting up to what appeared to be the front line, and the trench becoming shallow, convinced me that we must be in the vicinity of the dump. A newly dug trench on the right a few yards further on gave me the cue and crouching I stole along about one hundred and fifty yards to the end which finished off in a circle of about ten feet in diameter. Depositing the bombs I called on the others to come along. About five followed, laid down their bombs and hurried back. Finding no more coming I retraced my steps. After proceeding thirty yards or so I came across a couple of "Stokes," a few

[13] These would be the cast iron bombs for the 3-inch Stokes trench mortar. Production of this mortar began late in 1915. It was simple to construct, weighed about 36 pounds, and was a very practical weapon for trench warfare.

yards further on came across some more, at intervals of a few yards, more were seen. At once it was obseved the back of the party had developed nerves, got rid of their bombs and fled. Gathering them up I carried them to the dump then went back for more, repeating the trip several times, until I found the distance between the dump and bombs getting greater and greater. By this time I got "fed up," hopped over the remaining bombs, turned into the main trench and beat it out of the line myself.

Word had just eked out that we are in for our third engagement: first, St. Eloi; second, Third Battle of Ypres; and now the Somme, this time not as defenders, but as aggressors primed up for the event. The announcement that at 6:20 tomorrow morning we would make a charge, co-operating with the British and French created quite a stir. Some looked upon the matter in a serious light, others were indifferent while the remainder treated the whole affair in a humorous vein. A few discussed the mode of attack, chances of success, but the knowing felt and knew that the result depended upon the artillery. Exaggerated tales had reached us that the attacks on the Somme were a series of walkovers and there was nothing for us to do but gather in the spoils. I believe most of us hearing such stories, treated the defences with, if not contempt, at least with levity.

Personally, I did not sense the full amount of danger, though I realized it quickly when I was twenty yards over the parapet. Cpl. Recknell, who partnered me in the dug-out, was not feeling in the best of form, and apparently had a grudge at being sent up the line instead of Cpl. Woods. At this time the practice was to hold back in reserve a certain number of the battalion, particularly N.C.O.'s, so that if the worst happened, the battalion would have a nucleus to fall back upon. Woods did not require to go up this trip, but apparently it would not have mattered, for Recknell was killed the following day and Woods a week later.

Tomorrow was a fitting day for the attack for it marked the first anniversary of the Second Division's entry into France. The attack was planned on a large scale. The Canadians were to go over on the north with Courcellette as the objective. Imperials, Scottish troops principally, were to take Martinpuich adjoining in the south, and still further south the French were to carry the fight in the direction of Combles. Our 4th Brigade was to attack on the right of the Bapaume Road and the 6th Brigade on the left, while the 5th Brigade was to remain in reserve. The attacking forces of the 6th Brigade were the 27th, 28th, and 31st Battalions with the 29th in Brigade reserve. It was understood that the 27th Battalion was to take the right sector, the 28th the left sector and the 31st was to act as moppers up to both battalions, though in reality the 31st, or at least certain members, did not adhere strictly to operation orders, but went ahead on their own and penetrated further than their neighbours.

The frontage covered by the brigade was roughly 1,800 yards and the objective or furthest points about a mile, involving Sugar trench, Sugar refinery and ridge. Orders called for the 27th as the first attacking wave, followed ten yards behind by 3 and 4 platoons of the 31st Battalion, i.e., as far as our immediate front was concerned. Four waves were to be employed altogether in the first attack. The objective of the left half of the Company to which I belonged was Fritz's front line. We were entrusted with the job of cleaning or mopping up the trench, killing all those who showed fight or defiance, digging out the enemy from dug-outs and passing them out as prisoners; in short, disposing of all opposition and taking complete possession of the enemy front line, manning and consolidating it in event of a counter-attack being launched.

During the afternoon an extra supply of rifle shells, in bandoliers,[14] were handed out to us together with a couple of Mills bombs. With these bandoliers and a couple of gas masks hanging from our necks together with equipment, speedy manoeuvre was practically impossible. I, therefore, was glad to turn my overcoat over to the Q.M. to be obtained back at billets, rather than carry it during the attack, notwithstanding that it may be badly required later on.

Late at night (9:30) the sergeants in quiet tones softly told us to fall in. There was not much need for preparation, as each one had been ready long beforehand. We were on a mission which required not only alert faculties, but arms and equipment in order so that one could at least get a favourable and comfortable start off. Our attitude was possibly a little more serious and quieter than usual, but the humourists were still around. It was impossible to quell them, and when all is said and done, they are the best men to have in the ranks in modern warfare. A jovial temperament seems to be an antidote to morbid thought, fear or cowardice. Cutting to the left, platoon after platoon, in single file steal across the dip to the communication trench, while all around were scores of khaki clad men apparently bent on supporting the attack. The Field Artillery had crept up closer than ever. They had not much to be afraid of for the German airmen and sausage balloons were non-existent during the battles of the Somme. The British completely dominated the air and it was a rare sight to see the "eyes" of the enemy.

---

[14] A cloth bandolier contained 60 rounds of .303 ammunition, the total weighing seven pounds. Each Mills grenade weighed a pound and a half.

201

Skirting Pozières movements up the trench was slow. The communications were badly blocked, through parties coming down. Shelling, although intermittent, in no way delayed us. At last we reached the assembly trench on the right and filed along, allowing each soldier three or four yards space. It soon began to drizzle and rain and we became cold and numb, lying in the damp trench, trying to obtain forty winks. Several of us could have done with our overcoats. To make matters worse Fritz was indulging in scattered shelling. Fortunately, the range was long though a few fell in front and nearly rocked the trench. The shelling was sufficient, however, to keep us on edge.

As we lay shivering there in the darkness, the mind had every opportunity to run riot. I believe Thiebot, a dark-skinned Channel Islander, and one of our "tough guys" who always took a great delight in taunting and scaring the "drafts" with the remarks that they would last like a "snowball in hell" when Fritz got after them, and so forth, took a very serious, religious view of things, going even so far as to say that he knew he was going to get it, and turned over personal effects to one of his comrades. His premonition turned out correct for he was dead in No Man's Land a few hours later.

Shivering to the bone, we were glad to get the news about 3:30 a.m. to move out to the front line preparatory to attack. Stretching our limbs, we moved upwards, jumpled together with other units, to near the junction of trenches, when Charlie Knight appeared on the scene from the left trench in a great state, his face covered with blood, and his hands holding his chin and neck, elbowing his way, passed us in hot haste, his eyes staring wildly out of his head. It looked as if he had been hit a moment before and had not yet realized to the full what happened.

A few yards further on we became choc-a-bloc. It was impossible to move backward or forward. The trench was a jumble of soldiers. Our wrath as usual began to rise and imprecations were showered upon those in charge. The next moment saw those in the lead climb out of the trench into the open on the left, trying to make for our jumping off position in the line. The ground was a quagmire of shell holes and one had to move rapidly to keep up with his predecessor. Fritz, nervous and apparently under the impression that we were going to pull something off, was firing wildly over No Man's Land, and the bullets whistled around as we scrambled from shell hole to shell hole. Joe Saunders who was following a few paces behind me, was shot in the abdomen. Breathing heavily, he expired a few moments later, Fardell watching over him. Poor Joe, who was a 56th man, often remarked that Heiny would never get him. His death thoroughly angered us. It looked as if word had been given to every unit to make for their positions at the same time with the resultant jam that caused us to get out in the open in the vicinity of the front line. In the end we got into the trench, moved along a bit and got stuck once more. As it was becoming light, word was finally given to back up and remain where we were, mixed with the men of the 29th Battalion. Behind the parados, in shell holes, lay a number of 4 Platoon. My own platoon, No. 3, lost several in the scramble for position.

Two or three hundred yards ahead, and slightly down a slope, Fritz's line threaded its way along our front. The ground over which the attack was to be made was an expanse of pasture land torn by incessant shell fire and dotted closely with shell holes. Of growth there was nothing to be seen excepting tree trunks alongside the road running back from the enemy trench. There was the usual formidable support line, Sugar and Candy trenches, and the Sugar Refinery stronghold, several hundred yards in the German rear.

Our artillery preparation, I understand, took place the day before and ceased during the early morning of the 15th. I cannot recollect particularly heavy gunfire, and the concentration was certainly not on Fritz's front line in our vicinity, for when we entered it, it was absolutely intact. The opposition Fritz put up also pointed out that he had been severely left alone by the artillery until the last minute.

Whatever Fritz's thoughts were, they certainly were not of jubilancy. Since July 1st, regiment after regiment of Huns had been flung in the breach to stem the ever forward march of British battalions. From week to week and in some cases, day to day, he was recoiling backwards, squelched by an avalanche of iron and ground into the mire. With desperate efforts, goaded by the Higher Command, he tried to hold on, but all in vain, and unposted letters taken from the dead and captives bitterly told the tale of despair. Their letters were full of hunger, cold and death, with upbraidings of their airmen, who as one said, were spending their time in the theatres of Lille.

It was the same repetition in each letter—the British gunners are shelling their positions and communications so persistently and methodically that they dare not move backward or forward. No food or reserves are reaching them and they are gradually being killed off. The cry was, will we ever be relieved, will we ever emerge alive? Their letters were full of pathos, hopelessness and at times bitterness at their helplessness against us. Those opposed to us, however, were allowed to remain in their trenches without much molestation since the first week of August and in consequence had their lines in fine shape and dug-outs fairly deep.

The morning was opening out into a typical autumn one, sharp and slightly cloudy. No Man's Land badly furrowed and scarred afforded fairly firm footing but the innumerable shell holes and general unevenness of the surface foretold difficulties in crossing.

As zero hour approached I glanced around looking for signs to charge. The signal came like a bolt from the blue. Right on the second the barrage opened with a roar that seemed to split the heavens. Looking along the right, about forty yards away, I caught the first glimpse of a khaki-clad figure climbing over the parapet. It was the start of the first wave, the 27th Battalion. More Winnipeg men followed. Then glancing back over the parados I saw Sgt. Teddy Torrens rise up from a shell hole and wave his platoon forward. So quick, however, were the men of the 31st on the heels of the 27th that when I turned my head, those of my platoon beside Sgt. Hunter were actually up and over the parapet with a good five to ten yards start ahead of me. In a hurry to overtake them and carry the line as even as possible, I was up and over in a trice, running into shell holes, down and up for about twenty yards, until I found that if I continued this procedure and rate, loaded up as I was, I would be exhausted before I could get to grips with Fritz.

It was at this juncture that instinct told me to avoid the shell holes and move along the edges. I raised my head for the first time and looked at the Hun trench, and to my astonishment, saw Heiny after Heiny ranging along the line, up on the firing step, blazing wildly into us, to all appearances unmolested. Seriousness and grim determination took possession of me as I stared hard and menacing at those death-dealing rifles. Strange to say they all seemed to be pointing at me, an illusion but nevertheless that is how it appeared. My eyes were for a moment glued a little ahead to the right on Sgt. Hunter, who was leading with little Lt. Newlands beside him. He appeared a picture, heroic in the extreme; his rush had dwindled to practically a walk, and he strode forward with body erect, right in the forefront, a target for innumerable shots. As I was fast levelling up on the left, it seemed a thousand miracles that he was not laid low.

My wits sharpened when it burnt deeply into me that death was in the offing. At this stage an everchanging panorama of events passed quickly before my gaze, and my mind was vividly impressed. The air was seething with shells. Immediately above, the atmosphere was cracking with a myriad of machine-gun bullets, startling and disconcerting in the extreme. Bullets from the enemy rifles were whistling and swishing around my ears in hundreds, that to this day I cannot understand how anyone could have crossed that inferno alive. As I pressed forward with eyes strained, to the extent of being half closed, I expected and almost felt being shot in the stomach. All around our men were falling, their rifles loosening from their grasp. The wounded, writhing in their agonies, struggled and toppled into shell holes for safety from rifle and machine-gun fire, though in my path the latter must have been negligible, for a slow or even quick traverse would have brought us down before we reached many yards into No Man's Land.[15] Rifle fire, however, was taking its toll, and on my front and flanks, soldier after soldier was tumbling to disablement or death, and I expected my turn every moment. The transition from life to death was terribly swift.

Halfway across the first wave seemed to melt and we were in front, heading for Fritz, who was firing wildly and frantically, and scared beyond measure as we bore down upon him. Their faces seemed peculiarly foreign to me. Their trench was full and firing strong and as the remnants of us were nearing bombing reach, we almost, as one man, dropped into shell holes, a move wisely done and swiftly executed. Further progress and it is more than likely that we would have stepped into a volley of grenades. At this time, I had the shell hole to myself and took cover behind the left front edge, which was higher than any other part of the lip, and I could see without being seen from the immediate front, the flanks to the Hun line and the left rear right back to our trench. I was hardly down, when a man around the forty mark, medium-sized, well built, with a heavy sandy moustache, of Scandinavian appearance, came up on my left and stopped not a yard away. He seemed to be nonplussed as if wondering what came over those who were ahead of him a moment ago, as it suddenly dawned upon him that he was the nearest moving soldier to Fritz. I will never forget the look of bewilderment which came over his face, but it quickly changed to puzzled thought, as if wondering what to do next, when a rifle bullet caused him to shudder as if he had received an electric shock. In a flash another must have tore into his vitals for he winced with the shock, then his eyes opened wide and a terrified look of despair and helplessness crept over his features, his eyes rolled, and with a heart-rending shriek as he realized his end had come, he fell forward flat on his face, stone dead, almost on top of me.

It all happened in a twinkling, his death practically instantaneous, but that fatal moment, the wincing, the hopeless, piteous look, were indelibly printed on my mind forever. Glancing back I saw waves of men coming on, right away back to the parapet, but they were collapsing right and left and not a single one got as far forward as the remnants of our own Company. I saw one poor fellow stretched out,

---

[15] Firing at a rate of over 300 rounds per minute, the German Spandau machine-gun, if moved from side to side on its mounting, could act like a steel scythe cutting down exposed infantry advancing over open ground.

apparently dead, with a bullet wound in the head beside the ear, with a face waxen white, and a line of blood tracing down his cheek and neck. The moment after dropping into shell holes we started sniping. The target was so easy it was impossible to miss. The Huns, not many yards ahead, were up on the firing step, blazing in panic at the advancing men behind us, seemingly with only one thought, namely to stop those moving, and in their fright and fear, forgot our little band lying close at hand. Heiny after Heiny fell back in a heap as we closed upon the triggers.

On my left at the edge of the shell hole, a few inches from my shoulder a little ground flew up, and at once I saw I was observed and that a Fritz had just missed me. Pulling in my rifle I lay quiet. Looking back not a man was moving, the attack had stopped. By this time, Cross and Judge, formerly of the 56th Battalion, had jumped into the shell hole one after the other. Fritz finding no movement across No Man's Land, turned his attention to those nearest his line. Cpl. Recknell, who was in a shell hole about ten yards away on my right and very slightly ahead, got up on his knees and stretching his head, curious to see what was happening ahead, got slung in a second by a rifle bullet, quivered, doubled up and dropped forward, killed instantaneously. He appeared to have been struck in the body. Bobby Bisset, a stocky little Scotsman, who was lying in the same shell hole, crawled up on Recknell, caught him by the shoulders, as if to speak and shake him, and immediately his head fell and he practically lay dead on the top of Charlie. The next instant, adjoining Recknell, still further to the right, another soldier was killed as he peered over the shell hole. It looked like Thiebot. Nearer still and on my right was Grewzelier. He was sniping steadily. I saw him get shot also. Just when he was on the point of firing, a bullet got him and he rolled completely round on his back, stone dead. They were killed within a few moments of each other and I think by the same Hun.

At this time a strange incident happened; a German, without arms and equipment, climbed over the parapet on my right and ran into No Man's Land, shrieking and waving his arms, apparently stark, staring mad. He ran about twenty-five yards, wheeled round in a circle several times, the circles narrowing each time, then flopped dead. It was a weird and uncanny spectacle and I was held spellbound, watching his cantrips. I do not think any of our men shot him when he was in the open. He seemed to be in his death throes when he clambered over the parapet and reeled into No Man's Land. Thrilling sights passed before my eyes, during what must have been seconds though they could easily have been construed into hours, so great was the tension, and so miraculous was it that I and a few others in this vicinity escaped destruction.

Lt. Newlands rose up a little from me and gallantly endeavoured to signal us forward by a sweep of his hand, but the time was inopportune and no one moved. He himself was hardly up, when he was wounded and fell back into the shell hole. In the adjoining shell hole, almost touching ours, Lt. Foster got up almost simultaneously with Newlands and promptly collapsed back again, having been hit in the upper arm or shoulder. Freudemacher jumped in beside him to render first aid. It seemed that Foster was painfully hit, for I could see for a minute or two, an arm waving back and forward above the shell hole, as if he was in pain.

As the attack subsided and not a soul moved in No Man's Land save the wounded twisting and moaning in their agony, it dawned upon me that the assault was a failure and now we were at the mercy of the enemy. It was suicide to venture back and our only hope lay in waiting until darkness set in and then trying to win our way back. During this period of waiting, I expected we would be deluged by bombs, shrapnel and shell fire, and when darkness set in, ravaged by machine-gun fire, altogether a hopeless outlook, especially for our lot, who were lying up against his trench. The situation seemed critical and the chances of withdrawal to safety nigh impossible. So many things had happened, so many lives were snuffed out since I left the comparative safety of our front line, that I lost completely all idea of time.

Lying low in the shell hole contemplating events with now and then a side glance at my sandy moustached comrade, lying dead beside me, his mess tin shining and scintillating on his back, a strange and curious sight appeared. Away to my left rear, a huge gray object reared itself into view, and slowly, very slowly, it crawled along like a gigantic toad, feeling its way across the shell-stricken field. It was a tank, the "Creme de Menthe,"[16] the latest invention of destruction and the first of its kind to be employed in the Great War. I watched it coming towards our direction. How painfully slow it travelled. Down and up the shell holes it clambered, a weird, ungainly monster, moving relentlessly forward. Suddenly men from the ground looked up, rose as if from the dead, and running from the flanks to behind it, followed in the rear as if to be in on the kill. The last I saw of it, it was

---

[16] The tremendous casualties caused by the combination of machine-guns, trenches and barbed wire spurred the Allies into devising some sort of machine which would overcome all three. The result was the tank. The one seen by Fraser was a Mark I. It weighed 28 tons, had a speed of about 4 m.p.h., and was equipped with either machine-guns or two 6-pounder guns. It had a dramatic effect on the battlefield.

wending its way to the Sugar Refinery. It crossed Fritz's trenches, a few yards from me, with hardly a jolt.

When first observed it gave new life and vigour to our men. Seeing away behind men getting up, and no one falling, I looked up and there met the gaze of some of my comrades in the shell holes. Instinctively I jumped up and quickly, though warily, ran to where I could see into Fritz's trench, with bayonet pointing and finger on the trigger. Running my eyes up and down his trench, ready to shoot if I saw any signs of hostility, and equally on the alert to jump out of view if I saw a rifle pointing at me, it was a tense and exciting moment but I felt marvellously fit and wits extremely acute, for any encounter. I expected opposition and was ready for danger, but a swift glance, and to my amazement, not a German was staring at me, far less being defiant. Down the trench about a hundred yards, several Huns, minus rifles and equipment, got out of their trench and were beating it back over the open, terrified at the approach of the tank. Only a moment sufficed to show that it was safer in the German trench than being up in the open, where one may be sniped, so with a leap I jumped into the trench, almost transfixing myself with [my] bayonet in the effort.

In several seconds a few more of the Company were into the trench. With two others, I proceeded south to clean up the line. Going about fifty yards without encountering any opposition, and meeting some more of our fellows, we retraced our steps and ran back forty yards or so beyond where we entered the trench when we connected up with some more of our men. There was not a single German capable of offering fight. To the south in the open, I saw Sgt. George West driving about ten prisoners towards our line. A little fellow, I forget his name, a draft to No. 4 Platoon, was busy in the open and extremely keen on his job rounding up another batch of prisoners. Further away on the flanks more Germans were seen hurrying back to our lines, apparently quite anxious to be taken captive. Finding the trench completely in our possession, we started shaking hands and telling each other who was killed and wounded. Young Hayden arrived on the scene and overhearing that his brother was killed commenced sobbing, but controlled himself when his brother suddenly appeared in our midst. The latter complained of being hurt in the eye and beat it out shortly afterwards. The danger of being shot by the front line Germans being now over, several of us set about collecting souvenirs.

I tried to cut off buttons from the coat of a dead German but it was a tough job, as I found they were wired on. I chased up and down the trench looking for Iron Crosses. Two dead Heinies had the black and white ribbons, one with black and yellow also. I went through their pockets but could not locate them, so contented myself with taking a ribbon. Later I heard the crosses were usually attached to a chain, worn round the neck. One dead Heinie, doubled up in the trench, had attached to his belt a dagger, with a fancy tassel hanging therefrom, which appealed to me. I had quite a job loosening the belt from his body. He was equipped with a revolver, which I handed to Sgt. West, who appeared on the scene at the moment. Another dead German I rifled yielded a purse containing seventeen marks in paper and currency. A further one supplied a watch of the cheap variety. I got two helmets but discarded them later. I also passed up field glasses, but changing my mind I returned to Fritz to find, however, that somebody else got there in the meantime. I also took possession of a couple of Heiny Caps, one split new, and the other with a hole through it, and saturated with blood. The heavier stuff I placed in a sandbag and the smaller and lighter stuff I carried on my person. In a dug-out was found a raft of papers, letters and postcards. Three or four of us congregated and were examining the contents, when a soldier with a couple of sandbags appeared upon the scene, said he belonged to [the] Intelligence Department, and became thoroughly delighted when he saw the capture. When I moved away he was busy stuffing his sandbags. Ten to one Headquarters would have been so much enraptured with his booty that a D.C.M.[17] would be earmarked for him. From one dead Fritz, I took a postcard. It showed his name was Wilhelm Diercks, that he belonged to the 45th Reserve Division, Reserve Infantry Regiment 21, and what appeared to be 2nd Battalion, F Company. It was posted on September 9th, 1916, and sent by his sister, Vreda; the post stamp bore the Altrahlstedt.

The first thing that struck me was that this trench was hardly touched by our bombardment. It was deeper and much better constructed than ours, and that it had several dug-outs, one or two fairly deep. The trench was scrupulously clean, not a particle of filth, tins, paper or refuse of any kind was to be seen. Contrary to information handed out to us, Fritz himself was splendidly equipped. His uniform was in good condition and nothing was lacking in the way of equipment. Nearly every fourth man had a pair of glasses, revolver or trench dagger, the latter decorated with a tassel. There was no evidence of starvation. The trench and dug-outs disclosed all sorts of supplies. Brown bread was lying around, also cylindrical tins of meat paste. Boxes of dark, cheap looking cigars were here and there in the dug-outs and seltzer water was to be obtained in plenty. I was

[17] D.C.M.—Distinguished Conduct Medal.

rather chary about tackling his eatables but I did not pass up his white Rum. It was greatly appreciated but for taste, strength or quality, it was no match for our S.R.D. [Service Rum Diluted]. We were surprised to see Fritz so comfortable and well equipped and we so ragged and often pinched in our rations. Mr. German, however, got a rude awakening. In perfect health half an hour ago, he was now wallowing in death.

When I jumped into the trench, the sight I beheld, for sheer bloodiness and murder, baffles description. Apparently our artillery had sent over a last minute shrapnel barrage, for the Huns were terribly mangled about the head and shoulders which coupled with our sniping, completely wiped out every Heiny in the bays in front of us. Everyone of them was either dead or dying and the trench literally was running blood. As each bay contained three to five men, it required no imagination to picture the carnage. In the middle of a bay, a Heinie with a dark, stiff moustache, completely doubled up, was suspended, stuck between the parapet and parados. It seemed a peculiar and strange sight to see this Hun, head and knees almost touching, blocking the trench. A few feet north, at a corner, another Hun lay in the bottom of the trench, his head and face terribly lacerated, feebly groaning to death. Every soldier practically stepped on his face when passing south along the trench. Lying around a bend he was trod on before one was aware of his presence. Several times I ran over him. He appeared to be unconscious and was gasping his last breaths. A German with ruddy face, clean shaven and intelligent looking, was lying on his back on the firing step, minus equipment, as if he had been placed there. At first I wondered what happened to him for he appeared unmarked. His feet, however, were torn to shreds. He had a pleasant countenance and looked as if he was smiling in death. It was off him that I took the Iron Cross ribbon. A typical Hun, big, fat with a double chin, was sitting on the parapet in the south corner of the bay, his stomach so protruding over his thighs that very little of the latter could be seen, stone dead, and not a mark to be seen. There was no shell hole near him, so I conjecture he must have died of fright and not concussion. In the other corner of the bay, reclining back against the parapet, lay a young German, a bullet wound in the head, his face ashen white and with a look as if he sickened to death. How deadly the sprays of metal had done their work, how effective our sniping had been, was plainly discernible. In every bay lay dead and dying Germans, lying in grotesque shapes, and some huddled on the top of each other. Most of them had fearful wounds and the whole line resembled a shambles.

The survivors of the 27th and 28th Battalions, with odds and ends

210

of the 31st, jumped over Fritz's front line, and continued their way to the objective. The last I saw of them they were on the skyline, going over the ridge, their numbers pretty well thinned out. A few patrols of the 31st penetrated to the outskirts of Courcellette.

After we reached Fritz's front line a lull developed and during this period the timid found courage to come across and the stretcher bearers got breathing space to evacuate the wounded. Ridiculous instructions were issued to dig a communication trench in the direction of the enemy, commencing from the front line, by whose order I do not know. Lts. Newlands and Foster were wounded and Major Splane and Lt. Sharples, who were with 1 and 2 Platoons, were killed, the Major, I understand, being shot within seventy-five yards of our parapet. The only officers that appeared in our vicinity were Norris and Kennedy and they were attached to other Companies. Sgt.-Maj. Lawson put in an appearance, but had not a word to say, while Sgt. Wheatley lay in Fritz's trench feeling pretty sick. Sgt. Hunter was the active and most alive head. Spades were found and soon the dirt began to fly, but it was difficult to arouse much enthusiasm for the job, knowing there was a communication trench a little to the north and doubtless another one not very far south. We tackled a stretch of about 150 yards and got down to two to three feet, when a number of bullets came whistling in our direction. Thinking Heiny had found his bearings and was coming back on us we retreated into the trench, ready for defence. It was, however, a false alarm, so we returned to the digging.

The Hun command apparently realized the extent of our attack for shortly afterwards the hostile artillery opened up on his front line, right away back to our communications and belaboured these parts for a considerable period, sending us back for the second time and compelling us to seek safety in the snuggest portions of the trench. Holding our breath as shell after shell burst in and around, Fritz ultimately ceased. A party was organized to go forward and lend assistance further on. Sgt. Hunter led the way, while I took up the rear. Proceeding up the new trench we had dug we soon stopped and laid down, one behind the other. After a few minutes, I passed up the word, "Why the delay?" information coming back to the effect that so and so, the fourth man, had failed to connect up with those in front as they emerged into the open, so he lay down, the rest following suit. On enquiring what direction they took, another fellow and self set out after them, but could see no signs of either Hunter or the other two, so retraced our steps, expecting they would return and pick us up.

A few minutes later an officer of the 27th Battalion appeared on the scene, asked me what we were doing here and cursorily ordered us up ahead to help the 27th dig in. He was as drunk as a piper. I told him who we were and showed him a copy of operation orders, drawing his attention to the fact that our duty was to man Fritz's front line after it had been mopped up. He grabbed the sheet, looked at it upside down, muttered and cursed and commanded us to go ahead. It was most amusing; while this conversation was going on, one after another of our men, overhearing what had been said, quietly slid out of the road, back to the trench. He became angry and I annoyed, so I blurted out, in any case we could not go forward until I reported back to our officer in the trench. (We had no officer in the trench). "All right," he blurted out, then threateningly he fired back at me, "see you come back." Just as I reached the trench the balance of the company was filing out, going north, Sgt. Alec McDonald bringing up the rear, carrying a Heinie dress helmet. I asked him what was the matter. He responded, "Hurry out, we are relieved." Returning I told the officer that our lot was relieved and they were passing out at the moment. "Get up there," he said, pointing towards Fritz. Being sore and disgusted as the dickens, I flashed back, "All right, show us the way." He looked around, was at a loss for an answer, and at the moment a corporal of the 27th appeared on the scene and inquired about a supply of ammunition for the men. Without a word, the officer went away with the corporal. I stood, furious, looking at them hiking back over No Man's Land, then turning to young Hayden, who stuck to me like a leech, the others using discretion got out of the road one by one, said "To H--- with him, come on, beat it," and flung my spade as far as possible, utterly fed up with the gall of this strange intoxicated officer.

We chased back to the front line. Upon proceeding south a Hun shot his head above a shell hole, but promptly dropped it again as I caught a glimpse of him. By this time, I was passing three men of the relieving battalion lounging around the bay, and pointing told them that there was a very much alive Heiny in the shell hole over there. As I passed hurrying to overtake McDonald and the party, they stood up preparing to account for their shell hole neighbour. There was no signs of our men to be seen. All the information the newcomers could give us was that they had gone out. We struck a side trench which led into a circular machine-gun emplacement in No Man's Land, when we encountered a fellow, minus equipment, lying on his back yelling and kicking up a deuce of a row. At first I thought he was badly wounded; who did it turn out to be but Mackintosh of No. 4 Platoon, helplessly full of Fritz's rum, as happy as a lark, and trying to sing for all he was worth. Kennedy, a new officer, formerly of the 66th Battalion, I think, had lost himself, so joined Hayden and self at this point. I told him that we had been relieved and were going out. He

212

seemed to be uncertain what to do and was half afraid to go out in case he might get a slating from the colonel. He mentioned that this was his first engagement and he hoped he was doing right. We retraced our steps and made a fruitless attempt to find 31st men, and we got in contact with Sewell, a runner. Satisfied that they had gone out we made up our minds to return. By this time, Fritz recommenced shelling and we crossed No Man's Land, running from shell hole to shell hole, narrowly escaping disaster several times. One shrapnel bullet hit the field dressing at the corner of my tunic as we lay in a shell hole, getting ready for a run between the bursts. A number of our dead were passed and we heard one fellow yelling a considerable distance away.

Reaching our old front line we came across some of our machine-gunners. At this point we witnessed a fine sight. About 3:30 p.m. in extended order and in the middle of a bombardment the 42nd Battalion and the Princess Pats swept across our front, angling off to the left in great style and causing us to halt for a few minutes on our way back to witness this unexpected and alluring spectacle. One would have thought that Fritz was expecting them for the shelling was very severe at the moment, and though a number were falling, they moved evenly across in unbroken waves, apparently making for the northern flank, no doubt to protect the 5th Brigade. On the right, the latter was sweeping forward irresistibly on Courcellette, enveloping it and having it safely in their possession an hour and a half later.

Going down the trench we came across [Sgt.-Maj.] Lawson and a few others taking refuge in the narrowest and most secure looking part of the communications. While here, an officer, a little, middle-aged man, badly shell shocked, his mouth quivering, like a child crying, was being led out by a private, the latter holding his hand. He was a pitiable object. It was hard to believe that he could be reduced to such a state. Asking Lawson why they were staying there, I was told that Fritz was shelling the trench lower down badly and apparently they thought it was safer to remain where they were. Leaving the officer and telling Hayden to come on and take the risk, we beat it down in a series of spurts, flopping with each shell burst, ultimately reaching a deep dug-out at Pozières, pretty well pumped out. We waited here for several minutes, picking up Stretcher-Bearer Bamforth, and finally got out of the bombardment area, after experiencing several narrow squeaks and landed down at the position we vacated on the evening of the 14th, where we met the bulk of the survivors of the assault. After obtaining something to eat, Stretcher-Bearer Bamforth and self paired off into a little unoccupied dug-out, let the gas blanket down, and slept long and sound.

We awoke in the morning, made for the cook's limber with mess tins, and to our surprise found our limber had vanished and in its place was the cook limber of another battalion. At the moment our Company was on its way out to Albert. Minus breakfast we packed up and hiked along the valley towards Contalmaison, meeting MacNair of the police, who was left to inform the stragglers of the whereabouts of the battalion. Above Contalmaison we met the Company finishing their midday meal, and tried to obtain some scraps without success. I was rested not much more than ten minutes when Sgt.-Maj. Lawson appeared asking on behalf of the colonel for four volunteers to return to No Man's Land and bring in Major Splane's body. When he reached me nobody had volunteered, and apparently had anticipated trouble, for he looked rather wistfully at me after explaining his mission. I said offhand he could put my name down if he could not scratch the number. Returning later he intimated that he had been round the Company and only got one man. I told him I was ready, and the next minute collared Simmons as he was passing and said, "Come on, you'll come with me." "Sure," he said, "what for." And he did. Later another fellow was dug up. Simmons was originally a 66th man and was killed later on in the campaign. The other two were drafts named Campbell and Graham.

Informing us that we would go out under the white flag, we kicked over this, as we had not sufficient faith to believe that Fritz would pay much attention to any flag, if he had an opportunity to kill. So in the end we went fully armed. Talbordet, who knew where Major Splane was lying, was to accompany us. At the last moment we found out that four representatives from the other companies were on a similar errend to bring in their commanding officers who were killed: Capt. Boucher of "B" Company, Capt. Pinkham of "C" Company, the name of the officer of "D" Company I do not remember. Capt. Soley, an officer lately attached to the battalion, was in charge of our strange outfits. We returned to the line by way of Pozières and saw full evidence of the wreckage of the last twenty-four hours. At the side of the road were two of our men with their arms and legs broken and almost detached, mere trunks of men, and much more ghastly looking than the general run of dead. At the other end of Pozières we went off the road into a trench on the right and worked our way south. Parts of the trench were completely wrecked; the parapets being blown down, it was impossibly to pass along without exposing yourself. At these points, Fritz was sniping and we had a deuce of a time getting along and keeping contact. The going was so hard and risky that one Company's representatives turned back and left us. Not content sniping with rifle fire, it appeared as if Fritz was trying the same with whiz-bangs for they seemed to be following us as we struggled along. The whole thing was ridiculous. How we expected to get into No Man's Land and pick up the major when we had all we could do to handle ourselves in the trench, was hard to comprehend. At last we halted beside some Red Cross men and they asked us what we were doing here. Upon being informed of our mission they mentioned that they were up on a similar errand since an hour or two and found it hopeless to show themselves above the parapet. Returning, we had the job of dodging shells for several hundred yards and passed one of the tanks stuck in the communications [trench]. Our party scattered. Near La Boiselle I got a lift from a truck to Albert, where I hiked to the Brick Fields, arriving too late for supper, so crossed over the road to the canteen a little before closing time and had a scramble to get something to eat. I emerged, however, with a big tin of fruit and a couple of packets of biscuits and ate the lot, the first bite I had since twenty-four hours.

On reaching the camp, I made steps to obtain my pack and found the Q.M. [Quartermaster] busy sorting out those belonging to casualties. My attention was aroused when I overhear the remarks, "Look what Recknell has been packing around" and saw their eyes open wide when a sixteen pound iron ball was fished out of the pack. They looked surprised and wondered what the idea was. I suddenly remembered that Malcolm Maclean, myself and a few others, found the ball on the camping ground before we left for the Somme, had several putts at it, and then for devilment shoved it into Recknell's pack.

Sunday, September 17, 1916

Today we took stock of the casualties of the battalion and found 247 were put out of action, 78 belonging to "A" Company, a rather high percentage for a few hour's offensive. 7 officers were killed, 5 wounded and 1 missing. Of the rank and file of "A" Company, 19 were listed as killed, 11 missing and 37 wounded. The missing with few exceptions may be regarded as killed, while several of the wounded succumbed later. The killed to wounded showed an abnormally high ratio.

The casualties as taken from "Orders" are as follows:

Officers of the Battalion

Killed	*Missing*	*Wounded*
Major Splane	Lt. Keys	Lt. Newlands
Capt. Boucher		Lt. Millington

Killed	Missing	Wounded
Lt. Sharples		Lt. Holden
Lt. Swayne		Lt. Foster
Lt. Pinkham		Lt. McPherson
Lt. Toole		
Lt. Conrad		

Rank & File of "A" Company

Killed	Missing (Most of whom, if not all, should be dead)	Wounded
Forshaw*	Tyler	L/Cpl. Knight*
Dyer	Band	L/Cpl. Hayden
Oates	Gruzelier*	Carter
Clearwater	Light	L/Cpl. Goss*
Turner, W. M.	Barron	Bontheron
L/Cpl. Salter, J.*	Bisset	Whitbey*
Patton	Ashton*	L/Cpl. Desmond
Cpl. Recknell*	Doheny	L. McLean
Saunders	Grawberger	P. D. Stewart
Bell (M. Gun)	Hogarth	Jose
South	S. E. Johnston	Mould
Field		Sgt. P. Hunter*
Lloyd		E. Reed
L/Cpl. Williams*		Sgt. Torrens*
Stevens		L/Cpl. Toyne*
Matheson		Chapple
Sgt. Moore		Munghem
H. L. Smith		Embury*
Thiebot*		Hannah
		Griffith, E.
		Parsons*
		Maskell*
		Bowman
		Sgt. Hutchings*
		Tambling
		J. Page
		Moreau
		Gwillim
		D. R. Grant*
		Fardell*
		Shaw
		Cpl. Donaldson*
		J. A. Maclean
		Macdowell
		G. H. Martin
		Munro
		Pattern

Those marked with an asterisk were original members of "A" Company. Both Dave Grant and Teddy Torrens died from the result of wounds; the former an Edinburgh man had an arm shattered, while the latter, a little Englishman, had his jaw about torn off. It was also reported that Shaw had died and doubtless some of the other wounded also succumbed.

Ashton, who was reported as missing, had been attached to the Pioneers. He was returning to this unit from the base, but somehow got sidetracked and landed back at the battalion with disastrous results.

Thus ended the 31st Battalion's first trip to the Somme.

The Battle of Courcellette was fought in two actions; in the morning by the 4th and 6th Brigades and in the afternoon by the 5th Brigade, supported by the 7th. The glory of taking the final objective rested with the 22nd Battalion of Quebec and the 25th Battalion of Nova Scotia.

The 15th of September 1916 will go down in the annals of Canadian history as the day on which one of our principal engagements in the Great War was fought, being overshadowed only by the Battle of Vimy on account of magnitude of the latter undertaking, and by the Second Battle of Ypres on account of the critical situation existing at the time.

This afternoon we left the bivouac near Albert and proceeded through Warloy-Baillon, Vadencourt and Contay where we remained overnight. Three German prisoners, artillery officers, passed us at the latter place.

Monday, September 18, 1916

We are on the move again. This time by way of Val de Maison, Hérissart and la Vicogne where we were billeted for the night in very poor billets.

Tuesday, September 19, 1916

Today we passed Talmas, Bonneville, Montrelets and stopped at Fieffes. We were drenched to the skin during the march. Fieffes contains a very old church dating back to the 14th century. The pulpit is dated 1682. The statuary inside is rather nice, the statue of Joan of Arc being exceptionally well done.

Wednesday, September 20, 1916

The village is a very poor one and the billet cold and miserable.

Thursday, September 21, 1916

A large draft arrived today, a number being returned casualties. Before their arrival the [Sgt.-Maj.] tried to persuade me to accept another stripe, but I am afraid the ways of the army with its irksome ceremonial, nonsensical duties that masqueraded under the cloak of discipline, and distasteful petty annoyances so soured me, that I declined as gracefully as possible. Hearing the noise of marching feet the [Sgt.-Maj.] ran outside to the road to meet the draft. A few moments later Ritchie, who had previously been wounded, appeared at the entrance to the billet. Glancing around at the reclining men he spotted me and asking what happened to our crowd was told the last scrap pretty well extinguished them. He then said that as soon as his party was dismissed, the [Sgt.-Maj.] collared him and made him a corporal. A few days later, Ritchie was sent to "Kingdom Come." Ritchie was a Scotsman and one of our tug-of-war men.

I paid a visit to Canaples, passing a squad of German prisoners working at a pile of ammunition beside the road. In the evening with a "pal" we returned to Canaples, and feeling that we required a little pick-me-up, indulged in a mixture of hot coffee and rum, finishing up with cognac after sampling a wine called Cyrrh. It was a bit of "alright."

CHAPTER VII

With the 6th Brigade
Machine-Gun Company

Friday, September 22, 1916

I was asked to report at the Orderly Room, and found that Charlie Gordon, formerly of our Company, who lately put in for and obtained a Commission, was temporarily Acting Adjutant. He said they received a call from the 6th Brigade Machine-Gun Company for some assistance, and knowing that I was not keen on promotion, thought I would prefer machine-gun work as there was less fatigues and I would have a better time. Between killed, wounded, sick, and transfers, the Company had undergone a great change, so I thought it would be as well to tie up with the Machine-Gun Company as remain where I was. Receiving a note to be handed to the new O.C., I hurried off to Montrelet, an adjoining village, and was just in time to line up with my new associates and hike back to the front. We passed Bonneville and, at Val de Maison, passed the night in the loft of a barn.

Saturday, September 23, 1916

We are on the march once more. Herissort is passed and then Contay, where we remain for the night.

Sunday, September 24, 1916

At 9:00 a.m. our trek begins. We go through Warloy-Baillon and halt for a couple of hours on the right side of the road on this side of Albert. Proceeding, we march through Albert and pass a very tired out, sturdy-looking German peasant soldier who is being led back a captive. The day is very hot, my pack heavy, and as I developed a strained ankle, between pain and heat, perspiration poured out of me. For years afterwards, Willox, who was marching behind me, reminded me of that sweltering day, saying that each individual hair of my head stood straight out with a blob of sweat at the end, dropping down in tiny cascades. We enter the ruins of la Boiselle, and turning to the south, take up our quarters in scattered surface dug-outs in Sausage Valley, a few hundred yards from an enormous crater created by the explosion of a mine at the commencement of the Somme attack.

Monday, September 25, 1916

I circled around the area [where] the 34th Division fought on July 1, 1916. Prior to the assault, two great mines were blown, one of which containing the unprecedented amount of 60,000 lbs. of gun cotton, threw hundreds of tons of chalk into the air. In the bottom of the crater is a rude cross marking the grave of Pte. Moxham of the 6th Wilts Regiment. About one hundred yards on the Albert side of the crater is a wooden Celtic cross showing where Lt.-Col. Meredith Howard of the 24th Northumberland Fusiliers was killed and buried. In the same grave are Ptes. Bonner and McKeating who tried to save him. Not far away are crosses denoting the resting places of Capt. Murray and Lt. Charlesworth of the 25th Northumberland Fusiliers. In isolated places are the graves of Lts. Byrne and Burbureau of the 24th Northumberland Fusiliers, and of Capt. Baker and Lt. Eason of the 10th Lincolns. Numerous crosses in shell holes show where many of our men died, but there is no name to tell who is who. I presume they would have been buried several days after the fight and had no identification.

Tuesday, September 26, 1916

On our right a heavy bombardment is going on. I had another trip over the battlefield farther south in Sausage Valley near the crater. I went up one of Fritz's trenches. Deep dug-outs were encountered every thirty yards. There is much evidence that our fellows bombed them. German remains are strewn around.

The 27th Northumberland Fusiliers (4th Tyneside Irish) saw fighting here. Most of our dead were buried in shell holes with nothing but the bare cross to denote internment. Occasionally a cap, glove or tunic lay on the grave. In one instance a Christmas card was lying beside the cross. The inscription was from "Little Vera and Mamma to Daddy and Husband." On the cross hung a Balmoral bonnet. The occupant of the grave would therefore be a Royal Scot of the 34th Division. A huge German shell lying on the surface of the ground that did not explode had chalked thereon "One that refused to do its bit."

Today I took stock of my new comrades. I was allocated to Vickers Machine-Gun Crew, number 13. The section comprises nos. 13, 14, 15, and 16 Gun Crews. Most of my gun crew came from Nova Scotia, but the company was represented by men of nearly every province and was a youthful organization, being formed quite recently out of a nucleus of battalion machine-gunners and drafts from Canada-trained machine-gunners. The 31st Battalion was well represented. The Sergeant-Major was Teddy Bain of my old company, a former bank clerk. Carter, "Nifty" Clark, and Rush were others I spotted. I was told that Major Taylor, the O.C.,[1] had a preference for battalion men on account of their experience and knowledge of the line.

The first phase of the Battle of the Somme, affecting the 6th Brigade, took place on the 15th, to be followed by a second and final attack on the 26th. Briefly, the 29th Battalion was assigned the right flank of the front for the 2nd Division and the 31st Battalion the left. The latter had Courcelette Trench and two sunken roads on its front. In the afternoon of the 25th, German guns opened on the battle area and the 31st had over thirty casualties including three officers.

In the evening the battalion moved up to battle positions and took a long time to reach their quarters. The enemy kept up a steady fire on Courcelette and back areas. At 12:30 p.m. our artillery opened up with a terrific bombardment but the range was inaccurate and the enemy replied with a fierce barrage. In a haze of smoke our men went forward but had to seek protection in shell holes. Casualties were appalling. At 5:10 p.m. "A" Company's positions were assaulted but the foe was driven back. By the evening of the 27th the original objective was taken, and the 22nd Battalion relieved the 31st on the night of the 28th and the morning of the 29th.

On the 27th I began speculating on the attack and how our fellows fared. Rumours reaching me were that the 31st Battalion had lost about 375 men and the 29th over 400. The colonel of the 13th, the second in command, the adjutant and a number more were reported to have been killed by a bomb bursting in their midst.

Thursday, September 28, 1916

The Brigade Machine-Gunners came out tonight, being relieved by the gunners of the 4th Brigade. Two of our members were killed—

---

[1] The O.C., or Officer Commanding, was Major J. A. H. Taylor. He was replaced several months later by Major A. Eastham.

Cairns and Hubert—and two were shell-shocked. Fritz had been busy shelling between Pozières and Contalmaison and must have struck quite a number of our men as this was a crowded and busy quarter. Some of the French artillery in this area were knocked out. While returning after delivering rations, I stopped for a few minutes to watch the French gunners send over gas shells. They were a fast and energetic lot and compared favourably with our men for quick firing. Behind them was a heavy battery kicking up a deuce of a row. A Red Cross wagon was blown to smithereens by a shell killing the driver and wounding several others. Some shells dropped among members of a battalion on the move, causing about sixty casualties. Four of the 29th Battalion cooks volunteered for stretcher work. One of our gunners was watching them edging along near Courcelette when a shell exploded and they were blown completely away. I was at the 31st cook kitchen trying to glean information about the battalion but nothing trustworthy could be obtained. Very few had come back from the firing line and they had a hazy notion of what had transpired. What I could gather was that the 29th took their objective without too much trouble, but the 31st, who were in the vicinity of Courcelette, were in difficulties from the start owing to the heavy concentration of fire that was directed on them. They, however, went ahead only to find that they had run into barbed wire and a stretch of trench occupied by the enemy that our artillery had not touched. The Germans lined the parapet and caught our men stumbling across No Man's Land and trying to get through the wire. Machine-guns helped to create further damage, and very heavy casualties were suffered. Receiving more assistance, the battalion returned to the attack at night and ultimately gained the objective. Quite a lot of fatalities were inflicted on the enemy but our fighting strength had nearly disappeared. Later that night patrols went forward and returned with the news that the Germans had retired to further back positions.

Up to the present I have heard that Lt. Gordon, who belonged to my old company, was killed; also Lt. Arbuckle, who was formerly a private in my section. He was wounded at the St. Eloi engagement and had returned to the unit a few days ago. Both were very good officers, the latter especially so. Lts. Morgan, Living, and Norris were wounded on the way in. A report was received that Lt. Hanson died of wounds and that Capt. L'Amy was killed, but this was incorrect. The latter was buried by a shell but after a while was able to extricate himself and take part in the final advance. Two sergeants of the bombers were dead. One of them, Tom Avery, was an "A" Company man. His younger brother, of the same company, was wounded in an

222

earlier engagement. L/Cpl. Austin, to whom I handed over my stripe,[2] had his head blown off by a shell. Cpl. Ritchie, who received the promotion I declined and who had just returned from Blighty after being wounded at St. Eloi, was killed. Cpl. Roughton is wounded, Sgt. West got it in the chest and Sgt. Provan was wounded in two places, one wound in the face. He succumbed several weeks later. His brother, Jim, of "C" Company, also made the supreme sacrifice in this war, dying of wounds. They came from Galashiels in the Lowlands of Scotland. Little Dan Macleod is another listed as wounded; also, Jimmie Crerar, the scout. So far these are the company casualties that have reached me.

Saturday, September 30, 1916

Tonight I paid a visit to the battalion to ascertain further accounts of the fight. As expected, the reports were varied. The first I saw was Sgt.-Maj. Lawson who told me that they had a hard time of it getting in and going forward due to harassing fire. I found that the sergeant of my old platoon was the only original member left. Sgt. Wood was originally missing but has since been declared dead. He was a married man and had four of a family. Our married men have been hard hit. Maj. Gilker, a new arrival to "A" Company, and on the elderly side, was among the slain. Vernon Eccles, a ranker officer[3] from the company, was another of the fallen. Sgt. Donald Macrae, of my home town, was reported badly wounded. He had recently returned from Blighty after being wounded at St. Eloi. Two months later I heard he had been killed, his body being found in a shell hole by the 4th Division. He was the first in the battalion to receive a D.C.M.[4] Sgt. Porter was also wounded. Baker, Synnuck, Causche, and Slaven were also on the wounded list. Lt. Clements, one of our old sergeants, was wounded for the third time. Wiberg, a very quiet Scandinavian from Duhamel, Alberta, was killed. He had only been a short time with the

---

[2] Fraser, as we have seen, had been promoted to Lance Corporal, the most junior rank among the non-commissioned officers. Fraser had consistently refused to accept "stripes," an N.C.O. rank badge—one for a lance corporal, two for a corporal and three for a sergeant. Casualties among N.C.Os. and junior officers were very high. Fraser was well aware of this and acted accordingly. (See also his entry for 12 January 1917.)

[3] A "ranker officer" was one who had been commissioned as a lieutenant from the ranks. The battalion war diary lists a constant stream of privates, corporals, sergeants and sergeant-majors who had been promoted in this fashion. Some were sent to an officers' training school on promotion, returning to the unit one or two months later. Others received their commissions and remained with the battalion. The latter were men with the necessary education, experience and proven leadership qualities.

[4] D.C.M.—Distinguished Conduct Medal. As an award for bravery, it ranked between the M.M. (Military Medal) and the V.C. (Victoria Cross).

company. Having worked at the old Merchants Bank at New Norway, I mentioned quite a number of people whom I knew in his vicinity. This brightened him up considerably and he became quite a pal afterwards. Williamson, who like Ritchie, was previously wounded and had arrived back from England a few days ago, was also killed. He enlisted in 1914 when he was only eighteen years of age, and came from Hanna, being a clerk with the Canadian Bank of Commerce. Clarkson, an American who had been kept at the Reserve Base in England for nearly eighteen months, having found out that he was minus several toes and had broken down on route marches, also made the supreme sacrifice. He wanted badly to get to France. He said he would willingly return to Canada if he was only allowed to put his foot in France and make one trip up the line. He was on his way up when a shell came over and that was his finis. He never fired a shot. McDougall, our old stretcher-bearer, was one of the missing. Bignell, Stringer, and Angus were also wounded. Hardy Salter was wounded for the second time. Jack, his elder brother, was killed several days earlier.

As was to be expected, the latest drafts felt the shock of the fight. They were unnerved by the roar of artillery and noise of bursting shells and the thought of facing death was too much a strain on them and they failed to grasp the situation and understand that they had to go forward and tangle with the enemy. It was the first and last experience for many.

Monday, October 2, 1916

I had some trouble last night finding our quarters and nearly froze during the night. I met Tommie Law, our old Armourer Corporal near Pozières on his way out. He had been commissioned lately and said he was now acting O.C. of the Company, having had to take command on account of officer casualties. He told me only two officers came back intact from the line during this trip.

Our guns are still moving up and Fritz is falling back. To me the advance seemed a costly bit of business, but if Fritz is hit hard and pushed back I guess it satisfies the Higher Command despite tremendous casualties. The expenditure of shells is tremendous and damage to the enemy must be terrific.

An amusing incident occurred when one of our fellows was coming out of the line. An artilleryman lay on a stretcher wounded awaiting to be attended to and taken away. Fritz's artillery was on the active side and several shells fell in his vicinity. The wounded man with a "To Hell with this, it's too blood slow for me" got up and beat it away.

Tuesday, October 3, 1916

I saw a Heinie prisoner passing out. He appeared to be shell shocked as he had a vacant stare and was staggering. The weather is very wet and trenches muddy. We expect to come out tonight.

Wednesday, October 4, 1916

We left this morning for Warloy-Baillon passing through Burgencourt. The whole brigade moved today.

There were many changes in the battalion. Lance Corporals became Corporals and Sergeants and rankers got commissions. Recent awards, as far as I can remember, are a D.S.O. to Lt. Norris and M.C.'s to Lt. Millington, Sgt.-Maj. Lawson and Sgt.-Maj. Park [*sic*].

Of the men who had trekked southward from Belgium a few weeks ago, little more than one hundred marched back, and only a sprinkling of those who had joined up in 1914 were now in the ranks. The final casualty count, I understand, was 664. This turned out to be by far the most disastrous conflict in the battalion's history. Thus ended the 31st Battalion's contribution to the Battle of the Somme.[5]

As my connection with the 31st Battalion has been severed, I will no longer be able to follow its fortunes. However, I will still be operating in the general area of the 6th Brigade and expect to get news of the battalion's happenings from time to time.

Friday, October 6, 1916

We marched into Warloy today.

Sunday, October 8, 1916

Leaving Warloy we headed for la Vicogne passing en route Vadencourt, Contay, Herissart and Val de Maison. The previous day we were out on a route march to near Varennes. The 10th and 11th Brigades passed us today to continue the Somme Struggle.

Tuesday, October 10, 1916

We left la Vicogne for Bretel by way of Beauval and Doullens. At night I paid a visit to Hem.

[5] The Battle of the Somme, which raged during the summer of 1916, caused immense casualties to both the German and Allied armies. Estimates vary, but the Germans lost between 660,000 and 680,000; the British about 419,543 and the French 204,253. The Canadian casualties by the time the active fighting on the Somme had ceased were 24,029. (See G. W. L. Nicholson, *Canadian Expeditionary Force, 1914-1919*. Ottawa, Queen's Printer, 1962, pp. 198-200.)

Wednesday, October 11, 1916

On the hike again for Barly passing Hem and Risquetout. We were pretty well starved today, our company having lost contact with the commissariat. We roamed around the village trying to purchase food but could not get any—not even bread.

Thursday, October 12, 1916

We now head for Magnicourt, going through the villages of Neuvillette, Bouquemaison, Rebreuviette and Etrée Waimin.

Friday, October 13, 1916

Our travels now carry us to near Bajus through Maiziéres, Pénin, Tinques, Chelers, Magnicourt-en-Compté to Houvelin.

Sunday, October 15, 1916

On the move once again. The people in this part of France appear more prosperous. Their houses are more substantially built. Coal mining seems to be the chief industry. The roads are crowded with youngsters—mostly little girls. As usual they are not very tidy looking and their manners are not of the best. We passed La Comté, Beugin, Houdain, Maisnil and stopped at Barlin.

Monday, October 16, 1916

We underwent a most unusual experience. It was so novel that we could hardly believe our eyes. Fancy being ushered into an occupied brick house with doors and windows intact and no gaping holes in the roof or gables. True, the room we entered contained not a particle of furniture but the floor was "as clean as a whistle." We grinned as we slung our equipment off after several days' continuous hiking and laid down to rest. Furthermore, there was no crushing, only seven to the room—a gun crew. The women of the house lit a fire and made us very comfortable, giving us, into the bargain, a cup of coffee and later in the day, a bowl of soup. This was the best billet we had before or after. But our stay was of short duration and we could not tarry, much to our regret.

We are treading the road again on the way to a new front. Hersin Coupigny soon looms ahead and we realize we are in the midst of a coal area; slag heaps become a prominent picture in the landscape. Hersin is a brick town of fair dimensions and more prosperous looking than the towns and villages of the farming districts. Further on we halted at Sains-en-Gohelle where the sections split up and pursue their respective ways to the line.[6] Here the countryside becomes more hilly and patches of woodland dot the slopes and hollows. Next we pass the tiny village of Boyeffles in a picturesque setting. Most of the places around this part have double names, in fact, the smaller the village the bigger the name. The countryside from Bouvigny to Arras, embracing Notre Dame de Lorette and Vimy Ridge is somewhat pretty. Working our way up a fairly steep hill and round by a tower, the twin villages of Grand Servins and Petit Servins come into view on our right. Presently we circle through Gouy Servins and proceed down a fairly long pleasant stretch of road to Ablain St. Nazaire lying at the entrance of a valley between the ridges of Lorette and Vimy. On leaving Ablain we march straight down the road for several hundred yards, then sharply to the left for another few hundred yards and then a right angled turn takes to an outstanding landmark—the Church of Ablain St. Nazaire. Around here are scattered the ruins of quite a number of houses while the church itself is a mere shell. Rounding the church we have a fairly steep climb up the Lorette Spur and well up the slope of the ridge enter a communication trench known as Spur Alley. We now move along the slope parallel to the valley and overlooking the village of Souchez which has been blown away to its foundations. On the other side of the valley, opposite to us, is the Pimple, the northern end of Vimy Ridge, and occupied by the enemy. Our destination is a deep dug-out in Spur Alley trench. There are sixteen steps leading down into it, but the space therein is rather cramped. However, a crowded dug-out is a great medium for an introduction to one's comrades. I find I failed to jot down the name of our No. 1 on the crew who fires the gun, and at this date of writing, twenty-seven years later, cannot remember his name. He was from [the] interior [of] B.C. and was far from good-looking, had not much of a manner, but was fair in his dealings with the crew and was likeable. Then there was Starratt, a young fellow, not much more than a boy, from, I think, Stellarton, Nova Scotia; Harry Stevenson, another B.C. man, a transfer from, I think, the 54th Battalion. Had seen service in South Africa in the Boer War, but was not destined to see the end of this one. Ben Robinson, who was fairly old and had a quiet, pawky style, was the perfect peacetime soldier. He took great care of himself and his belongings, kept everything in ship-shape and was always ready and on time. He never seemed to have occasion to

6 In brief, whereas an infantry company of about 100 men would occupy a section of a trench, the machine-gun company was broken down into machine-gun crews and sections, each crew siting its gun behind the front line to cover several hundred yards of frontage. In action, the gun-crews of the company would cover the brigade front.

hurry and was always ahead of the next move. Steeves, a big, red-faced, healthy-looking fellow from Moncton, New Brunswick, later on tired of the crew and joined the transport. Wolfenden, easy-going, laughing, talkative, and very sloppy, was perfectly at home in any sort of billet and in any kind of weather. He was always the centre of conversation. These, then, were my first co-workers in the Machine-Gun Company. By the time I was knocked out of the great adventure, they were killed, wounded or transferred, and I was associated with an entirely different lot.

From our position a great view is obtained. Down below in the middle of the valley is the Sugar Refinery around which a tremendous battle took place in May 1915 between the French and the Germans. It might be said to have been the centre of the Artois Struggle which consisted of trying to drive the enemy from the Lorette and Vimy Ridges on a front ranging from near Loos to Arras. It was only partly successful and had to be broken off on account of appalling losses. The Lorette promontory had been the scene of such frequent and bloody combats that the French called it the Butte de la Mort, or Ridge of Death. The result of such heavy fighting was the capture of the Lorette Plateau and villages of Ablain, Souchez, Carency, La Targette and Neuville St. Vaast.

The Sugar Refinery, which lay halfway between Ablain and Souchez, was a veritable German fortress, and when it was finally captured on June 1, 1915, it cost around 17,000 French lives. The Battle of Artois incurred a French loss of nearly half a million consisting of 143,000 dead and captured and 297,000 wounded. In this region we could hardly move a few yards without stumbling across French and German bodies, some lying in the open and others half buried.

Straight ahead, over the valley, we watched the German positions on the Pimple. Sheltering behind this elevation and nestling by a wood lay the village of Givenchy. To the north, near Fosse 6, hidden among the trees, Fritz's artillery barked out many shells in our direction. Fronting Lorette Plateau, the town of Angres stood out as a protection bastion for the city of Lens which lay behind. Tagged on to Lens on the south was the town of Liévin. Lens itself was split into several sections under the name of "Cité," such as Cité St. Pierre, Cité St. Jeanne D'Arc, Cité St. Emile, and others. Most Canadians only knew Lens as the hometown of Georges Carpentier, the French boxer of several years ago. To the north of Angres, where the German line took a sharp turn, was a famous stronghold known as the Double Crassier. These were the places our eyes rested on for the next few months.

228

Tuesday, October 17, 1916

Since we arrived it has been very quiet and if this continues we should have quite a home here. Artillery does not appear to be much in evidence, but on the other hand, a fair amount of trench mortar work is carried on, the resultant explosions having a tendency to create a bad attack of nerves.

It has been reported that saccharine was first manufactured in the Sugar Refinery lying below us. As it is a by-product of coal tar, the raw material could be obtained by the refinery's back door so to speak. This quarter is thickly populated and the Germans work the mines that dot the horizon. They are referred to as Fosses and on the maps are numbered for military reasons.

Sgts. Tucker and McGirr and Cpl. Hun have been awarded M.M.'s in connection with the Somme offensive.

Wednesday, October 18, 1916

The weather has turned very bad and walking on the greasy, chalky soil is difficult. When out roaming in the vicinity of the trench, I came across French and German skeletons with rotten clothing and equipment hanging on them.

Thursday, October 19, 1916

It is a wet, disagreeable day. We received our pay in the trenches, which is something unusual. Things being quiet proves that we have been sent to this front for a rest-up.

Friday, October 20, 1916

Another fellow and I from the gun crew paid a visit to Sains, several miles away, for the purpose of making purchases. Between Goay Servins and the Tower we came across a motor lorry with a cable attachment holding a sausage observation balloon about 300 yards aloft. There were about thirty men of the Royal Flying Corps in attendance waiting around the road to have the balloon down in a hurry in the event of danger. On the north side, a hundred yards away, was a machine-gun in readiness to ward off hostile planes. At Boyeffles further on, I was told that two hundred civilians were killed by enemy shells within fifteen minutes prior to the enemy being driven back in the middle of 1915.

Coming back over the Lorette Plateau we passed a finely kept French cemetery containing about eight hundred graves. Their occupants belonged to one division and fell when storming the plateau. A couple of miles nearer Boyeffles was another French cemetery where about two hundred soldiers are buried. The trek back through a varied stretch of woodland was quite enjoyable.

Saturday, October 21, 1916

A landmark near Souchez was known as the Iron Post. One of our gun crews had a position near here. It was, as its name suggested, an iron pole and it was badly marked and chipped by bullets, shrapnel balls and shell splinters. At nights we used to rake around the Refinery heap trying to find wood and coal for cooking and heating purposes but, as it had been well pawed over, we never got very much. It was reported that at Ablain and Souchez the enemy was particularly bestial, murdering, mutilating, and outraging the civil population. Many tragedies were enacted in this area.

I was down for rations tonight and after waiting for six hours had to retrace my footsteps. Near headquarters at Ablain former members of British troops had executed a variety of carvings on chalks.

The trenches around here are infested with rats, principally black ones. Food not in cans has to be hung up in the dug-outs to avoid being spoiled. The rats are a perfect nuisance, running in and out of the dug-outs, along the trenches and up and down the parapet in their hundreds.

Tuesday, October 24, 1916

We are having a pretty fine time of it doing our own cooking and no fatigues. Every fourth day finds one of us officially cooking and going for rations, the other three days being blank except two hours guard per day and night.

It was foggy this morning, so I took advantage of the situation and went over the ridge to explore our surroundings. I came across a dead Frenchman half buried. His skull had fallen off showing the spinal bones at the neck. I obtained a couple of buttons off his tunic. In his breast pocket was a pipe and smoking material. Underneath, in his side, was a piece of shell which must have been responsible for his death. Close by lay another dead soldier clothed in a brownish uniform. He appeared to be a French Colonial, a Moroccan, and the brass buttons on his tunic had queer markings reminding me of foreign writings. I removed a few of the buttons. As the fog soon lifted, I had to beat a hasty retreat to the trench.

Friday, October 27, 1916

On the way out of the line we passed what we thought was only a boot, but, on closer inspection, found a leg bone in it. I heard that they were burying the remains of about two hundred civilians including women and children who were gassed in the town of Souchez.

Tuesday, October 31, 1916

Along with another fellow, I paid a visit to Hersin and Barlin. At Hersin we had our photos taken at a place [which] we found out later, was of ill repute.

Wednesday, November 1, 1916

Last night we visited Bully-Grenay and were surprised to see so many lights when the place was almost within shell fire range.

Information reached us that Leo Clarke of the 28th Battalion was awarded the Victoria Cross. He is the first of the 2nd Division to obtain the coveted honour.

Going along the main street in Bully-Grenay I stopped to look at a crowd entering the Y.M.C.A. building and then followed in after them. A padre was talking. He spoke in a very serious tone. Wondering what he referred to when he said, "He was very penitent towards the end," I asked a soldier beside me what he was talking about. He replied that a fellow of their battalion, the 25th, named Young, an original, was shot for desertion.

On the way to Bully I had a look round a cemetery adjoining the road. Although it was only nine months old, it contained over one thousand graves.

The coal mines in our vicinity are worked during the night and close down in the daytime so as not to attract the attention of the enemy.

Friday, November 3, 1916

I am acting runner until the section comes out of the line. This morning I was up at French Dump on the Arras Road opposite Angres having a very easy time. The trenches, however, are in very bad condition.

Tuesday, November 7, 1916

When out for rations, Benham of No. 14 Crew was wounded. The weather was wretched, rain falling every day and flooding the

231

trenches causing them to cave in. Rubber boots are being used and working parties are kept busy day and night.

The unfit and undesirables are being weeded out. Five have gone to the base and three were returned to their respective battalions. Five men from the 28th Battalion have replaced them.

Friday, November 10, 1916

Coming back from French Dump I saw a weasel at the side of the road. With so many rats around I should fancy it would have a picnic of a time.

The trenches are getting worse and worse. Our fellows are awful looking objects caked with mud from head to foot. The new men are having their eyes opened to winter conditions. Movement in many parts is overland. The Arras Road is preferred to the communication trench, notwithstanding that bullets whistle past you the farther up you go. The rain washes down the soil, reveals new corpses and rifles daily. One of our planes was brought down in our lines today.

Sunday, November 12, 1916

Along with another fellow, I went down to Aix-Noulette to purchase food supplies. On the way back, about halfway up the communication trench, we came across the Corps Commander, Lt.-Gen. Sir Julian Byng, with several of his staff who were on their way to visit the 31st Battalion lines. They were resting at the side of the trench strung out about fifty yards. When we were passing them they got up to continue their way. I got wedged in between the Corps Commander[7] and General Ketchen, the Brigadier of the 6th Brigade. After trudging along slowly for two or three hundred yards, Sir Julian, who was leading, turned round and said to me, "You better go ahead as you are quicker than I." The Brigadier also stepped to the side and let my pal pass. That was the first and last time I had seen "Byng." I knew him from photos I had seen. He was quite a big man, dark, good-looking, with a pleasant manner.

Tuesday, November 14, 1916

A number of the 31st Battalion fired at a flock of geese passing overhead and brought several down in the lines of the 5th Brigade.

[7] The former commander of the Canadian Corps, Lt.-Gen. Alderson, was appointed Inspector General of the Canadian Forces in England in the Spring of 1916. He remained in that post until November of the same year. Lt.-Gen., the Honourable Sir Julian H. G. Byng, a British cavalry officer, took over the Canadian Corps from Alderson. He was to be replaced in 1917 by Lt.-Gen. Sir Arthur Currie, a Canadian.

One of our men, who is now with a Salvage Company, received quite a scare. He thought one of the falling birds was a "rumjar" and rushed to cover as fast as he could.

Saturday, November 18, 1916

Snow is on the ground this morning and the air is cold.

A German deserter came into our lines the other day. As usual he was questioned and gave valuable information, though he contradicted himself several times and his statements could not be relied upon in their entirety. He made up his mind to desert and at night passed along his lines into another battalion's front, finally going over the parapet at a place he knew. He told what battalions held the line, supports, reserves, their billets, stores, dumps, artillery and machine-gun emplacements. He said they had no gas on their front. Their scouts recently reported that we had gas cylinders on our front line, which was false, which made them stand to with their gas helmets ready for forty-eight hours. He complained about the quantity and quality of their food and bullying attitude of their officers. Out of 120 in his company he said 110 were willing to give themselves up but were afraid of crossing No Man's Land.

There is considerable trench mortar activity on both sides.

Friday, November 24, 1916

Enemy machine-gunners are daily becoming more active, sweeping the Arras Road at night and making working and ration parties somewhat nervy as the bullets whistle and whine through the air. Last night one of the salvage men was shot in the head above French Dump while coming down in one of our limbers. The bullet passed through his steel helmet.

Monday, November 27, 1916

My period of running ended today and I was detailed to return to the crew who were going into the line tonight.

As we would be in view of the enemy going in in daylight, we had to wait until it was dark before we left the communication trench and proceeded overland to our position. The last few hundred yards took some manoeuvring. There was no defined path and it was with difficulty that we picked our way round shell holes and over old trenches, slipping and floundering on the way in and hustled by stray fire. The position was located in an old trench. It was not an established emplacement and it seemed as if an order was given to

233

place a gun somewhere in the vicinity. The situation was most unsatisfactory. Out in the open without shelter from cold, rain, or snow, no place to sleep but in the bottom of the trench and entirely trapped in the day time. The sergeant of the section did not put in an appearance tonight, having failed to find us.

Tuesday, November 28, 1916

Dissatisfied with the location and determined to find a better place, I crawled around a maze of old trenches to the edge of the ridge and went up a trench vertical to the line. Observing what seemed to be an opening into the side of the hill about two and a half feet high, and noticing several yards further on a similar hole, both being blocked at their entrance by an accumulation of soil, curiosity caused me to examine them. With the assistance of another gunner, we cleared the earth away and crouching low entered the first aperture.

Lighting a match we found ourselves in a large roomy cave. At the far end were six bunks, two at one side, two at the end, and two at the other side, one bunk above the other. Further digging around the entrance and we were able to get in and out with only a little stooping. The place was absolutely dry and atmosphere fresh and clean. It was built by the French in 1915 and used as a dressing station, and apparently became derelict when the line moved forward. Meeting with such success, we turned our attention to the other hole and soon cleared the entrance of its accumulation of soil and entered it to find another cave-like room entirely bare. Between the two was a ten-yard passage but it was so low that you could only get back and forward by crawling on your hands and knees. Seemingly, it was constructed for air circulation only. What a home! A room with sleeping accommodation and another for cooking purposes. We were not long in notifying the others. The gun was quickly removed closer to our abode and a new post established. We were now in clover and could have stayed there for the duration.

As we were in view of the enemy in the day time, we could only get out at night and had still to clamber in and out overland. An ungodly number of rifle and machine-gun bullets pinged into the hillside when darkness set in. The first thing we did when we changed over was to apportion off guard duties. They were pencilled down on a piece of paper and showed who were on duty during the wee, small hours. As we deemed that neither the officer nor the sergeant dared come near the place during the day and would never in a blue moon locate our den at night, duties were completely ignored and we all slumbered long and peacefully despite possible gas or other attacks. However, a few nights later the officer and sergeant, after various attempts to find us, at last succeeded by means of the tell-tale gun to locate our hideout and we were caught asleep at the switch. Inquiring who was supposed to be sentry, the slip of paper told the story—it was Red Driscoll—there and then he was penalized double duty in the line which meant that when our crew was relieved, he had to stay in for another trip. Less than a year later Red stayed in the line for keeps—Passchendaele got him.

As soon as we were settled down in our new home, my failing exerted itself[8] and when I noticed the sky was downcast and the lighting poor, I set out on the prowl to reconnoitre the ground for evidence of fighting. We were at the tail end of a dark ravine and a series of old fallen down trenches crisscrossed from one side to the other. Bending low I had only gone a few yards when I came across a couple of graves, one containing the remains of an unknown Frenchman, and the other that of a Foot Chasseur. As the light further waned and I could expose myself more, evidence of terrific fighting revealed itself. French and German dead lay around in strange confusion. I was kept busy cutting buttons off their tunics for souvenirs. Rifling the dead used to be considered in pre-war times a ghoulish business, but over here the dead are of no account, they are scattered all over the battle area. Unless the enemy is pushed far enough backward it is too dangerous and risky trying to recover the bodies for decent burial so they lie where they fell. After the Battle of Vimy, when the enemy was forced to retire from this front, I paid the ravine a visit, so that I could go over the ground in safety, and piece things together, but I was too late for civilians started a cemetery and several dozen bodies were already interred. A pile of letters, cards and odds and ends taken from their pockets lay on the ground, while a sandbag was stuffed with other articles. Nearer the Arras Road an old Frenchman was searching the ground.

I made a cursory exploration of several hundred yards, carefully picking my way along the trenches. There were several crosses here and there, but most of the dead were unburied and though there were many Germans, the French predominated. Seventy yards away was a German cemetery. Most of the crosses were broken. The inscriptions showed that the deaths occurred in August of 1915. At one corner, where two trenches met, was an upright granite slab about three feet long by one and a half feet broad and nine inches thick, and inscribed thereon in German in gold lettering, words to the effect that

---

[8] Fraser's "failing" was his insatiable curiousity and his desire to collect souvenirs, especially buttons and badges from dead soldiers.

so and so of the German Army, belonging to the family of "Gesleys" in Mannheim was killed there. Apparently, this German was of some consequence.

Proceeding up the ravine along a broken-down trench, I observed a row of dug-outs built against the side of the ridge. The first dug-out had a corrugated iron roof pretty well smashed in by a shell. Peering in through the entrance I was astonished to see, almost in the skeleton stage, a man in underclothes reclining on a bed. Below on the floor lay the remains of two other Germans. They must have met death suddenly. I cut three buttons off the tunic of one of them. Several of the other dug-outs that were smashed in contained more bodies, or rather skeletons. The dug-outs were lavishly furnished with beds, dressing tables, chairs and rugs, obviously stolen from neighbouring French houses. The Germans must have been caught in a surprise attack for most of them were half dressed, and apparently those that escaped destruction, ran away for good when their comrades were left where they fell. Even to one nerved to the sight of dead, it was a peculiar experience peeping into dug-outs in this quiet and dark ravine and witnessing the result of tragedies enacted over a year ago. I am perfectly sure I was about the first to explore this ravine since the attack swept forward and left it a second No Man's Land. A little distance away a cross was seen stating that underneath were buried seven Frenchmen and eight Bosches.

Last night the 31st Battalion went over on a raid on our front and returned without losing a man. The raiding party consisted of Lt. Curtis, a corporal and twelve men. They made their way over the desolation of No Man's Land under [a] rifle grenade barrage. On entering the German line, the officer with six men proceeded down the trench on the left about forty yards without encountering the enemy. The corporal, with the balance of the party, took the right and met up with five Germans manning a post. Opening fire at once, two of the Germans were killed and a third wounded. The two dead men had no identification, so they were dragged to the wire, but the officer appearing [he] ordered withdrawal with the result that useful information was not obtained.

Tonight our artillery opened up all of a sudden on the Pimple and sent a hurricane of shells into Fritz's positions, finishing up with exploding a mine and the 8th Battalion rushed in and occupied the crater. After a while the front quietened down.

Where we are is a regular hotbed of stray shots. They hit ground near our position. We were up observing when a couple whizzed past us. At first we considered we were sniped at, but it appears we are in direct line of fire from the Angres-Lievin Front.

236

Wednesday, November 29, 1916

Once again under cover of fog I went on a discovery expedition, this time heading north across the ravine. Here and there around the parapets were numerous bottles resembling old-fashioned, lemonade bottles. They contained what looked like cotton wool and powdery substances. I wondered what they were intended for. It later dawned on me that they were home-made French bombs. Upon explosion the glass would be splintered into many pieces causing painful and dangerous wounds.

Nearing a corner of the trench, I could see several dead Frenchmen; rounding the bend lay a group of dead Germans. The situation explained itself at once—a battle royal took place at the corner of the trench, the opposing parties bombing each other for possession, with the above result. Passing further along, evidence of fighting lessened, and still further away only a few bodies were sighted. A trench running vertical to LaPrada had been well explored some time before, some keen hunters going the length of partially disinterring the bodies to find relics. The colour of the uniforms, red and blue, disclosed that the French who fought here belonged to the old time regulars. The later regiments were clothed in the dress known as invisible blue.

I went down to French Dump for rations. Apparently, the enemy has a clamped rifle trained on a spot near the dump which he fires periodically at night for a bullet whirred over the road close to me. This has occurred several times lately.

Wednesday, December 6, 1916

Paid a visit to Bethune, thirteen kilometers distant, passing through Sains, Noeux where there are several mines, and then Verquin. Bethune, in size, is somewhat similar to Bailleul and Poperinghe and lies directly west of La Bassée, one of the best known towns of the early part of the war.

Friday, December 8, 1916

Returned to the line today. The weather is wet and cold.

Friday, December 15, 1916

Came out tonight after a fine spell. Since the last few nights it has been very dark and overland travelling was not very pleasant.

Wednesday, December 20, 1916

We are back in the line again. As we went all the way in by communication trench, we started early and actually relieved the other gun crew in daylight which is something unusual. Our position was known as Dug Out position. It is perched on the top of the Lorette Ridge facing Angres and overlooks a great stretch of country reaching from the double Crassier to Vimy Ridge. The gun is mounted day and night. Our position is a very uncomfortable one. There are only two small, leaky dug-outs and rat infested at that. They can only house four and we have six on the crew. My sleeping accommodation is the gun emplacement, and I have to lie huddled up so sleep is out of the question. Part of a trench mat, balanced on one side on a step and on the other on a ricketty stool, serves as my bed. A rat occasionally visits me and, as it is cold, I have a hard time coaxing myself to sleep. When [the] 6:00 a.m. shift comes along I have to get up and out of the way to let the cook get on with his duties. A gun emplacement, a bedroom, and a kitchen all in one, but not at the same time—enough to satisfy a real estate salesman. One has to be careful that he is not in line of the firing aperture when rifle or machine-gun fire is coming in this direction.

In the afternoon, on the south, a heavy bombardment started and continued for a few hours. I have not heard the official results, but rumour states a strong party of C.M.R.'s made a trench raid and roped in quite a number of prisoners and killed and wounded about two hundred. Another version mentioned that the Imperials made the raid. Several days later I saw in the papers the outcome of this raid. The C.M.R.'s took fifty-eight prisoners including two officers. They penetrated into the supports and bombed the demolished dug-outs and machine-gun emplacements.

Thursday, December 21, 1916

About midnight Fritz started traversing our quarter with a machine-gun, the bullets skimming over our heads.

Friday, December 22, 1916

The weather is miserable as usual. The line is becoming a bit livelier and trench mortar activity is increasing on both sides.

Saturday, December 23, 1916

Aeroplanes are fairly active today. Fritz's are flying very high and therefore cannot do much scouting. In the evening one of our planes hovered low over Fritz's lines and a hurricane of rifle bullets were sent after him. It was extremely daring of the pilot and he was lucky to get away unscathed.

Sunday, December 24, 1916

Quite a racket was kicked up around the Calonne Sector. For a time there was a great display of fireworks. Heard the 22nd Battalion had carried out a raid.

Monday, December 25, 1916

This is Christmas Day and the weather is wretched. I have tired of sleeping in the gun emplacement and have started digging a deep dug-out. The other two dug-outs are leaking like a sieve, so had no trouble in obtaining assistance.

Word reached us that the 27th Battalion was going to make an attack tonight. Just as I was preparing to settle down for the night, rifle and machine-gun fire opened up all of a sudden and a flood of bullets poured over our parapet making us keep our heads down. It was apparent a raid or simulated attack was on and Heinie was lining his parapet and shooting like mad. Soon this fire gave way to trench mortars and from that to light and then heavy artillery. The enemy was evidently scared or peeved for he lifted his fire and shelled Arras Road and its vicinity. Soon he began to scatter his fire and when a couple of heavies hissed over our trench and burst twenty yards beyond throwing a shower of mud over our emplacement making the stove dance and knocking out the candle light, we beat it to our partly made dug-out. There we sat still expecting every moment to be our last. But, after what seemed a long time, the shelling quietened down but not before we had many narrow escapes. No sooner did the enemy cease firing in our direction when our artillery took up the challenge and thundered out crushing stuff. Heinie shifted his attention to them and our immediate area lapsed into quietness again, much to our relief.

A very amusing incident occurred during this lively bombardment when two of our gun crew tried to escape the shelling which very nearly got them. They occupied one of the dug-outs adjoining the communication trench about twenty-five yards away. A shell exploded within fifteen feet of them, throwing a fountain of earth up in the air to fall on the top of their dug-out. We said to each other, watch Aimoe and McCormick get out of the dug-out in a hurry, but there was not a stir. In a few minutes another one came over and just missed them. In a flash McCormick rushed out of the dug-out, down the trench towards us and turning sharply into the short trench leading to the emplacement, threw himself into it. He was immediately followed by Aimoe who had his tunic on his arm, his braces streaming in the wind and he was in such a hurry to get round the bend in the trench that he did a perfect Charlie Chaplin on one foot. No sooner did he land in the emplacement when a third shell exploded right in front of it wrecking the emplacement and tossing the gun out of the way and scattering corruption all over them. It was a scream to see them, consternation and fright written all over their features. Scrambling from the emplacement they literally flew up the trench a couple of hundred yards away, finally taking refuge in a deep dug-out in the battalion's quarters. They did not put in an appearance for quite a while afterwards. Although it was a serious situation and their plight desperate, it was impossible to refrain from laughter.

Tuesday, December 26, 1916

This morning I went down the trench to see what damage was done. Ablain Lane was demolished in one place and the Arras Road trench was caved in where it adjoined Ablain Lane in two places by a couple of shells which burst on the parapet. Between the road and our emplacement were several new shell holes; there were also new shell holes all round our emplacement. Tonight Fritz sent over whiz-bangs when the ration limber came up the road at 12:00 p.m. Heiny got busy again with trench mortars and artillery.

Wednesday, December 27, 1916

Trench mortar duels still continue.

Thursday, December 28, 1916

Fritz was very active tonight and dropped several thousand gas shells in the vicinity of Bully-Grenay and Aix-Noulette. Six civilians belonging to one family were gassed.

Friday, December 29, 1916

It started raining tonight and did not stop until 9:00 a.m. The trenches are in a fearful mess. Ablain Lane has caved in almost completely and we will have to go overland tomorrow for rations. The Arras Road communication trench has fallen in in several places and is full of water. This is the opportunity for sniping and indirect machine-gun fire. The other night, while emptying sandbags, a bullet whistled past Driscoll's head and struck corrugated iron a few inches from my feet sending sparks flying.

Tuesday, January 2, 1917

The weather is still wet and miserable and the trenches are in a deplorable condition. Artillery and trench-mortar fire is increasing. We are having quite a time with our deep dug-outs. I am afraid our relief will have to finish it. Heiny was busy this forenoon when dinner was being cooked. He sent over about fifteen heavies and they dropped fairly close to us, the nearest one alighting about three yards from the dug-out. We had to take refuge in our new shelter. It is easily seen that in the event of an attack we would be out of luck as he has a perfect line on our quarter. There is no question but the gun should be moved to a more isolated spot.

Wednesday, January 3, 1917

Fritz has been busy again and managed almost a direct hit on our emplacement. The emplacement is wrecked, but luckily the gun is intact. However, he has demolished our cook kitchen burying brazier, utensils, fuel and rations. Another couple of shells all but got our dug-out.

Our new officer, Lt. Williams, who had not been under fire before, was down in the Bajolle trench visiting some other crews with Sgt. McGirr, and on his way to our position got caught in the shelling. The sergeant presently appeared and told us that Williams was down in the trench a bit stuck in the mud, and almost all in. Laughingly, he said, "I don't think he will bother you again about being good soldiers in the trenches." Williams was well groomed in peace-time soldiering and expected us to keep ourselves shaved, buttons polished and clothing clean when in the line despite conditions created by the weather and the enemy. We resented this from a newcomer who had yet to obtain battle experience and be able to differentiate between important and unimportant things. A few moments later he appeared round the corner of the dug-out and collapsed. He was in quite a state and looked as if he had undergone a great ordeal. Mired up to his knees with shells exploding all around him quite unnerved him—it was an effective cure. There was no more word about being fancy-line soldiers.

He was the son of a Hamilton, Ontario minister. I was told that the lovely, home-knitted, pure wool socks and other comforts that came our way were donated by his father's congregation. I froze on to the socks and washed and rewashed them in shellhole water as they were far superior to the issue socks and I had no desire to lose them. However, it is a shame how unappreciative some soldiers are—some of our men made use of them for a few days, threw them away and put in for others. When Williams left us a few months later, all Hamilton donations stopped.

Thursday, January 3, 1917

Heiny was busy today shelling Ablain and North Alley trenches.

Friday, January 5, 1917

An extra fine day today. Our artillery opened the day's proceedings by hammering at the enemy for several hours, paying particular attention to Fosse 6 where a troublesome battery is located.

Saturday, January 6, 1917

The enemy was very quiet throughout last night and this morning. Very few lights were thrown up and there was no artillery, trench-mortar, machine-gun or rifle fire. Owing to this unusual circumstance, word was pased round to all to be on the alert. The gun section at the billets was ordered up to the line and stood to outside in the rain in readiness for eventualities. Nothing, however, occurred. Perhaps Fritz was scared at us being so silent or he was changing over. Anyway, there was some reason for the quietness.

Sunday, January 7, 1917

Our trench mortars were active today especially on the Pimple. I watched them being fired and followed their course through the air. The explosions were terrific and beat everything I had seen. A mule that broke loose is parading the Lorette Plateau in full view of the enemy.

Monday, January 8, 1917

At 7:30 p.m. we were relieved. One of the relieving party had his foot injured by a limber on the way up and had to return for treatment.

Tuesday, January 9, 1917

Our quarters are situated in Noulette Woods and belonged originally to the French. The way to them was extremely muddy.

I paid Bully-Grenay a visit today. A soldier of the 22nd Battalion ran amok and began firing his rifle at all and sundry. There was quite a stampede around the Y.M.C.A. Someone shot him in the leg. I saw him being carried away on a stretcher.

Friday, January 12, 1917

The weather is extremely cold. I was offered an easy job—Orderly Room Clerk. This carried three stripes—but, refused—too dull and uninteresting.

Saturday, January 13, 1917

I heard that ten Germans escaped from the prisoners' camp at Bruay, but were recaptured at night in our front lines.

Sunday, January 14, 1917

We had an easy time going into the trenches tonight. The last few hundred yards we travelled overland. The location is known as the Bojolle line and is down in the flat parallel to the Arras Road near Souchez. Our dug-out, though dry, is cramped for room. Duties are easy but awkward, having to wade through mud to gun positions.

Monday, January 15, 1917

As usual, I have started to investigate the neighbourhood. Skulls and bones protrude from the parapet every few yards. Most of the remains were those of Frenchmen, their uniforms being the old dark blue. The Bojolle line seems to be one long cemetery. Most of the crosses simply mentioned "Francais."

Near the path down to Souchez a few hundred yards away, equipment, bits of clothing, skulls, bones in long boots (German) were very noticeable.

Tuesday, January 16, 1917

A heavy fall of snow made the surroundings look dismal.

Since a week past, rumours have been flying around that a big raid is to be carried out by the 4th and 5th Brigades, while the 6th Brigade is to make a feint attack. At 3:00 p.m. we were notified that in an hour and a half the raid would be carried out. We had to take the gun down to its position and three thousands rounds of indirect fire were to be directed along a road 2,300 yards away to the left of Fosse 6 in the vicinity of Angres.

Thirteen hundred yards away is the Pimple and it is expected that trouble will come from the enemy at this point if our movements or fire are observed. The light, however, was bad and retaliation did not develop. The artillery opened up right on the dot and our machine-guns set up a barrage on their objectives while the front liners threw over smoke bombs. Phosphorus shells were also sent hurling into Fritz's lines. To the north a couple of mines were exploded and the 4th and 5th Brigades went over. So far, no authentic news has reached us, but we have had varying reports of the result. The commonest version is that Fritz was aware of the raid and his lines opposite the 5th Brigade were heavily manned. A limited number reached his wire, threw bombs and retired. The 4th Brigade got into his lines, but found no troops, the enemy having retired to the supports.

A few days later I received what appears to be the correct result of the raid. It took place at Cité Calonne. Prisoners numbered one hundred including one officer; they were Poles and Silesians. Our losses were slight. In four minutes the enemy front line was reached and in twenty minutes we were in to his supports to a length of three hundred yards—the whole frontage covered 750 yards. About sixteen hundred men took part. The enemy dug-outs were blown up and set afire by throwing in Stokes' bombs with petrol cans of oil attached, creating considerable casualties. Trenches were demolished. One of our sergeants, who was in Bully-Grenay, saw between 25 and 30 of the prisoners—he said they were a miserable-looking lot, many being mere boys.

Wednesday, January 17, 1917

Our spell in the Souchez-Angres Sector has come to an end and tonight we we were relieved by the gunners of the 1st Brigade. The relief was a good one and we were glad to pull out of the snow and slush of the Bajolle line. We were mushing it along the Arras Road by 7:00 p.m. In an hour's time we reached Sains and went into billets.

Thursday, January 18, 1917

At 9:00 a.m. we start on the march. Hersin is soon reached, then on to Barlin where we saw a peculiar incident. A woman in mourning with a black veil over her head was walking along the street followed by her husband who carried a little coffin containing the body of their child.

Preceding her was a priest in black and white robes with a few boys in front, one carrying a black cross with a metal crucifix in the centre. A few paces behind him another boy walked, holding a cross to which was attached a wide pale blue ribbon made up into a big bow. It was a strange sight and I thought an exceedingly poor custom to influct on the bereaved parents.

Marching was extremely difficult owing to the road being so slushy. Our feet were as wet as could be before we had gone very far. From Barlin we went through Houdain and then on to Division. Thence our route lay through Ourton to Dieval, our quarters. Roughly we tramped about thirteen miles. It was bitterly cold when we reached our journey's end. A tot of rum, and then after waiting a couple of hours for supper, we toppled over to sleep. The billet is an old barn and is very draughty. I see where there will not be much comfort.

Saturday, January 20, 1917

I visited the village of Bours, 2½ kilometers away.

Monday, January 29, 1917

Today the brigade marched past the Corps Commander, Sir Julian Byng, a few miles from Dieval on the road to St. Pol.

Tuesday, January 30, 1917

We left our billets after being nearly frozen for several days, and headed for our next quarters at Burbure, passing en route Ourton, Dicion, Bamblain, Chatelain and Cauchy-a-la-Tour, a distance of about twelve miles.

Wednesday, January 31, 1917

We went for a short route march to Auchel.

Thursday, Feburary 1, 1917

I visited Lillers today. It is a fair-sized town much the same as Bailleul and Poperinghe.

Some soldiers has a narrow escape when a motor car, occupied by Frenchmen, skidded. It was followed by a car containing three German prisoners. Canadian Army Headquarters was located at Lillers.

Saturday, February 3, 1917

We went on a route march today by way of Lillers and Allouagne.

I paid the 31st Battalion a visit and was told that Ross of my old company was killed near Souchez by a "sausage."

Sunday, February 4, 1917

At Auchel several rather amusing boxing bouts were seen.

245

Monday, February 5, 1917

We lined up and trooped to the Colliery Baths at Auchel, the best shower we have had so far. Our badge, the arrow, was given to us today.[9]

Tuesday, February 6, 1917

All the originals of the 6th Brigade had their photos taken. They were a sadly depleted lot. Headquarter units would probably comprise 85% of the number.

Thursday, February 8, 1917

I hiked today to Bruay to see the finals of the 2nd Division Boxing Tournament. The prize winners came from the 2nd Pioneers, 6th Canadian Engineers, 6th Brigade and 4th Brigade. Bombardier Wells, a tall, lanky, fair-haired Englishman, gave an exhibition of boxing. He seemed a very skilful boxer, but he did not look rugged enough for world championship calibre.

Friday, February 9, 1917

Two of us set out for Lillers for the purpose of getting a decent meal. Decent meals are scarce but this time we were in luck. Entering a restaurant we were served pork chops garnished with beans and chipped potatoes, and liberally washed down with coffee. The price was two francs. So, it is about the best meal I have had in France.

On the way back we dropped into a little store which had a sign in the window "English spoken here." A woman was in charge and from her I elicited much interesting information concerning the earlier part of the war in this and the adjoining area. She was English born, married to an Englishman, and lived in France for twenty years, paying a visit to England regularly every year before the war. She appeared sensible, level-headed and gave us a good account of happenings when she fled from La Bassée where her husband was manager and head brewer of a brewery belonging to a firm whose principals resided in Lille and Paris.

La Bassée, before the war, had a population of around 4,000 and when they left it had dwindled to 900. She said the civilians did not

---

[9] This was a brown, cloth badge sewn into the centre of the 2nd Division's blue divisional patch. All machine-gunners in the machine-gun corps in each division wore the same badge.

know very much of what was taking place. French soldiers passed through the town to the line and that was practically the last they saw of them. The artillery kicked up a terrific noise and the continuous bombardment startled them. Her husband, however, paid little attention, expecting that the Germans would be driven back and went on with his duties as usual. The people gradually pulled out, provisions became scarce, and shells were occasionally reaching the town. The climax came when she went to the butcher's shop for meat. On the way she overheard two soldiers saying that they were surrounded. When she got home she told her husband what she heard. For the first time he became serious and anxious. He had only finished a big brew when he called the hands together and told them how to proceed until he got back from seeing his wife and children in safer quarters. He then got out the pony and trap, threw in a few valuables and necessaries, including the meat. His wife and children jumped in and in a few minutes they were fleeing along the road which was a moving mass of refugees all bent for various places. They had in mind the town of Merville. French soldiers warned them on the road they had to take devious courses to escape the cordon. Soon they were augmented by crowds escaping from other fronts and the roads became blocked with people of foot and in various conveyances. Many were heading for Bethune. They said a great many wandered into the enemy's hands, many of them young men who today should be in uniform fighting for their homeland. Everything was in a tumult and she later heard that when the Germans reached La Bassée they began firing down the roads. Many left their own houses to seek shelter with relatives or to inform them that they were leaving, with the result that families became separated and to this day traces cannot be found of thousands.

She, herself, saw a woman shot within a few yards of her. Several hundred stayed behind in La Bassée taking refuge in cellars. Many were killed between the opposing bombardments, and the Germans must have captured a large number. These civilians were sent inland to work on German farms and to make munitions. Letters have trickled through from some they thought were lost. Only a fortnight ago a woman, who had stayed near her in La Bassée, arrived in Lillers, clearing through Switzerland. She failed to recognize her, her features were so changed.

From La Bassée this English person ultimately reached Lillers. Her husband never returned. He obtained work in a brewery in town, but, of course, his position is nothing to what it was. His men fled La Bassée. The Germans took possession of the brewery and quartered themselves there. Fearing the beer was poisoned, every drop was

247

poured away. A few months previous to the war, new machinery, copper tanks, etc. were installed. All this was removed and shipped to Germany. She stated that near the road where we were billeted refugees squatted there in thousands. Ultimately, they found accommodation. Some obtained government work, others started little buisnesses, while a number did odd jobs. She did not know how half of them existed. The government granted them a franc per day for an adult and half a franc for a child, but she mentioned this was insufficient to keep body and soul together.

When questioned regarding the attitude of the civilians towards the refugees, she startled us by saying with few exceptions they would do nothing for them; on the other hand they put difficulties in their way. It was claimed that the refugees interfered with their trade and employment. She, herself, thought that they were jealous of the industry and energy that some of the refugees displayed. A number of the refugees were forced to hawk goods to make a living. Many sold cakes, fruit and confectionery to the soldiers, sometimes following a brigade for miles.

On asking her what the French people thought of the British efforts, she remarked that many French were badly informed, that they did not read the papers very often and did not take a deep interest in matters. Consequently this class, and they are in the majority, is not well satisfied with what Britain had done. The educated classes, who realize all the difficulties, on the other hand, thought she had done all she could. Confronted with German fighting power, British power seemed weak. The French do not think anything extraordinary about the British or Colonial Forces, but she attributes this to nature. She said the French think they are the best fighters and each nationality thinks the same. Anyway, she concluded with the remark that she heard a French soldier tell a shopkeeper that the British were taking over their lines in the Somme and would likely lose them, though perhaps they might regain them in a counter-attack. He did not seem to have much confidence in the British making an advance.

When asked about atrocities, she said she was firmly convinced that in the majority of cases the stories circulated were quite true. She was not very sanguine about our attacks. In her view we do not utilize enough men. Since the Germans took La Bassée they have held it despite repeated British attacks. Several time, she said, our men were almost into the town but could not hold their ground. Once, she said, the enemy almost captured Bethune. She mentioned that one time the number of refugees in and around Lillers numbered eight thousand.

Monday, February 12, 1917

We left Burbure today for a new part of the line, our destination being the Neuville St. Vaast Sector near Arras. On the way we passed through Allouagne, Marles, Bruay, and stopped overnight at Hondain.

Tuesday, February 13, 1917

From Hondain we proceeded south by way of Rebreuve, Gauchin-Legal, Estreé Cauchie, Camblain l'Abbé, finally reaching Ecoivres where we remained in billets for the next several days. Between us and the line lay the straggling village of Mt. St. Eloy. A huge double tower, the remains of a church of former times, perched on an eminence stands out as a prominent landmark against the horizon. When at Ablain, I was told that the ruins were caused by a German bombardment during the Franco-German war of 1870. The surrounding villages were declared out of bounds on account of an outbreak of mumps and smallpox. Burbure, which we left, had an epidemic of cerebral-spinal meningitis and diphtheria. Three hundred of the brigade were quarantined.

Wednesday, February 14, 1917

Both armies are displaying great activity on this front. Raids and counter-raids occur with increasing regularity.

Everything points to a big push in this area. The roads are crowded with guns, trucks, limbers, and troops. Munitions are being accumulated. The adjoining woods are crammed with troops, horses, mules, supplies and all the paraphernalia that is required by the artillery and infantry. Even the tanks were congregating in the vicinity. New roads and light railways were being constructed. Engineers are busy and dumps are everywhere. I even saw a company of black troops going on fatigue.

Between Mt. St. Eloy and Ecoivres is a military cemetery containing about 2,500 graves. The last two to be buried were members of the Canadian Black Watch, the 42nd. They were interred yesterday. A few days before an unknown German soldier was buried beside his opponents.

When out for a route march this afternoon we passed several parties of German prisoners. They were of good physique. A few officers were with them. Our fellows fancied their quarters—good huts, water handy and plenty of fuel.

Thursday, February 15, 1917

I have just been informed that Swenton of my old company, who was granted a commission last September and became attached to the 50th Battalion, was killed two days ago on the way up to the line.

Friday, February 16, 1917

We were awakened this morning by the noise of bombs exploding, the bombs having been dropped from a German aeroplane. We could distinctly hear the whirring of the plane as it passed over us. Three bombs in all were dropped, killing two men and two children—French civilians.

Sunday, February 18, 1917

I visited the village of Acq today. It is a small, poor-looking place of no interest whatsoever.

Thursday, February 22, 1917

I obtained a day pass and went sight-seeing. Leaving Ecoivres we went to Acq, then pursued our way to Frevin-Capelle and on to Capelle-Fermont. From here we headed for Aubigny passing on our right the village of Agnières. Aubigny is a fair-sized place, but of no outstanding interest. Gangs of German prisoners with the number nine in red on the back of their tunics were working on the roads. They appeared to be well pleased with themselves and cast insolent looks at us when we passed them. From Aubigny we went to Savy, then retraced our steps and cut over to Haute Avesnes and back by Acq to Ecoivres. At night we went to Acq and enjoyed ourselves immensely at the Military Theatre, the actors and singers being members of the Highland 51st British Division. They gave a very good display.

Friday, February 23, 1917

We went up the line today for a six days' trip in the reserve and another six in the supports. There are a great number of Kilties[10] around here. We came across a unit of the Seaforths coming out. They were peculiar looking objects. Mud from head to foot—layers and layers of it. They were unwashed and unshaven, and a sorry, tired-looking lot. To reach our quarters we had quite a distance to go, and it

---

[10] Kilted soldiers from Highland regiments.

appeared we took a round-about route. The first place passed was Marcocuil. A huge gap in a building marked where a shell had exploded. Next we make for St. Aubin. Further on we reach Anzin where the limbers were unloaded and picking up the tripod, gun, repair parts and ammunition, we string out in twos and threes and cross the Arras-Souchez Road to our dug-outs beside Ecurie which village is levelled to the ground.

We are in a deep dug-out constructed by the French out of chalk and capable of holding thirty-six men. There are two entrances at the ends which creates a strong rush of air through the interior making the place on the cold side and very draughty. Two tiers of wire bunks run from end to end.

A lot of gas has been sent over this sector according to reports. Lately the enemy has been dropping confectionery over our lines from aeroplanes. They are highly poisonous and we have been warned against eating them. When found they have to be turned over for analysis.

When sitting in the trench beside the dug-out, a company of Kilties lined up in the trench behind us. This trench formed a semi-circle and the bulge almost touched the dug-out. A Kiltie told me that their sudden appearance was nothing more than a practice manoeuvre, and they did not take very kindly to such movements. Our next door neighbour on the south is the famous Scottish 51st Division we heard so much about throughout the Campaign. We are on the extreme right of the Canadian line.

Sunday, February 25, 1917

Tonight I shot away a couple of thousand rounds of indirect fire. Indirect firing is not very satisfactory—you cannot see your target and, of course, do not know what damage, if any, is done. Besides, the belts have to be refilled and it is a blistery job forcing the shells in with the palm of the hand without a protective covering.[11]

Monday, February 26, 1917

It is a very fine day today. I saw the village of Thélus in the German lines. It is only from the ridge around here that the enemy can observe us. Loitering in the vicinity of the dug-out, we were suddenly roused from our lethargy by the appearance of observation planes.

---

[11] The Vickers Machine-Gun was a belt-fed weapon. The ammunition had to be properly placed in a webbing belt, and the belt, containing hundreds of bullets, fed into the mechanism of the gun. When fired the shell casings were automatically extracted, leaving an empty belt to be re-filled by hand.

They were busy observing during the whole forenoon. One plane in particular defied Heiny's anti-aircraft. It lazily hovered over his lines, and this was its undoing. A Fokker came over scattering several of our planes, then got after the easy-going plane and finally sent it to earth. Luckily the pilot was able to plane down. Heiny flew over us very low and our machine-gunners got after him but he escaped.

Once more our estimation of the German airmen has risen. He certainly did daring and effective work. Tonight I heard our plane was badly smashed when landing. The Observer had bullets in the neck, leg, back and head, and died at night surviving several hours. The Pilot was slightly wounded.

Wednesday, February 28, 1917

I am cook today and this is the menu:

Breakfast: Rolled Oats, Bacon, Bread dipped in bacon fat. Tea.

Dinner: A Mulligan made from meat, crushed hardtack, rolled oats and oxo cubes, seasoned with salt and mustard.

Supper: Bully Beef fried with bits of bread. Bread with plum jam and lemon marmalade, cafe-au-lait.

The rolled oats, oxo cubes and cafe-au-lait were either purchased privately or obtained from parcels received from relatives and friends.

We have been feeding pretty good since the last few days.

We are doing quite a lot of indirect fire on dumps, communications, etc.

Thursday, March 1, 1917

While on guard between 4:00 a.m. and 6:00 a.m. the line livened up on our left. We could hear the noise of rapid fire. Soon afterwards, red lights seemed to be fired into the air frantically. After the rifle fire had ceased and the raiders returned, our artillery opened up and a display of fireworks ensued, apparently an attack or raid had been carried out.

A few days later a report reached us that the assaulting battalions were the 47th and 54th of the 4th Division. They went over the bags[12] after discharging gas and took the front line without much trouble. Going further on the gas blew back and, in addition, they ran into their own barrage. Fritz, who was expecting them, was reinforced, and heavy casualties were suffered to the number of six hundred

---

[12] This is over the top of the trench which was lined with sandbags.

including forty-one officers. In fact, further reports had the casualties as high as nine hundred. A truce of two hours was arranged on the morning of the third from 10:00 a.m. to 12:00 noon under the Red Cross flag, to bury the dead and collect the wounded. Two of our colonels were said to have been killed. It was rumoured an investigation was being made because of the disastrous raid.

Today we went into supports at "Spooner" about 375 yards from Fritz's front line. Near us is the "Labyrinth," a perfect maze of trenches radiating and circling in all directions. It figured largely during French occupation.

Saturday, March 3, 1917

I had an interesting evening yesterday watching our own and Fritz's trench mortar units duelling. We have a very good position here and can roam overland at will provided the atmosphere is not clear enough for observation from the village of Thélus on Vimy Ridge. I have just heard that the Jocks over in the 51st Division will raid the Hun trenches tonight. Later a message was received from our signalling station that the Argyles made the raid at 6:00 a.m. and it was highly successful, over eighty prisoners being captured, including three officers, four machine-guns and two trench mortars. A further report credited the 6th Gordons as the raiding party and that the enemy put up a stiff fight and a considerable number of them were killed in the trenches. Our casualties were represented as three killed and seventeen wounded.

Monday, March 6, 1917

Last night we received quite a scare. Two of our crew were on guard and the others, including the writer, were in a deep dug-out sleeping. Suddenly those above excitedly shouted an alarm and there was a scramble to get into our clothes and equipment. Rushing upstairs, the gun was quickly mounted, bombs brought up and rifles loaded and bayonets fixed. Fritz's artillery opened up on our trenches sending shrapnel in all directions. We thought he was attempting a raid and anxiously waited for him to lift his barrage and isolate our front and support lines, but his artillery gradually slackened and no raid was made. It appeared that the 8th Battalion, who relieved the 29th that day, fired a few shots frightening Heiny and causing him to send up his S.O.S., and then the music started. It was reported that the result was one officer killed and three men wounded of the 8th.

253

Thursday, March 8, 1917

We left Mt. St. Eloy for Servins passing Villers-au-Bois. The billet is a poor one.

Our Section Sergeant visited his brother at Bricay. He was one of the participants in the big raid that was pulled off a few days ago and was wounded and slightly gassed. He belonged to the 54th. He mentioned that, including the Colonel and Second-In-Command, 420 went over the parapet after a couple of waves of gas were wafted over No Man's Land. The wind became unfavourable and the gas blew back and down No Man's Land, gassing a number of our own men. The artillery thundered out a seven minute barrage, then the barrage lifted and the men of the 54th went over. They were immediately mown down and only five, including the narrator, reached Fritz's front line. Three of them got up on the parapet and were immediately shot. The other two beat it back taking cover in shell holes. The raid ended in disaster, the Colonel and Senior Major being slain.

The 75th Battalion on their flank was more successful and obtained prisoners, but suffered heavily. The captives numbered eleven, including a sergeant-major and two stretcher bearers. The latter had huge red crosses on their arms, were fully armed and were seen operating a machine-gun. The Sergeant-Major said they were aware of the projected raid and ordered the Prussian guards into the line to meet it.

Of the 420 of the 54th that took part, 360 were casualties. Both Colonels Kimball and Beckett were killed. I noticed reference to the attack in the papers today, but, as usual, the account was coloured up.

Saturday, March 17, 1917

We have been having an easy time lately. Time [is] principally occupied in practice shooting and manoeuvres.

This afternoon I paid Hersin a visit, passing Coupigny. I had a first-rate meal. Anything out of the ordinary in meals is of special note to us—a couple of eggs, beans, custard and fruit, tea and bread.

Monday, March 19, 1917

I had a letter from Nan Proven saying that her brother, Billy, who was wounded while with my old company on the Somme on September 26th last, had died of wounds.

Wednesday, March 21, 1917

One of our aeroplanes came down in a field beside us owing to engine trouble. Both occupants were unhurt though the plane was badly damaged. It was equipped with a couple of machine-guns—a Vickers in front and a Lewis behind.

Friday, March 23, 1917

We left Petit Servins today for Mt. St. Eloy passing Camblain l'Abbe en route.

Saturday, March 24, 1917

There was much aerial activity today. A German plane passed over our heads flying very low and if it regained its lines the observer should be in a position to impart valuable information. Several of our planes went after it but were unable to bring it down. Shortly afterwards, Mt. St. Eloy and surroundings were heavily shelled. It was rumoured that 56 were killed near our quarters. A shell went through the roof of one of the 31st Battalion's transport huts, burying itself without exploding. Another shell got its mark, a direct hit on the 29th Battalion water cart, blasting it to smithereens, killing two men, wounding a third, and causing the death of three horses.

Tonight we went into the line and had a long trek before reaching our position at Zivy 1, which was located forty yards behind the front line. The dug-out is a deep one with two entrances and we are crushed in it like sardines.

Sunday, March 25, 1917

I went out this morning for water and had to hike quite a distance for it. Trenches are numerous in this area and it is somewhat difficult finding one's way around. Some of the better known trenches are named Territorial, Elbe, Vistula, Mercier, Guillermot and Ashton. There is considerable artillery activity. Neuville St. Vaast is in ruins. Heiny pays special attention to the roads leading in and out.

Not being far away from the enemy lines, special attention is being paid to guards. Raids by ourselves and the enemy have been frequent of late: the 18th Battalion lost several men as prisoners.

Monday, March 26, 1917

It is a disagreeable day and trenches are in a fearful mess—mud everywhere. We have been shelling the enemy incessantly with light and heavy guns and trench mortars and he has countered with similar weapons.

Tuesday, March 27, 1917

Another cold, wet, wintry day. I have heard that there were forty casualties around Mt. St. Eloy yesterday. We have continued our shelling today and pounded the hostile lines mercilessly. The enemy front line has now gaps in it in many places.

The 27th Battalion went over on a raid. They had no casualties and captured no prisoners. They got into the enemy firing line but found no Heinies. There were no dug-outs and his line was badly mired. It looks as if he moves his men back and forward to escape casualties.

Fritz came back pretty strong this afternoon and gave Neuville St. Vaast quite a strafing. He caused quite a bit of damage and registered several casualties, wounding one man of my old company. A crew of Imperials, who were helping out our trench mortar men, had decidedly hard luck. A premature burst occurred, killing a Sergeant, a D.C.M. man and a L/Cpl. and wounding two others. I saw the L/Cpl. being carried out.

Tonight a number of us were detailed to carry ammunition (rifle shells) from a dump beside a road leading out from the north side of Neuville St. Vaast to a point several hundred yards further up Vimy Ridge. As the roads and terrain were in a sodden, muddy condition, we were directed to a spot in a trench where several pairs of long rubber boots lay and were told that we better make use of them when packing up the boxes of shells. We looked them over carefully and found that they were for most, partially filled with mud and water and decided against their use. However, a few hardy souls struggled into them. We started together on the job, but it was not very long before we separated and got strung out. Up and down the trail we went, sliding and slipping and emitting curses in the darkness until we found that Moodie, one of the rubber boot fanatics, was in dire distress. Then our misery turned to levity. We razzed him every time we passed. He was all in due to trying to keep upright on his slippery rubber boots, but he was determined that he would not discard them. Wearily he struggled on. Bud Willox particularly took great pleasure in taunting him. Of course it was pitch black and the area was not very healthy; bullets were hissing and pinging around every few moments and we were glad when we saw the last of the boxes. We had

256

carried 144,000 rounds. It was a fatigue that we will not readily forget.[13]

Wednesday, March 28, 1917

It has turned out a fairly good day and the trenches are slowly drying up. There is quite a lot of aerial activity. Fritz brought down one of our planes in flames over his lines. We appear to be getting the worst of aerial exchanges. Our airmen are courageous enough, but due to lack of skill or cunning, or inferior machines they somehow do not measure up to requirements to beat the enemy.

As usual, the bombardment is going on with short rests in between. Fritz replies at times.

Thursday, March 29, 1917

Another of our planes was brought down yesterday. Fritz has been shelling today rather heavily and has knocked out a fair number of our men. Five of the 31st Battalion were killed and five wounded. In the machine-gun company we had two wounded, another accidentally shot and a fourth damaged his leg and had to go to hospital. The weather was again very disagreeable.

Friday, March 30, 1917

A raid was carried out by the 31st Battalion today. I have not heard the result yet. Shelling has been constant all day. Our dug-out has had a little jarring and the candles went out. So far, the information gleaned about the raid is that five prisoners were taken, but three were killed with their escort while crossing No Man's Land. Six of our men were killed or missing, including one officer, Lt. Appleby, and fourteen were wounded. Next night one of our men, Pte. Painter, came in after lying out all day in shell holes. Three officers and sixty other ranks took part. The prisoners claimed that they were unable to get supplies for three days.

One of our gunners was wounded today in Neuville St. Vaast.

[13] This, of course, was in preparation for the attack on Vimy Ridge. During the last two weeks of March, those in the Machine-Gun Company not on duty at the front were busy training for the attack. (War Diary, 6th Canadian Machine-Gun Company, 15-31 March 1917.)

Sunday, April 1, 1917

Another dismal day. A further member of the Company was wounded in the knee tonight at Neuville St. Vaast.

Monday, April 2, 1917

There is much aerial activity today. One of our planes made a poor attempt at fight and displayed a lack of wits. The machine was the usual patrol or observing plane and not much good for speed or fighting. Heiny, who was high up in the sky, was slowly approaching our plane as it patrolled over the enemy lines. Seeing his chance he quickly dropped and started firing at our machine which circled lower and lower, ultimately diving to earth in the German lines. If our man was at all watchful, he could easily have withdrawn to our lines and flown low for ground protection.

The bombardment has been continuous today and it looks as if we have commenced a softening-up process. Fritz has retaliated, but his fire cannot compare with ours. Our trenches are badly knocked about.

Wednesday, April 4, 1917

One of our aircraft was forced down today by machine-gun fire. It landed safely near Mt. St. Eloy. Fritz accounted for another of our machines today. We were relieved tonight by the 4th Machine-Gun Company. It was a very late relief. We reached billets at 4:00 a.m.

The weather has been atrocious—mud is everywhere and roads are badly cut up.

Thursday, April 5, 1917

Most of the day had been spent cleaning up.

Friday, April 6, 1917

Fritz sent over a solitary shell which crashed into the middle of a hut occupied by a party of Royal Engineers, killing fourteen and wounding eighteen. I happened to be looking at the spot when it struck. It is about three hundred yards away and below Mt. St. Eloy.

Saturday, April 7, 1917

An enemy aeroplane stole through the clouds this afternoon and fired at one of our observation balloons. When I rushed out of the billet the balloon burst into flames and fell to the ground. Fritzie immediately headed home as fast as he could. The occupants of the balloon were not caught napping. They promptly jumped out. The descent of the parachutes was graceful to watch. The 'chutes swung daintily and lightly to earth. It was a smart piece of work by the enemy and he made good use of the clouds.

CHAPTER VIII

The Capture of Vimy Ridge

Monday, April 9, 1917

We now enter into a conflict that became one of the major engagements of the war. It was known generally as the Battle of Arras, but most Canadians, in their enthusiasm for their own troops and the part they took in it, thought only of it as the Battle of Vimy. It was the biggest and most important struggle that the Canadians were ever in and involved the whole four divisions in the line at the same time on a frontage of nearly four miles. Hitherto, the chief actions such as the Second Battle of Ypres, St. Eloi and The Somme, engaged only part of the Dominion Forces and, consequently, the operations were not on the same gigantic scale as at Vimy.

When the guns thundered out in the early morning of Easter Monday, it spread a conflagration that blazed from Lens to near Croisilles, a distance of around twelve miles and enveloped five Corps under the leadership, from north to south, of Generals Hollands, Byng, Fergusson, Haldane, and Snow, involving the First and Third Armies of Horne and Allenby.[1]

The region of Vimy Ridge was allotted to the Canadians and units of the 13th British Brigade which partnered our 6th Brigade on the north. The lineup from north to south comprised the 4th Division whose chief objective was Hill 145; the 3rd Division which had to

---

[1] Lt.-Gen. Sir A. E. A. Hollands commanded I Corps; Lt.-Gen. Sir J. H. G. Byng (later Governor-General of Canada) commanded the Canadian Corps; Lt.-Gen. Sir Charles Fergusson commanded XVIII Corps; Lt.-Gen. Sir J. A. L. Haldane commanded VI Corps; Lt.-Gen. Sir Thomas D. Snow commanded VII Corps; Gen. Sir H. S. Horne commanded the First Army; and Gen. Sir E. H. H. Allenby commanded the Third Army.

overcome the strongly held position of La Folie Farm; the 2nd Division with the village of Thèlus on its front; and the 1st Division with Hill 140 to surmount, [and which] had the Scottish 51st Highland Division on the right.

The ridge was only about 450 feet high and sloped gradually from the west, but dipped rather sharply to the east. It was crossed by the Lens-Arras Road which ran through the hamlet of Les Tilleuls. The trees of Goulot Wood, Bois de la Ville and Farbus Wood partly draped the reverse or eastern side. The 2nd Division front included the highest point of the ridge. The length of its front was 1400 yards and the depth, 2300 yards which was considerably longer than the other divisional fronts. Section 4 of my company was given the task of finishing the day's objective at the furthest point and had to cover the outward and inward flanks of the 27th and 29th Battalions. My gun crew took up its position near the inner edge of Bois-de-la-Ville.

Vast preparations had been made for the attack. The array of artillery, principally British, was so great that one gun had only to cover a frontage of 27 yards. Silent batteries[2] took up positions within one hundred yards of the front line. Eight tanks were to be employed to break down enemy wire and dispose of troublesome machine-gun nests. A heavy accumulation of munitions had been assembled at various forward dumps. When at Servins a month ago, we marched to fields where a plan of our front was laid out to match as near as possible the terrain we had to cover. The principal features that we would meet on the actual battle field were marked out. This rehearsal gave us a very good idea of the distance we had to travel, and when the actual test came I had absolutely no difficulty in making for my objective without the least deviation. Everything loomed up as clear as crystal—the wire, the roads, the village, the cemetery, the separate woods and the railway embankment beyond.

The manner of fighting was to be on the leap frog system and the area was to be divided into four distinct objectives or lines, which for convenience went under the colours of black, red, blue and brown. The first, or black line was allotted to two battalions each of the 4th and 5th Brigades, the second or red line was to be captured by further battalions of the same brigades. The blue line, where most trouble was expected, was given over to the 31st, 28th, 29th Battalions and two battalions of the British 13th Brigade. The final objective, the

[2] That is, artillery batteries which, under cover of darkness, were brought close to the front, dug in and camouflaged but never fired any shells prior to the actual attack— thus silent. The closer the guns were to the front line, the greater the range the guns could reach behind the enemy front.

brown line, was to be taken by the 27th Battalion, and, according to my notes, by part of the 29th. This line ran through the woods already mentioned, on the down slope of the eastern part of the ridge. As my gun crew was attached to the 27th Battalion for this action, I traversed the full distance of the battle area and passed through all the units employed.

On the night of the eighth we hung around the billet close to Mt. St. Eloy waiting for word to get ready and move up for the attack. The minutes seemed to drag as we watched an aeroplane with lights moving around the heavens like a will-of-the-wisp. The appearance of the 27th Battalion along the road was the signal to fall in and we crossed to the road and followed in its wake. The night was frosty. We passed through Mt. St. Eloy and moved slowly along. Getting away from the beaten path, we took a short cut through the fields and stopped frequently for rests. Apparently, there was no hurry. As we conversed with each other in the darkness one could tell that this was no usual hike to the line. A tenseness pervaded the atmosphere and a seriousness seemed to creep over our features as we tried to sense the outcome and analyse what chances we had of returning alive, but these matters lay in the lap of the gods. A shell which swept through the air above our heads and burst about three hundred yards beyond told us that the Bosche was still alive. We were following the tracks of the eight tanks. Reaching the Neuville St. Vaast-Arras Road we moved along it southward for a few hundred yards and then crossed overland and took up our assembly or jumping-off position in an old trench behind the support lines. There we lay shivering in the cold and wet. The weather was atrocious, alternating rain, sleet and snow which was driven by a chilling wind that cut to the bone and we became still and numb. It was a long, tedious wait as we moved up and down the trench trying to keep warm. There were no dug-outs and not such a thing as sleep.

As the zero hour of 5:30 a.m. approached we came to life and gazed intently towards the German line. A terrific crash that resounded to the heavens heralded the attack. The barrage had begun. A constant stream of 18-pounder shells was sent pouring down on to the enemy front line amidst ear-splitting explosions and smashed and scattered the trench to the winds. Heavy shells would rock the earth and create enormous craters. The noise was bedlam. The Germans frantically fired their S.O.S. lights into the sky vainly calling to their guns for help. Lights of every hue in the rainbow flashed up from their line. Their trench and the vicinity was alive with fire and appeared a blazing inferno as the shell bursts spat out long tongues and jets of flame. It was a pretty although grim sight to watch a regular fireworks

262

deluxe. Our eyes were glued in wonderment to the line and we felt that ungodly havoc was being wrought on the Hun. The shelling was so intense that the line was illuminated nearly all the time.

The barrage had hardly lifted when the men of the 4th and 5th Brigades were into the German front positions and, after a short, severe struggle in parts, the objectives were taken. By this time the first batch of prisoners began trickling past us mingled with our walking wounded, mostly 1st Division men. An hour or so later and the second line was captured. More preparation was required for the storming of Thèlus and prolonged light and heavy fire were directed on the blue area. We could see our men moving steadily ahead in the rear of the creeping barrage. Progress seemed to be slow but regular. Fritz by this time had found his bearings and a considerable amount of scattered shelling took place. The walking wounded were quite numerous and we joshed them in the passing.

It seemed to become colder and sleety snow driven by gusts and squalls soon melted making the ground extremely muddy and slippery which proved a great hindrance when we went forward. At 9:00 a.m. we were ordered to get ready to move. Picking up our respective loads we quickly climbed out of the trench into the open. The ground was soft and shell holes were everywhere, which proved a trying ordeal and called up all the stamina and perseverance which the body and mind could muster. However, we were glad to be moving, if for no other reason than to get the circulation going and warmth into our bodies.

When in line with Neuville St. Vaast bordering Guillermot trench the enemy sent over a few shells bursting a hundred yards behind us. At first we took them for whiz-bangs on account of their rapid flight and did not pay much attention, but as the range was being lessened, the writer and a few others dropped into a shallow trench a little to our rear. Pausing there for a minute or two I was on the point of climbing out of the trench when a shell with a dull pop burst on the parapet almost in my face. My breathing stopped at once. With mouth open I could neither breathe in nor out. Breathing was paralysed. It was a peculiar sensation. In a flash I knew it was a gas shell and it completely fouled the air. In a fraction of a second, in fact my quickness astonished me, I had my respirator on and was breathing freely, but not before I caught sight of Porter on my left, who looked as if he was a goner and had not the strength to do anything. He was on the elderly side and I thought should not have been in this action. However, we were signalled at the moment to move on and I expected to hear later that Porter had breathed his last.

Prisoners were passing us on their way to the cages. They were a miserable-looking lot and were in a hurry to get off the ridge. Some were helping their wounded out. Several wore steel helmets but most of them had the usual caps, the majority with a white band round them. Two Germans voluntarily gave a hand in carrying out one of our men. About two hundred prisoners had passed us since the commencement of the attack. On the left, heavy stuff was falling in the outskirts of Neuville St. Vaast near where a score of horses were tied to trees. They were stampeding badly and tried to free themselves. As we struck the tram line, the enemy shelling became worse and wounded and dead were more frequent.

Soon we reached our front line and then crossed No Man's Land to Fritz's line. The terrain from now on was one mass of shell holes. Several contained dead, principally our own men. The German line was so flattened that it was scarcely recognizable. Further on we came across the 5th Brigade in shell holes, the limit of their objective. The 4th Brigade did not appear to have suffered badly. On my left was a hollow which ran up the ridge at right angles in which a number of 5th Brigade men had fallen. It seems as if they had taken this sunken route for safety and the enemy had anticipated the move and posted a machine-gun at the upper end. It was at this point I saw most of our slain. Still the casualties could not be compared to the Somme.

At this stage the going was very difficult. The mud was thick and heavy, the shelling so severe that we began to scatter. Many were exhausted, but could not halt, the shells were dropping and we were still within the portals of the barrage. The route lay between the wounded and the dead, and as we slowly dragged ourselves along our eyes rested on the fallen. Within a few hundred yards of the Lens-Arras Road the worst case was seen. A 5th Brigade man was struck on the head by a piece of shrapnel which knocked his brains out. They were lying two feet away and resembled the roes of a fish.

On the other side of the road we halted for a breather till the rest of the section came up. The enemy barrage had been passed by this time. After a short spell, we got on the move again and made for a sunken trail to the north of Thèlus. Looking around I noticed that Thèlus was a village no longer, just a mere shell with scarcely the wall of a building standing higher than six feet. Our heavies must have deluged it with shells. Wounded men of the 6th Brigade were now passing us on the way down to Neuville St. Vaast. Moore, of my old Company in the 31st Battalion, was hobbling out with a gunshot wound in the leg.

We were now near the crest of the Ridge and splendid view was obtained of the right. Our 1st Division and the adjoining Scottish Division were making very fine progress. In extended order with few blanks they were following close behind a rolling barrage.[3] The barrage showed up as a wall of smoke and so perfect were the shells laid down that there were no gaps and the line was kept as straight as a die, as the saying goes. It showed the artillery at their very best. The movable wall of bursting shells outlined by smoke was a pretty sight to watch.

After a halt at the sunken path, we went forward on the heels of the 27th Battalion who were to complete the objective, leaving behind on our left a line of 31st men who had reached their final positions. In a little while we met up with the 27th and settled down in shell holes till our barrage lifted. Before us are broad lines of barbed wire hardly touched, a striking contrast to the wire we had already passed. Our artillery did splendid execution on the wire above the road. It was literally hacked to pieces.

After waiting for a while the barrage showed signs of lifting and we struck ahead again. A few cracks from rifles showed that enemy snipers were busy. Several of the 27th men, in their eagerness to keep up with the barrage, got caught by shells which fell short, sending them scurrying backwards. Presently the right barrage began to move and then they left. Down the ridge we ran. A perfect panorama enfolded before our eyes. The wide Douai plain stretched to the horizon devoid of woods. Nestling below the ridge was Farbus, Vimy and further north Givenchy and Lens. Beyond Farbus was Willerval and on the horizon could be discerned several more villages. When nearing a communication trench leading up to the ridge, a hostile machine-gun opened fire and immediately everyone in the vicinity dropped to the ground and took refuge in shell holes, but it only required a few moments to put the gunner out of action.

The shelling became hotter again and realizing that it was unsafe lying in shell holes in the open, a couple and myself ran to a dug-out a few yards away from which smoke issued. One entrance was blown in. I only went down two or three steps when I was forced back by the smoke. McDermid, a Nova Scotian, was not satisfied with my effort and he decided to enter the dug-out. Meanwhile I returned to near the shell hole that I left. McDermid could not stand the smoke and followed me stopping about two yards behind, when shrapnel came

---

[3] A rolling barrage was one where the artillery shells would fall along a specified line covering the front of the infantry attack. A few minutes later, the range of the guns would be increased by 100 or 200 yards, allowing the infantry to advance further under their protective shellfire which kept the enemy's heads down. Then the barrage would "lift" or the range increased yet further. The intent was to give the constantly advancing infantry protection. Knowing this, the enemy's artillery would fire behind the rolling barrage, hoping to catch as many of the advancing infantry as possible, especially as they were walking in the open.

over our heads and burst, as I thought, a considerable distance behind me. McDermid uttered a cry, and as I turned he had a despairing look in his eyes. Thinking he was shell-shocked or frightened out of his wits, I felt slightly disgusted and paid no further attention. A moment later, observing that there were signs of a forward move, I went back to our gun crews in the shell hole and collected my load. It transpired later that McDermid was mortally wounded having received shrapnel in the lower part of the body and the upper part of the thighs. He died later at the base. His brother was killed further along the ridge on the same day. Two German prisoners filed up the ridge past us, one an oldish man with a black beard. Two hundred yards away several Fritzies were running towards our lines like mad, evidently in a hurry to be taken prisoners and to get out of their own shell-fire.

As word was given to advance, my gun crew, No. 14, headed to the left to take up a position on the north end of Bois-de-la-Ville. As the area looked suspicious, snipers being busy, we spent no time in getting down the slope. We passed a few 27th men shot dead and one Heinie. Seeing an artillery emplacement, we ran into it at an angle and met a German machine-gunner face to face. He was a tall man with an overcoat on, apparently, a new one, and on his sleeve he had a machine-gun badge mostly of silver thread and very pretty.

He was very pale and blood was trickling down one cheek. As I advanced back a few yards after passing him, I saw steps leading down to a dug-out and on one of the steps lay a belt with a dagger and fancy tassel attached. One could read the move. The gunner, knowing his game was up, swiftly got rid of his arms and tried to throw them down into the dug-out to show he was unarmed. I marked well the spot and also where the other German lay so that I might get souvenirs, but when I returned I found I was too late. The gunner held us at bay a few minutes earlier but someone must have winged him and no further attempt at fight was made.

Seeing the Germans retreating over the plain, McCormick and I grabbed the German gun, a heavy and clumsy thing it was, and carrying it about fifteen yards, turned it around with the intention of shooting the enemy when we found it was out of action. Thinking the belt was stuck, we cut it and tried to re-thread it, but it would not run. At this point Sgt. McGirr of our section jumped in between us from the rear and tried to get away a burst, but it was useless. A closer inspection revealed that the block was removed and, apparently, thrown away. McGirr had a piece of chalk and when we left him he was writing on the gun "Captured by the 6th Brigade Machine-Gun Company." I heard later that this was rubbed out and the capture was claimed by the 27th Battalion.

A few days after my return to Calgary in the middle of 1918, I read in the Free Library, in an issue of the Vancouver Daily Province, an account of the presentation of medals to Mrs. McGirr, the sergeant's mother. McGirr had been awarded the M.M., French Croix-de-Guerre and the D.C.M. Describing the exploit that earned him the D.C.M. I was surprised to read that on Vimy Ridge he captured an enemy machine-gun and, turning the gun around, shot the retreating enemy. It took a minute or two to sink in that this referred to the incident already mentioned that McCormick and I were mixed up in. However, McGirr was a first-class lineman and was ready for any occasion. In fact, he did not require to take a part in the Lens action as he was supposed to leave at the time for a commission. In his anxiety to get into the show, he persuaded Sgt. Ball to change places with him, so Ball stayed back at Headquarters and McGirr went forward to meet his doom.

We angled to the south from the emplacement into Bois-de-la-Ville and selected a suitable position for the gun. We started digging right away and it took quite a time before we had everything straightened out and the gun set up. Next we made a couple of funk holes and smoothed the position over to our satisfaction. Meanwhile the 27th Battalion threw out patrols a hundred yards or so in front with the intention of clearing the wood and Farbus village. Prisoners in twos and threes were being unearthed from the dug-outs and gun emplacements in the wood and sent to the rear. For a short time Fritzie was doing considerable sniping, one of our fellows being shot dead in the gun emplacement beside us. By this time the enemy noticed we had slackened, having gained our objective, and collected on the plain about a mile beyond. Coming towards the ridge in a vertical line one behind the other, they broke into extended order and advanced slowly past the telegraph poles in a line parallel to the ridge and towards the railway embankment where they stopped and, apparently dug themselves in.

Our artillery fire fell away completely, our forward troops having out-distanced the range. An occasional shell came over our heads and fell aimlessly down in the wood doing no damage. On account of the boggy nature of the terrain it was impossible for the guns to move forward and take up new positions, consequently, the enemy gunners took advantage of our temporary helplessness, and with the little artillery he had in hand, fired point blank into the wood, the shells kicking up a deuce of a racket as they crashed into the trees. He had a whiz-bang battery straight ahead on the plain beside a road that ran parallel to the ridge several hundred yards away and it was most disconcerting to watch him firing into our positions. Another battery, or part of a battery, was located in the wood around the village of Willerval on our right that fired heavy stuff. Having observation, good shooting resulted and soon there were many casualties in the ranks of the 27th Battalion. His artillery fire drove us from our machine-gun position and we sought refuge a few yards away in a short trench where we watched the firing and then crouched low to the side of the trench to await the explosions. That was the first and last time I saw point blank firing by the enemy.

An artillery observation officer, an Imperial man with two wounded stripes on his sleeve and a Military Cross ribbon on his breast, appeared on the ridge above us, and was frantic because he could not get in touch with his battery. So well he might, for he was ideally situated to direct fire. Shortly afterwards he was killed by a shell and his signaller was wounded. The latter was in the war since the commencement in August 1914 and this was his first injury. Porter, who I mentioned was gassed when he commenced to move forward, later caught up with us much to my surprise. He said he recovered from the gas attack, but the sergeant had to carry his load on the way forward as he was all in. The tanks were a complete fizzle and got stuck early in the fray around No Man's Land.

Between the shelling, McCormick and I made frequent visits to our gun to see that it was still there and intact. Casualties from the 27th were gathering around our quarter, most of them walking cases. They were anxiously waiting for the shelling to cease to that they could get away. One poor fellow, a big chap, was crying like a baby with shell-shock. His nerves and control were absolutely gone and he was yelled at by everyone to shut up the moment he whimpered. Ultimately the artillery fire slackened off and they disappeared over the ridge and another batch of casualties crept in. One, a Scotsman, had shrapnel in him on the left side from head to foot. Asking a Red Cross man who seemed to be in charge of these casualties, why he did not get him out of there, he whispered to me that he was fatally wounded and would peg out any moment. When we were relieved he had been lying there for twelve hours almost dead with the cold. Many dead and wounded were lying down in the wood in the snow.

Several times a scare would develop by those in front running back to our position, but I could observe no effort by the enemy to attack, and there was no concerted rifle fire by our men to indicate an attack.

Colonel Daly of the 27th Battalion suddenly appeared from behind and became quite excited when he peered at the plain. He yelled to me, "See the Bosches" as he pointed to them on the flats in front, as much as to say why don't you do something. I had seen them moving forward since the last hour or more, and as they were so far away did not consider it was worth while wasting amunition. Besides, our function was defence. He asked me if I knew where any of his officers were. I told him there were some in a dug-out about twenty yards away and pointed to the place. When he reached the dug-out I heard him bawling them out at the top of his voice for staying in the dug-out when he thought there was so much to be done outside. He seemed to think that the enemy was going to attack us. Fritz's position, once we could get our guns up, was absolutely untenable. This surmise proved correct for he retired before many hours had elapsed to a line further back on the plain. At this stage two German officers on horseback rode along the flat from behind Vimy to Willerval trying to take in the whole situation, while small groups of Germans edged towards the embankment from near Willerval.

The 27th Battalion moved down the ridge slightly, pushing the Germans towards the railway line where they were throwing up flares all night. Number 13 Gun Crew on our right, about two hundred yards away, were very fortunate. They found a German dug-out full of souvenirs. It was the abode of artillerymen and signallers and contained swords, bayonets, revolvers, compasses, Heinie caps, photos, correspondence, etc. They came across Germans in another dug-out and took them prisoners. One of them could speak good English and said he was glad he was a prisoner for he knew he would get good treatment. He thought it was absurd killing each other for no reason whatsoever. He added the German army would soon be defeated and it was not the army it used to be. He said that as soon as our bombardment started, their officers ran away.

Wednesday, April 11, 1917

Word was passed around that the 4th Brigade Machine-Gun Company would relieve us tonight.

In the darkness we stole away over the snow. Fritzie was shelling pretty stiff, but we managed to find a quiet route out by Thèlus. Thèlus stood out like a spectre against the sky, gaunt, ruined, dead. The shell holes around it were veritable craters.

The damage done in so short a time was almost unbelievable. The roadway could hardly be detected for shell holes. Fritzie had a splendid dump here and evidently intended doing a lot of work on his trenches. It was quite an ordeal getting around the cross-roads at Les Tilleuls. The roadway here was over a foot deep in mud. It was a long and weary trek out and we passed about forty stretcher bearers with stretchers for the front line. The men were utterly exhausted. After a while we passed the enemy's original support and front line and

269

reached our original trenches where, after much straggling around, we crawled into empty dug-outs which we found and from pure tiredness slept in every conceivable position.

Next day we wandered out to Mt. St. Eloy, passing over forty dead horses at the side of the road, mainly killed by exhaustion. When we reached our billets we were famished with hunger, but there was nothing available to eat for several hours.

I understood our Company's casualites were twelve. Horsfall, French and a new battalion man who was attached to us were killed. McDermid died of wounds at the base. Eight were wounded. Horsfall, was sturdily built, was teased quite a bit by his Section Officer who usually referred to his short, thick neck. Curiously enough, Horsfall was killed by shrapnel slitting his throat. The casualties of the 31st Battalion were reported to be eighty-nine including two officers, one being Donald Forbes, formerly a private in my old company who was killed near Zivy Cave. He was from Greenock, Scotland and was a great friend of the writer. He confided greatly in me and his intention upon conclusion of hostilities was to settle down in Scotland as a C.A. [4] and marry a certain girl he was engaged to. He was a great admirer of his native town. Davenport, another old timer in my former company, was also killed. When found he was in a reclining position in a shell hole with his head resting on his arm. He was thought to be asleep, but instead he was stone dead with a bullet through his heart.

The engagement was the easiest and most successful that I ever was in. The going was arduous and tough, but the opposition was negligible, although after consolidation one was lucky to escape death from shell fire in Bois de la Ville.

Thus ended the storming and capture of part of Vimy Ridge by the Canadian 2nd Division as seen by a participant.

Thursday, April 12, 1917

Tonight we slept in a wine cellar at Mt. St. Eloy near the Towers.

Friday, April 13, 1917

Today was a day of rest and cleaning up. We obtained a bath and were paid.

[4] Chartered Accountant.

Saturday, April 14, 1917

We have headed for the line again, stopping tonight in Neuville St. Vaast.

Sunday, April 15, 1917

Tonight we moved up to relieve the 5th Brigade Machine-Gun Company. Gangs of soldiers were busy clearing the roads on the Ridge, shovelling the mud away, filling in shell holes, and removing debris. The weather was extremely wet and the area is a quagmire, almost impossible for movement of artillery and ammunition. The work, however, is going on rapidly and guns are slowly getting forward. Many dead horses lie around and a number of our dead are still unburied. On the south of Neuville St. Vaast we are practically out of the shell zone, but Fritz is still close enough to us on the north.

Passing through Neuville St. Vaast, I saw the cemetery for the first time. It was hardly recognizable. One could discern that the grave-stones on the whole were much bigger and costlier than the average stones in other French villages. At Les Tilleuls we turned north and, after going several hundred yards, we moved into dug-outs beside the road where it curved down to Petit Vimy. It was here that machine-guns were massed, as it was considered the likeliest spot for a counter-attack.

Our home is a leaky German dug-out full of German jam tin stick grenades. After some clearance it was made habitable. On the road we passed one of our aeroplanes brought down by Fritz. A few hundred yards away was another one which was shot down yesterday. The two occupants lay there riddled with bullets. Further back is another of our planes with the two airmen burnt to death. Our air service certainly needs overhauling either in the way of planes or better training.

Richtofen's Circus[5] is operating in this area and they are making a bloody mess of our airmen. They know they have the superiority by far and do not waste much time dickering for position. Richtofen, himself, flies a blood red plane and upon conclusion of the war it was found that he shot down more planes in the month of April 1917, than in any other month, his score being twenty-one. Having a powerful

---

[5] Baron von Richtofen, who was later to command Fighter Wing No. 1 of the German Air Force, had painted his aircraft red. This garish colour, and variations of it, were later copied by other German squadrons. Richtofen's squadron was at first easy to identify, and because of the colours the collection of aircraft was commonly termed a "circus." Richtofen, of course, was a famous German ace who shot down 80 Allied aircraft before he was killed. Major W. A. Bishop, a Canadian pilot in the R.A.F., had 72 victories to his credit by the end of the war.

little telescope, I witnessed many air battles and could see them well over the enemy area when it was almost impossible to see them with the naked eye. Knowing by the colour of the planes who they were, made it much more interesting. Our planes all looked alike and were drab in comparison. The Circus planes were a riot of colour, one would be pink with a green nose, another black with yellow wings, a further one with a blue body and orange tail. Their best known men seemed to have had red as the basic colour. Richtofen's brother, Lothar, flew a red plane splashed with yellow; Schaefer's plane was red with a black tail, and Almenroder's was red with a white tail, but Richtofen's the daddy of them all, was a glaring blood red. Wolff, Festner, Krefft and Kleinhenz were other well-known members of the Circus.

Monday, April 16, 1917

The weather has changed and the sun is shining today. Fritz is paying attention to our vicinity and is dropping heavy shells with great regularity.

Tuesday, April 17, 1917

Fritz has observation on the road beside us, and his artillery is shelling continuously. Men and transports are taking great risks going down to and returning from Petit Vimy direction. The bend in the road beside us is fast becoming a Hell Fire Corner or shrapnel corner. Our heavies will have to get busy soon and knock his batteries out of commission or else the road will become impassable. We, ourselves, do not relish our position and we cannot expose ourselves without drawing fire.

Wednesday, April 18, 1917

Gangs of men, principally the 116th Battalion and 2nd Pioneers, are busy getting the roads into shape for the transports. So far, mostly pack mules and horses pass our way with munitions and supplies. Good weather is badly required to dry up the mess and enable our artillery to move forward.

Thursday, April 19, 1917

The enemy is still shelling the road in front of our position and killed one man and three horses this morning. Eckford and Williams of our No. 2 Section, when changing relief, were killed during the morning by a shell bursting beside them. I went for water today to the Zivy

Cave which is situated near our old front line. It is an old French mine with galleries running underground. Fritz has been seen in the Lens District and it is surmised that he is burning the town. Reports have reached us that Grenay, Angres, Lieven, the Double Crassier and Cité St. Pierre have fallen into our hands.

Near where we are is where the 13th British Brigade units advanced. Several men of the King's Own Scottish Borderers lay dead below the road.

Friday, April 20, 1917

The gun crew of No. 8 gun were practically cleaned up today. While they lay sleeping in their improvised dug-outs, a shell landed and the whole six of them were wounded, three rather badly—Cpl. Hunn, Kelly and Murphy. They would never have been noticed if it were not for an Observation Officer who happened to pass and thought there was something strange about the place. Going over, he found them in a sorry plight.

Our section moved forward to the railway embankment a little to the south of Vimy. On the way across we halted at an observation post and evidently we were seen by the foe for a shell whizzed into us and burst a little ahead sending showers of earth over us. We scattered immediately and ran forward with Fritzie gunners having the time of their lives sniping at us with artillery fire. Three hundred yards in front of our new post is a wrecked British plane.

Saturday, April 21, 1917

The enemy is shelling our line consistently and the front liners are having a hard time of it. Casualties must be fairly numerous as we are not having much artillery support. Last night the railway embankment was heavily bombarded.

We witnessed a very unsatisfactory spectacle this morning—an air flight between three German and two British planes. The enemy simply fought our men to a standstill. They were all over them and had our men in difficulties in a twinkling. Pitching into the Britishers, they forced them down and round in circles firing at them unmercifully. One of our planes caught fire and tumbled in flames to earth. One of the occupants threw himself out of the plane. The other plane, which was no match for Heiny, was forced to the ground beside us. Heiny followed him down to about fifteen feet from earth firing all the time. He then swerved upwards and passed us, but we were caught napping—nobody seemed to have had firearms handy and notwithstanding the shouts for guns and belated shooting, he got safely away.

273

Our airman, however, was very courageous. He made a perfect landing under extreme difficulties, and as soon as he touched ground he immediately fired off a burst from his gun when Heiny passed over him. The other occupant was wounded. As the plane was in good shape, I expected word would be sent to the Flying Corps in order that it might be picked up and taken away, but it was left there and within a few days it became a wreck, being battered by shells that burst in its vicinity. In our sector alone we lost six planes to his one, also an observation balloon.

We were relieved by the 4th Brigade Machine-Gun Company tonight and had a long trek to Aux Rietz, arriving in the early hours of the morning. On the road we noticed everything was in pretty good shape, the light railway extended and well laid, the roads in good condition and tents well advanced. Our big guns were into position once more and seemed to be more numerous than ever. The racket the guns kicked up kept us from sleeping when at Rietz.

Sunday, April 22, 1917

Another nice day but cold. Planes are busy again. Fritz, however, has measure of us and we find safety in numbers. We were shelled today by a long-distance gun which made us scatter.

Monday, April 23, 1917

This morning at dawn our artillery opened proceedings with a terrible roar. I never heard a bombardment like it. As I write, it is still going on on our right. It appears the bombardment was a preliminary to an attack on Arteux-en-Gohelle which was captured along with Oppy by the British and Canadians by the evening.

I visited my old battalion company and was told that Percy Craine was killed. It was he who gave me the idea of keeping a diary.

At Mt. St. Eloy today I saw about three hundred prisoners pass through on their way to Aubigny. They were the third batch to pass through and were captured by the Imperials in the fight at Oppy and Arleux. It was reported that the 27th Battalion Signalling Officer was severely wounded by a premature[6] from a naval gun. Our camp was shelled heavily during the night.

---

[6] That is, a premature explosion of the shell before it reached its target.

Tuesday, April 24, 1917

The enemy shelled our camp today and we had to move further back. Fortunately, no one was killed although one of our fellows was wounded. A shell skimmed over my head bursting twenty yards away and splattered me with earth.

Wednesday, April 25, 1917

Near Villers-au-Bois I saw a batch of German prisoners, about one hundred. Word has been received that Keyhoe of the Machine-Gun Company, who was reported missing, has been found killed and is buried at Thèlus. He was an ammunition carrier with the company on the 9th.

Thursday, April 26, 1917

When the sky was cloudy and three of our observation balloons were up, a German plane emerged from the clouds and flew past a balloon, firing at it with the intention of igniting it, but missed. After going half a mile away, the machine returned and had another shot at it but missed again. The next time he got it and it fell in flames to the ground. A few minutes afterwards about eight of our planes appeared.

Once more we moved forward a little and went into dug-outs around Neuville St. Vaast. When there, we saw a couple of our planes brought down. We went up the line with ammunition tonight and had a few scares from shell fire.

Friday, April 27, 1917

The First Division is going to attack on our immediate right, east of Willeval, for the purpose of straightening out the line. On account of this, orders have been given to us to move forward to the railway embankment to support the 5th Machine-Gun Company which has gone ahead. On the way in we came across another of our planes brought down within the last few days. It came down in Goulot Wood below the ridge. A few nights ago the enemy shot up a magnificent parachute flare. It lighted up the country like daylight for at least two miles.

Saturday, April 28, 1917

At 4:30 a.m. our artillery opened up an attack and our forces went over on our right. I have not heard the result but the current report is that the objective was reached. Our casualties appear to have been heavy for I have seen stretcher after stretcher going to the rear since the last several hours. Fritz is retaliating with quite a barrage. A couple of tall, slim Germans passed us on the way out as captives.

A 5th Brigade fellow who came down from the line this morning with a wounded officer related what occurred to him early this morning when out with the officers in front of the supports. While digging themselves in, they noticed a small body of about a dozen men a little ahead of them. Thinking they were our own men they paid no attention till a flare went up from the party towards our front. Being a little suspicious, they moved forward when they were imme- diately challenged in German and fire was directed at them, wound- ing the officer badly in the legs. Each of the enemy fired a round and then bolted. The 26th Battalion man returned the fire, hitting an officer and another two. His officer comrade told him to make sure his men and, as one of them showed signs of movement, he took no chances and polished him off.

Saturday, April 29, 1917

At 4:00 a.m. when on guard, our distress signals were sent up and the artillery got busy. A counter-attack had been expected as it was observed yesterday afternoon that enemy troops were being massed.

A few days ago copies of a German document for the edification of their troops was found in a German dug-out and it referred to statements made by four Canadian prisoners of the 2nd C.M.Rs. and P.P.C.L.I. captured in the latter end of March. They gave away information very liberally and indicated Division Headquarters, billets, machine-guns in the line, and also stated that an attack was impending and that they had trained for it.

This morning's S.O.S. was nothing more than the outcome of a scare. Fritz thought that we were going to attack and barraged No Man's Land. Naturally we thought likewise; hence the S.O.S. for retaliation. Both sides were very nervous. The positions, funk holes, do not offer much protection.

Monday, April 30, 1917

It was rather interesting yesterday evening watching aeroplanes manoeuvring for fight. Our planes were in force and made Fritz keep away at a respectable distance. We had several very fast planes. It looked as if a fight would develop. One of our planes, fairly high up, raced for Fritz, swooping down on him. Fritz accepted fight, but our plane backed out.

About 11:00 last night the enemy sent over gas shells and kept it up until about seven this morning. They came over in hundreds and hundreds as if fired from machine-guns. The air above the flats in front of the embankment was drenched with gas. I happened to be in a dug-out in the embankment and had to keep my respirator on all the time. At various times I would go out and remove the respirator for a few moments but the air was vile and my eyes would smart and coughing start so that I was glad to put it back on. All night long the shells were popping and it was impossible to sleep, masked with a respirator. It was a night to be remembered and it stirred more hate in us than at any other time. The weather has been delightful for a week and it is glorious to be out in the sun.

CHAPTER IX

Fresnoy, Hill 70 and Lens
The Summer of 1917

Tuesday, May 1, 1917

There was considerable aerial activity this afternoon. Two of Fritz's "Red Bellies"[1] got after one of our observation planes. It was pitiful to see how helpless our machine was. The German machines overhauled it in a trice and swooping down, flew right into it firing all the time. We could see the path of the tracer bullets—streaks of smoke. The tracers are for the purpose of observing and controlling one's fire. Every moment we expected to see our plane fall in flames to earth, but luckily another of our machines hove in sight and coming to the rescue, the Germans retired. Earlier in the day I heard that one of our triplanes brought down a Fritz but soon afterwards was shot down itself.

In the evening a few of the 5th Brigade brought in a wounded man. When passing us I saw he was an airman. He was one of the occupants of the triplane and lay wounded in our lines for several hours. I noticed a plane being shot down tonight. It seemed to be a Fritz.

About 9:00 p.m. fireworks broke out on our right and our artillery got busy. Soon the S.O.S. went up all along our front and then the artillery beside us commenced banging out the stuff. It continued quite a time and was pretty hot while it lasted.

Tonight we left the railway embankment and moved straight across the plain with a view to reaching our positions for a further engagement which was scheduled to take place on the 3rd and became known as the Battle of Fresnoy. On the way across gas shells were landing in our path and our officer had the temerity to suggest

---

[1] Doubtless one of the colourful German aircraft as described earlier, these two with the underside of the aircraft painted red.

that we take up a temporary position on the plain beside a lone tree. By this time the area in the vicinity was reeking with gas and the shells were popping in muzzled explosions all around us. It was a stupid idea and was resented by everyone. Continuing, we crossed the road which, if I remember rightly, was known as Vancouver Road, and dropped into holes on the other side evidently dug out by battalion men lately. These holes, two yards apart, were about four feet deep. There was no overhead cover. The location was a poor one. If it rained, the hole would fill up. We could not lie in it as it was too small. We would also be a beautiful target for enemy airmen. By taking up these positions we placed ourselves in a helpless situation. Lots of groans were let out when we heard these holes were to be our dwellings for tonight. We stayed there for two hours. Those to the south got out of their positions and moved along the road. Before I was able to get my equipment on and step on to the road, the man ahead of me had vanished into the darkness. Hurrying along trying to catch up with the Section, I observed lying at the side of the road, reclining in various positions, what seemed to be part of a platoon of men resting. I was on the point of asking if they saw any machine-gunners pass down the road, when to my amazement I saw they were dead men. This apparently was a collecting point for those killed.

Twenty-seven years later when talking to a co-worker, John Wilson of the 31st Battalion, he told me he was one of a party who packed out these casualties and he remembered the fatigue as a tiresome and harassing one. There were eighteen of them.

Further down the road, near old German gunpits, we took up our abode in cubby holes. A German plane was up at the break of day hovering low over our lines so we had to hide ourselves.

Yesterday the enemy spotted one of our advanced gun positions and pounded it mercilessly. The artillerymen were noticed running away to the flanks. Coming back later they were sent off in a hurry again.

Wednesday, May 2, 1917

In the evening, at dusk, we moved forward in the open over a mile to an old German line near a sunken road. Southeast in a hollow lay the village of Arleux. The trench appeared to belong to a system of trenches known as the Arleux loop and is about two hundred yards from our front line. A considerable number of German rifles were strewn around and several of the dug-outs were deep ones. Others were lately started.

Since the enemy was dislodged from the ridge, our division has pushed him back or caused his evacuation from, first, the railway embankment and then various parts of the plain. Our men have had arduous tasks creeping up in the night and digging themselves in as best they could. The 5th Brigade have had a hard time around the Arleux-Fresnoy Sector. Their progress was slow and casualties heavy.

Thursday, May 3, 1917

A further attack was planned for today as a continuation of the Battle of Arras. The objective was a line running south to Cherisy from Fresnoy. The 1st Division was chosen to capture the latter village and the 2nd Division was selected to overcome the northern section of the Arleux loop, the 27th Battalion taking the right and the 31st, the left. Our machine-gun company had to support the attacking party with overhead fire. It had been ascertained that the enemy were aware of the attack and in consequence were in strength.

It was early in the morning when we took up a position in an old Fritzie trench. We immediately began to build an emplacement a few yards in front of the trench, also cubby holes for belt filling. We were somewhat rushed as there was not very much time to get the work completed and be ready for the music. There were woods behind the enemy line where it was expected troops would likely mass for a counter-attack, so were registered to sweep this area.

Promptly at 3:45 a.m. our guns roared out their fury and our machine-guns cracked the air in unison. The infantry climbed the parapet and over they went. Before many minutes had passed, about sixteen Huns came running towards our gun with their hands up. This looked very promising. As they approached closer and saw our guns spitting fire, up went their hands still higher. They were taken captives by a couple of our men and it was amusing to watch their cunning. They were delighted with themselves, smiling and wanting to shake hands. The picture was ludicrous. Only a few moments before they were trying their hardest to kill us and now you would think they were our long lost brothers. The leader came towards me with his hand extended, crying in broken English, "You ween, you ween (win)." All you could do was smile, it was so funny. If they only looked sullen and threatening you would feel like strangling them, but coming forward minus firearms and so pleased! Later on several more batches passed us and then our own wounded walking cases began to appear. One of the first was McIlveen of the 31st. He received a wound in the leg and was greatly tickled with himself. "Never no more," he said to me, "It is Blighty this time and there will be something wrong with my head if I come back again." I think this was about the third time he had been wounded.

Before our barrage opened up, the enemy bombarded our front line causing many casualties and took the edge off the attack.

The 31st Battalion on our front went forward in the darkness, stumbling over debris and falling in shell holes in the face of enemy shelling and machine-gun fire, some losing direction and others stopped by uncut wire. A number in confusion kept going and walked completely into German hands and were taken prisoners. Apparently our artillery did not get enough time to register on their targets, with the result that the barrage was a poor one, starting behind the enemy line and outstripping our men whose function it was to keep close to the barrage. Those that got through lost contact with each other and were stranded in shell holes and helpless. They had to retire as best they could to a line further back. Considering the number of casualties and the small amount of territory gained, the action was entirely on the debit side. The casualties of the 31st Battalion were about 48% of their effective strength at the commencement of the engagement.

Friday, May 4, 1917

The enemy began dropping shells in our lines and things were assuming a serious aspect. Our men had practically no cover and had to lie tight and take full punishment. Enfilade fire was coming from the direction of Mericourt in the northeast and one particular gun had a perfect register on our trench. It soon became very noticeable. Starting on the north, a shell would explode in or near the trench; the next one would drop about ten yards further down, the third would alight a similar distance away. A series of explosions at very short intervals occurred for a distance of about three hundred yards. Then the fire would be reversed and shells would burst on the way back. Up and down the trench with perfect regularity, shells were bursting with the result that the battalion men were shifting and bunching up and down the trench trying to keep ahead of the bursts, while a limited number, as soon as the shell burst, would race past the place of explosion to get on the other side. We were completely at the mercy of the artillery. Our crew had to keep close to the gun; consequently, we ran the gauntlet every time the explosions neared us. The suspense was unnerving as the bursts neared you on the left, but when the shell passed over you and exploded on the right, the tension was released and you breathed again freely. Up and down the trench the enemy kept this type of shelling for a long time, making the situation almost unbearable. Much more of it and we would have had to retire.

Saturday, May 5, 1917

Very little information reached me as to how our company fared. The crews, being located a fair distance apart, it is difficult to know what is transpiring elsewhere. Three are wounded in No. 2 Section, including Keenan. Some of the crews became separated and members were arriving back claiming they were the sole survivors; others stated they did not know what happened to their comrades. Here and there they were disorganized by the shelling. No. 1 Section had a similar number of wounded. In No. 3 Section Branion, who was wounded on the Somme, was killed, while another was wounded.

Sunday, May 6, 1917

Lt. Waddington of No. 1 Section passed out wounded today, pretty badly I understand. Hostile shelling has been gathering in severity. Six 29th Battalion men, a few yards away from us, were wounded by the same shell. Cullen, a battalion man temporarily attached to our unit, was wounded tonight when out for rations.

The Hun still maintains his ascendancy in the air and our Flying Corps is falling into disrepute with our fighting men. This morning Fritzie in all his glory was roaming around our front line. I counted about twenty hostile planes. One Huge German scout with pennants flying, evidently a commander's plane, was being escorted through space by a battler which was flying a short distance behind.

Monday, May 7, 1917

Things in the aerial world revived a little today. One of our fast planes brought down three enemy balloons and a plane, while Fritzie shot down two of our planes within our view.

A singular and lucky thing occurred today. Heiny was bombarding us and was coming too close to be pleasant, with the result that we took shelter in a German dug-out. McCormick and myself were the first to get into the dug-out, but in a few minutes six battalion men crowded us down to the bottom. It was originally intended to be a deep dug-out, but Fritzie only got time to construct about eight steps and a landing. I was sitting on the bottom step and the others sprawled right on the top. As we lay there waiting for a let up in the shelling, a shell bounced off a dug-out beside us and slid into our dug-out, from the northeast corner, curved round the shoulder of the top man on to the lap of another and settled down on the third bottom step. Fortunately it did not explode or we would have been blown into minced meat. A yell was let out as the shining, silver-coated shell slid into our midst, and immediately one after another, holding their breath, beat it up the steps and bolted down the trench. When McCormick rose to get up, I saw the shell lying on the step and yelled at him to take the thing out. You would have thought he was hypnotized, for automatically down went his hand instantly and he picked up the shell and, climbing up the steps, [he] gingerly laid it down at the entrance to the dug-out and ran away. The rest of the day the battalion men gave it a wide berth.

Towards evening word was received that we would be relieved tonight. As I was one of the advance party, I started out early. Going down the trench, I came across a few men trying to dig out eight men who apparently were killed or died of concussion when a shell made a direct hit on their dug-out. We had quite a time getting out. Things looked pretty hot as we neared the embankment. Heiny was sending over heavy stuff which burst in our path. Taking devious turns, and as Heiny did not alter his range or direction, we got through but not without a few scares.

Since the last several days the enemy had been playing the dickens with the embankment. A shell had landed on our gun emplacement blowing the tripod away. Our dug-out could hardly be got into for wreckage and rubbish, while the latrine was no more.

After a long, unpleasant spell with heavy casualties and fate swinging to and fro, the units were relieved. The action was a most unsatisfactory one. Insufficient time was given to the artillery for preparation and counter work. The enemy was aware of the coming attack and having, as you may say, an open northern flank, their guns in that direction were in a position to concentrate on our front. Notwithstanding the smallness of the operation, the casualties of the 31st Battalion were nearly three times that suffered at Vimy.

Tuesday, May 8, 1917

As we had not shaved since over a week, we were an unkempt looking crowd, dirty and weary and eager to get out of the line for billets. Last night Fritz kept sending over gas shells by the thousands and we had a time of it lying with our gas masks on and unable to sleep. The smell of gas was abominable. Our brigade was relieved by the 4th and they were in difficulties at the start. The enemy counter-attacked their sector and the adjoining sector and forced a retirement. Fresnoy had to be given up. We were immediately sent for for assistance and at night went up to help. The 19th and 21st Battalions, if I remember rightly, went over that night but got messed up and demoralized and had to retire. It was reported that the Colonel of the 19th was killed.

283

Next morning the 20th Battalion was ordered to go over, but orders for cancellation came through when time was up and they were partly over before each company was acquainted with the fact.

Wednesday, May 9, 1917

Our guns are packed in one trench ready for a counter-attack. Later at night skeleton crews went into the line.

I paid Willerval a visit for water. A shell had nearly knocked the well out of commission and it took a good fifteen minutes to fill a petrol can. An artillery battery was approaching our direction from the north. The men and horses were nearing the cross roads about fifty yards away. I happened to be looking towards them, having finished pumping water, when over in the fading light came a Fritzie "heavy" landing among them with a terrific crash and igniting timbers of a nearby house. A melee ensued. The rear limbers dashed down the road to the west in the scramble. Three or four more shells followed. Thinking the enemy was possibly bent on wiping out Willerval, we beat a hasty retreat. Right in our path lay the victims among the wreckage, evidently stone dead—three men and two horses. A mule with a load of ammunition bolted past us. A quick glance at the fallen served to increase our anxiety to get away for fear of a follow-on burst.

Thursday, May 10, 1917

We are back again in our original positions which does not reflect very much credit on those whose duty it was to see that sufficient power was made available to make the action a successful one. When our men were pushed back, the British, who held the adjoining sector, relieved part of the impact and suffered heavily, the 12th Gloucesters, and 1st East Surreys being the victims.

The enemy has been sending gas shells over since the last ten days. They are fired from high velocity guns a considerable distance away. Our first spell of gas was when our crew were at the railway embankment near Vimy Station. I was on guard outside the dug-out when shells came flying over, striking the ground with a thud and exploding in a puff. Feeling my eyes smarting and a disagreeable sniff in the air, I awoke the others speedily. For ten hours we had our masks on and could not sleep. Thousands of shells were lobbed into our vicinity, presumably to render the artillery men useless. Shells came over so thick it was dangerous to be outside. The nights being mild and calm, the gas hung around a long time.

There is a dead 31st man lying out twenty yards in front of me. He appears to have been dead since several days, and is a big, husky and seemingly a new man, for he has the green Calgary badge on his shoulder.

German prisoners were kept busy as stretcher bearers. Two Germans came limping through the shelling into our lines on their lonesome. An officer, who was taken prisoner, was disposed to be talkative and gave his belongings to all and sundry. One of our gun crew got his whistle, another received his compass. Later on he repented of his benevolence and said our soldiers stole everything from him. Another soldier, an N.C.O., mentioned that he was in the American Navy before the war.

A shell burst yesterday, partially buried Willox and Moodie, but they were freed without difficulty. The same day our new officer, Locke, was wounded by shrapnel above the eye. Tonight, at 7:00 p.m., as we were waiting for our relief to come along, the enemy dropped heavy stuff into Arleux. Things looked suspicious so we watched silently for a few minutes, then the hostile shelling opened up in all its fury, throwing a barrage between the front line and the back of our trench. In an instant our guns blasted out their messengers of death and we jumped to our machine-guns and swept the path in front of Fritz. The enemy, however, did not come over and in a short time the bombardment settled down, our guns getting the last shot. No sooner were we finished when Fritzie switched his fire a little south at Oppy, the bombardment on our front apparently being a feint. Late tonight reports reached us that the German attack was beaten back with considerable slaughter.

Friday, May 11, 1917

We were relieved at midnight and had a long, tedious march to tents, arriving about 3:00 a.m. For the first time in an age I saw the papers. A lengthy description was given of the fighting around Fresnoy. The headlines were immense and referred to the action as the Battle of Fresnoy.

Saturday, May 12, 1917

On skyguard today near Neuville St. Vaast. This means that I have to keep a sharp lookout for enemy aircraft and have to fire at them if they come within range.

Mention was made in the papers that the German ration of bread was reduced to one loaf for three men per day. I am afraid we would regard this as a luxury. We never have more than a loaf between three and the loaves are small specimens at that. Often they are smashed to pieces when handed to us. Many times we have had to be content with hardtack (biscuits).

Sunday, May 13, 1917

I visited the 31st Battalion lines to ascertain how my old company fared during the recent attack between Fresnoy and Acheville and was told that the total casualties for the battalion were 229 including twelve officers. Lt. Percy Kingsmith, who was originally a ranker in my company, was killed. Scotty Mearns, one of "A" Company characters, and Mitchell, were also killed. Sgt. Newton was wounded for the third time, this time rather badly. Others wounded were Crerar, Doyle, Bateman, McIlveen, Bell, Luther and Freademacher. Lt. Newlands received his second wound. Sgt.-Maj. Lawson and Kirk Owen have gone for commissions. It was rather amusing how Luther was wounded. He stopped to gaze at a movie man taking pictures when he was knocked out.

A 31st fellow was buried by a shell but managed to dig himself out and skedaddled from the spot. Later on he came back and, seeing fellows digging at the place, asked them what they were after. Much surprised when they turned round, they told him they were digging for him.

Monday, May 14, 1917

Last night we moved up once more towards the line, this time as far as Neuville St. Vaast where we took up quarters in musty cellars below wrecked buildings. It was cold during the night and sleeping was out of the question. This afternoon I saw a weasel on the hunt amidst the ruins. The other day I was talking to Lt. Hall of an entrenching or labour battalion. He was originally a ranker in my section of the 31st Battalion. A year ago he left for Blighty, shell shock. At present he is in charge of a working party labouring in Vimy. He had one hundred men but between killed, wounded, gassed and sick, the number dwindled down to thirty and he had to take them out. When he met me he was looking for a padre to officiate at the burial of two of his men.

Tuesday, May 15, 1917

We reached the railway embankment last night. We have now guard duties to do for both day and night, sky guard during the day and

S.O.S.[2] at night. Our position is in a long trench about three hundred yards in front of the embankment. Yesterday the enemy hurled about thirty-five heavies on the railway line vicinity and I was told that thirteen of our men were killed. I was also informed that in some of the captured artillery dug-outs in this neighbourhood, Fritz had electric light installed and that women's apparel had been found. Lt. Hardiman was slightly wounded today. He received a piece of shrapnel in the head.

As my gun crew happened to be located beside my old company in the battalion, I sought out some of the fellows I knew, though at this date they were few and far between having been replaced by drafts of various battalions. However, I soon located Sgt.-Maj. Barrons and had a long talk with him, principally about the old boys and their fortunes, or rather misfortunes. Being in the May 3rd scrap, I was anxious to get his version of the attack. He was somewhat bitter in his denunciation of the whole affair. He condemned the whole proceedings. In the first place, he considered it was useless to advance until the right had progressed, for we were in a position to be enfiladed from either side. There was practically no preparations and details of what should be done were lacking. The artillery bombardment was poor and inaccurate, the heavies bursting too far behind the enemy lines and the whiz-bangs were out of range. Anyway, the German wire was untouched and the enemy uninjured by shell fire when our men attacked. All they had to do was to line their parapet and blaze away at us which they did causing heavy casualties. As the advance was not carried out evenly, those parties that went ahead and reached their objectives suffered severely from sections where the enemy were left in possession. Part of a company of the 27th Battalion went over the parapet only to run back again, thus leaving a space open in the attacking line. When part of the 31st reached their objective, it was found that "C" Company was caught in the wire and got badly cut up by pockets of the enemy. Only thirty-five answered the roll call later on. There was a gap of 350 yards between the 27th and 31st Battalions. They only held their positions for a very short time. New Fritz troops, fresh from Belgium three days ago, with hot coffee in their bottles and sandwiches, new clothes and new equipment came over, jumping from shell hole to shell hole in bunches of about a hundred. By force of numbers they compelled our men to fall back. Our gunners and riflemen opened up on them and many of the enemy

---

[2] "Sky-guard" meant being prepared to use the machine-gun against attacking enemy aircraft; "S.O.S." duty meant being prepared to fire the machine-gun, usually along pre-fixed lines, should the men in the front line send up certain coloured flares as a signal they were being attacked and needed assistance.

were killed and wounded. If orders were promptly given and men, if available, transferred to fill the gaps in the line, the Sgt.-Maj. thought that the front could have been held at least for a time, though he was of the opinion that the position was untenable once organized fire was poured in from the front and flanks.

Captain Blair gave the order to retire before it was necessary and in consequence they had to abandon about one hundred wounded. Thirty to forty, however, crawled back at night. Lt. Newlands, who was wounded in the face, lay in the German wire for sixteen hours. He said our wounded were flinging grenades into the German trench while the rest of the battalion was back in the sunken road. The enemy must have taken a lot of our men prisoners.

The 31st was relieved by the 28th who made a feeble bombing attack which came to nothing. Another attack was on the point of being organized when artillery officers noticed the condition of the wire and, seeing it uncut, had the attack cancelled. The Sergeant-Major considered the whole business a failure, badly organized, badly carried out and should never have been instituted as this part of the line was too far ahead already. The talk also of the enemy being starved and living in discomfort was a complete falsehood. They had a perfect home, lots of food was lying around, cigarettes, cigars and even books were there. The 31st had to attack, consolidate and this was a big item, and afterwards they had to carry out the wounded and even the dead. The men were absolutely all in and the rations were not the thing for the work they had to do. Our command have a lot to learn about how to conserve the energies of the men with a view to keeping them in fighting trim.

The Sgt.-Maj. was awarded the M.M. I chaffed him quite a bit over it. He said he got it because he was first at the "ration limber." Sgt. Talbourdet was also awarded it.

Saturday, May 19, 1917

Quite a lot of aerial activity took place today. Both Fritz and our men were chasing each other, but no fatalities resulted. Looking through my telescope at the German planes, I saw they were varied in colour. One was bright scarlet. This was flown by the famous Baron Richtofen. Another was red with a black tail. A third was white and black. A couple had red bodies with yellow stripes around the centre, while wings and tail were white.

288

Sunday, May 20, 1917

Jacklin of "A" Company of the 31st was killed early this morning. He was on gas guard when a shell burst a considerably distance away from him. A tiny piece of shrapnel, however, pierced his heart. He was buried close by.

We went up the line tonight, relieving the 5th Brigade Machine-Gun Company while the 4th Brigade Company took over our old position. One of the 5th was killed before we arrived. Two officers of the 28th Battalion were killed in our trench.

Monday, May 21, 1917

I saw an aerial fight today between four of the enemy battlers and four of our old fighting machines. It was a poor display and distinctly showed the superiority of the Hun machines. Our planes were slow, clumsy and difficult to manoeuvre for firing positions. Fritz would dart in and out at leisure, firing as he went. Our men were being hustled all over the sky. How they escaped damage puzzled me. One of our machines seemed to be out of control or its pilot was off his head. It ogled towards the German line being escorted by a Fritz and passed out of sight over German territory. The fight was a disgraceful one and as far as the enemy was concerned, it was like taking candy from a kid.

Bailleul was badly battered today by the enemy. The air overhead was thick with dust and smoke.

Tuesday, May 22, 1917

It rained heavily last night. This afternoon three of our triplanes got after six German machines and brought three down in splendid style. A fourth Hun plane made a beautiful nose dive and got clear away. It was quite a sight watching tracer bullets fired at our machines soar up from the ground. Little specks of light stealing up the sky marked their course. The shooting was very good. The enemy was evidently peeved, for soon afterwards half a dozen of his battlers arrived on the scene from the direction of Lens. They were to tackle our "tripes" (triplanes), but when they saw our men did not intend to budge, they turned around and headed for home. It was a welcome change and gave us great satisfaction.

A sergeant of the 28th Battalion was wounded by shrapnel beside our position.

Wednesday, May 23, 1917

I have just heard that young "Cupid" Jull of my old company in the 31st, who lately obtained a commission and was transferred to the 28th, was killed on the 3rd.

There was quite a lot of aerial sparring today. Five of our new planes made eight of the enemy turn tail, but they returned afterwards. A lot of manoeuvring took place but I lost sight of them in the distance. Later, looking away over Lens, a fight seemed to be developing. I had only time to get my telescope on a machine when the tank must have exploded or it got in the path of a shell for the wings were shot clean off into space together with what seemed the occupants. A few minutes later I made out a couple of Fritzies hovering about the spot. There was no triplane of ours to be seen, while earlier there was one around, so I presumed our plane was the victim.

Our planes went home early today and for the rest of the day the Huns had glorious innings all to themselves. They came over our trenches and observed everything that was to be seen; they even dipped low and strafed the men in the trenches. One of their planes went after our observation balloons and made the occupants of two balloons parachute to safety.

The only originals left in "A" Company of the 31st Battalion who go into the firing line are Sgt.-Maj. Barrons; Sgt. Ferrie, formerly Canteen Sgt.; Thatch, originally a bomber; and Maclean, previously a battalion detail man. Whitley and Musgrove are back again after being wounded, and also Sgt. Angus.

This evening one of our planes, heading for home after flying over German territory, was being chased by five Hun planes. The enemy fliers had the edge on him for speed and were pressing him hard. He was rising, falling, and twisting in his endeavours to keep them off his tail. There was a running fire all the time. Just when we expected to see him catch fire and crumple to earth, the foremost hostile plane crashed headlong to earth. Time and again they almost had him, but he went through the whole gamut of acrobatics and was under them and over them, behind them and in front of them in turn and put up a most magnificent defence. His trickery was superb. The last I saw of him, it looked as if they had forced him to land somewhere in the Lens area and it seemed doubtful if he reached our own lines.

Friday, May 25, 1917

Another lovely day. Our aircraft was out in force in the evening. I saw a German machine chasing one of ours which was heading back towards our lines. It was quite exciting watching our plane trying to shake his opponent off. Fritz was too fast for him so he had to manoeuvre all the way. Fritz was sending bursts after him, but our man handled his machine dexterously. His evasive tactics were marvellous. Once it appeared he was struck for his plane fell over and over as if completely out of control, and I thought he was heading for a crash and fires, but a short distance from the ground he straightened out and streaked for home leaving Fritzie nonplussed. It was a very fine getaway. However, later on I witnessed a poor display. Above No Man's Land was a Fritz plane and at a higher elevation were three of our triplanes who all practically had him at their mercy. One of our craft made a half-hearted attempt to shoot him down.

Sunday, May 27, 1917

We came out of the line tonight being relieved by the 4th Machine-Gun Company. I had a long tramp to tents near Mt. St. Eloy.

Monday, May 28, 1917

For the second time we had to shift our camp, having been shelled out. One of our fellows, when going for a bath, was hit by a piece of shell fired by one of our anti-aircraft guns.

Tuesday, May 29, 1917

Today great preparation took place for an inspection by Brigadier Ketchen, which was scheduled for tomorrow. We had a regular cleanup and our buttons were polished as never before.

Wednesday, May 30, 1917

The inspection duly came off and it was a relief when the ordeal was over. As a rule these inspections cost money. A full kit is required and as there are always shortages, it means a parade to the quartermaster's stores.

An engagement of consequence is usually followed by a list of awards, so today we were notified of the Vimy honours for the company. Decorations are fast falling into disrepute as most of them by far are given for no outstanding service, and as a certain number of awards are allotted to each unit, they have to be distributed. At Vimy there was absolutely nothing out of the ordinary done by our fellows. The artillery took such good care of the enemy that there was nothing much for us to do but to move to our objective with little opposition. In spite of this Lt. Williams was given the Military Cross, Sgt. McGirr the D.C.M. (he had already the M.M.), and Cpl. Hunn the D.C.M. (he also has had the M.M.), while L/Cpls. Olmstead and Dincen were awarded M.M.'s. It is too bad that the decorations are not granted for bravery exclusively.

Thursday, May 31, 1917

This forenoon we left for our rest which is to be spent at Gouy-Servins.

Friday, June 1, 1917

Some more decorations have been given away, this time for the Fresnoy engagement. Cpls. Beard, Clapp and Morrison [were] the receivers. Morrison was in the transport and his activities are always in the rear. No one, not even ourselves, knew what the medals were for.

Saturday, June 1, 1917

Another beautiful day. Most of the time is occupied in drilling and machine-gun work.

Wednesday, June 6, 1917

We went our on a route march via Camblain l'Abbe.

Friday, June 8, 1917

Reports have reached us that our old stamping ground in front of Wyschaete has been captured. A crushing blow was delivered yesterday when Messines Ridge was erupted by the explosions of twenty mines. The accumulation of guns was even greater than that employed at the Battle of Arras and on a shorter front. The massed fire absolutely smothered the enemy and the Ridge was wrested in the matter of three hours. Prisoners of over seven thousand were taken. The villages of Messines, Wyschaete and Oostaverne were over-run. The Bluff and St. Eloi, places where much fighting had taken place and where thousands had been killed, at last fell into more peaceful times. Australians, New Zealanders, Tasmanians, Irish and British troops shared in the attack.

Saturday, June 9, 1917

Early this morning there was a severe bombardment beyond Lens.
    I paid a visit to Aubigny by way of Cambligneul and saw a large number of troops entrain for Blighty on leave.

Monday, June 11, 1917

Word has reached us that Rosengrein, who was wounded in the Vimy advance, died of wounds.

Much rain fell today.

Saturday, June 16, 1917

Brigade sports were held today. The weather is still oppressively hot. We were inoculated yesterday.

Sunday, June 17, 1917

I visited our old positions near Souchez. A civilian with two youngsters was roaming around the Lorette Plateau above Spur Alley. Recognizing the remains of a German soldier, he struck it several blows with his stick and turning to me exclaimed, "allemande no bon."

Weeds were growing profusely in every place but the Pimple.

Sunday, June 24, 1917

I visited Bethune today passing en route Bouvigny, Boyeffles, Sains, Noeux and Veruin and returned by way of Hersin. Fritz was shelling Noeux with long-distance "Crumps" when I passed. At Bethune groups of Portuguese soldiers were strolling around. They looked a very poor type of soldier—small bones, slow and lethargic. Their uniform was almost the same as Fritz's in colour and were far too tight for comfort and active service.

Tuesday, June 26, 1917

We were inspected today by the Divisional Commander, General Burnstall.[3] It meant a lot of polishing up.

The members of our Company who chose Paris leave, as Blighty leave was too long in coming, had hot times in the gay city. The life proved too fast for them and Paris leave was cancelled shortly afterwards.

Tuesday, July 3, 1917

We left for the line tonight passing through Bully-Grenay and crossed the old German line. Fritz had a regular stronghold here. The

[3] Major-General Sir H. E. Burnstall took over command of the 2nd Canadian Division on 15 December 1916. An artillery officer, he had commanded the artillery in the 1st Canadian Division until 1915 when he was promoted to command the Canadian Corps artillery. The former divisional commander, Maj.-Gen. R. E. W. Turner, was appointed to command all Canadian troops in Great Britain.

Crassier was located on a ridge. He had deep dug-outs, cement machine-gun emplacements, tunnels, and his trenches were untouched. It would appear as though his flanks had been penetrated and he was forced to withdraw. A frontal attack on this point looked like suicide. We passed through Cité St. Pierre, a suburb of Lens. Our officers and sergeant who led us in had a very hazy idea of the location of the position we had to occupy. It was clear that they had lost their way and after walking us around several streets, finally decided that we position the gun in a vacant space adjoining a villa. We relieved nobody. We are supposed to be in supports. The gun position was ridiculous. McCormick and I soon decided that we would find a proper position before long. All that concerned the officer and sergeant was to get away.

The hostile line is difficult to figure out as Fritz has outposts around buildings. The trench system has broken down. We sleep in cellars and observe from the ruins of houses. Both sides, therefore, are in precarious positions and may be said to hold their lines in little groups, disconnected for most and liable to surprise attacks.

The suburbs of Lens are rather pretty and contain well-laid out streets lined with semi-contained, brick villas with nicely laid out gardens behind, bordered by high brick walls. The boulevards have a row of trees on both sides. Where we are, the buildings are compara-tively new. Every house is damaged and only a few are occupied by the troops.

At night the enemy sent over shrapnel and machine-gun fire knocked sparks off the buildings. Troops skulk around the houses watching from corners and door entrances. We were supposed to relieve Imperial troops, the Sherwood Foresters, but whether the gun crew beat it away or we could not locate them is a mystery. I am inclined to think we landed on the wrong street and we were left to make the most of it.

Wednesday, July 4, 1917

In the early morning I started down the street with a view to finding a basement for shelter and sleep. The first two I looked into were too badly damaged to get in and out; the third had an accumulation of debris and rubbish, but the fourth was the very thing the doctor ordered. It was clean as a whistle. We soon made a change over and as McCormick's whole idea of army life was a suitable place to stay and sufficient time to play cards therein, he was in his element with the location and in a few minutes he unearthed the cards and was calling for a game.

The next thing to do was to find a suitable emplacement for the gun. I ran out by the back door and looked around and presto! There was a position before my eyes. At the right-hand corner was a little brick outhouse. From there one had a clear view to a street in Lens about three hundred yards away, running at right angles to our position. The intervening space was completely open and branched in width from one hundred yards to two hundred yards at the upper end. It constituted a perfect field of fire. In a matter of a few minutes we knocked out a few bricks in the wall of the outhouse and trimmed the hole to look as if it had been made by a shell. This was to serve as a firing aperture. A hole was also made in the wall for a lookout. The whole crew surveyed the emplacement and smiled in satisfaction.

We did not maintain fixed guards. Every now and then we would make a trip through the back garden to the gun to see everything was all right. The garden contained currant and gooseberry bushes and also rose bushes, so we were in surroundings very much above the usual. In fact, we could very well have stayed there for the duration.

We noticed a group of headquarters officers edging along the buildings and apparently coming in our direction. As they approached closer I could see that our officer and sergeant were with them. Fortunately we were noticed and, as it turned out later, we saved our officer's bacon. Headquarters were making a survey with a view to establishing official machine-gun posts and had a couple of men carrying white painted stakes which were lettered and numbered. Our officer and sergeant were in a blue funk. First of all, they were afraid they would be unable to find us and secondly, if they did, that we might be asleep with the gun lying beside us. The staff officer in charge, who had maps of the area, asked immediately to be shown the gun position. I took them through the building across the back garden to the outhouse and pointed to the gun all set up with the belt threaded and ammunition and spare parts lying handy a yard away. I drew their attention to the range of territory the gun covered, to the camouflaged firing hole and to the observation slit. The response was—splendid, capital, an ideal position—and a stake was immediately deposited beside the gun and the position officially noted. Our officer was congratulated all round. His fears were groundless after all.

Thursday, July 5, 1917

Fritz did considerable shelling at night and his machine-guns were quite active.

Friday, July 6, 1917

Early this morning a 27th Battalion man passed our position after being wounded and was later followed by another man who was gassed.

An incident I have witnessed very often occurred today. One of our scouts was shot down. Hearing the noise of firing, I scanned the heavens and saw three German battlers high up in the air come swooping down on one of our scouts. Our plane flew for our lines, but Fritz was faster and soon overhauled him, shooting all the while. In a few moments our plane crashed to earth at a fairly steep angle. The plane flew as if it were undamaged. Our airman gave a very poor display of manoeuvring. Instead of dipping and zigzagging, he flew straight, giving the enemy a fine lead for accurate shooting. These displays very much disgusted our troops. We cannot understand why our scouts are not protected by fighters or why they do not display more wariness in watching for hostile craft. Later on a fight took place between three German planes and five of ours. A mixup ensued for several minutes but no damage resulted.

Word was passed around that an attack on our front was expected tonight and everyone was to be on the alert. Previous to this a hostile patrol of about seventy ventured too far towards our front and the 27th Battalion opened up on them with disastrous results. They retired leaving dead and wounded. This was the occasion for Fritz to become peeved and his artillery and trench mortars belaboured our front with gas shells and sausages.

Saturday, July 7, 1917

Both the 27th and 31st Battalions were bombarded with shells and a considerable number of casualties were created.

Sunday, July 8, 1917

On our left a bomb and rifle grenade scrap developed, which lasted for fifteen to twenty minutes and resulted in some more casualties. A dud landed beside our position.

Monday, July 9, 1917

In the early morning we bombarded the German lines on the right. This evening, for the first time, the Germans shelled our immediate vicinity. We had a narrow escape—a shell went through the side of our villa covering us with dust and sending pieces of brick flying around the room. Another shell burst on the other side of the street. We are still having a good time among the black currants.

Tuesday, July 10, 1917

We have started skyguard again, but Fritz has not given us much opportunity to get him as he keeps flying high.

Thursday, July 12, 1917

A quiet day. Some sky fighting. Rations extremely good since a few days. Authorities seemingly have wakened up to the fact that their fighting men require food to be in battling trim. Anderson was slightly wounded last night when going for rations. A hostile plane was brought down above Lieven, both occupants being riddled with bullets.

In the evening, while on skyguard, five enemy machines high up spotted three of our planes and came swooping down from behind firing into them. I thought we were in for it. Fritzie was all over them, was much faster and had the more compact and easier handled machines. He was very confident and bustling. Our men, however, stood up to them and exchanged courtesies. Suddenly one of the German planes turned round and beat it for home as fast as he could, planing down all the way at a very steep angle. Whether he made a good landing or not I could not say. Apparently one of the fliers was hit.

While out for rations tonight, Fritzie opened up with a machine-gun and almost got us, the bullets plugging into the earth at our feet.

Friday, July 13, 1917

One of our planes was brought down this morning. Yesterday two of our balloons were brought down in flames, the occupants escaped in parachutes.

We changed our front tonight by side-stepping to the south of Liévin near Hill 65. We had a long, round-about trip through the trenches and arrived late at night. The buildings in this quarter are badly wrecked and wicked smells abound. Civilians appear to have been living here till lately for there is no end of furniture, clothes, beds, cooking utensils, etc. in the houses. Fritz apparently had not time to collect the booty after sending the civilians inland. Fighting appears to have been exceedingly severe. Shell holes were numerous and lots of grenades were lying around. Where two of our section guns were located, the place was rotten with dead. The Germans appear to have been severely handled and their dead were still lying unburied while steel helmets, rifles and equipment were everywhere.

Several of our fellows had to go with fever. We are doing a twenty-four hour shift which shows that our quarters are not exactly comfortable and healthy. There are a few graves beside us marked by crosses, but no writing thereon. Rifles, equipment and cap are laid on the graves. They belonged to Imperial soldiers. It would appear that the enemy buried them.

Saturday, July 14, 1917

I had a bathe in a pond beside a slag heap.

Sunday, July 15, 1917

It rained heavily in the early morning which caused a number of our men to get out of their shelters.

Along with another gunner, I went up on a twenty-four hour shift to take up a position above the railway line. We have a little chalky dug-out, a sort of a recess dug into the bank that affords very little shelter. The position is a joke. In the event of an attack we have to lug up the gun, tripod, etc. for about 150 yards over barbed wire into the open, set up the gun and lambast the enemy. While doing this, you can guess his artillery would barrage our area making any forward movement on our part extremely difficult and risky.

During the day the enemy sent over several 43's[4] and as they were landing perilously close we left our position and side-stepped to the north until the shelling ceased. In the evening we were relieved.

Monday, July 16, 1917

When dusk set in, myself and Reid, who was No. 4 on the gun,[5] were detailed to take over another twenty-four hour position on Hill 65 which lies above the Green Crassier and overlooks a stagnant, slimy pond. We went up on the night before with the previous relief and an officer and guide in order that we might know our way in. I told Reid to pay special attention as there would be no one with us tonight, but when we got back he said he had no idea where the dickens we went to. I had only a hazy idea myself. The position was in a shell hole in a sea of shell holes in the open. In the darkness we started out carrying

[4] Fairly large shell.
[5] A gun crew was composed of eight men. Each had his special job, but all were trained to replace anyone who became a casualty.

tripod and gun, crossed the derailed railway truck and ascended the face of the ridge. Proceeding along a small path for several hundred yards which we could not see but knew by the feel of our feet that so far we were on the right track, we struck off to the right among a maze of shell holes that touched and ran into each other. A ruined building on the tip of the Crassier that showed up vividly on the skyline was the only guide mark, but to get the right angle from it was the trouble.

We wandered around and around but yet we could not see the couple we had to relieve and they, of course, were naturally on the lookout for us. It was pitch dark and unless we could get within twenty yards or so of the shell hole we would be missed. At last we decided to return to the path and strike out again from there. This we did and once more we headed towards at least the right direction, but had little luck. We seemed to stumble all around the area and yet we could not connect up on our men. As it was getting late and the light was beginning to change, we became anxious and started whistling quietly to obtain a response. After much wandering, at last we struck the place. One of the men was standing up and we spotted him. I could have sworn that I passed the vicinity at least a dozen times. We uttered sighs of relief for we thought we would never find them. They were packed up and ready to go since a couple of hours. In a moment they were out of sight in the darkness and we took over.

Reid was a new man and had only recently arrived. He was red-haired and came from Ayr, Ontario. The position was a middle-sized shell hole. The centre was cut out after the manner of a trench and was about five feet long by three feet wide. There was no shelter what-soever and we would be here, wet or dry, for twenty-four hours without means of getting away in the day time without being seen. We set up the gun and lay back for eventualities. It was nothing more than a sacrifice defence position. All we hoped for was that it would not rain—as it was, the hole was on the damp side. Apart from being cramped and stiff our shell hole did not distress us very much. Towards dusk, however, the enemy became active and sent several shells into our vicinity and lobbed over small sausages, but none found their mark. I noticed three-fourths of them were duds.

Tuesday, July 17, 1917

When daylight broke we had to watch for planes and cover up when they were around.

Expecting to be relieved about midnight, I had the gun packed up and in readiness to be taken out. When the graveyard hour was reached Heinie all of a sudden launched a bombardment on our front line barraging towards us. In a few moments our distress signals went up. Unwrapping the gun we got busy trying to set it up for action and at the same time keeping low for the air was alive with whiz-bangs which screeched past us as fast as lightning. This was Reid's first experience of fire and I had a job keeping him quiet in the shell hole. He wanted to get up and see what was taking place and would not keep still. As the noise of rifle fire and bombing did not follow and the bombardment slackened, I concluded Heiny was only after casualties and a little nerve shaking, so took down the gun and once more recovered it to take away. We were relieved about 3:00 a.m. and as it was showing signs of brightness we hurried out.

Wednesday, July 18, 1917

After being relieved we headed for billets at Bouvigny which we reached at 7:00 a.m., after passing through Liévin, Angres and Aix-Noulette.

Saturday, July 31, 1917

I was down at the 31st Battalion billets to see how they fared during the recent trip in the Lens area. They had a fairly stiff spell, having had about seventy casualties. Musgrove, a well-known member of my original company in Calgary, was killed. He was badly wounded at St. Eloi and returned to the line recently. He should not have been posted back as he was unfit with a foot injury, but rather than put up with the annoyance and ceremony of the base, he demanded a transfer to line duty in France. Sgts. Wheatley and Sewell, two of our 56th Battalion draft, were wounded, also Wingrove.

Sunday, July 22, 1917

Fritz has been busy shelling the back area and has caused casualties in both Bully-Grenay and Sains. A piece of shell tore one of the breasts of a French woman. Fritz had also been firing at one of our balloons and brought two down. Tonight one of his bird men stole across the sky and shot another down in flames.

Monday, July 23, 1917

We are up in the line again tonight and took over No. 16 crew's old position. Nearing our quarters, Fritz sent over some heavy stuff which made us step lively. Twice during the early morning he kicked up quite a shindy, but our artillery did not think it worthwhile retaliating.

Wednesday, July 25, 1917

Several times during the night Fritz's artillery came away strongly but his fireworks were not of long duration.

Thursday, July 26, 1917

At 2:45 a.m. a company of Royal Engineers put over gas from 1200 projectors containing 15½ tons of gas, on the suburbs of Cité St. Laurent and Cité St. Theodore. At the same time smoke and gas shells were hurled by Stokes mortars into the enemy trenches.

I have just received word from a runner that I have to go to the French Coast for a fortnight's rest. This was a surprise, especially as I am the only one in the unit to go. With a "ta-ta" to the rest of the crew, I beat it out to Sains passing Bully-Grenay on the way.

Tuesday, July 31, 1917

Last night Heinie sent over some long-distance stuff that burst in the fields a few hundred yards away.

At 2:30 p.m. those for coast leave were whisked away in motor transports for Calonne Ricouart by way of Hersin, Barlin, Houdain, Divion and Camblain Châtelin, staying overnight at Calonne where it was raining and the billet was uncomfortable. There was nothing to see and it was difficult getting a decent meal. Some of the estaminets had penny-in-the-slot musical machines which played dance music. The village folk—fat, French girls and thin, pale-faced weedy fellows smoking cigarettes—waltzed around until the estaminets closed.

While walking on the station platform, a railway worker came along and opened a closed-in truck and signalled me to come forward. Inside was a huge butt of wine. He knocked the bung out and tilted the cask to one side where I placed my mess tin which was soon filled, in fact more was spilled than went into the tin. Some of the fellows noticed what was taking place and rushed over to the platform, but the porter closed down. It was an unexpected drink and was very welcome.

Wednesday, August 1, 1917

At 7:45 a.m. prompt, we were marched up to the station to entrain for Wimereux on the English Channel a little south of Boulogne. We stayed there in the rain for four hours before the train arrived. We were then ushered into box cars that never seemed to have been cleaned out and it took us about twelve hours to reach our destination. By then we were as stiff and wet as could be. It was here at Wimereux that Lt.-Col. John McCrae, the author of that well-known piece of verse "In Flanders Fields" died. We marched from Wimereux through the rain to beyond Ambleteuse, six kilometers away to our camp which consisted of a collection of tents. There were no floor boards and as the rain had found its way into a third of the tent we crowded into the driest part.

Thursday, August 2, 1917

It is another disagreeable, wet day and the place is dull and forlorn looking. I visited Ambleteuse and Audresselles. The former was quite a summer resort in peace time. A number of Heinie prisoners were working in this area.

Friday, August 3, 1917

The day opened wet and windy.

Tuesday, August 7, 1917

We have had very wet, disagreeable weather and half of our trip is over. Yesterday I walked to Boulogne but there was nothing much to be seen. Prisoners fresh from the Ypres front arrived near Wimereux yesterday. The town is very cosmopolitan—Australian, Canadian, American, Portuguese, British and French troops were to be seen on the streets.

Today a couple of French women were up in our lines to identify a soldier who had broken into their estaminet and stolen between one and two hundred francs. It was the queerest inspection that we were ever subjected to. The culprit was identified quickly. He belonged to the 4th Division and looked a regular Bill Sykes.[6] Wimereux and Boulogne are full of British girls in khaki. They seem to be having the time of their lives. Many are homely and plain looking, but quite a number are pretty. Some are quite young. Their dress does not show them off to advantage. On the whole, they are a sensible-looking lot. The nurses dominate the atmosphere. With so many hospitals in this quarter their word is law.

Tuesday, August 14, 1917

We left this morning for our last front after having a fair time. The situation of the camp was first rate and attractions in the way of concerts and moving pictures were good. Sports, such as running,

[6] The criminal character in Charles Dickens' novel *Oliver Twist*.

302

jumping, tug-of-war, etc. were held. I saw Tom Longboat,[7] the Indian, running and long-jumping. He was beaten, however, by a big, broadly-built Scotsman of the Old Country Black Watch. Longboat had a long, steady, rakish step and looked every bit a runner. The camp disadvantages were: the tents were too crowded and it was difficult getting a decent, comfortable sleep; the blankets were moving, fatigues were too numerous. Restrictions as to walks were absurd. We were practically confined to the camp. Passes were few and not easy to get.

We had a fairly good journey back as there was less waiting and side-tracking. Motor-buses were on hand at Bethune and we arrived the same night at our destination. On arrival, I heard that the much talked of attack on Lens would be pulled off in a few hours, so I see where I will be roped in for the consolidation after all.

Wednesday, August 15, 1917

The general attack on Lens commenced today at 4:25 a.m. by the 1st Division on the left, then the 2nd Division, and on the extreme right, the 4th Division, our Brigade, the 6th, being in divisional support. The attack was ushered in with the usual heavy barrage, then over the top went the infantry.

So far no definite news has reached us regarding progress. This morning prisoners have been trickling in, batches of 14 to 72 having passed through Sains. Ambulances, principally Scottish, apparently loaned to the Canadians, have been busy carrying out casualties, mostly from the 5th Brigade.

Sains was shelled today. The first official report of the action states that Cité St. Laurent, Cité St. Emilie, Cité St. Elizabeth and Hill 70 have been taken, involving an advance of 1,200 yards to one mile and that fifteen officers and 282 men were captured.

We left tonight for Fosse 11 where my section slept in cellars of the mine building.

Thursday, August 16, 1917

I have heard that the enemy has made several ineffectual attacks. Several prisoners have passed us on the way out.

At 9:00 p.m. we moved forward, two crews of our section taking up advanced posts 50 to 100 yards behind our front line. When we

---

[7] Tom Longboat was a Canadian Onondaga Indian who became internationally famous as a long-distance runner at the turn of the century. Longboat volunteered for active service in January 1916 and served with various regiments during the war. He was twice wounded.

arrived at Company Headquarters, Fritz put up a barrage and immediately our signals of distress from the front line went up and a reply from our artillery and machine-guns followed. For a considerable time there was a terrific noise and one could not hear himself speaking. Fritz, however, did not attack and when the bombardment quietened down, our crews went forward but were caught in a second barrage. Everyone escaped with the exception of Elmer Bishop who received shrapnel in the back killing him. One of Section 3 guns was knocked out. Later in the morning the enemy attacked and was able to get into Chicory trench, but a counter-attack cleared him out and a number of his men were made captive. I saw eight of them. The current report was that sixty were taken. They bombed their way to within thirty yards of our positions. Later on in the morning we relieved the 4th Machine-Gun Company. When changing over, Campbell, who took my positions when I was away on rest, was killed. He was standing inside the building when a piece of shrapnel came through some open space in the ruins hitting him in the region of the heart and lungs. He only lived about ten minutes. It was a peculiar casualty. Most of the fellows were bunched up around the entrance engaged in conversation only a couple of yards from Campbell when the fatality occurred. There was no noise of the impact and no cry from Campbell. It happened so quietly that we did not notice at the moment what took place. We were somewhat puzzled how he got hit as he was in a more sheltered position than any of us.

Friday, August 17, 1917

This morning a party went forward and brought out one of our guns that had been smashed by shrapnel, the muzzle cap being broken and the jacket perforated. The crew obtained a gun from the 4th Machine-Gun Company. Later on in the day another lot went out to look for Elmer Bishop but it appeared a burial party had picked him up. Quite a number of our dead were lying around. In addition to Campbell and Bishop, Muirhead was slightly gassed and Drysdale and Forbes were wounded.

There has been quite a scrap in this push and the 4th Machine-Gun Company are full of incidents relating thereto. One of their crews took possession of a cellar and found ten Germans therein. Four hour later they found a Fritz minus his boots under a bed. This Heiny acted rather peculiar. He struck a match and as he had no cigarettes or pipe the conclusion drawn was to attract the attention of the enemy. He was told to desist. However, he did the same thing a second time so the officer was advised. He came upstairs and promptly plugged him with his revolver.

304

Saturday, August 18, 1917

Fritz came away with a bombardment this morning but did not attack. It is apparent that he is afraid that we are going to essay an advance, and this is his means of nipping it in the bud.

Sunday, August 19, 1917

The next official account of the Lens engagement is that we have taken 896 prisoners including 22 officers. Many Heinies have been noticed lying around killed by machine-gun fire. We have been putting up increasingly good machine-gun barrages, so woe betide the enemy who are not under cover.

Monday, August 20, 1917

Early this morning a shell struck the roof of our building and bricks and dust fell downstairs into the cellar beneath, making us wonder what in the duece would happen next. Luckily no one was upstairs. He repeated his performance in the forenoon, so it seems he has a line on us.

Tuesday, August 21, 1917

At 4:35 a.m., the 27th, 29th and 50th Battalions went over on an attack supported by the artillery which brought down a heavy bombardment. Unknown to us, the enemy had an attack timed almost exactly and we were astonished at the quickness of his reply. Both sides met one another in No Man's Land and a battle royal took place. After bombing and bayonet work, we slowly forced the enemy back, meeting another line later on. After some desperate fighting we were supposed to have reached our objective, but with sadly depleted forces. We had, however, to pack back leaving outposts composed of bombers and Lewis gunners to hold the line.

A little behind were the 6th Machine-Gunners, our section gunners being positioned in buildings beside the Lens-La Bassée Road. Throughout the day the enemy kept up a vigorous bombardment and it was with great risk and difficulty that the wounded were brought out. The 50th Battalion had practically to retire at once and it was early seen that we would soon be in difficulties, and to avoid being made prisoners orders came out to retire at dusk. Fritz was known to be gathering strength and as he had us nearly surrounded, the order did not come too soon. Within twenty-four hours we were back in our old positions. The action, therefore, may be termed a complete failure—heavy casualties and nothing tangible to show for it. The

305

ordinary soldier, of course, blamed the staff. The attack was on too small a scale and on too narrow a frontage. There were not enough moppers-up to attend to the disposal of the enemy in cellars and dug-outs and there was an insufficient supply of bombs sent forward. Since the fifteenth it has been reported that we took in this area 1,378 men, 34 machine-guns, and 21 trench mortars.

Our section was unlucky; a shell exploded and mortally wounded Sgt. McGirr, badly wounding Harry Stevenson, slightly injuring Ben Robinson, and shook up Lt. Wallbridge. The sergeant was notorious for his recklessness. Previously he was chasing and firing at a Heinie who disappeared among some buildings. It was intended that he stay back at the transport lines as word was expected that he would go out for his commission, but he insisted on getting into the scrap despite remonstrances.

Word was sent down to our position, which adjoined the communication trench, for four stretcher bearers to carry Harry Stevenson out. This was the second call on our gun crew for assistance. A little while before an officer appeared in our cellar and said he required a couple of men to replace casualties, one of which was Elmer Bishop. He looked around and spoke to Ladd and Reid telling them to get their equipment on and be ready to go up to the front in a few minutes. Ladd took the matter philosophically, but no so Reid. The order stunned him. He looked at me and in a quivering voice said he did not see why he should have to go because he was a new man and did not have any war experience. McCormick piped in, "Now is your opportunity to get the experience." Reid's gloom only deepened. He looked disparingly at me and said, "Besides, I am not feeling very well." At this moment the officer breezed into the cellar and called out. "Are those two fellows not ready yet?" Reid had to jump to in a hurry. He reached into his pocket and pulled out fifteen francs and in a shaky, whimpering voice full of pathos and dejection, said, "Here, Fraser, take this and if I don't come back keep it." Seeing the condition he was in I told him to buck up and not take it that way, that it would not be as bad as that. In a moment they were off with a guide to the fray.

The officer appeared again and as mentioned before, asked for four of us to go up as stretcher bearers and bring out Harry Stevenson who was very badly wounded. McCormick, Jackson, Nick and I responded to the call. Nick, with another man, was loaned to us by the 31st Battalion about three weeks ago as ammunition carrier for the Lens scrap. He was either a Greek or an Italian, I forget which, but we promptly dubbed him "Nick." He was little, dark and stocky and very keen to do any sort of work, but his pet wish was to mix it with the Germans. McCormick, so far, toned him down by telling him not to

306

be in a hurry as he would get lots of opportunities to close with them. Anyway, he was pleased when I said to him that now we were going to get into it.

Manville was our guide. A bombardment by Fritz was on when we started up the communication trench and it increased in intensity the further up we went. Altogether we had about a mile to go. The trench, an old German one, was wide and not very deep, badly knocked about by shell fire and in parts full of broken strands of wire which proved troublesome. Snipers were busy. Shells were either whizzing past us or dropping all around, miraculously missing us. We overtook the other party and I was a little in the rear of Ladd when a shell roared by Ladd missing him by the barest inch and crashed into the foot of the side of the trench—a dud. Ladd pulled in his stomach as if to dodge it and slowly turning round revealed the whitest face I ever saw in my life. He tried to grin, but it was a very, very sickly-looking grin.

We hurried past the spot in case of a delayed explosion. A little further on we became so exhausted with stooping and rushing that we dropped into a dug-out on the left to catch our breath. After a very harassing time, we made another stop at section headquarters about seventy yards to the left of the communication trench. Here several of our men were located along with an officer. They appeared to be quite worked up. They told me the attack was unsuccessful and that the battalion had retired and all that was left out in front were details such as bombers, Lewis gunners and our own gunners. On both sides of us, a little distance away, were buildings occupied by the enemy and we were warned not to show ourselves or attempt any shooting. The whole idea was that as soon as Harry Stevenson was picked up and taken away, the gun crews would retire as we were surrounded.

Glancing up at the top buildings, I could see and hear Germans looking out furtively and then realized why everybody seemed to be so serious. After a short rest it was agreed that we should push on, but only one at a time. Manville, the guide, led the way. One by one over the open they went a short distance and then dropped into the trench. I was last to leave. After getting into the trench I soon lost sight of my predecessor and when I struck a side trench on the right where the infantry had fallen back and were crouching in funk holes in uneasiness, my puttee got caught on some trench wire and I bent down to fix it. All this time shells were falling and the atmosphere was thick with brick and plaster dust from the buildings as they crumpled under shell fire. At this point Manville arrived back on the scene and told me to hurry, that the crews were all packed up and ready to leave, warning me that as soon as we reached the Lens-La Bassée Road, a sunken road, to cross quickly to the other side and sneak along it as Fritzie had observation on the nearer side and his snipers would plug us if seen.

Soon we reached the end of the trench which terminated at the road, and right in the trench at the corner lay a dead Canadian and a dead German not more than a yard apart. Manville jumped over them and ran quickly to the other side of the road and I followed him. About seventy yards further down the road, we entered a wrecked building through a hole in the wall. Here all our fellows were packed and very anxious looking. They were fidgetting to get away. In fact, most of them were in a blue funk asking where abouts Heiny was. Various buildings were pointed out to me in which they had been noticed. In fact they said Fritzie was all around them and this was the cause of their anxiety. Some of the late arrivals were lying on the floor exhausted. I spotted Reid and asked him if he wanted his fifteen francs, but he was too far gone to even answer or smile.

A council of action was held and in a few minutes it was decided that, as soon as possible, two with a stretcher would run to an old German dug-out about fifty yards away where Harry Stevenson lay grievously wounded and pick him up and bring him in. Bud Willox and Elwood volunteered for the job. Both were husky, resolute fellows. In a moment or two the place became enveloped in a fog of smoke and brick dust caused by exploding shells and the two dashed out with the stretcher and in a few minutes reappeared with Harry who was absolutely all in. After that it was decided that McCormick and Jackson would lead off with the stretcher and fifty yards would be followed by Nick and myself as relief stretcher bearers and later on one by one of the crews would beat it out. Jackson and McCormick grabbed the stretcher and away they went, then Nick. When I reached the entrance to the trench, I turned round, waved to those behind and was gone.

After a long, arduous spell with many squeaks and narrow shaves and the lives almost scared out of us, we reached the dressing station. One has to go through such an experience to really understand what it is to carry a wounded man through a double bombardment and without supporting straps.[8] We were scarcely away when our outposts fell back and Heiny attacked with murderous fire. Looking back we saw our distress signals go up and then our artillery started. The roar and hiss of the shells with the accompanying explosions was terrific and the noise was tremendous as it echoed and reverberated around

---

[8] Supporting straps ran from the handles of the stretcher up and over the shoulders of the bearers, thus helping to ease the burden of carrying the wounded over a considerable distance.

the buildings. It was a laborious and slow job getting down the trench as the shells were flying from both sides and at nearly all conceivable angles. One could not distinguish a single shell in the turmoil, so we just kept crawling through, impervious to everything but getting out unscathed. I regard it as a miracle.

Before long Nick and I had to relieve the other two. After several exchanges Nick's fingers lost their grip entirely and he dropped his end of the stretcher shaking up Harry badly. The three of us handled the situation for the rest of the way. During the last few hundred yards McCormick kept yelling at Jackson and myself "Stick to it, stay with it, you have only a little way to go now" as if he were a cheer leader at some sporting event. At that, it took all the guts we could command to pass through that inferno of din and explosion. If we had delayed our departure from the outpost a few minutes longer, I am afraid Stevenson's fate would have been sealed as he would have been abandoned. A few days later information reached us that Harry died at Etaples.

We passed a stretcher case on the way out. A Bosche prisoner was one of the stretcher bearers. They were all in. In certain places along the trench the stench arising from the dead was such that one had to hold his breath when passing. There were some Heinies, but most of them belonged to our 4th Division. One case told its story very plainly—a stretcher with a man on it with a hole through his face from side to side. A common occurrence—a wounded man being carried out struck by shrapnel and killed. It was in this trench that Bishop was killed. During the time it took to go up the trench and return it was so badly battered that it was difficult to realize that it was the same trench.

After turning Harry over to the Red Cross, we retired to our cellar and were given a tot of rum. Never did rum taste so good!

The 5th Grenadier Guards and the 29th Battalion met in an attack but the 29th were unable to dislodge them.

One of the most unfortunate cases I heard of was when a Red Cross man, who was attending to two wounded men, had his hand blown off when a shell burst. This was told to me by the fellow who came to their assistance.

Tuesday, August 22, 1917

Nick, the firebrand who failed as a stretcher bearer, was observed last night to have turned very quiet and contemplative and this morning he was the same. Asking him how did he like his trip up the line in the shelling, he replied that he was not afraid of the Germans, but, oh, the dead! the dead! Apparently Nick had a nightmare. McCormick, upon hearing him, shouted over in disgust, "Never mind the dead ones, it's the live ones you want to keep your eyes skinned for." A few days later Nick and his lanky pal, who about died of fright getting to the outpost, were returned to the battalion.

Wednesday, August 23, 1917

The scrapping quietened down considerably last night. Word was received that Kitson, Esty, and Curly Elwood were wounded and Urquhart was missing. The battalions have been relieved.

Thursday, August 24, 1917

Early this morning we were relieved and another fellow and I reached the billets at Sains first, arriving around 2:00 a.m. Manville was wounded coming out and Orr was slightly gassed.

I have just seen the official Intelligence Report which mentioned that the enemy which fought our brigade was comprised of units of four divisions, 7th, 11th and 4th Reserve Guards and the 220th. Since the fifteenth no fewer than fifty-nine battalions have been engaged by our Corps. Prisoners have been taken from the 1st Prussian Guards. The majority of the troops who met us in No Man's Land were the 5th Grenadier Guards.

Thus ended the part we played in the Lens engagement. It also terminated my diary. Several weeks later I went on leave to Blighty where all my notes up to this date were left with my sister at Inverness, Scotland.

Particulars were jotted down in a new note book up to November 5th when I was wounded, but this was lost or confiscated from my pack when I became a casualty. Further information will, therefore, be given from memory so I will be unable to furnish dates, places, minor events and casualties; consequently, there will be little more to relate, as memory, particularly at this late date, is fickle.

CHAPTER X

Passchendaele—and a Blighty

The next month (September) the Brigade was pretty well occupied in Reserve, resting and training and in the interval brigade and divisional sports were held. We moved to the Estrée Cauche area. I remember being put on a strange guard. Some of the troops had stolen a barrel or two of ale from the local brewery and I had a spell of guard to see that no further thefts were made.

Towards the end of September, we went into Avion-Mericourt sector taking up positions alongside the battalions. We had a very long trek over the Ridge to the line. Nothing very eventful happened that I can remember. There was more or less intermittent shelling which is incidental to all fixed positions. Several days later we were .back on the Ridge, where it was cold, wet and muddy. When here, a runner arrived to tell me that I was scheduled for Blighty leave, so left promptly for Headquarters and later hiked to Aubigny to entrain. I was soon across the Channel and up to London where a short pact for a few hours was made. Catching the Scottish train, I sped northwards to Edinburgh and the following day found me on my way to Inverness in the Highlands of Scotland.

[On my return to the front I found] the 31st Battalion was located not very far away. I hunted up "A" Company and found it billeted in a building beside the road, at least the greater part of the company appeared to be billeted here. I walked in and carefully looked around, but I could not recognize a single individual, not even one from the earlier drafts. All those that were with me to the Somme seemed to have disappeared.

While watching one of our planes flying low and approaching my direction, something suddenly exploded and the wings shot apart and the machine fell to earth. Apparently an internal explosion took place for it was too far back to be either affected by enemy fire or to be in the way of one of our shells.

Around the beginning of November found us on the march to a camp of tents between Ypres and Potijze. It was announced that an attack on Passchendaele would be made on November 6th at 6:00 a.m., but that our Section No. 4 would be held back in reserve as most of our gun crews in the section had played an active part at Vimy, Fresnoy and Lens and it was considered our turn to have an easy time.

Due to the lateness of the season, the weather was on the wet side and the terrain soft. We had not settled down very long before we found that Fritz's artillery had a fondness for our camp. Three or four times during the night he almost landed his shells on our tents. Having been kept awake most of the night and finding the spot a bit unhealthy and the tents bunched too closely together, our gun crew resolved to flit elsewhere. In the morning we looked around and found a spot about two hundred yards away that contained a much lesser number of shell holes than where we were, so we pitched our tents. It was more satisfactory, although about 60 yards away, during the next morning, a shell landed on a small shelter built against a low embankment killing the two occupants who were asleep. They never knew what happened. Expecting to remain here until the end of the Passchendaele action, I found time to check up on the crew and the gun and noted the following:

No. 14 Gun Crew
1. Fraser, D.
2. Ladd, Wm.
3. Reid
4. Linden
5. Orme
6. Goodman, C. W.
7. Bartley
8. Fage

Gun Particulars:
1. Tripod and Crosshead C48348
2. Gun L862
3. Field Mount C79931
4. Lock A313
5. Lock (Spare) 47734
6. Feed Block 41788
7. Feed Block (Spare) A45

Crew numbers 4, 5, 6 and 7 were new men and at the present date I have no recollection of them. Although I was the longest in France and Belgium Fage was longer with the Machine-Gun Company and was latterly transferred to my crew from No. 15.

On the evening of the 4th, our transport went up the line and met with such opposition that a number were wounded and others so badly shaken and shell-shocked that they were either unfit or unwilling to proceed on the following night. Our crew was, therefore, called upon for assistance. Leaving Fage in charge of the tent and belongings, the rest of us assumed our new duties and new they certainly were. For the first time we had each to lead up a horse to a forward dump carrying an assortment of goods. The transport men left behind soon had the horses loaded up and ready. Roughly there must have been something like 14 or 15 in our little convoy.

I observed that we had an officer in charge, a man that I had not seen before, and concluded that he was a late arrival. We started out and I found myself second last in the line. My horse was loaded up with cans of water, four on each side. They formerly contained gasoline. Up the road we went. We soon passed Potijze. Further on the countryside became bare and open and looked as if it had been fought over recently. Shell holes were everywhere and most contained slimy, muddy water. The terrain was a wilderness of mud. Thank goodness, however, the road was fairly firm. We were warned to space out which caused quite a distance between the first and the last man.

Next we came across our artillery in the open only a few yards away from the road. Apparently, it was impossible for them to take up positions far from the road as the guns just sank in the quagmires. The artillery was firing as we passed and Fritz was returning the fire. We soon saw that it would take practically a direct hit to do any damage. We watched the shells send up fountains of mud and water as they exploded. For quite a distance you could see eruptions taking place at various points resembling geysers or mud volcanoes. As it was still bright, we crawled slowly along and so far did not anticipate much trouble. The shelling was scattered. Some shells fell short and others went over our heads before exploding.

In the distance we could see a gradual rise in the land culminating in a ridge and obliterating all view beyond. Near the top, shells were falling beside the road. As we neared the base of the ridge, a substantial-looking Fritzie cement block house appeared on the right in a hollow, showing a large Red Cross beside the entrance. When quiet, this, apparently, was the furthest up point ambulances would come to pick up casualties. According to the map, I would say that we were in the vicinity of Zonnebeke.

Emerging from the hollow, we crept slowly up the ridge. When Fritz's artillery sent over a salvo, a quick one, two three, four bursts around the road at the top of the ridge, I said to myself this is where we stop until the shelling blows over. It was the usual and logical thing to do, but no, our officer was prepared to walk us through it. Another salvo came and those in the lead passed over the pinnacle of the ridge where the shells had fallen. We were gradually getting through, when I sensed it was about time the next salvo was coming and with it trouble, and sure enough the shells came.

I was thrown by the force of the explosion on to my face into the gutter at the side with the rest of me sprawled around the edge. The first thing that surged through my mind was "Am I dead, am I dead?" I was badly dazed and partially choked by mud and water when I went face first into the ditch but my mind quickly cleared and I looked around and saw my horse lying dead half over my right thigh and pinning me down. We were tossed from one side of the road to the other. Glancing ahead I observed the horse in front dead and its attendant also. He was Joe Bishop, a brother of Elmer who was killed several weeks before at Lens. Joe was taken off the gun crew and given a supposedly safety job with the transport. Ahead of him was Ladd. His horse was dead also and he, himself, was wounded and trying to rise. I turned around to see how the fellow behind me fared. I saw him and his horse motionless in death. Four horses killed, two men killed and two men wounded was the result of the senselessness of the officer who led us in. He certainly played us into the hands of the enemy.

After squirming for several minutes, I managed to pull my leg from under my horse and astonishing to say it was not sore, let alone injured. The right side of my face, however, was burning and stinging as if someone had stuck hot needles into it. It was full of tiny bits of metal. My chin, lip, nose and the inner corner of the eye was hit, besides the cheek, ear, jaw and also the fingers. I knew from the burning that my face was plastered, but that was all as far as I felt. Ladd shouted that he was hit in the leg. Getting up, I said I would bandage him and then tried to extract the bandage from the frontal corner of my tunic, but at this moment another salvo came over and the explosions so disturbed the air that I had difficulty in breathing for a minute or two. The shells fell short and the small embankment above the ditch seemed to waver before my eyes as the earth erupted. Ladd cried out that he could not make it and sank to the ground. I shouted back that I would send stretcher bearers as soon as I could. Then, for some unaccountable reason, I got mad and swore a volley of oaths in Gaelic. I was mad not only at Heinie for getting me, but also at myself for being so easily caught and wounded in such a simple fashion.

314

I started down the road feeling as strong as an ox, not even the least bit sickened, and after going about twenty yards, looking down I observed my tunic and pants were streaming with blood. I never noticed until I had gone a few yards further that my right arm was shattered at the shoulder, completely twisted around and dangling. There were five other wounds, but I did not know of their existence until later. In a temper I skedadled down the road holding up my right arm as the way it was dangling I thought it would fall off.

About two hundred yards further down the road, two men from our transport approached and when I neared them I shouted rather forcibly to them to clear out. It was a picture to see their faces. They stopped, looked at me for a moment and in sheer fright turned round and ran away as if the devil was after them. My face, which was plastered with mud and blood, must have scared the daylights out of them.

Reaching the base of the ridge I walked right into the cement blockhouse and told the Red Cross men that Ladd was lying wounded at the top of the road. They went out with a stretcher but waited up the road a bit for about ten minutes until the shelling ceased and soon afterwards Ladd was brought in. I looked at the M.O. and recognized him immediately. He was Hart who enlisted from the Youngstown or Hanna District as a private and came to my Company. After a while he got tired being kicked around and blossomed out as the 25th Battalion M.O. His first words to me were, "Good God, Fraser, are you still around the line?" In a few minutes an ambulance appeared and four or five of us piled in and away we went.

Our first stop was Potijze where we were given hot cocoa and the right sleeve of my tunic was cut away. The next stop was Ypres where the driver had to report. Later on a further stop was made at the western end of Vlamertinghe where we were stripped of our uniforms, put into flannels, tagged and had a visit from a padre who asked for the names and addresses of our next of kin. In quick time we were into another ambulance and whisked away to a casualty clearing hospital beside Poperinghe. It was operated by the Australian Medical Corps and consisted of several large tents. We were dropped off here and in a matter of minutes I was under the X-ray machine. When an anaesthetic was being given, the last words I heard were spoken by an elderly doctor to his assistant when he said in soft encouraging tones, "That's it, Donie, that's it."

Later I awakened in a tent in a dim light where about thirty fellows lay on stretchers moaning and groaning. A bag containing the shrapnel taken from my shoulder was pinned to my clothes, while the left arm was wreathed in bandages and the other wrapped the same

315

way but, in addition, strapped to my body. At this stage I was very dazed and sore and if I felt strong after I was hit, I felt the opposite now. During the later hours of darkness the noises, sighs and groans arising from pain and distress sounded as if we were in purgatory. Two or three times I called out Ladd's name, but apparently he was not in the tent, for no response was received.

In the morning a Red Cross train was at hand and in a short time the carriages were filled. Two nurses came into my carriage and sat about ten feet away on the opposite side. I could tell by the sinister way they looked at me every now and then that they expected me to peg out.

As the train slowly sped away and I realized that my fighting days had passed forever, I silently said farewell to the line that had been my home for the last two years and two months.

The Infantry Battalion
of the Great War

The infantry was the arm around which the Canadian Corps was built. It fought the battle, captured enemy positions and held them when taken.

A battalion was the unit of infantry and its lowest sub-unit was the infantry section, commanded by a corporal, which consisted of ten men armed with rifles initially and later with some light machine-guns. Four sections were grouped into a platoon commanded by a subaltern officer (Second Lieutenant or Lieutenant) with a small headquarters of a platoon sergeant and a runner. Four rifle platoons were grouped into a company commanded by a major or captain. Company headquarters also contained a Second-in-Command (normally a captain), a Company Sergeant-Major, a Company Quarter-Master Sergeant, a Company clerk, cooks and runners.

Four companies under a battalion headquarters formed the infantry battalion. It was commanded by a lieutenant-colonel. His headquarters consisted of the battalion Second-in-Command (a major) who was the Commanding Officer's understudy. Routine administration was handled by two captains, the Adjutant and the Quartermaster. The Adjutant was responsible for preparing orders, supervising dress and discipline and all matters dealing with personnel as well as overseeing the Orderly Room which dealt with routine orders and correspondence. He was assisted by an Assistant Adjutant (a lieutenant), an Orderly Room Sergeant, several clerks and the provost sergeant who commanded the Regimental Policemen.

The Quartermaster was responsible for all logistic and supply support for the battalion including food, forage, fuel, arms, clothing, ammunition, equipment and stores. He was assisted by his understudy, the Regimental Quartermaster-Sergeant, and controlled the unit cooks, butcher, shoemaker, master tailor and postal non-commissioned officer. He also directed the Transport Officer (a lieutenant) who was responsible for all horsed transport, including the care of the animals, assisted by the Transport Sergeant.

As the war progressed certain special duties evolved at battalion headquarters. These included the Signals Section, commanded by a lieutenant with a sergeant understudy. Its responsibility was to maintain communication by the most expeditious method possible, be it telephone, visual wireless or runners. This section had an establishment of 53 signallers with a variable number of runners. The Intelligence Officer, a lieutenant, was responsible for the collection, collation an dissemination of tactical information. He was assisted by a staff of Scouts, Snipers and Observers. The Lewis Gun Officer, lieutenant, was responsible for the technical training on that weapon, assisted by a sergeant. The Bombing and Works Officer was responsible for the training of all ranks of the battalion in the use of grenades and supervised all battalion construction, whether in the trenches or out of the line. He was assisted by the Pioneer Sergeant, his section of Pioneers and the Sanitary Corporal. This section also found stretcher bearers. The Gas Sergeant was responsible for gas training within the battalion and the maintenance of respirators.

The Regimental Sergeant-Major was the connecting link between the non-commissioned officers and the men of the battalion and the commanding officer. He was responsible for drill, discipline and deportment as well as supervising all duty rosters and the Regimental Police.

Attached to the battalion headquarters was a Medical Officer from the Canadian Army Medical Corps, with a small staff of medical assistants, and a Chaplain from the Canadian Chaplain Services.

A sketch of the battalion organization follows overleaf.

Source: Canada, Ministry, Overseas Military Forces, *Report of the Ministry Overseas Military Forces of Canada 1918*, London, 1918.

An Infantry Battalion—1914-1918

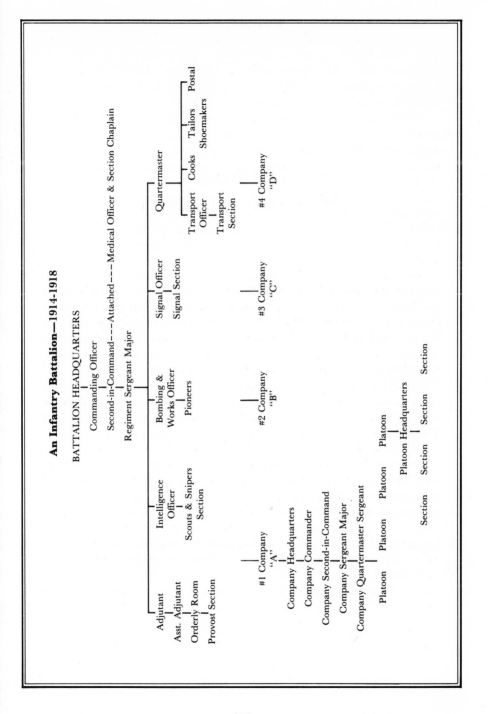

BATTALION HEADQUARTERS

Commanding Officer

Second-in-Command – – – Attached – – – Medical Officer & Section Chaplain

Regiment Sergeant Major

Adjutant
Asst. Adjutant
Orderly Room
Provost Section

Intelligence Officer
Scouts & Snipers Section

Bombing & Works Officer
Pioneers

Signal Officer
Signal Section

Quartermaster

Transport Officer
Transport Section

Cooks   Tailors   Postal
      Shoemakers

#1 Company "A"

Company Headquarters
Company Commander
Company Second-in-Command
Company Sergeant Major
Company Quartermaster Sergeant

Platoon   Platoon   Platoon   Platoon

Platoon Headquarters

Section   Section   Section   Section

#2 Company "B"

#3 Company "C"

#4 Company "D"

The Brigade
Machine-Gun Company

Brigade machine-gun companies were organized in November 1915 on the basis of one for each brigade—four in a division. They were initially equipped with the Colt machine-gun until this was replaced during the summer of 1916 with the Vickers Light Machine-Gun—a water-cooled, belt-fed, .303 caliber weapon. The organization outline below was used within the Canadian Corps until March 1918 when all medium machine-guns were restructured into machine-gun battalions, one for each division, and Corps machine-gun motor brigades—increasing the number of machine-guns in the division from 64 to 96.[1]

The Brigade Machine-Gun Company, commanded by a major, was composed of a company headquarters—including a second-in-command, a company sergeant-major, a company quartermaster sergeant, a transport sergeant, cooks, clerks and orderlies—and four sections of four medium machine-guns each. Each section was commanded by a subaltern officer and each gun was manned by a crew of one sergeant and five rank and file. Two sections of guns (eight) were often employed together to act as a machine-gun battery, particularly on indirect fire tasks.

The outline organization of a machine-gun company is shown below.

[1] Nicholson, *op. cit.*, p. 383.

320

A Brigade Machine-Gun Company
November 1915-March 1918

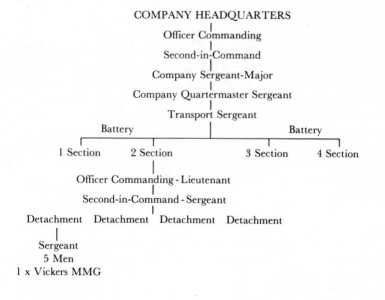

COMPANY HEADQUARTERS

Officer Commanding

Second-in-Command

Company Sergeant-Major

Company Quartermaster Sergeant

Transport Sergeant

Battery   Battery

1 Section   2 Section   3 Section   4 Section

Officer Commanding - Lieutenant

Second-in-Command - Sergeant

Detachment   Detachment   Detachment   Detachment

Sergeant
5 Men
1 x Vickers MMG

Historical Outline of the 31st Battalion, 1915-1917

COMPARATIVE EVENTS

September 1915 — October 1917

Month/Year	31 BN	Cdn Corps	Other Events
SEP 1915	18 Sep - brigade arrives in France 19 Sep - move to St. Sylvester Cappelle 20 Sep - familiarization and training 25 Sep - goes into line Kemmel lower slopes Wytschaete Ridge Trenches muddy, in poor condition in many parts and badly in need of repair. Area littered with corpses from earlier battles. In support line.	Cdn. Corps formed and HQ opened (Lt.-Gen. Sir E. A. H. Alderson, KCB, at Bailleul on 13 Sep '15 as result of decision to send 2 Cdn. Div. to France. 1 Cdn. Div. held line from Ploegsteert Wood north-west 4,400 yards to Wulvughein-Messines Road. On 22 Sep two brigades of 2 Cdn. Div. occupied area from north of 1 Cdn. Div. to three miles north to the Vierstraat-Wytschaete road. Corps under command Second Army, General Sir Henry Plumer, Corps troops contains eight battalions, which were to become part of 3 Cdn. Div. and Canadian Cavalry Bde. Strength 1,354 officers; 36,552 other ranks. 25 SEP - feint attack to support Battle of Loos.	Bulgaria enters war on Great Britain's side. Germany ceases offensive in Russia. Austrian offensive fails 25 SEP - Battles of Loos; First Army
1 OCT 1915 6 OCT 12 OCT 18 OCT 24 OCT 30 OCT	First day in first line trenches Relieved to reserve Relieves 28 Battalion—takes part in Cdn. Corps demonstration Relieved by 28 Battalion to reserve Relieves 27 Battalion in forward trenches Relieved by 28 Battalion to reserve Locre	13 OCT - Another demonstration in sp. of British attack at Loos, - Smoke screen laid for deception.	British and French divisions sent to Salonika Cardona offensive in Italy launched Austro-German offensive against Serbia launched.
5 NOV 1915 11 NOV 17 NOV 21 NOV 25 NOV	Relieves 28 Battalion at Kemmel Relieved by 28 Battalion, to Kemmel Shelters Relieves 28 Battalion Relieved by 28 Battalion Relieves 28 Battalion—left section of line	Canadian Corps continues to hold line in Ypres Salient from St. Eloi in north to Ploezstreet Wood in south. 17 NOV - first raid by 5 Brigade and 7 Brigade near Petit Douve and Seaforth Farm.	NOV-DEC - Two inter-Allied conferences at Joffie's HQ at Chantilly to plan for 1916—a general offensive by France, Britain, Russia and Italy.

Month/Year	31 BN	Cdn Corps	Other Events
1 DEC 1915	Relieved by 28 Battalion—to Brigade Reserve	No major change in corps situation	Canada agrees to field four divisions in France
3 DEC	Relieves 24 Battalion—left section of line	14/15 DEC - another raid by 5 Battalion	Cardona offensive halted—a failure
9 DEC	Relieved by 28 Battalion	22 DEC - 7 Brigade formed—RCR, PPCLI, 42 Bn, 49 Bn.	Kut invested by Turks
15 DEC	Relieves 28 Battalion	28 DEC - 8 Brigade formed—1, 2, 4, 5, CMR	19 DEC - Sir Douglas Haig replaces Sir John French as Commander in Chief, British Expeditionary Force
21 DEC	Relieved by 28 Battalion	24 DEC - 3 Cdn. Div. formed—Maj.-Gen. M. S. Mercer, CB.	
27 DEC	Relieves 28 Battalion	Artillery support provided by guns of 3 (Lahore) Division	
2 JAN 1916	Relieved by 28 Battalion—to Division Reserve	2 JAN - Raiding activity continues—25 Battalion (5 Brigade)	9 JAN - Dardenelles evacuation complete
8 JAN	Relieves 28 Battalion in left sector		1 JAN - Sir Robert Borden pledges Canada to 500,000 men in uniform
14 JAN	Relieved by 28 Battalion		Great Britain introduces conscription
20 JAN	Relieves 28 Battalion in left section		
26 JAN	Relieved by 28 Battalion—to Division Reserve	31 JAN - 6 Brigade raid	
1 FEB 1916	Relieves 28 Battalion	9 Cdn. Brigade joins 3 Div. —43, 52, 58, 60 Battalions	21 FEB - German offensive against Verdun begins
7 FEB	Relieved by PPCLI to Corps reserve—Beethen	German diversionary attacks on 5 British Corps cause Corps area to be extended to include St. Eloi	25 FEB - Fort Douamont falls to Germans
25 FEB	Moved to Brigade reserve—Scherpenberg		
27 FEB	Relieved 24 Battalion on right sector line.		
3 MAR 1916	Relieved by Royal Canadian Regiment —to brigade reserve		
5 MAR	Moved to Corps reserve—Berthen		6 MAR - Germans widen their attacks at Verdun to west bank of River Meuse
9 MAR	Moved to divisional reserve—Locre		Russia launches abortive attack at Lake Norocz, near Vilna.
13 MAR	Relieves 28 Battalion at Kemmel		
20 MAR	Relieved by 28 Battalion—to Brigade reserve	27 MAR - 3 (British) Division attacks south of St. Eloi after six mines exploded.	Italians make another vain attack on Isonzo front.
25 MAR	Relieves 28 Battalion at Kemmel		
31 MAR	Relieved by 4 Yorks—to Div. reserve —Locre		

Month / Year	31 BN	Cdn Corps	Other Events
1 APR 1916	Moves to Corps reserve—Bailleul	Steel helmets issued, 50 per company, to the forward units	Allies continue to attempt to relieve pressure on French at Verdun but no immediate avail.
2 APR	Moves north to Ouderdon		
3 APR	Relieves a British brigade in trenches near St. Eloi in confused circumstances to the east of craters	4 APR - 2 Cdn. Division assumes command of crater—St. Eloi sector. First instance where an entire corps relieved another	
6 APR	Assist in defeat of German attack by counter attack but mistakenly occupies craters 6 and 7, not 4 and 5.	6 APR - 6 Brigade loses craters 2, 3, and 4 to German attack. Fighting very confused because of lack of information and absence of maps.	Easter Rebellion in Ireland.
7 APR	Relieved by 19 Battalion, with some difficulty—180 casualties.	7 APR - 6 Brigade relieved. 617 casualties after 4 days in line.	
8 APR	Reorganizing and refitting in Ouderdam Working parties forward to strengthen line.	8 APR - 4 Brigade attempts to recapture craters 2 and 3 but is repulsed	
18 APR	Moves into Brigade support line near Scottish Woods to relieve 25 Battalion —4 Brigade	9 APR - 4 Brigade repulsed again in attempt to recapture craters.	
21 APR	Relieved by 18 Battalion to Divisional reserve.	15 APR - further attacks on St. Eloi craters, stopped.	
		26-27 APR - Germans attack 1 and 2 Cdn. Divisions but are beaten off.	29 APR - British forces in Kut surrender to Turks.
1 MAY 1916	Relieves 24 Battalion in Scottish Wood	Corps experiment with use of wireless to control artillery fire.	
2 MAY	Relieves 25 Battalion in front line.		
6 MAY	Relieved by 29 Battalion—to brigade reserve at Scottish Wood		
8 MAY	Move to divisional reserve at Reninghelst.		14 MAY - Austrians launch offensive in Italy.
22 MAY	After 16 days rest moved to brigade reserve at Scottish Wood		
27 MAY	Occupy centre sector of front line at Hooge	28 MAY - Lt.-Gen. Alderson relieved of command of Corps and replaced by Lt.-Gen. the Hon. Sir Julian H. G. Byng	
31 MAY	Relieved by 25 Battalion—to divisional reserve, Reninghelst.		31 MAY - 1 JUNE - Battle of Jutland. "Mincing machine" battle of Verdun continues.

Month/Year	31 BN	Cdn Corps	Other Events
6 JUN 1916	Relieves 9 Cdn. Infantry Brigade in apex of Ypres salient between Zoave Wood and Sanctuary Wood. Hold off German attack which captures Hooge.	2 JUN - Germans attack 3 Division positions at Mount Sorrel and Sanctuary Wood behind heavy bombardment and four mine explosions. Canadian line pushed back about 700 yards but PPCLI saved the situation and Germans did not exploit. Canadian counterattack, unco-ordinated, only partly successful.	5 JUN - Buisiloo offensive begins with unexpected initial success at Luck against Austrians.
8 JUN	Relieved by 27 Battalion—to Brigade support in Ypres.		5 JUN - Lord Kitchener killed at Sea.
11-12 JUN	Relieves 27 Battalion in centre sector.		8 JUN - Germans launch fresh offensive against Verdun on east bank of Meuse but suspend attack to send 7 divisions to Eastern Front.
13 JUN	Demonstration in support of 1 Division attack.	13 JUN - 1 Division recaptures Mount Sorrel and Tor Top for remainder of summer—until September.	
14 JUN	Relieved by 27 Battalion—to brigade reserve, Ypres		
15 JUN	Moved to Reninghelst and reorganizes	Cdn. Corps remained in Salient—"stationary but aggressive."	17 JUN - Cardona checks Austrian attack in Italy.
21 JUN	Moved to Dickebusch in brigade support		
28 JUN	Relieved in brigade supp. by 25 Battalion (5 Brigade) and returns to Reninghelst.		
	6th Infantry Brigade Machine-Gun Coy		
2 JUL 1916	Vickers machine-guns issued and Colt weapons turned over to infantry battalions. Company spends month in and out of line by sections firing indirect shoots.	Canadian Corps continues to hold line.	1 JUL - Haig launches British offensive on Somme, with minor French attack on his southern flank. The first day's action a complete failure with 60,000 casualties. JUL - Somme offensive renewed. Germans abandon offensive in Verdun sector

Month / Year	6th Infantry Brigade Machine-Gun Coy	Cdn Corps	Other Events
8 AUG 1916 19 AUG 20 AUG	Warned of pending move to Somme sector Lee-Enfield rifle issued Began march to Somme sector halted at Epelersques for training.	By end August, 2 and 3 Divisions equipped Lee-Enfield rifles. Ross rifle withdrawn 4 Cdn. Division reaches Corps area under Maj.-Gen. L. J. Lipsett, CB. KMG. 30 AUG - Canadian Corps relieves 1 ANZAC Corps about Pozieres Division, Brigade and unit patches issued to Cdn. Corps after arrival in Somme sector	7 AUG - New Russian offensive in Galacia 6 AUG - New Italian offensive on Ixonzo front. 27 AUG - Rumania declares war on Austria and enters on Allied side. 28 AUG - Von Falkenhayn replaced as Chief of German General Staff by Field-Marshal Paul von Hindenberg with his deputy Lt.-Gen. Erich Ludendorff.
4 SEP 1916 5 SEP 10 SEP 15 SEP 17 SEP 25 SEP 26 SEP 29 SEP	Company moves by train from St. Omer to Candas In billets. Relieved 1 Cdn. Machine-Gun Company in area Baillis Wood. Sections deployed in reserve, with 27 and 28 Battalions and with 1 Motor Machine-Gun in support. All sections of company relieved and move to Warloy Company moves back into firing line Supports 6 Brigade attack Relieved by 4 Brigade Machine-Gun Company	3 SEP - Cdn. Corps assumes command of Pozieres sector as part of Gough's Reserve Army. 1 Division holding line, 2 and 3 Division preparing for battle. 15 SEP - Battle of Flers-Courcelette, attack by 2 Cdn. Division on Candy Trench and Seeyou Trench supported by seven tanks. Attack very successful on 6 Brigade front. Follow up attacks by 5 and 7 Brigades have difficulty. 16-22 SEP - 1 and 3 Divisions capture Courcelette objectives 26-28 SEP - Battle of Thiepval Ridge—attacks by 1 and 2 Divisions meet heavy resistance and fail to capture Kenora and Regina Trenches.	18 SEP - Flakenhayn begins Austro-German offensive against Rumania. 20 SEP - Buisilov offensive ends in east.

Month/Year	6th Infantry Brigade Machine-Gun Coy	Cdn Corps	Other Events
1-3 OCT 1916 4-5 OCT 8 OCT 16 OCT 31 OCT	In support with indirect fire In reserve at Warloy Move begins to La Vicogne and Lens sector Company complete in Bailin and relieves 63 (Brigade) Machine-Gun Company in line. Front very quiet. Company in and out of line.	1 OCT - Battle of Ancre Heights—2 and 3 Divisions attack Regina Trench and defeated. 8 OCT - Corps reserves attack after raid on Regina Trench. 1 and 3 Divs. assault and beaten back. 10 OCT - 4 Cdn. Division relieves 1 and 3 Divisions 17 OCT - Corps, less 4 Division and Corps artillery withdrawn to First Army area between Arras and Lens 21 OCT - 4 Division partially captures Regina Trench 27 OCT - 44 Cdn. Battalion destroyed in attempt to capture remainder	
NOV 1916	A quiet month of trench routine.	11-18 NOV - 4 Cdn. Division complete capture of Regina and Desire Trenches. It was relieved on 26/28 NOV to rejoin Cdn. Corps	Inter-Allied Conference in Chantilly to discuss plans for 1917 on 15-16 NOV. 16 NOV - Sir Sam Hughes replaced as Minister of Militia.
DEC 1916	A quiet month of trench routine.	Canadian Corps sector quiet except for trench raids.	13 DEC - Joffee replaced as Commander-in-Chief French Armies by Gen. Robert Nivelle 6 DEC - Lloyd George becomes new British Prime Minister in Coalition government 5 DEC - HQ Overseas Military Forces of Canada opens in London 6 DEC - Germans capture Bucharest. Rumania effectively out of the war.

Month/Year	6th Infantry Brigade Machine-Gun Coy	Cdn Corps	Other Events
JAN 1917	Normal trench routine of relieve and be relieved. Quiet.	Cdn. Corps continues to hold on Artois front between Arras and Lens. Trench raid on 17 JAN by 20 and 21 Battalions successful. 19 JAN - Planning begins for capture of Vimy Ridge.	Germans alter their defensive tactics to fighting an elastic defensive battle in depth. Inter-Allied conference in Rome followed by approval of Gen. Nivelle's plans for 1917.
FEB 1917	Normal trench routine of relieve and be relieved. Quiet.	Successful trench raid by 10 Brigade on 13 FEB.	1 FEB - Germans begin campaign of unrestricted submarine warfare at sea. 13 FEB - 5 Cdn. Division founded in England Kut recaptured from Turks 4 FEB - German High Command issues orders for withdrawal to Hindenberg Line in March.
5 MAR 1917 10 MAR 23 MAR 27-28 MAR	Fired in support of trench raid by 1/6 Gordon Highlanders. Normal trench routine until 7 MAR. Training begins for coming offensive and continues. Relieved 5 Machine-Gun Company in Neuville Straast Support raids by 27 Battalion.	28 FEB - 1 MAR - Largest Cdn. Trench raid by 4 Division a disaster—687 casualties for 37 prisoners. Sir Robert Borden visits Corps. 5 MAR - Byng issues "Scheme of Operations" for Vimy attack. 20 MAR - Corps begins preliminary bombardment of Vimy Ridge.	12 MAR - Russian revolution begins and Czar abdicates on 15 MAR. 10 MAR - British capture Bagdad. 15-19 MAR - Germans withdraw 29 Divisions to Hindenberg Line.
4 APR 1917 9 APR 11 APR 12-30 APR	Company moves to Mount St. Eloi to prepare for Vimy operations in rain and snow. Easter Sunday—Company fires barrage in support of attack and has sections moving with 27 and 29 Battalions. Company moves to support lines In and out of line supporting brigade	9 APR - Cdn. Corps attacks four divisions up. All objectives except the Pimple captured by last light. It falls to 10 Brigade on 12 APR 28 APR - 2 Infantry Brigade attacks Arleux and captures it.	6 APR - USA declares war on Germany 9-14 APR - Third British Army attack on Scarpe 16 APR - Nivelle offensive begins on the Aisne. It fails with only limited gains. It continues until 5 MAY. 17-19 APR - British attack on Gaza fails.

Month/Year	6th Infantry Brigade Machine-Gun Coy	Cdn Corps	Other Events
1-3 MAY 1917	Company supports attack of 31 and 27 Battalions on Fresnoy	3 MAY - 1 Brigade and 6 Brigade attack Fresnoy. Partial success—fighting continues to 8 MAY	3 MAY - Mutinies begin in French Army.
8-9 MAY	Company supports 4 Brigade who defeat counter-attack against Fresnoy	5-6 MAY - 10 Brigade attacks near Avion.	15 MAY - Petain replaces Nivelle as French commander. Mutinies in French Army spread to 55 divisions by end of June.
10 MAY	Company relieved and moves into rest near Aux Rietz. Remainder of month spent in routine.		15 MAY - Italians attack again on the Isonzo
			16 MAY - Borden tells House of Commons conscription will be needed.
1-30 JUN 1917	Company in training for entire month.	4 Division continues attacks near Avion with 9 Cdn. Brigade between 2-28 JUN.	7 JUN - Second British Army (Plumer) captures Messines Ridge in first phase of Haig's offensive in Flanders.
		6 JUN - Maj.-Gen. Sir Arthur Currie assumes command of Cdn. Corps. Maj.-Gen. Macdonell assumes command of 1 Cdn. Division	25 JUN - First US Army units land in France.
		9 JUN - Currie promoted to Lt.-Gen.	10 JUN - Italians conduct successful attack on Trentino.
			29 JUN - Kerensky offensive in Galacia.
3 JUL 1917	Company moves with 6 Brigade to relieve British units in front of Lens—in the Avion sector from Mericourt to Souchez River.	7 JUL - Cdn. Corps warned to capture Lens and Hill 70.	21 JUL - Preliminary bombardment for Flanders offensive begins.
13 JUL	Company moves to Lens sector and continues in line.	10-16 JUL - 1 and 2 Divisions relieve 1 (British) Corps from Souchez to Loos with 3 Division on south flank.	31 JUL - Flanders offensive opens with little success.
18-22 JUL	Company at rest in Bouvigny huts.	23 JUL - 116 Battalion conduct successful diversionary assault on Mericourt Trench.	18 JUL - Germans crush Kerensky offensive.
23 JUL	Company relieves 5 Brigade Machine-Gun Company in Laurent sector.	Weather bad on front.	
24-31 JUL	Company remains in line holding positions.		

Month/Year	6th Infantry Brigade Machine-Gun Coy	Cdn Corps	Other Events
AUG 1971	Company continues alternate tours of line and reserve firing indirect support missions into Lens.		
15 AUG	Company provide indirect support and continued in line during subsequent attacks.	15 AUG - 1 and 2 Divisions attack Hill 70 behind excellent artillery barrage and counter-battery fire, with 4 Division providing a diversion directed at Lens. Attack was successful in achieving objectives.	16-18 AUG - Battle of Pilckem Ridge in Flanders. By end of month British advance up to three miles in the rain.
30 AUG	Company moves into rest at Camblain L'Abbe.	19-25 AUG - attacks continue against Lens by 4 Division.	French launch limited attack near Verdun on 20 AUG. It had recovered from Nivelle offensive.
SEP 1917		Cdn. Corps front remains quiet and units conduct training in preparation for future operations.	1 SEP - Germans capture Riga. 20 SEP - British capture Gheluvelt Plateau. 26 SEP - British capture Polygon Wood.
17 OCT 1917	Company begins move north to Ypres Salient	3 OCT - Lt.-Gen. Currie warned to have two divisions ready to go to Flanders. Currie objects to serving under Gen. Gough and to splitting his corps.	4 OCT - ANZAC Corps capture Gravenstafel Ridge.
25 OCT	Company entrains for Cassel.	18 OCT - Cdn Corps relieves ANZAC Corps in mud west of Passchendaele.	24 OCT - Germans rout Italians at Battle of Caporetto.

Index

331